Inequality

INEQUALITY

What Can Be Done?

Anthony B. Atkinson

Harvard University Press

CAMBRIDGE, MASSACHUSETTS
LONDON, ENGLAND
2015

First printing

Book design by Dean Bornstein

Library of Congress Cataloging-in-Publication Data
Atkinson, A. B. (Anthony Barnes), 1944–
    Inequality : what can be done? / Anthony B. Atkinson.
    pages cm
    Includes bibliographical references and index.
    ISBN 978-0-674-50476-9 (alk. paper)
    1. Income distribution. 2. Poverty. 3. Equality. 4. Welfare economics. I. Title.
    HC79.I5A822 2015
    339.2'2–dc23
    2015000848

To the wonderful people who work in the National Health Service

Contents

Acknowledgements

This book is the result of research on the economics of inequality carried out since I graduated as an economist in 1966. In nearly fifty years, I have accumulated many debts—to those with whom I have worked, to colleagues around the world, to students, and to writers in different fields. I can single out only a few. Over a long period, I have collaborated in the field of income inequality with (in alphabetical order) François Bourguignon of the Paris School of Economics; Andrea Brandolini of the Bank of Italy; Andrew Leigh (now Member of the Australian Parliament); Eric Marlier of CEPS, Luxembourg; John Micklewright of University College London; Brian Nolan of Oxford; Thomas Piketty of the Paris School of Economics; Emmanuel Saez of the University of California, Berkeley; Amartya Sen of Harvard; Tim Smeeding of the University of Wisconsin–Madison; and Holly Sutherland of the University of Essex. In recent times, I have worked with Rolf Aaberge and Jørgen Modalsli at Statistics Norway; with Facundo Alvaredo, Salvatore Morelli, and Max Roser at the Programme for Economic Modelling at INET at the Oxford Martin School; with Jakob Søgaard of the University of Copenhagen and the Danish Ministry of Finance; and with Charles Diamond, founder of *Inequality Briefing* (http://inequalitybriefing.org/). In Nuffield College, an ideal research environment, I have enjoyed discussions with, among others, Bob Allen, Christopher Bliss, Duncan Gallie, John Goldthorpe, David Hendry, Paul Klemperer, Meg Meyer, and John Muellbauer. I owe a great deal to all those listed above, and I would like to say what a pleasure it has been to work with them. In writing this book, I have benefitted much from having recently edited, with François Bourguignon, the second volume of the *Handbook of Income Distribution,* published by Elsevier in December 2014. I express here my gratitude to the more than fifty authors who contributed to that work.

This book grows out of two public lectures and an article: the Arrow Lecture "Where Is inequality Headed?" given in May 2013 at Stanford University; the plenary lecture "Can We Reduce Income Inequality?"

given at the annual meeting of the Nationalökonomische Gesellschaft/ Austrian Economic Association in Vienna in May 2014; and the article "After Piketty," which appeared in a symposium on Thomas Piketty's *Capital in the Twenty-First Century* (Cambridge, MA: The Belknap Press of Harvard University Press, 2014) in the *British Journal of Sociology* 65 (2014): 619–638. These were prepared while I was a Centennial Professor at the London School of Economics, and I am most grateful to the school and to my colleagues there for their support while I worked on these projects, and during the period when I have been only a virtual participant. In the course of expanding the content, I have drawn on ideas developed while I held an ECFIN Fellowship in 2012–13, and I am grateful to the European Commission for supporting my research in this way.

In preparing the book, I have been helped by many people, but I should make special mention of the fact that the calculations in Chapter 11 were made by Holly Sutherland and her colleagues Paola De Agostini, Chrysa Leventi, and Iva Tasseva of the University of Essex. In 1983 Holly and I began working on TAXMOD, a micro-data-based tax-benefit model for the UK, as part of the ESRC-funded programme on Taxation, Incentives and the Distribution of Income, directed by Mervyn King, Nick Stern, and myself. At that time, together, in friendly rivalry, with the Institute for Fiscal Studies, TAXMOD was setting the pace internationally, and Holly has subsequently developed the research into the remarkable EU-wide model EUROMOD. The calculations in Chapter 11 use the UK component of the model. It goes without saying that the Essex team are not in any way responsible for the contents of that chapter, but without their willing and insightful cooperation it could not have been written.

In the book I make reference to the great improvement that has taken place in the availability of data since I began studying the distribution of income in the 1960s. In constructing the graphs in the book, I have drawn particularly on the *Chartbook of Economic Inequality* that Salvatore Morelli and I have constructed, on the World Top Incomes Database for which Facundo Alvaredo is responsible, and on the LIS Key Figures published by the LIS Cross-National Data Center in Luxembourg (of which I am proud to be president). But there are many other bodies who make data available, and, though too numerous to be named, they should also be thanked.

I am most grateful to the following people who have read part or all of the manuscript, often under great time pressure, and have encouraged me with their interest in the project: Rolf Aaberge, Facundo Alvaredo, Charles Atkinson, Estelle Atkinson, Judith Atkinson, Richard Atkinson, Sarah Atkinson, François Bourguignon, Andrea Brandolini, Zsuzsa Ferge, David Hendry, John Hills, Chrysa Leventi, Ian Malcolm, Eric Marlier, Claudine McCreadie, John Micklewright, Salvatore Morelli (who also helped with the graphs), Brian Nolan, Maari Paskov, Thomas Piketty, Max Roser, Adrian Sinfield, Tim Smeeding, Holly Sutherland, and Iva Tasseva. Their comments have greatly improved the book, leading in some cases to major rewriting. I have had fruitful discussions about aspects of the book with Julian Le Grand, Ruth Hancock, and Wiemer Salverda. Charlotte Proudman aided me at the early stages. Maarit Kivilo very efficiently helped me with the preparation of the references in the endnotes. It has been a pleasure to work on the book with Ian Malcolm, editor for Harvard University Press, and his colleagues; they have been most helpful and encouraging.

In the work that lies behind the book, I have been greatly assisted by my colleagues in the Inequality Group that forms part of the EMoD programme supported by INET at the Oxford Martin School, and is now linked to the Employment, Equity and Growth programme at INET at the Oxford Martin School. I am particularly grateful to David Hendry, who not only made space for the Inequality Group and supported the work over the past eighteen months while I have been secluded at home, but also first suggested that I write a book that brought together my thinking on different aspects of inequality. Of course, neither he nor anyone else thanked here should be held responsible for the errors of analysis or for the opinions expressed.

Royalties received for this book before 2020 will be donated to the following charities: Oxfam, Tools for Self Reliance, Emmaus UK, and the Quaker Housing Trust.

Inequality

Introduction

Inequality is now at the forefront of public debate. Much is written about the 1 per cent and the 99 per cent, and people are more aware of the extent of inequality than ever before. The president of the United States, Barack Obama, and the head of the International Monetary Fund (IMF), Christine Lagarde, have declared rising inequality to be a priority. When the Pew Research Center's Global Attitudes Project asked respondents in 2014 about the "greatest danger to the world," it found that in the United States and Europe "concerns about inequality trump all other dangers."[1] But if we are serious about reducing income inequality, what can be done? How can heightened public awareness be translated into policies and actions that actually reduce inequality?

In this book, I set out concrete policy proposals that could, I believe, bring about a genuine shift in the distribution of income towards less inequality. Drawing on the lessons of history, and taking a fresh look—through distributional eyes—at the underlying economics, I seek to show what could be done now to reduce the extent of inequality. I do so in a spirit of optimism. The world faces great problems, but collectively we are not helpless in the face of forces outside our control. The future is very much in our hands.

Plan of the Book

The book falls into three parts. Part One is concerned with diagnosis. What do we mean by inequality and what is its current extent? Have there been periods when inequality has declined, and, if so, what can we learn from these episodes? What can economics tell us about the causes of inequality? One chapter leads to another, without chapter summaries, though I provide a "Summing-Up So Far" at the end of Part One. Part Two sets out fifteen proposals indicating steps that countries can take to reduce inequality. The full set of proposals and five further "ideas to pursue" are listed at the end of Part Two. In Part Three, I consider a range of objections to the proposals. Can we level the playing field without losing jobs or slowing down economic growth? Can we afford a programme to reduce inequality? "The Way Forward" summarises the proposals and what can be done to bring them about.

Chapter 1 sets the scene with a discussion of the meaning of inequality and a first look at the evidence about its extent. There is much talk about "inequality," but there is also much confusion, as the term means different things to different people. Inequality arises in many spheres of human activity. People have unequal political power. People are unequal before the law. Even economic inequality, my focus here, is open to many interpretations. The nature of objectives, and their relation to social values, has to be clarified. Are we concerned with inequality of opportunity or inequality of outcome? With which outcomes should we be concerned? Should we focus just on poverty? When presented with data on inequality, the reader has always to ask, inequality of what among whom? The chapter goes on to present a first picture of economic inequality and how it has changed over the past 100 years. This serves not just to highlight the reason inequality is today high on the agenda but also to introduce the key dimensions of inequality considered.

One of the themes of the book is the importance of learning from the past. It may have become a cliché to say, as Santayana did in *The Life of Reason,* that "those who cannot remember the past are condemned to repeat it," but like many clichés, it contains a great deal of truth.[2] The past provides both a yardstick by which we can judge what could be attainable in terms of reducing inequality and clues as to how it could be achieved. Fortunately, the historical study of income distribution is an area of economics in which considerable progress has been made in recent years, and the writing of this book has been made possible by the greatly improved empirical data, described in Chapter 2, on economic inequality over time in different countries. From these data we can learn important lessons, particularly about how inequality was reduced during the postwar decades in Europe. This decline in inequality occurred during the Second World War but was also the product of several equalising forces in the period from 1945 to the 1970s. These equalising mechanisms—including conscious policies—have subsequently ceased to operate or gone into reverse, in what I call the "Inequality Turn" taken in the 1980s. Since then, inequality has risen in many countries (but not all, as I discuss in relation to Latin America).

The forces that led to reduced inequality in the postwar decades provide a guide to designing policy for the future, but the world has changed dramatically since that time. Chapter 3 considers the economics of inequality today. Here, I start from the economics textbook story focused on the twin forces of technological change and globalisation—forces that are radically reshaping the labour markets of rich and developing countries and leading to a widening gap in the distribution of wages. But I then depart from the textbooks. Technological progress is not a force of nature but reflects social and economic decisions. Choices by firms, by individuals, and by governments can influence the direction of technology and hence the distribution of income. The law of supply and demand may place limits on the wages that may be paid, but it leaves plenty of room for the operation of wider considerations. A richer analysis is needed that takes account of the economic and social context. The textbook story concentrates on the labour market and fails to treat the capital market. The capital market, and the associated question of the share of profits in total income, were in the past a central element in the analysis of the distribution of income, and they should be again today.

After diagnosis comes action. Part Two of the book sets out a series of proposals that together could move our societies towards a significantly lower level of inequality. These span many fields of policy and are not confined to fiscal redistribution—important though this is. The reduction of inequality should be a priority for everyone. Within government, it is a matter for the minister responsible for science as well as for the minister responsible for social protection; it is a matter for competition policy as well as for labour-market reform. It should be a matter of concern for individuals in their roles as workers, employers, consumers, and savers, as well as taxpayers. Inequality is embedded in our social and economic structure, and a significant reduction requires us to examine all aspects of our society.

Accordingly, the first three chapters in Part Two deal with different elements of the economy: Chapter 4 with technological change and its distributional implications, including its relation with the market structure and countervailing power; Chapter 5 with the labour market and the changing nature of employment; and Chapter 6 with the capital market and the sharing of wealth. In each case, market power and its location play a significant role. The distribution of wealth may have become less concentrated over the twentieth century, but this does not imply that there has been a transfer of control over economic decision-making. In the labour market, developments over recent decades, notably increased labour-market "flexibility," have involved a transfer of power from workers to employers. The growth of multinational companies, and trade and capital-market liberalisation, have strengthened the position of companies vis-à-vis customers, workers, and governments. Chapters 7 and 8 take up the issues of progressive taxation and the welfare state. A number of the measures proposed, such as a return to more progressive income taxation, have been widely debated, but others are less predictable, such as the idea of a "participation income" as the underpinning for social protection.

The standard response to the question "How can we fight rising inequality?" is to advocate increased investment in education and skills. I say relatively little about such measures, not because I feel they are unimportant, but because they have already been widely canvassed.[3] I certainly support such investments in families and in education, but I would like to highlight more radical proposals—proposals that require us to rethink fundamental aspects of our modern society and to cast off political ideas that have dominated recent decades. As such, they may at first sight appear outlandish or impractical. For this reason, Part Three is devoted to objections and to assessing the feasibility of the measures proposed. The most obvious challenge is that we cannot afford the necessary measures. Before coming to the budgetary arithmetic, however, I consider the more general objection that there is an inevitable conflict between equity and efficiency. Is it necessarily the case that redistribution causes disincentives? This discussion of welfare economics and the "shrinking cake" is the subject of Chapter 9. A second set of objections to the proposals outlined is that "they are fine, but the extent of globalisation today means that a country cannot embark on such a radical path." This potentially serious argument is discussed in Chapter 10. In Chapter 11, we come to the "political arithmetic" of the proposals: the implications for the government budget, taking the United Kingdom as a specific case study. Some readers will turn to this first. I have left the subject for last, not because I believe it unimportant, but because the analysis is necessarily more specific in terms of place and time. The revenue from the proposed taxes and the costs of social transfers depend on the institutional structures and other features of a particular country. My aim is therefore to explain the way in which economists assess the feasibility of policy proposals, illustrated by what can be done today in the UK. For some of the proposals, it is not possible to carry out such calculations, but I have tried to provide a broad indication as to how they would impinge on the public finances.

What to Expect

The book is a product of my reflections, not only on the causes and cures for inequality, but also on the state of contemporary economic thinking. In the English novel *Cold Comfort Farm* by Stella Gibbons, 1932, the author adopted (no doubt tongue in cheek) the practice of marking with stars "the finer passages," with the aim of helping the reader who was not sure "whether a sentence is Literature or . . . just sheer flapdoodle."[4] I had thought of adapting her example, marking passages where I deviate from the conventional wisdom, so that readers fearing "flapdoodle" could be on the alert. I have decided against introducing such stars, but departures from the mainstream are signalled. I should emphasise that I am claiming not that the approaches adopted are necessarily superior, but that there is more than one way of doing economics. I was taught, in Cambridge, England, and Cambridge, Massachusetts, to ask, "Who gains and who loses?" from an economic change or policy. This is a question that is often missing from today's media discussion and policy debate. Many economic models assume identical representative agents carrying out sophisticated decision-making, where distributional issues are suppressed, leaving no space to consider the justice of the resulting outcome. For me, there should be room for such discussion. There is not just one Economics.

The book is directed at the general reader with an interest in economics and politics. The technical material is largely confined to the end-notes, and I have included a glossary of some of the main terms employed. There are a number of graphs, and a small number of tables. Detailed sources for all the figures can be found in the Figure Sources at the back of the book. I have been mindful of the dictum of Stephen Hawking that "every equation halves the number of readers." There are no equations in the main text, so I hope that readers will make it to the end.

Part One

DIAGNOSIS

Chapter 1 ::

Setting the Scene

This book is concerned with ways of reducing the extent of inequality, and we need to be clear at the outset exactly what is, and what is not, meant by this goal. Let me begin by removing one possible misconception. I am not seeking to eliminate all differences in economic outcomes. I am not aiming for total equality. Indeed, certain differences in economic rewards may be quite justifiable. Rather, the goal is to *reduce* inequality below its current level, in the belief that the present level of inequality is excessive. I have stated this proposition deliberately in terms of the direction of movement, not of the ultimate destination. Readers may well disagree as to how much inequality is acceptable while agreeing that the present level is intolerable or unsustainable.

In this chapter, I explore the reasons we should be concerned about inequality and its relation with underlying social values. I then take a first look at the empirical evidence. Just how unequal are our societies? By how much has inequality increased? Once we have seen the broad patterns, however, it is necessary to probe more deeply. Just what is being included in the statistics and what is missing? Who is where in the distribution?

Inequality of Opportunity and Inequality of Outcome

On hearing the term "inequality," many people think in terms of achieving "equality of opportunity." This phrase occurs frequently in political speeches, party manifestos, and campaign rhetoric. It is a powerful rallying call with long roots in history. In his classic essay *Equality*, Richard Tawney argued that all people should be "equally enabled to make the best of such powers as they possess." In the recent economics literature, following the work of John Roemer, the determinants of economic outcomes are separated into those due to "circumstances" that are beyond personal control, such as family background, and "effort," for which an individual can be held responsible. Equality of opportunity is achieved when the former variables—circumstances—do not play any role in the resulting outcome. If some people work harder at school, pass their exams, and get into medical school, then at least part (but not necessarily all) of their higher salary as a doctor can be attributed to effort. If, on the other hand, their place at medical school is secured through parental influence (for example, preference being given to the children of alumni), then there is inequality of opportunity.[1]

The concept of equality of opportunity is an attractive one. However, does it mean that inequality of outcome is irrelevant? In my view, the answer to this question is "no." Inequality of outcome is still important, even for those who start from concern for a "level playing field." To see why, we need to start by noting the difference between the two concepts. Inequality of opportunity is essentially an ex ante concept—everyone should have an equal starting point—whereas much redistributional activity is concerned with the ex post outcomes. Those who think inequality of outcome is irrelevant regard concern for ex post outcomes as illegitimate and believe that, once a level playing field for the race of life has been established, we should not enquire into the outcomes. To me this is wrong for three reasons.

First, most people would find it unacceptable to ignore completely what happens after the starting gun is fired. Individuals may exert effort but have bad luck. Suppose that some people trip and fall into poverty. In any humane society help will be provided to them. Moreover, many believe that this help should be offered without enquiring into the reasons the person fell on hard times. As the economists Ravi Kanbur and Adam Wagstaff note, it would be morally repugnant to "condition the doling out of soup on an assessment of whether it was circumstance or effort which led to the outcome of the individual . . . to be in the soup line."[2] The first reason, then, that outcomes matter is that we cannot ignore those for whom the outcome is hardship—even if ex ante equality of opportunity were to exist.

But the significance of outcomes goes much deeper than this, leading to the second reason that inequality of outcome matters. We need to distinguish between competitive and noncompetitive equality of opportunity. The latter ensures that all people have an equal chance to fulfill their *independent* life projects. To pursue the athletic analogy, all can have the opportunity to acquire swimming certificates. In contrast, competitive equality of opportunity means only that we all have an equal chance to take part in a race—a swimming competition—where there are unequal prizes. In this, more typical case, there are ex post unequal rewards, and this is where inequality of outcome enters the picture. It is the existence of a highly unequal distribution of prizes that leads us to attach so much weight to ensuring that the race is a fair one. And the prize structure is largely socially constructed. Our economic and social arrangements determine whether the winner gets a garland or $3 million (the top prize in the U.S. Open Tennis tournament in 2014). The determination of the prize structure is the principal concern of this book.

Finally, the third reason for concern about inequality of outcome is that it directly affects equality of opportunity—for the next generation. Today's ex-post outcomes shape tomorrow's ex ante playing field: the beneficiaries of inequality of outcome today can transmit an unfair advantage to their children tomorrow. Concern about unequal opportunity, and about limited social mobility, has intensified as the distributions of income and wealth have become more unequal. This is because the impact of family background on outcome depends both on the strength of the relationship between background and outcome and on the extent of inequality among family backgrounds. Inequality of outcome among today's generation is the source of the unfair advantage received by the next generation. If we are concerned about equality of opportunity tomorrow, we need to be concerned about inequality of outcome today.

Instrumental and Intrinsic Concerns for Inequality

Reducing inequality of outcome matters, therefore, even to those for whom equality of opportunity is the ultimate objective. It is a means to an end. In the same way, influential books such as *The Price of Inequality* by Joseph Stiglitz and *The Spirit Level* by Kate Pickett and Richard Wilkinson have identified other instrumental reasons we should be concerned about inequality of outcome.[3] They argue that we should reduce inequality of outcome because it has bad consequences for today's society; they blame increased inequality for lack of social cohesion, increased crime, ill-health, teenage pregnancy, obesity, and a whole range of social problems. Political scientists have identified a two-way relationship between income inequality and the role of money in determining the outcome of democratic elections, characterised by the "dance of ideology and unequal riches."[4] Economists have placed worsening economic performance at the door of increased inequality. In her speech to the 2012 Annual Meetings of the IMF and the World Bank, Christine Lagarde spoke of her "third milestone: inequality and the quality of growth in our future world." She went on to say that "recent IMF research tells us that less inequality is associated with greater macroeconomic stability and more sustainable growth." The extent of consequential benefits from reducing inequality can be much debated, and I return to the relation between inequality and economic performance in Chapter 9.

The case for reducing inequality does not, however, depend solely on its having adverse consequences of the kind described above. There are *intrinsic* reasons for believing that the current degree of inequality is excessive. These reasons may be framed in terms of a broader theory of justice. For economists writing on these issues a hundred years ago, it was natural to think in utilitarian terms. Summarising individual well-being in terms of the utility level attributed to each person, they argued that excessive inequality reduced the sum of total utility, since the value of an additional unit of income (or economic resources more generally) was lower for the well-off. As it was put by Hugh Dalton, British economist and postwar Labour Chancellor of the Exchequer, transferring £1 from a rich person to a less well-off person would, other things the same, reduce inequality and raise the sum of utility for society as a whole.[5]

Utilitarianism has been much criticised, not least for being concerned solely with the sum of individual utilities, and being, in the words of Amartya Sen, "supremely unconcerned with the inter-personal distribution of that sum. This should make it a particularly unsuitable approach to use for measuring or judging inequality."[6] It is for this reason that distributional weights are applied when measuring inequality, with more weight attached to those who are less well-placed. These distributional weights incorporate our social values regarding redistribution and provide an intrinsic basis for concern about inequality. Just what these weights should be is a matter over which people differ, as may be seen from the "leaky bucket experiment" described by the economist Arthur Okun. He asked what would happen if some of Dalton's £1 transfer were to be lost on the way. From the answer given, Okun deduced how much more weight would have to be attached to the income of the recipient, compared with that of the donor. If half of the transfer leaked out of the bucket, then we would need to give twice the weight to the income of the recipient compared with that of the donor. People giving greater weight to poorer recipients would favour more redistribution; they would go further towards reducing inequality. In the limit, all the weight would be given to the least well-off, a position often associated with *A Theory of Justice* by John Rawls, although there is much more to his theory than is captured by this limiting case.[7]

The "Rawlsian" position of favouring the least advantaged may sound quite radical. However, it is not far removed from the statements of politicians who argue for income tax cuts on the basis that these would stimulate economic activity and hence increase revenue that could be used to raise the incomes of the poorest among us. As this argument illustrates, there is nothing intrinsically egalitarian about the Rawlsian objective. Maximising the well-being of the least advantaged may lead to a quite unequal distribution. More radical in this sense than Rawls was Plato, who expressed the view that no one should be more than four times richer than the poorest member of the society.[8] On this egalitarian view, inequality matters on account of the distance between rich and poor, and there may be a case for action even where there is no gain to the poorest.

A Theory of Justice by Rawls initiated a wide debate among moral philosophers about the nature of social justice. Of particular relevance here is Rawls's framing of the principles of justice in terms of access to "primary goods": "things which it is supposed a rational man wants whatever else he wants," listed in broad categories as "rights and opportunities and powers, income and wealth."[9] As Sen has argued, this takes us well beyond utilitarianism but stops short of considering the "wide variations [people] have in being able to *convert* primary goods into good living."[10] Sen has proposed that we should move on from primary goods to "capabilities," defining social justice in terms of the opportunities open to people according to their functioning. The capability approach differs from Rawls's approach in two respects. It focuses on what goods can do for people in their particular circumstances, taking into consideration, for example, that people with disabilities may have higher travel-to-work costs than able-bodied people. It is concerned not just with the achieved outcomes, but also with the range of opportunities, which Sen regards as an essential element of personal freedom (hence the title of Sen's book, *Development as Freedom*).[11] In practical terms, the capability approach has broadened the dimensions of social and economic performance under examination, notably influencing the Human Development Index launched twenty-five years ago by Mahbub ul Haq (the index ranks countries according to their level of development, looking at education and life expectancy, as well as income).[12] In the present context, the capability approach brings us back to instrumental reasons for concern about the inequality of economic resources, but now within a coherent set of principles of justice.[13] Within such a framework, income is only one dimension, and differences in income should be interpreted in the light of differing circumstances and of the underlying opportunities. But it remains the case that achieved economic resources are a major source of injustice. That is my reason for concentrating here on the economic dimension of inequality.

But what do economists have to say about inequality?

Economists and Income Inequality

Some two decades ago, I gave my presidential address to the Royal Economic Society titled "Bringing Income Distribution in from the Cold."[14] The title was chosen to underscore the way the subject of income inequality had become marginalised in economics. For much of the twentieth century the topic had been ignored, whereas I believed that it should be central to the study of economics. I started that address by quoting the same concern expressed earlier in the century by Dalton, who said that as a student he had been especially interested in the distribution of income: "I gradually noticed, however, that most 'theories of distribution' were almost wholly concerned with distribution as between 'factors of production.'" He went on to say that "distribution as between persons, a problem of more direct and obvious interest, was either left out of textbooks altogether, or treated so briefly, as to suggest that it raised no question, which could not be answered either by generalizations about the factors of production, or by plodding statistical investigations, which professors of

economic theory were content to leave to lesser men."[15] The same remained true when I reviewed the economics literature in the 1990s. In his
account of the history of economic thought on income distribution, Agnar Sandmo observes that "the connection between resource allocation
and the distribution of income was not given much attention in modern
general equilibrium theory; in the influential presentation of the theory
by Gerard Debreu [Nobel Prize–winning economist], the term 'distribution' does not even appear in the index." Later he notes that economic
theory has begun "to catch up on its neglect of the determination of income distribution. But this neglect is still visible in the allocation of space
in introductory textbooks and books on microeconomic theory."[16] A
glance at today's best-selling textbooks shows that the structure has remained much the same as in the past, with discussion of inequality kept
separate from the central chapters on production and the macroeconomy. For example, the *Principles of Microeconomics* by Harvard professor
Greg Mankiw has an excellent chapter titled "Income Inequality and Poverty," but it is separate from the earlier chapters (and from the companion
Principles of Macroeconomics). Perhaps more telling is the fact that, when
it comes to compressing the book into the *Essentials of Economics,* the
inequality chapter does not make the cut, the criterion for which is, to
quote the author, "to emphasize the material that students should and do
find interesting about the study of the economy."[17] Apparently, inequality
does not qualify.[18]

The implication is that distributional issues are not of central interest
to economists. Indeed some economists hold the view that the economics profession should not concern itself at all with inequality. This has
been expressed forcefully by the Nobel Prize–winner Robert Lucas of the
University of Chicago: "Of the tendencies that are harmful to sound economics, the most seductive, and in my opinion the most poisonous, is to
focus on questions of distribution. . . . The potential for improving the
lives of poor people by finding different ways of distributing current production is nothing compared to the apparently limitless potential of increasing production."[19]

Lucas is right to emphasise the great contribution of economic growth
to improving the lives of many poor people all around the world. If cast
in sustainable form (an important "if"), then future growth offers the
prospect both of reducing international inequality and of helping the

least advantaged within countries. But I disagree with him in two respects. First, distribution and redistribution of the current total of income *do* matter to individuals. The extent of differences has a profound effect on the nature of our societies. It does matter that some people can buy tickets for space travel when others are queuing for food banks. A society in which no one could afford to travel privately into space, and in which everyone could afford to buy their food from ordinary shops, would be more cohesive and have a greater sense of shared interests. Second, total production is influenced by distribution. Understanding the distribution of income is necessary to understanding the working of the economy. As we have learned from the recent economic crisis, it is not enough to look simply at macroeconomic aggregates. Economic differences among people are of first-order importance. As the Nobel Prize–winner Robert Solow of the Massachusetts Institute of Technology (MIT) says in his critique of the models that have dominated modern macroeconomics: "heterogeneity is the essence of a modern economy. In real life we worry about the relations between managers and shareowners, between banks and their borrowers, between workers and employers, between venture capitalists and entrepreneurs, you name it. . . . We know for a fact that heterogeneous agents have different and sometimes conflicting goals, different information, different capacities to process it, different expectations, different beliefs about how the economy works. [The] models exclude all this landscape."[20] Questions of distribution and differences in outcomes for individuals are not the sole part of economics—to suggest that would be unwarranted—but they *are* an essential part.

Distributional issues are central to this book, and I seek to show how they relate to our understanding of how the economy works. But first we need to consider the results of the "plodding statistical investigations" in which I and my colleagues have been engaged. Just how unequal are our societies? How much has inequality risen in recent decades?

A First Look at the Evidence

The broad picture with regard to economic inequality in the UK and the US over the past 100 years is summarised in Figures 1.1 (US) and 1.2 (UK).

I start with the evolution over time of overall inequality in the distribution of household incomes. The definition of household income is described in more detail in the next section; for the present it can be thought of, in the US case, as the number a person would enter on their income tax return. Inequality is measured by the Gini coefficient, which is a single-number summary index of inequality ranging from 0 to 100 per cent, popularised by the Italian statistician Corrado Gini.[21] Implicit in using such an index are distributional weights, as discussed above, but these may not be evident to the countless researchers who use the Gini coefficient. In fact, by employing the Gini coefficient, they are implicitly weighting an extra £1 to a person a quarter of the way up from the bottom at three times the weight of an extra £1 given to a person a quarter of the way down from the top.[22] In terms of the leaky bucket experiment, one could lose two-thirds of the transfer and still regard the transfer as worthwhile. I take the Gini index here, since it is widely used and the available statistics are presented in this form, but we need to remember that the index converts a whole distribution to a single number and that there are many different ways in which such a conversion can be made.[23]

The graph for overall inequality in Figure 1.1 provides a long-run perspective, from which we can see that the distribution of income in the US has gone through a sea change. At mid-century, it looked as though incomes were over time becoming more evenly distributed. Herman Miller of the US Census Bureau said in 1966 that "this view is held by prominent economists and is shared by influential writers and editors," quoting the statement by *Fortune* magazine that there had been a distributional revolution "though not a head has been raised aloft on a pikestaff, nor a railway station seized."[24] The Gini coefficient had fallen by some 10 percentage points from its peak in 1929. From the end of the Second World War to the late 1970s, there followed a period of little change in overall inequality, prompting the US economist Henry Aaron to famously joke that following the income distribution statistics in the US "was like watching the grass grow." Then, in the 1980s, the grass shot up. This was the "Inequality Turn" in the US. Between 1977 and 1992, the Gini coefficient rose by some 4.5 percentage points; and since 1992 it has increased by a further 3 points. Overall inequality is not back to the levels reached in the Jazz Age, but it is more than halfway there.

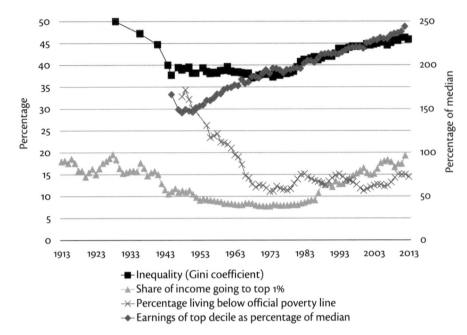

FIGURE 1.1: Inequality in the US, 1913–2013

Overall inequality (squares) is measured by the Gini coefficient, based on household gross income equivalised (adjusted) for household size. The percentage of total gross income (excluding capital gains) that goes to the top 1% is shown by triangles. The percentage of the population living below the official poverty line is represented by X's. Using the scale on the right-hand side, the diamonds show the earnings of the top decile (the person 10% from the top) relative to the median (the person in the middle of the earnings distribution) of full-time workers.

At the top of the distribution, the share in total gross income of the top 1 per cent increased by one-half between 1979 and 1992, and by 2012 it was more than double its 1979 share. Even allowing for the effect of changes in income tax (the Tax Reform Act of 1986 led to income shifting between the corporate sector and individual tax returns), this is a remarkable increase. For the top shares, we can go back in time before the Second World War to see an overall decline for the first fifty years. The fall initially took place during the First World War, although the decline in the share was recouped by the end of the roaring 1920s, and then again after the Great Crash of 1929 and during the Second World War. Today,

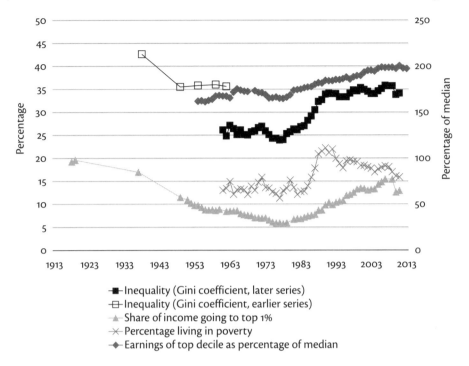

- ■ Inequality (Gini coefficient, later series)
- □ Inequality (Gini coefficient, earlier series)
- ▲ Share of income going to top 1%
- ✕ Percentage living in poverty
- ◆ Earnings of top decile as percentage of median

FIGURE 1.2: Inequality in the UK, 1913–2013

Overall inequality, measured by the Gini coefficient, is shown by squares. In the earlier series (open squares), the Gini is based on after-tax income, not adjusted for tax unit size. In the later series (solid squares), Gini coefficients are lower because they are based on disposable household income equivalised (adjusted) for household size. The percentage of total gross income going to the top 1% (triangles) shows an increase between the 1980s and 1990s. This increase may be due in part to a change in the taxation system in 1990, from treating couples as a tax unit to an individual base. The percentage living in poverty (X's) is the percentage of individuals who live in households with equivalised disposable income below 60% of the UK median. Using the scale on the right-hand side, the diamonds show the earnings of the top decile (person 10% from the top) as a percentage of the earnings of the median (the person in the middle of the distribution) of full-time adult workers.

the share of the top 1 per cent has returned to its value of 100 years ago. The top 1 per cent in the US now receives close to one-fifth of total gross income—meaning that, on average, they have twenty times their proportionate share. Within the top 1 per cent, too, there is considerable inequality: the share of the top 1 per cent of those within the top 1 per cent (that is, the top 0.01 per cent) is also around one-fifth of the total income of this group. This means that 1/10,000 of the population receives 1/25 of the total income. The upper tail of the distribution has some resemblance to a Russian matryoshka nested doll: wherever we slice the distribution we find the same inequality being reproduced within the remaining top part.[25]

Trends in the US and the UK Compared

How does the experience of the UK compare with the changes in inequality that have taken place in the US? It is often suggested that the situation in the UK is a pale imitation of what is happening in the US, and that the UK chart can be obtained by simply replacing "S" by "K" in the heading. There is some truth in this. As shown in Figure 1.2, the UK overall inequality series, which begins in 1938, showed a fall of some 7 percentage points when the series restarted after the Second World War. (In looking at these charts, the reader should focus on the *changes over time*; the levels of inequality are not fully comparable across the two countries, as income is measured differently in the US and the UK.) Overall inequality then rose in the 1980s. There was a similar post-1979 "Inequality Turn" in the UK. The top shares fell up to the late 1970s and then started rising. The share of the top 1 per cent in gross income was 19 per cent in 1919 and fell to some 6 per cent by 1979; it has since more than doubled. The share of the top 1 per cent in the UK is lower than that in the US, but this group still receives one-eighth of total gross income.

It is not surprising, therefore, that Robert Solow, writing in 1960 about the distribution of income, drew attention to "the similarity of British and American experience in the twentieth century."[26] But differences have emerged since then. In the 1980s the rise in overall inequality in the UK was much larger than in the US. Between 1979 and 1992, the rise in the Gini coefficient in the UK was some 9 points, twice that in the US. In contrast, after 1992 there was little increase: the coefficient in 2011 was essentially the same as it had been twenty years earlier. The differing time pattern, as well as the total overall increase, shows that the UK and the US were not following identical paths, and the differences provide us with valuable information about the underlying forces. Studying "differences in differences"—the *differences* across countries in the *changes over time*—is a valuable source of insight in our search for explanations of rising inequality.

Readers concerned about the UK may draw some consolation from the fact that the last twenty years have seen no increase in overall income inequality as measured by the Gini coefficient. It is the case, however, that the level of inequality remains stubbornly above its level in the 1960s and 1970s. To get back to where we were when the Beatles were playing, we have to reduce the Gini coefficient by some 10 percentage points. What does this mean? To get some idea, suppose that we seek to achieve such a reduction through taxes and transfers alone. Based on reasonable assumptions about tax rates and government spending, the tax rate increase required to reduce the Gini coefficient for disposable income from 35 to 25 per cent would be 16 percentage points of income.[27] The magnitude of the required increase in the tax rate points to the fact that reduced inequality cannot be achieved solely through fiscal measures, a conclusion that is reinforced once we take account of the likely impact of such a tax hike on incentives. This is why many of the policy measures proposed in this book are directed at making the distribution of market incomes less unequal. It is also why a radical policy to reduce inequality has to engage the whole of government. But for the moment, we can see that we are facing a major challenge.

Inequality around the World

The extent of the challenge becomes clear when we compare income inequality across a range of countries. Figure 1.3 shows the Gini coefficient for equivalised disposable household income for countries ranging alphabetically from Australia to Uruguay and in terms of their overall income per head from India to the United States. Making such comparisons is not easy, and in the next chapter the sources of the data are discussed in greater detail.

In China and India, the Gini coefficient shown in Figure 1.3 is close to 50 per cent, or around double the values found in the Nordic countries at the top of the graph. (In South Africa, it is close to 60 per cent.) The coefficient is also high—above 40 per cent—in the Latin

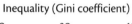
Inequality (Gini coefficient)

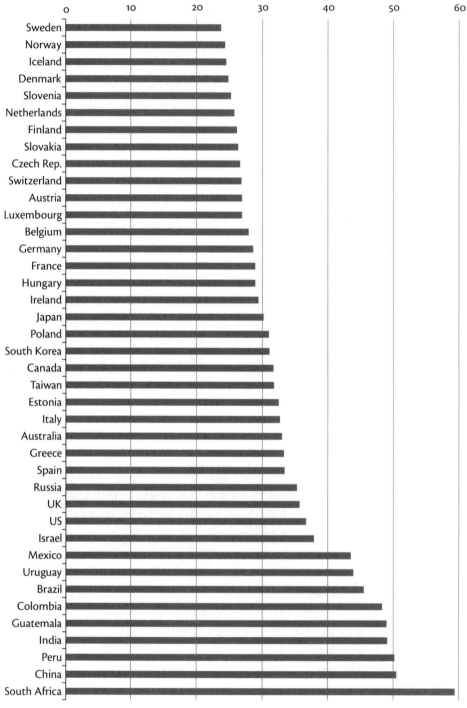

American countries shown, such as Brazil and Mexico. Next (after Israel) comes the US and then the UK. (The value shown for the US is lower than that in Figure 1.1 since the latter measured income before deduction of taxes.) These Anglo-Saxon countries have much higher overall income inequality than Continental Europe and still higher than the Nordic countries.[28]

The cross-country comparison shows what is implied by the challenge of reversing the rise in income inequality that has taken place since the 1970s. For the UK, the challenge of reducing the Gini coefficient by 10 percentage points means making the UK like the Netherlands. For the US, a reduction in the Gini of 7.5 percentage points would mean making the US like France. For other countries in the Organisation for Economic Co-operation and Development (OECD), the distance is smaller. In Australia, the Gini coefficient has risen since 1980 by 4 percentage points, and France would again be the target.

Should We Just Focus on Poverty?

So far, I have discussed the evidence about income inequality. Martin Feldstein, the Harvard economist who has pioneered research on the economics of social security, argues strongly that "the emphasis should be on eliminating poverty and not on the overall distribution of income or the general extent of inequality," and this is a widely held view.[29] I share his concern with what is happening at the bottom of the income scale. It was the rediscovery of poverty in Britain in the 1960s—specifically, the publication on Christmas Eve 1965 of *The Poor and the Poorest* by Brian Abel-Smith and Peter Townsend—that led to my research on poverty and my first book, *Poverty in Britain and the Reform of Social Security*.[30] Fifty years later, the fight against poverty is now firmly on the political agenda, with national governments setting explicit goals. Following the 1995 United Nations (UN) Social Summit in Copenhagen, the Irish govern-

---

FIGURE 1.3: Inequality in selected world countries, 2010

Inequality is measured by Gini coefficients based on equivalised household disposable income (income after taxes and transfers). The coefficient in Sweden is 23.7%, which may be compared with 59.4% in South Africa.

ment set a national poverty-reduction target as part of its 1997 National Anti-Poverty Strategy. In 1999 under Tony Blair the UK government adopted an official target for the abolition of child poverty, with the aim of eradicating child poverty by 2020; Blair's successor, Gordon Brown, enshrined this ambition in law in the Child Poverty Act 2010. The European Union (EU) in its Europe 2020 Agenda set the goal of reducing by at least 20 million the number of people who are either at-risk-of-poverty, severely materially deprived, or living in "jobless households" (the current EU total population is approximately 500 million).[31]

Despite these good intentions, progress towards reducing poverty in rich countries has been slow. The evolution of poverty over time in the US and the UK is shown in Figures 1.1 and 1.2. In the US, the poverty threshold has been held constant in terms of purchasing power, contrasting in this respect with the threshold in the UK and the EU.[32] It is not therefore surprising that the official poverty rate in the US fell from 33 per cent in 1948 to 19 per cent at the time President Lyndon Johnson launched the War on Poverty in 1964. Poverty continued to fall until the late 1960s, but since then there has been little overall improvement in the poverty rate, and the absolute number has increased as the population has grown: today some 45 million Americans live below the official poverty line.

In the UK (Figure 1.2) the poverty rate, measured according to a threshold expressed as a proportion of median income, was reduced from 22 per cent to 16 per cent between 1992 and 2011. This decline, which began under the Conservative government of John Major, is a substantial one. It demonstrates that poverty can be reduced. Does this then justify the "focus on poverty" strategy? The decline in poverty in the UK was accompanied by a marked rise in top income shares. The New Labour government was "intensely relaxed" (a contradiction in terms?) about people getting rich. However, the fall achieved in the past twenty years—for which credit must be given—still leaves the current UK poverty rate above the level of the 1960s and 1970s, a level that was regarded at the time as profoundly shocking. The Child Poverty Action Group was founded in 1965 when the poverty rate was 3 per cent lower than it is today.

In the EU, the at-risk-of-poverty rate has risen in recent years.[33] The

Social Protection Committee reported in 2014 that "the latest figures on living and income conditions in the EU show that the EU is not making any progress towards achieving its Europe 2020 poverty and social exclusion target." Quite the reverse: "There are 6.7 million more people living in poverty or social exclusion since 2008, a total of 124.2 million people for the EU28 or close to 1 in 4 Europeans in 2012. Poverty and social exclusion has increased in more than 1/3 of the Member States in both 2011 and 2012."[34]

There is still a long way to go. In my judgement, the eradication of poverty in rich countries requires us to think more ambitiously, beyond the strategies employed to date. We have to view our societies as a whole and to recognise that there are important interconnections: economics tends to assume away or downplay any interdependency between the economic fortunes of individuals (or households), but John Donne was right when he wrote that "no man is an Iland, intire of it selfe." What happens at the top of the distribution affects those at the bottom. As Tawney wrote a century ago, "what thoughtful rich people call the problem of poverty, thoughtful poor people call with equal justice a problem of riches."[35]

Put more pragmatically, we can ask whether countries can achieve low rates of poverty at the same time as having high top income shares. To examine whether this is the case, I have assembled in Figure 1.4 the evidence for fifteen OECD countries. The lines in the graph divide the countries into groups according to whether they are above or below the median country. Eleven of the fifteen countries are found in the top right-hand or the bottom left-hand boxes. Only Switzerland appears to have achieved below-median poverty while having above-median top income shares. Higher poverty tends to go together with larger top shares.

Rising Earnings Dispersion

The title of this section refers to "dispersion" to underline the obvious—but often overlooked—fact that not all differences in economic outcome represent unjustified *inequality*. Some people are paid more than others for perfectly justifiable reasons, such as working longer hours or doing unpleasant jobs or taking on more responsibility. Among the most im-

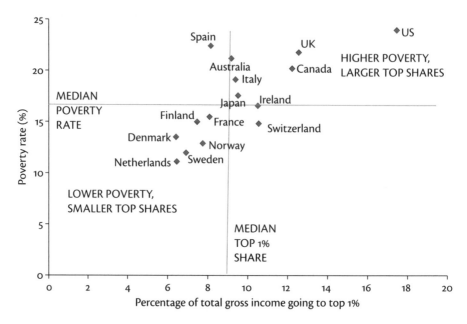

FIGURE 1.4: Poverty and top income shares in selected countries, c. 2010

In the US in 2010 the relative poverty rate (percentage living on incomes below 60 per cent of the median) was 24.7%, and the share of total gross income going to the top 1% (excluding capital gains) was 17.5%.

portant justifications for differences in earnings is that some people have invested in training for occupations that require more skill. Such a "human capital" explanation of pay differences is of ancient vintage. In *The Wealth of Nations,* Adam Smith stated this clearly: "A man educated at the expense of much labour or time . . . must be expected to earn over and above the usual wages . . . the whole expenses of his education, with at least the ordinary profits of an equally valuable capital." This simple statement of what underlies the college-wage premium explains both why differences do not necessarily imply inequality *and* why it is not necessarily the case that all of the observed difference can be explained in this way. It is quite possible that the investment in human capital by a higher-educated worker earns more (or less) than the ordinary profit on capital. A pioneering study by Nobel Prize–winners Milton Friedman and Simon Kuznets of professional earnings in the 1930s in the US concluded that "the actual difference between the incomes of professional and non-professional workers seems decidedly larger than the difference that would compensate for the extra capital investment required." To this extent, the difference *did* constitute inequality.[36]

The long-run evolution of the earnings distribution in the US and the UK is depicted in Figures 1.1 and 1.2 (earnings at top decile). The graphs are best understood by imagining all those with earnings being lined up in a parade in order of how much they earn. The statistician then divides them into tenths and asks the person at the start of each tenth to step forward. The person at the start of the sixth tenth is the *median*—the person in the middle—and the person at the start of the top tenth is the *top decile*. What the graphs show for each year is the ratio of the earnings of the top decile to the earnings of the median. So in the US in 1952 the top decile earned some 150 per cent of the median. This graph extends further back in time than is commonly the case in studies of wage dispersion, which tend to focus on what has happened since the 1970s. It is, however, important to set the experience of recent decades in historical context. We can see that, in the US, the rise in top earnings began long before 1970. Between 1952 and 1972, the relative advantage of the top decile rose from 150 per cent to 194 per cent of the median, a rise as large as that which took place between 1972 and 2012. The experience of the UK was different. In the 1950s and early 1960s, earnings dispersion was widening, but from the mid-1960s to 1979 the top decile fell relative to the median. How this was brought about is discussed further in the next chapter. Not only is the time-path different, but also the overall increase is smaller in the UK than in the US—in contrast to what we have seen to be the case for overall income inequality. In the UK, earnings dispersion increased less, but overall income inequality more, than in the US.

We are therefore telling a more nuanced story than simply "rising inequality." As summarised in Table 1.1, there are differences between periods, between countries, and between individual earnings and household incomes. These differences help us understand the determinants of inequality. We can learn from the episodes circled in Table 1. How did the US maintain a broadly stable level of household income inequality in the 1950s and 1960s, despite widening earnings dispersion? How did the UK reduce earnings dispersion from 1965 to 1979? Why did income inequal-

TABLE 1.1. *A brief postwar history of inequality in the UK and the US*

	1950 to mid-1960s	Mid-1960s to end of 1970s	1980s	1990 to today
Individual earnings dispersion	Rise in UK	Fall in UK	Rise in UK	Rise in UK
	Rise in US	Rise in US	Rise in US	Rise in US
Household income inequality	Stable in US	Stable in US	Rise in US	Rise in US
	Stable in UK	Fall in UK	Large rise in UK	Stable in UK

ity rise much more sharply in the UK in the 1980s? These questions, together with the experiences of other OECD countries, are taken up in the next chapter.

The Dimensions of Inequality

We have taken a first look at the evidence about inequality; before going further we need to take a step back and clarify the concepts underlying the statistics. There are many dimensions to inequality, and some important ones have so far been missing. Indeed, even within the field covered, the reader may well have been wondering just what is or is not included. Graphs such as Figures 1.1 and 1.2 lead one to ask, inequality of what among whom?

Inequality among Whom?

So far I have talked about households and, when discussing earnings, about individuals. But there are other possible units of analysis. Within the household there may be distinct families, and within the family there may be distinct generations. Which of these should be used? The answer depends in part on the extent to which members of the household share equally in its resources. If there is full sharing, then the calculations described above, based on total household income, would be appropriate. Where sharing is incomplete, we can make a case for considering the different spending units, or nuclear families, that constitute the household. On a family basis, we would treat separately grown-up children still living at home, and elderly parents living with their children would constitute a separate family unit within the household. For many years, poverty in the UK was calculated on such a family-unit basis, yielding figures that were higher but showed a less steep increase than that shown in Figure 1.2. The figures were higher because each family unit within the household was assumed to have to get by on its own income. On the other hand, today's method of counting may understate the true extent of poverty since it assumes that resources are fully shared. It may conceal poverty arising from inequality within the household. Put differently, if young adults return to the family nest when economic conditions deteriorate, household-based measures may conceal the extent of the rise in inequality.

The choice of unit depends not only on how much income is shared but also on our notion of control over resources and whether we are concerned about the degree of individual dependence. If we believe, for example, that young adults should be independent of their parents, then this is a reason for adopting an inner-family unit, based on adults plus their dependent children but not including grown-up children still living at home. Such a move would raise the measured extent of income inequality and poverty because, even if incomes are pooled, the sharing of resources would not be taken into account. This issue is often neglected in public discussion. Reference is made to "benefit dependency" but not to dependency on other household members. Yet in the past it was an objective of public policy to secure financial independence for the elderly so that they were not reliant on their children. Issues of social values and expectations lie behind what might otherwise appear to be a purely statistical question: whether we should measure inequality or poverty in terms of households or of families.

Inequality of What?

Overall inequality is measured in Figure 1.2 for the UK in terms of household disposable income adjusted for household size and composition (the US measure in Figure 1.1 is for income before taxes). The composition of household income is set out schematically in Figure 1.5, which I have referred to as a "guide to household income." For readers who—understandably—find the different concepts confusing, this guide may be

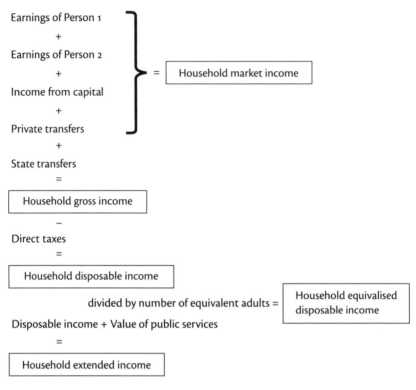

FIGURE 1.5: Guide to household income

helpful at a number of stages in the book. (The terms are also defined in the Glossary.)

To begin with, since we are thinking in terms of a whole household, we have to add up the earnings of everyone in the household. A person with low earnings may be married to someone who is much better paid: a church minister may have a wife who is an investment banker. The guide shows two people, but there may of course be several in the household. Earnings include not only the wages and salaries received by employees but also the incomes of people who are self-employed (this source of income differs in that it includes a return to both the hours put in and the capital invested). To this, we add income from savings, which may take the form of interest on bank accounts or on bonds, or may be dividends on shares, or rent on property owned. We add transfer payments received from private bodies, such as a pension, and state transfers from the government. This yields the total household gross income. Subtracting income tax and other direct taxes, such as social security taxes, gives disposable income. The next stage shown in the guide takes account of differences in household size and composition. One household's income means less if it has to provide for a family of two children than if it accrues to a single person. As a colleague of mine used to say, "with two children, a penny bun costs four pence" (his wife got one too). In practice, the adjustment made to allow for differing family size is not made on a per capita basis, since there are economies of scale. My colleague did not have four central heating boilers. Rather, an "equivalence scale" is applied that allows for the fact that not all spending has to be increased per person. One simple scale is the square root of household size, so that the income of the family of four is divided by 2 (which is the square root of 4), but the statistics presented earlier use a slightly more complicated scale (known as the modified OECD scale), which gives 1 for the first adult, 0.5 for subsequent adults, and 0.3 for each child.[37]

The purpose of the guide is to help the reader understand the makeup of household disposable income adjusted for household size and composition, referred to below as household equivalised income. But its usefulness goes further. From the scheme set out in Figure 1.5, we can see the different elements that potentially contribute to explaining the evolution of household incomes. But first we have to ask, what is the principle behind the list of income items in Figure 1.5? The definition usually adopted by economists is that income is the sum of all receipts, whether monetary or in kind, that accrue in a given period, or, equivalently, the maximum amount of resources that the household could exercise in consumption while holding constant its net worth: that is, without reducing the value of assets minus liabilities. The definition is *comprehensive* in its coverage and goes beyond the scope of most definitions of income for income tax purposes. In principle it includes all income in kind, including the vegetables grown in your garden (in which the tax authorities are not usually interested). It certainly includes benefits in kind provided as part of employment, which can be substantial. In principle, it includes the income in kind received by homeowners from the services of their accommodation. Owning a home does not yield cash income but has the equivalent effect in that it saves the owner from having to pay rent. For this reason, the application of the comprehensive definition of income indicates that we should impute an income, referred to as "imputed rent." Such an item is included in the national accounts (see the next section) and is sizeable: in the UK in 2012 it represented about 10 per cent of Gross Domestic Product (GDP). The same consideration applies to other assets, such as furniture, home IT equipment, and consumer durables, but their quantitative significance is likely to be much less. In the distributional statistics quoted earlier, imputed rent is not included, but it is certainly relevant to policy reforms that impinge on the housing market.

Missing from the distributional statistics is a further important source of income in kind: the value of public services, such as health, education, and social care. These are shown in Figure 1.5 as adding to household disposable income to give household "extended income." Public services are not easily valued, but they undoubtedly add to the resources available to households. If, for example, public education were not provided, parents would have to finance private schooling for their children out of their disposable income. Countries differ in the extent of the provision of public services, so that their omission affects the comparison of inequality across countries. As we shall see later in the book, countries with less public spending tend to have higher private spending, although the distribution is likely to be different. Valuing the public services at their cost to the government, the measured inequality in extended income in European countries is considerably less than that in disposable income.[38]

Adoption of the comprehensive definition of income implies that full account be taken of changes in asset values: the fact that assets may have gained or lost in value over the period of measurement. Such changes do not enter the measurement of national income, but in terms of the household balance sheet they certainly affect spending capacity. If the value of the shares you own has risen during the year, then you can spend that amount without reducing your net worth. We need to distinguish between accrued and realised gains (and losses). The former are gains on paper; the latter are gains that have been turned into cash by sale of the asset. It is the latter that are typically taxed and that appear in some income-distribution statistics. Capital gains can make a noticeable difference, particularly to measured top income shares. In the US, the share of the top 1 per cent excluding capital gains (as in Figure 1.1) in 2012 was 19.3

per cent, but the share including realised capital gains was some 3 percentage points higher at 22.5 per cent.[39] To the extent that realised gains fall short of the total accrued (since many holders of the assets have not sold), the increased inequality is understated. On the other hand, the calculation does not allow for inflation, and by counting the monetary gain it overstates the real gain. If prices have risen during the period, then the purchasing power (referred to as the "real value") of your assets has declined. So if your $1,000 shares have increased to $1,200, you have made a money capital gain of $200, but if prices have risen by 10 per cent, then the real gain is only $100. This raises a more general point. The comprehensive definition of income refers to holding net worth constant, and this means the real value. Anyone holding assets is subject to a capital loss on account of inflation. The person with a bank account paying zero interest is suffering the same reduction in purchasing power. Conversely, in the case of liabilities, there should be an addition, since the obligation to repay is reduced in terms of its purchasing power. It has always surprised me that so little attention has been paid to these adjustments for inflation, which are very apparent to small savers, who even at low rates of price increase are seeing their wealth eroded.

What about Inequality of Consumption?

So far I have been discussing the distribution of outcomes in terms of income and earnings, but these may—quite reasonably—be regarded as means to an end, not ends in themselves. Silas Marner, in George Eliot's novel of that name, may have derived pleasure from counting his gold, but most people look beyond their bank account—as he too later did.[40] The end that many economists have in mind is consumption. And it is not just economists. In his review of Thomas Piketty's book *Capital in the Twenty-First Century,* Bill Gates, while agreeing with the book's main conclusions, criticises the author for "neglecting consumption altogether."[41] If we consider consumption rather than income, then the findings with regard to inequality and poverty can be different. Dale Jorgenson of Harvard has argued that "official U.S. poverty statistics based on household income imply that the War on Poverty ended in failure . . . However, poverty estimates based on household consumption imply that the War on Poverty was a success." Bruce Meyer and James Sullivan conclude that "moving from traditional income-based measures of poverty to a consumption-based measure and, crucially, adjusting for bias in price indexes lead to the conclusion that the poverty rate declined by 26.4 percentage points between 1960 and 2010, 8.5 percentage points of which has occurred since 1980."[42] As far as overall inequality is concerned, Dirk Krueger and Fabrizio Perri have suggested that "the recent increase in income inequality in the U.S. has not been accompanied by a corresponding rise in consumption inequality," but other authors have reached a different conclusion. Orazio Attanasio, Erik Hurst, and Luigi Pistaferri find that "consumption inequality within the U.S. between 1980 and 2010 has increased by nearly the same amount as income inequality."[43]

The consumption-based research is valuable, but, as with income inequality, questions need to be asked. First, what is being measured in the consumer surveys? We observe not consumption but rather consumption expenditure, which is not the same, as is illustrated by the services from owner-occupied housing discussed above. In that case, consumption exceeds consumer spending; in other cases, as when the household has bought a durable good, spending in a given period may exceed consumption. Different authors have adopted different approaches to spending on education and to spending on medical care. Second, how accurately is consumer expenditure measured? It is well known that certain items, such as alcohol and cigarettes, are under-reported in consumer surveys. What about the total? The key issue is whether the degree of under-reporting has been changing over time. As Mark A. Aguiar and Mark Bils have noted, if consumption inequality has been rising less than income inequality in the US, the mirror image is "a growing gap in savings favoring high income households. Based on reported consumption expenditures, the high income group increased their savings rate from 25 percent to 38 percent between 1980 and 2007, while the low income group maintained a savings rate of roughly −30 percent over this period." They go on to say that the implied savings rates are "implausible."[44] In fact, total consumer expenditure reported in the surveys declined as a percentage of that estimated in the national accounts. A study by the Federal Reserve Board found that the ratio declined by some 10 percentage points between 1992 and the early 2000s. Although the percentage reported in the surveys is now stable at around 78 per cent, this could in part explain the different findings over the longer period.[45]

We have to ask similarly about the population coverage. The study by Krueger and Perri that found less increase in consumption inequality was restricted to a subsample of the population, excluding all rural households, all households with a head aged under twenty-one or over sixty-four, all households in which after-tax labour earnings plus transfers were zero, and all households in which weekly wages were below half the minimum wage. This is not comparable with figures for income inequality covering the whole population. Looking at the whole US population, Jonathan Fisher, David Johnson, and Timothy Smeeding found that "income and consumption inequality increase at approximately the same rate between 1985 and 2006 but diverge during the period of the Great Recession (between 2006 and 2010)," with consumption inequality lower in 2010 than in 2006.[46]

The choice between consumption and income depends on the purpose of the analysis. In the case of poverty measurement, the answer depends on which of two different conceptions we espouse. The first concept is concerned with the *standard of living;* the second concept is concerned with the *right to a minimum level of resources.* Historically, studies of poverty have adopted the first approach, and those that measured income did so on the grounds that low levels of income allowed little scope for saving, so that the income provided a good basis for measuring consumption. Seebohm Rowntree, an early-twentieth-century British social researcher (and chocolate manufacturer), compared the incomes of households with the poverty line set at the level sufficient "to obtain the minimum necessaries for the maintenance of merely physical efficiency."[47] Over time, however, attention began to shift to a broader definition of poverty based on the capacity to participate in the life of society, and with this came interest in the concept of minimum rights to resources, the disposal of which is a matter for individual decision. The difference between the two approaches can be illustrated by the measurement of poverty for men and women. On a standard-of-living approach it may be legitimate to set different poverty lines for men and women, on the grounds that women have on average smaller nutritional needs, and this was indeed the case with the US official poverty line in its early years. The poverty line for 1963 set by Mollie Orshansky for non-farmers under the age of sixty-five was $1,650 a year for a single man but only $1,525 for a single woman.[48] On a minimum-rights approach, such differentiation would be unacceptable.

The use of consumer spending as an indicator of poverty or overall inequality is open to the objection that spending, like income, is a means to an end. Crucial inequalities can arise in the process of consumption: in the activity of converting money into goods and services. These include differential access to goods and services on account of different prices: for example, it has been argued that the "poor pay more" because of their use of neighbourhood shops rather than out-of-town supermarkets. The rental practices of landlords may mean that low-income tenants face higher energy prices, for example, because they have to use coin meters. The inequalities may be the result of the non-availability of goods and services. As societies have become richer, shops may have ceased to stock cheaper varieties or qualities of products. Services, such as transactional banking, may not be available in certain areas. The poor may be excluded from bank loans by credit scoring. All of these issues need careful consideration before we can reach conclusions about the changing pattern of the inequality of consumption.

Considerations of access to goods and services have led to proposals that we should contemplate the distribution of "certain specific scarce commodities," as Nobel Prize–winner James Tobin of Yale put it in what he called "specific egalitarianism." He cited, among other goods, food, housing, education, and medical care.[49] In the same way, the approach to measuring poverty and social exclusion in Europe from 2009 included indicators of material deprivation. One of the three components of the Europe 2020 target for poverty and social exclusion is a measure of "severe deprivation," defined in terms of the enforced lack of four items from a list of nine. These nine items include "avoiding arrears with housing costs," "affording meals with meat, chicken or fish," and "keeping the home adequately warm."[50] An interesting difference between Tobin's list and that of the EU is that the former includes education and health, the provision of which Europeans would regard as primarily the responsibility of the state. On the other hand, at the top of the income scale, a telling indicator of "voluntary exclusion" is the capacity of rich people to opt out of state provision into private schooling and health care. In the words of the British philosopher Brian Barry, "if the wealthiest fraction of a society feel that they can afford to insulate themselves from the common fate and buy their way out of the common institutions, that is also a form of social isolation."[51]

The multifaceted nature of consumption, and the differing concerns that it evokes, mean that a consumer spending measure is not demonstrably superior to income as an indicator. I continue to focus on income as an indicator of potential control over resources. The use of income is indeed recognition that the use of resources goes beyond consumption. When measuring inequality, we are concerned not just with the consumption of the rich—important though this may be—but also with the power that wealth can convey. This power may be exercised over one's family, as with the passing on of wealth to heirs, or more generally in such ways as control of the media or influence with political parties. A good example is provided by charitable donations. Putting a coin in a bucket conveys little such power, but the establishment of charitable foundations can have a profound impact on the lives of others, as indeed has been well demonstrated by the Gates Foundation. The impact can be highly beneficial, but it represents nonetheless the exercise of power in a way that is not captured by the measurement of consumption. Income is indeed a means to an end, but its reach goes much wider than consumption.

Who Is Where in the Distribution?

Barbara Wootton, an English economist and social campaigner, wrote that one of the incidents that led her to write *The Social Foundations of Wage Policy* was the discovery that the elephant giving rides at Whipsnade Zoo earned the same amount as she did as a senior university teacher.[52] I have often wondered about the relevance of this particular comparison, but there is no doubt that people like to know where they are in the income distribution.[53] There is also little doubt that many people, particularly those near the top of the distribution, believe that they are lower down than they really are. Jan Pen, the Dutch economist who invented the "parade of incomes" to represent the income distribution, "once asked a medical specialist, who is probably among the top 0.3% of the income pyramid, which part of the population he thought were above him. He considered the question and answered: 20%."[54] More recently, Polly Toynbee and David Walker asked a similar question of top city lawyers and bankers in London who were comfortably in the top 1 per cent of earners. The lawyers and bankers overestimated by a factor of 4 the earnings required to be in the top 10 per cent. When asked to fix a poverty threshold, this elite group set it at a level that turned out to be "just under gross median earnings, which meant they regarded ordinary earnings as poverty pay."[55]

Numbers in the income distribution can quickly become out of date, even with modest rates of inflation, but it may help the reader to know who was who in 2013. At that time, the US Census Bureau put median household income at $51,939 a year, and the poverty threshold for four people (below which 14.5 per cent of the population was living) was $23,834 (or 46 per cent of the median). These figures refer to money income before taxes and do not include the value of noncash benefits such as food stamps. Moving up the distribution, we learn from the Census Bureau that $150,000, some three times the median, places a household in the top 10 per cent, and the estimates of Emmanuel Saez of Berkeley, on a somewhat different definition, suggest that the top 1 per cent began at around $400,000.[56]

In the UK, official figures show that the median household disposable income adjusted for household size and composition in 2012–2013 was £15,300 a year for a single person, £22,950 for a couple, and £32,125 for a couple and two children. (In comparing these with the US figures, bear in mind that direct taxes have been subtracted in the UK case but not for the US figures.) The poverty threshold is set at 60 per cent of the median: that is, £9,180 a year for a single person. The upper tail in the UK is less spread out, so twice the median (£64,250 a year for a couple and two children) would put a household on the verge of entering the top 10 per cent.[57]

So far I have focused on the vertical dimension of inequality—between rich and poor—but there are important horizontal dimensions as well. In the Gini coefficient or a top 1 per cent income share, people appear anonymously, but we may be concerned with how unequal income is across various groups, such as by gender, location, or ethnic group.[58]

We may want to make allowance for differences in needs. For example, the figures for income inequality presented above take no account of geographic differences in prices. The cost of living in Boston, for example, is rated at 132.5, whereas that in Topeka, Kansas, is rated at only 91.8.[59] Another significant difference is needs on the grounds of disability; valuable research makes the case for including these needs in the equivalence scales used to calculate equivalised income. Asghar Zaidi and Tania Burchardt show in the case of the UK how failure to take account of the costs of disability leads to a significant understatement of the extent of poverty among people with disabilities. In what follows, I consider three horizontal dimensions: gender, generational, and global.

Gender

The figures above showing the dispersion of earnings did not distinguish between those of men and women or tell us anything about the gender pay gap. In the United States, the US Census Bureau figures show the female/male average (measured by the mean) earnings ratio for full-time year-round workers. In 1960, the ratio was 60 per cent, but by 2013 the ratio had risen to 78 per cent. This is a distinct shift, but it still means that men earn on average one-fifth more than women. Moreover, the rise has not been a steady one. The ratio was stable from 1960 to 1980, then increased over the next two decades. Since 2000 there has been little change.[60] In their review of the evidence for eight OECD countries, Sophie Ponthieux and Dominique Meurs conclude that "the gender wage gap has been decreasing more slowly since the late 1990s (except in the UK and Japan, where the narrowing has continued at the same pace) or stagnating, and even increasing in Italy."[61]

In considering the trend in the gender earnings gap, we need—as with the distribution of earnings in general—to distinguish between differences attributable to characteristics such as educational attainment, which may justify differential pay, and those that reflect discrimination. Historically, a major factor behind the general narrowing of the gender wage gap has been the increase in women's educational levels. In the US the college graduation rate for women in 1950 was around half that for men (although, interestingly, this is a phenomenon that dates back only to the 1930s; for birth cohorts 1910 and earlier the difference was small). After 1950, the graduation rate for women began to rise, and women are now the majority of US college graduates. This reversal of the gender education gap has been observed in most OECD countries. Women now outrank men in twenty-nine of the thirty-two OECD countries.[62] The role played by education and other labour-market–relevant characteristics, as revealed in more than 1,500 studies of the gender wage gap, covering sixty-three countries over the period from the 1960s to the 1990s, has been summarised by Doris Weichselbaumer and Rudolf Winter-Ebmer as follows: "The bulk of [the decline in the gender wage gap] must be attributed to better labor market endowments of females which came about by better education, training, and work attachment. Looking at the published estimates for the discrimination (or unexplained) component of the wage gap yields a less promising perspective: There is no decline over time."[63] Standardising for data selection and for differences in statistical methods "gives rise to a slightly more optimistic picture," but this still implies that it would take roughly sixty years for the gap they attribute to "discrimination" to be reduced by 10 percentage points.

Differences by gender remain an important source of concern.

Time and Generations

Figures 1.1 and 1.2 for the US and the UK presented a sequence of "snapshots," showing the circumstances in that year of the entire population present at the time. We do not get to see the whole movie. We do not know whether the people in the upper ranges are still there next year; we do not know how many of the families in poverty were able to escape the next year. This matters for three reasons. The first is that there is year-to-year mobility, and it is possible that the observed increase in inequality is due to increased volatility. That is the way macroeconomists have tended to interpret the rise in top income shares. In the UK, the extent of income mobility has been investigated by Stephen Jenkins, who finds that there is "a substantial degree of income mobility between one year and the next," but he qualifies this statement by saying that "most mobility is short distance rather than long distance." He gives a graphic description of the underlying process: "Each person's income fluctuates about a relatively fixed longer-term average—this value is a tether on the income scale to which people are attached [as if] by a rubber band. They may move away from the tether from one year to the next, but not too far because of the band holding them. And they tend to rebound back towards and around the tether."[64] Has mobility increased? In the US, Peter Gottschalk and Robert Moffitt found that increased transitory variations in earnings could account for half of the increased dispersion in the late 1970s and early 1980s, but the effect then levelled off.[65] Over the period 1970–2004 as a whole, Wojciech Kopczuk, Emmanuel Saez, and Jae Song concluded that "virtually all" of the increase in the variance of earnings was due to the increase in the variance of permanent earnings. They found that "mobility at the top of the earnings distribution is stable and has not mitigated the dramatic increase in annual earnings concentration since the 1970s." This is consistent with the conclusion of Gottschalk and Moffitt that increased earnings instability was concentrated among the least-skilled, so that it was less relevant to the rise in the top decile earnings ratio shown in Figure 1.1.[66] In the UK Jenkins found that transitory volatility had not changed much between the start of the 1990s and the mid-2000s. It appears that, at least in the US and the UK, increased volatility is only a modest part of the story.

The second reason we need to follow people over time is that there are predictable life-cycle variations in income. For many people, income follows a broadly hump-shaped pattern, rising as their career progresses and falling as they retire and run down their savings. Such systematic life-cycle differences could explain part of the observed rise in inequality if there has been a shift in the demographic structure. To these may be added the changes in family formation, notably the increase in the proportion of one-parent families. In 1960 the US Census reported that 9 per cent of children lived in a family with one parent; by 2010 this had increased to 27 per cent. In the UK today, there is a similar proportion: one child in four lives in a one-parent family. In the US, Rebecca Blank, labour economist and former member of President Obama's Cabinet, examined how far changes in demographic and family structure could account for the increase in the Gini coefficient between 1979 and 2007. She found that demographic shifts played a role, but the contribution was small: on the order of 1.25 percentage points.[67] In the UK, Jenkins had earlier identified only a modest contribution of demographic shifts over the period 1971 to 1986. Shifting demographic and family structure is undoubtedly important in terms of policy design, but again it does not contribute much towards explaining rising inequality.

The third reason for following individual lifetimes is that there may be significant inequality between generations. If, as in the past, real incomes are rising over time, those born later enjoy higher lifetime incomes. Such a rise is built into the standard approach to the evaluation of public investment decisions. When a government is considering a long-term project, or the benefits from the mitigation of climate change, a social discount rate is applied, and this discount rate is made up of two components: a pure discount factor for the distance in time, and a factor that reflects the expectation that future generations will be better off.[68] In other words, a lower valuation is attached to the incomes of future generations, just as a lower valuation is attached to the better-off when measuring inequality at a point in time. But such an expectation may no longer be warranted. If we now expect the growth of average incomes to be slower, or nonexistent, as we seek a sustainable path, then we should not discount future generations in this way. We should not assume that they will be better off than we are today and therefore regard them as "less deserving" (which is what discounting means). They may be no better off and perhaps even worse off. The issue of intergenerational justice has therefore greater priority than when we believed that "life could only get better," and it should be one of the factors by which we judge the choice of measures to reduce the current inequality of income.

Global Inequality

Inequality among all the world's citizens reflects the combined impact of the inequality within countries and the inequality between countries. Seen this way, the simple story of global inequality over the last hundred years is that there was first a period when inequality within rich countries was falling but inequality between countries was widening, now replaced by a period when inequality within rich countries is rising but inequality between countries is narrowing. Inequality within countries has followed a U-shape and inequality between countries has followed a ∩-shape.

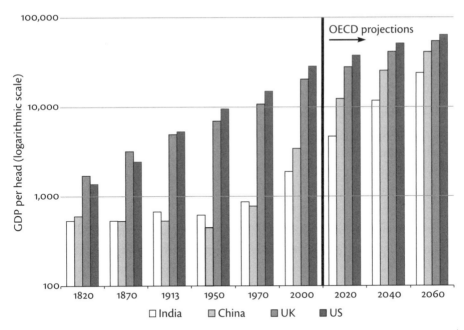

FIGURE 1.6: Global divergence then convergence: GDP per capita, 1820–2060

In 1820, the GDP per capita in PPPs (Purchasing Power Parities, which are exchange rates adjusted for differences in purchasing power) was $533 in India, $600 in China, $1,376 in the US, and $1,706 in the UK.

The ∩-shape—divergence between countries followed by convergence—is illustrated by four countries in Figure 1.6, which shows the absolute differences in national income (GDP) per head in India, China, the UK, and the US, as they emerged historically and as they are projected to evolve according to the OECD. In each case national income is expressed in terms of purchasing power, where this takes account of the rising cost of living over time and the differences in purchasing power across countries (that a dollar buys more in Delhi than it does in New York). It need hardly be stressed that such comparisons across time and space can only be approximate, but they suffice to show the broad picture. From 1820 to 1970, the gap widened between India and China, on the one side, and the UK and the US, on the other. Income per head in the US rose by a factor of more than 10; the UK grew rather less over this period, having started off ahead but then been overtaken by the US. From 1970 to the present, India and China have been closing the gap, and the OECD projects that this will continue through the present century.

The ∩-shape for the distribution between countries is usually advanced as furnishing grounds for optimism that the global distribution will in the future show less inequality. There are, however, two reasons for caution. First, while the gap is narrowing in relative terms, the absolute differences in purchasing power are continuing to widen. China may be growing faster in percentage terms, but that growth applies to a much smaller base. As projected by the OECD, the absolute difference in income per head between China and the United States will widen until 2057. Second, while China and India have been growing rapidly, other developing countries have achieved slower rates of growth. It is for this reason that, although most of my proposals relate to inequality within countries, I discuss in Chapter 8 the global responsibilities of OECD countries to do more to redistribute current income among countries.

Chapter 2

Learning from History

Income inequality has risen in many countries in recent years, but the trend has not always been upwards. For this reason alone, we need to look back in time and examine the historical record about inequality. When in the past has inequality fallen? What can we learn from such periods? To answer these questions, we need a long run of data measuring income inequality. Fortunately, we now have such data. Using today's methods, researchers have examined historical records and constructed estimates of income inequality covering more than a hundred years. Such research is exciting because the historical perspective allows us to understand better how the present inequality arose and how income inequality might be reduced in the future.

In seeking to draw lessons from statistics on inequality, we have to be confident in the quality of the data we are using. This is why I begin this chapter by describing and evaluating the sources of evidence on which scholars of inequality can draw. Such scrutiny is essential. All too often economists race ahead, drawing conclusions from figures that happen to be there, without asking whether the data are suitable. This is all the more important given the explosion of data. The famous study in the mid-1950s by Simon Kuznets, the Nobel Prize–winning Harvard economist, of the evolution of income inequality over time was based on a handful of data points for a small range of countries.[1] Today there is a profusion of data-sets. This represents a great improvement and is a tribute to the substantial effort of statistical offices and individual researchers. At the same time we risk being overwhelmed. Just to give one illustration, the December 2012 issue of the *Journal of Economic Inequality* includes one article that starts from the observation that income inequality is higher in the US than in Japan (as was shown in Figure 1.3, where the Gini coefficient for the former is some 7 percentage points higher) and goes on to provide an explanation. But a reader of the *Journal* would be puzzled to discover that another article in the same issue uses a dataset that shows no real difference in the Gini coefficients of the two countries: US (37.2 per cent) and Japan (36.6 per cent). We need to ask, where do the different data come from? and why, as in this case, do they sometimes seem to be telling different stories?[2]

Sources of Evidence

Household Surveys

The principal source of evidence about income inequality today is the household survey. The figures announced by the US Census Bureau each September on the extent of income inequality and financial poverty are derived from the Current Population Survey, a regular monthly household survey with an annual supplement, centred on March, that collects information on the income of the household in the previous calendar year. Some US readers may have taken part in this survey, although you should not be too disappointed if you have not been chosen, as only some 60,000 households are selected each year (around 1 in 2,000). The UK figures shown in Figure 1.2 are derived from the Family Resources Survey, a survey of more than 20,000 households that similarly asks detailed questions about income and household circumstances. The European Union Statistics on Income and Living Conditions (EU-SILC) cover all member states (and Iceland, Norway, Switzerland, and Turkey) and are the basis for the EU social indicators, such as the proportion of people living at risk of poverty or social exclusion.

As a result of the investment made by national statistical agencies and other bodies, we now know from these household surveys a great deal more about income inequality than when I first began research in the 1960s. At that time, relatively little information was collected and, where data were collected, little was released to researchers. It was virtually impossible to make comparisons across countries. Today we have data sources designed for this purpose, such as EU-SILC, which now covers more than thirty countries. Independent research centres such as LIS (the Luxembourg Income Study) make data available for researchers on a harmonised basis, covering nearly fifty countries (these data have been used above in Figure 1.3). Collections of secondary data such as the World Income Inequality Database assembled by United Nations University–World Institute for Development Economics Research (UNU-WIDER) cover more than 150 countries from Afghanistan to Zimbabwe.

Comparability is key to this research. The statement that inequality in one country is lower than in another is of limited meaning if the underlying statistics are not collected on a comparable basis. We cannot draw immediate conclusions about differences in inequality if in country A incomes are recorded in a household survey for the household as a whole, whereas in country B they are drawn from individual income tax records. We cannot say that pay is less dispersed in one country if the statistics leave out all farm workers or public-sector employees, or if the survey is confined to urban areas. In what follows, I have tried to use a comparable definition across countries and, where that is not possible, to signal the likely consequences of the differences. Of course, 100 per cent comparability is impossible. The same information may be collected in all countries, but its significance depends on the context. Inequality of money income is of less concern where the state provides services such as education and health care free to all, and where housing and transportation are subsidised. There will, moreover, always remain differences between statistical sources, and it is a matter of judgement whether they are salient. I was once told that one particular country included in household income the value of honey produced from bees kept at home. Even as the son of a beekeeper I did not feel that this would materially affect the comparison with the UK.

Comparability is just as important over time. Our ability to say more about inequality today stems not just from the fact that surveys are better and more comparable than ever before, but also from the fact that they have been operating over decades. Moreover, resources have been invested in rendering them broadly comparable over time. Again, full comparability is not possible. Survey methods improve over time, and we cannot go back to redo the surveys from the 1970s. Changes in methodology affect the conclusions drawn. In 1993 the US Current Population Survey changed from paper and pencil to computer-assisted interviewing; it also changed the maximum amounts that could be entered. Before 1993 earnings were top-coded at $299,999, which was high enough not to affect most people but meant that top earnings were understated (after 1993 the limit was raised to $999,999). Over the years, there have been many other changes in methodology: the source of the US data has no fewer than twenty footnotes detailing changes in different years. The cumulative impact of these changes is hard to assess, but those in 1993 seem to be the most important because there was a large rise in recorded inequality in that year. The US Census Bureau counsels that users should "exercise caution" in comparing years before and after 1993, and I have adjusted Figure 1.1 accordingly.[3]

LIMITATIONS TO HOUSEHOLD SURVEYS

Household survey data are now widely used to study inequality, and the figures for different countries shown earlier in Figure 1.3 are based largely on this source. But there are several potential limitations. To begin with, they are *household* surveys and therefore exclude people who do not live in households. Those not covered include people living in institutions like students, school boarders, and military personnel, and those in hospitals, hostels, shelters, refuges, or reception centres. Household surveys leave out older people living in care homes or nursing homes, children taken into care, and those living on the streets. These omissions matter because some of the groups not covered are likely to be concentrated in the lower ranges of the income distribution. This may be compounded by the bias that arises when the listing from which the sample is drawn fails to be representative of the household population. The classic example is the use of telephone interviewing back when telephones were far from ubiquitous, which led to opinion polls overestimating the Republican vote in US presidential elections.[4]

Complete coverage is hard to achieve, since in most countries participation in surveys is voluntary, and people can refuse to take part. The rate of nonresponse for the Family Resources Survey in the UK in 2010/11 was 41 per cent. This means that, for every six people who took part, there were four others about whom we learned nothing. When asked about the reason for refusal, 23 per cent said that "they could not be bothered." The rise of nonresponse is worrisome: in the late 1990s nonresponse was 34 per cent. In the US the response rate is much higher, with nonresponse in 2013 just over 10 per cent, but there too nonresponse has risen in recent years. The declining response rate is an issue that should concern the statistical agencies.

Why does this nonresponse matter? Low response rates do not in themselves mean that we should reject the findings. Even surveys with low response rates can be representative if nonrespondents are no different, in the relevant characteristics, from respondents. However, with questions on income and wealth, there are good reasons to suppose that rates of nonresponse are systematically higher among the well-off. Those with more complex financial circumstances may, for understandable reasons, be less willing to devote the time required to answer detailed questions on their income and wealth. The Federal Reserve, when conducting the US Survey of Consumer Finances, draws both a standard geographically based random sample and a special "list sample," selected from statistical records derived from income tax returns (under strict rules governing confidentiality) to include disproportionately families that hold a relatively large share of such thinly held assets as noncorporate businesses and tax-exempt bonds. The Federal Reserve reports that "in both 2010 and 2013, about 70 percent of households selected for the area-probability sample actually completed interviews. The overall response rate in the list sample was about one-third; in the part of the list sample containing the wealthiest families, the response rate was only about one-half that level."[5] There are, therefore, good reasons to suppose that the upper tail of the distribution is under-represented in household surveys. In the UK, the series for overall inequality shown in Figure 1.2 in the previous chapter is taken from the work of the Institute for Fiscal Studies, which makes an adjustment using data from income tax returns (see below) to correct for the problems in obtaining high response rates to the underlying household survey from very rich individuals and the volatility in their reported incomes.

Adjustments to household survey data are also required to correct for "response bias," where people take part but provide answers that are incomplete or incorrect. In some cases this may be beyond their control. Participating in an official survey in the UK a few years ago, I realised that an answer I had given to an earlier question left out one source of income, but I was told firmly that the computer-based interview would not let me return to an earlier question, so my original answer had to stand. When using survey data to examine the distribution of income, it is important to examine how far the recorded totals of income match up with those known from external sources. In the case of the EU-SILC, a comparison with the national accounts (allowing for the differences in definitions) found that in 2008 wages and salaries had the highest coverage rate, followed by social benefits in cash and taxes. Coverage was poor for self-employment income and property income. These categories of income are, on average, located higher up the distribution, so that their under-recording in household surveys tends to cause inequality to be understated.[6]

Household surveys are an indispensable source of data, and it is vital that statistical agencies continue to invest in their operation and development. The information they provide is essential to the creation of policy to reduce inequality. Nevertheless, we must treat the findings from surveys with appropriate caution. For this reason, they are increasingly being used in conjunction with administrative data.

Income Tax Data

If the income distribution data do not come from household surveys, where can we find them? The main answer is from administrative records, as they came to contain information on how individual families were faring. There were earlier "social tables" in which pioneers such as Gregory King constructed income distributions for England and Wales (for 1688), but these were not based on data for individuals. Not until the advent of the personal income tax (at the beginning of the nineteenth century in the UK) could genuine estimates of income inequality be assembled from verified data on individual incomes. Such distributional data can be combined with external control totals, from population data and from the national accounts, to estimate the shares of different groups in total income. This way the shares of the top 1 per cent in Figures 1.1 and 1.2 relate to the top 1 per cent of the total adult population (or total tax units, as appropriate) and give their share of total household income as estimated in the national accounts. The totals are not limited to those reported by taxpayers.[7]

Initially the personal income tax covered only a small minority of the population, and the series for top income shares commence before we can make estimates for inequality in the whole population (the Gini coefficient). Coverage of the income tax data has since expanded, notably during and after the Second World War, so that the administrative data now cover the great majority of the population. Even for individual taxpayers not filing tax returns, collection of income tax at source means that the coverage of the tax records is extensive. Nevertheless, in using data from income tax records, we must bear in mind that they are not purpose-designed; the data are a by-product of an administrative process. The form and content of the data reflect the tax legislation. In the US, for example, the tax unit refers to the combined incomes of couples (and their dependents), whereas in the UK since 1990 people have been taxed as individuals, and the resulting distribution relates to individual incomes.[8] The definition of income for tax purposes may depart significantly from the comprehensive definition described in the previous chapter. It may allow the deduction of interest paid on a house purchase or on personal loans. In some cases, it may approach the comprehensive definition more closely than household surveys, for instance, the inclusion of imputed rent on owner-occupied housing (as used to be the case in the UK) or of realised capital gains. In all cases, the coverage of the income tax data is potentially seriously affected by the "nonresponse" of taxpayers in the form of tax avoidance and evasion. Studies of top incomes based on income tax records have typically paid considerable attention to the possible impact of avoidance and evasion.[9]

Data on Earnings

Both household surveys and administrative records provide sources of data on individual earnings, the latter typically in the form of social security tax collections. The range of possible data sources is, however, larger in the case of earnings, since information can be collected from both sides of the labour market. Countries may employ different sources. The earnings data for the US in Figure 1.1 come from the same source as the income inequality series, that is, the Current Population Survey, which is a household survey, whereas the data for the UK in Figure 1.2 come from employers, the Annual Survey of Hours and Earnings. The earnings data for France in this chapter come from tax declarations. Comparisons of different sources for the same country suggest that the findings are reasonably coherent.[10] However, the difference of perspective between employee and employer may lead to systematic differences on certain variables, notably hours, where employers may report contractual hours and employees report those actually spent on the job. There may also be important differences in coverage. The coverage of the statistics based on the French tax declarations excludes agricultural workers, civil servants, domestic workers, and those working less than full-time, with the result that the coverage in 1995, for example, was around two-thirds of all employees. The EU Structure of Earnings survey excludes public administration as well as enterprises with fewer than ten employees.

The variety of sources means that the data on earnings are often richer than data mined from household surveys, but it may also mean more difficulty ensuring consistency across countries and across time. The user has always to check that like is being compared with like.

Data on Wealth

In the case of wealth, there is an even larger range of possible data sources. There are household surveys of personal wealth, such as that conducted by the US Federal Reserve, and those recently introduced by the European Central Bank, of which the UK component is the Wealth and Assets Survey. As noted, such surveys are subject to nonresponse, which cannot be fully overcome by oversampling rich people. The very rich are the subject of a different kind of investigation, which is the construction of lists of large wealth-holders, such as the Forbes List of the World's Billionaires and the Sunday *Times* "Rich List," which has been compiled by Philip Beresford in the UK. There are multiple potential sources of administrative data. These include the tax returns from an annual wealth tax where such a tax exists, and the indirect information such as the investment income recorded on income tax returns, the income being multiplied up to yield estimates of the underlying wealth, where the multipliers take account of the variation in taxable return with wealth size and other characteristics. Indirect evidence is provided by the administrative data on estates at death, often associated with the operation of inheritance or estate taxation. In this case, a different kind of multiplier is applied. In effect those dying in a given year are treated as a sample of the living population. Death is not random, so the multipliers vary according to age and gender. They also allow for the fact that the wealthy typically have lower mortality. In this way the distribution of estates in a year are converted into estimates of the wealth of the living. It is evident that the multiplier procedure is surrounded by a margin of error, and that, as with the income tax data, the results are constrained by the definitions embodied in the legal structure and may be affected by the avoidance and evasion of taxation. As in the case of the income tax data, the wealth estimated from tax data can be expressed as shares of the national total by making use of external information about total personal wealth. The estimates of total personal wealth come from national balance sheets, which in the UK form part of the national accounts.

Going Back in Time

The sources of data have been described in contemporary terms, but an important contribution of recent research has been to go back and resurrect data from the past. In some cases, this means using data on individuals from the past, but this process is typically very time-consuming and rarely used.[11] More common is the use of published tabulations, which show how many people received incomes in different ranges. This information was routinely published by the income tax authorities in many countries, often in considerable detail. In the Netherlands, for example, such sources show that in 1933 just one married couple had an income between 800,000 and 900,000 guilder; and since there was only one, we know from the row average that their taxable income was exactly 874,000 guilders—or more than 800 times the average income.[12] In the early years—around the beginning of the twentieth century—economists made use of the income tax tabulations, but there followed many years of neglect. Only recently has this rich source been exploited. By combining the tabulated data with newly constructed control totals for income, it has been possible to construct series dating back in some countries to more than 100 years.[13]

To sum up, there are many sources of information from which we can learn about the distribution of income, earnings, and wealth. If you appear in the statistics that follow, it may be because you have taken part in a household survey; it may be because your employer made a return as part of a survey; your income tax records or your social security tax records may have been an input into the estimates; or you may appear in the Rich List! The important point to take away from this account of the sources underlying the evidence is that all data are imperfect, and that we have to make the best use we can of these flawed materials. I like the image of economic data described by the Harvard economist Zvi Griliches: "The available economic statistics are our main window on economic behavior. In spite of the scratches and persistent fogging, we cannot stop peering through it and trying to understand what is happening."[14]

When Has Inequality Fallen in the Past?

In this chapter, I am seeking lessons from periods when there has been a salient reduction in inequality. What do I mean by this? What constitutes a "salient" change in inequality? We know that the summary measures of inequality, such as the Gini coefficient, vary from year to year. How much does the figure have to fall for us to say that there has been a salient reduction? The standard answer people give to this question is in terms of the sampling error, or the variation that can be expected from collecting information on only a sample as opposed to the whole population. Statistics Canada, for example, suggests that, with a sample of some 35,000 households, a change in the Gini coefficient of 1 percentage point or more can be considered statistically significant.[15] It is, however, the policy salience that concerns me here. Making the same kind of calculation as that in the previous chapter, linking changes in the overall tax rate to changes in the Gini coefficient, we can see that a 5 percentage point rise in the tax rate would bring about a fall of 3 percentage points in the Gini coefficient.[16] Since a 5 percentage point rise in the tax rate would be a major step for any minister of finance, a 3 percentage point reduction in the Gini coefficient does not seem unreasonable as a criterion of salience, and it is employed here—although it is, of course, only an indication. Referring back to the country comparisons of Gini coefficients in Figure 1.3, we can see that a 3 percentage point reduction would render the UK less unequal than Australia, and France and Germany less unequal than Finland.

What about the other inequality indicators? For the poverty rate, we may note that the Europe 2020 target for combating poverty and social exclusion over the present decade aims, in round numbers, at a reduction of one-sixth. Applied to the at-risk-of-poverty rate (rather than the extended measure of poverty and social exclusion), this too would imply in rounded terms a reduction of 3 percentage points. For top income shares, there is no obvious metric, and I take the same figure of 3 percentage points. Finally, for the top decile of earnings, expressed as a percentage of the median, I take a 5 per cent change as salient, which would mean that a fall from, say, 200 per cent to 190 per cent of median earnings would register. In each case the change is measured over a period when the indicator was proceeding in a clear direction, but without regard to the length of the period. I am seeking periods of change, not speed of change.

Changing Inequality from 1914 to 1945 and the Role of War

In *Capital in the Twenty-First Century,* Thomas Piketty says of his native France that "it is striking to see the extent to which the compression of income inequality is concentrated in one highly distinctive period: 1914–1945. . . . To a large extent, it was the chaos of war, with its attendant economic and political shocks, that reduced inequality in the twentieth century. There was no gradual, consensual, conflict-free evolution towards greater equality. In the twentieth century, it was war, not harmonious democratic or economic rationality, that erased the past."[17] The evidence about France on which Piketty draws for this period is that on top income shares. There are eight other countries for which we have evidence on top shares for 1914 and 1945, and for all but two (Norway and South Africa) the share of the top 1 per cent in total gross income was by 1945 at least 3 percentage points lower than in 1914.[18] In Japan, the share of the top 1 per cent fell from 18.6 per cent to 7.4 per cent, numbers virtually identical to those for France (where the share fell from 18.3 per cent to 7.5 per cent). What is more, in these two countries the fall between 1914 and 1945 accounted for almost all of the total fall in the twentieth century. A difference begins to emerge, however, between France and Japan, on one side, and the other seven countries for which we have data covering the period. In Denmark, the Netherlands, Norway, South Africa, Sweden, the UK, and the US, there were salient declines in top income shares after 1945. The reduction in inequality was not confined to the period 1914 to 1945.

To understand more clearly the role of the world wars, we need to examine in more detail what happened in the period 1914 to 1945. Beginning with the First World War (1914 to 1918), we can see that top income shares in the UK were lower after the war, reflecting among other things the loss of overseas assets: the share of the top 0.1 per cent fell from 10.7 per cent in 1914 to 8.7 per cent in 1918. But there was no salient reduction in the other combatant countries such as Japan or the US. In France, the share of the top 1 per cent was 18.3 per cent in 1915 and 17.9 per cent in 1920. In noncombatants, such as Denmark and the Netherlands, the top income share actually rose during the First World War. As has been shown in the events to mark the centenary of 1914, the war had profound consequences, but these did not include major redistribution away from rich people. There were indeed calls after the war in the UK and other countries for a capital levy to deal with war profiteering. Sir Josiah Stamp remarked in his lectures *The Financial Aftermath of War* that "there was a great clamour for attacks upon *increase* of capital wealth made during the war" (his italics).[19]

For the interwar period, we have evidence for more countries: for the years from 1920 to 1939, the evidence on top income shares now covers fifteen countries, extending to India and Zimbabwe (then Southern Rhodesia). Of the fifteen, nine, including four Anglo-Saxon countries (Australia, Canada, the UK, and the US) and Denmark, Japan, and Sweden, did not exhibit a salient overall change in top shares between 1920 and 1939. In only four was there a salient decrease over the period as a whole: France, the Netherlands, New Zealand, and South Africa. In his discussion of the French experience, Piketty stresses the complexity of the interwar period and the existence of countermovements superimposed on the overall pattern of change. One was the deflation between 1929 and 1935, the distributional consequences of which were offset by the election of the Front Populaire in 1936, with the subsequent tax changes and the

Matignon Agreements on workers' rights.[20] There were considerable differences across countries in the distributional impact of the Great Depression that started in 1929.[21]

In the Second World War (1939 to 1945)—in contrast to the First World War—inequality fell widely. For all except two of the seventeen countries for which we have top income share data, there was a fall in inequality between 1939 and 1945 (the exceptions were South Africa and Southern Rhodesia). In eight of the seventeen countries, the fall was sufficient to qualify as salient. It was not just in occupied or defeated countries that inequality fell. The time paths are shown for a selection of countries in Figure 2.1. As indicated, the shares of the top 1 per cent fell to a similar extent in all countries shown—with the exception of Switzerland. It is also possible to bring to bear evidence about overall inequality, in the form of the Gini coefficient, shown by the solid lines in Figure 2.1. In the UK, the Gini coefficient after the Second World War was a full 7 percentage points lower than in 1938; in the US the difference between 1936 and 1944 is of a similar order of magnitude.

The Second World War was different in that there was a more general reduction in income inequality. In some cases, this was the product of the "chaos" of war and occupation, or of the structural breaks imposed by the postwar settlement. But even in countries where there was continuity of government major changes took place as a result of new social attitudes and a greater sense of social solidarity. In the UK this had already led during the war to the 1944 Education Act, and, more generally, as Richard Titmuss described in his history of social policy during the war, "by the end of the Second World War the Government had . . . assumed and developed a measure of direct concern for the health and well-being of the population which, by contrast with the role of the Government in the nineteen-thirties, was a little short of remarkable."[22] The year 1945 saw the election of the postwar Labour government, which created the National Health Service and a unified system of National Insurance along the lines proposed by Beveridge. In the US, Claudia Goldin and Robert Margo, who characterise the reduction in wage dispersion as the "Great Compression," highlight the role of labour -market intervention in the form of the National War Labor Board.[23] More generally, Paul Krugman has cited

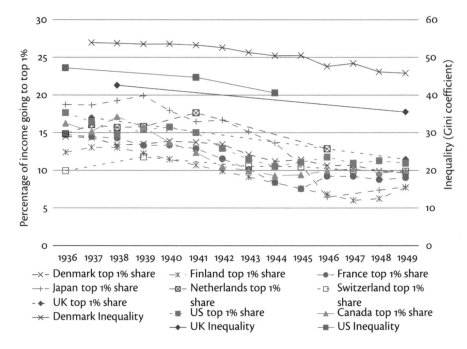

FIGURE 2.1: Inequality and the Second World War, selected world countries

The share of total gross income going to the top 1% (left axis) and overall inequality (as measured by the Gini coefficient; percentage on right axis) fell in most countries during the Second World War.

the other New Deal and Second World War policies of President Roosevelt, and the strengthening of trade unions.[24] But the question then arises, how long did this last?

After the Second World War in the US

What happened next? Quite soon, in the US, the earnings distribution began to widen. As we saw in Chapter 1, the rise in top US earnings can be traced back to 1951. This had nothing to do with globalisation or new computer technologies. The pay distribution began to widen before there was a single commercial computer in operation: the first were delivered in that year (Ferranti Mark 1 in the UK, followed by UNIVAC 1 in the

US). But what is striking is that this widening of the pay distribution was not accompanied by a rise in the inequality of household incomes. It was much later—in the 1980s—that household inequality began to increase. We tend to talk as though wider pay differentials must automatically lead to greater income inequality, but this US experience of the immediate postwar decades tells us that the link can be broken.

How was this achieved? It is useful to go back to the Guide to household income (Figure 1.5). From this, we can see that several different elements intervened to ensure that rising dispersion of individual earnings did not lead to an increase in the Gini coefficient for overall incomes. The first stage is the move from individual earnings to total household earnings. Here, the postwar period saw major developments. The 1980 study by the National Bureau of Economic Research titled *The American Economy in Transition* found that in the labour market "the most important change was the influx of women into the job market, particularly of married women with children." In 1947, one-fifth (22 per cent) of married women (living with their husbands) were in the paid labour force; thirty years later, the figure was close to one-half (47 per cent).[25] The composition of household income was therefore changing. How did this affect inequality? The distribution of the sum of household earnings depends on the degree to which the earnings of husbands and wives are correlated. By the same token, the impact of increased labour-market participation depends on who was entering the labour force. Inequality could be moderated or enhanced. In the immediate postwar period, it appears that increased participation enhanced the earnings of households in the lower part of the distribution. Summarising the postwar US experience, Nan Maxwell writes that "for husband-wife families prior to 1970, equalizing impacts stem from relatively high participation rates of women married to low-earning men." However, after 1970, "increased participation came mainly from women with above-average earnings growth who were married to high-earning men. Hence, continued increased female labor force participation may increase inequality for dual-earning husband-wife families."[26] Lynn Karoly and Gary Burtless have documented how the correlation between male and female earnings was negative in 1959 but by 1989 had become positive. It was then the case that "the growing correlation between husbands' and wives' earnings tends to boost overall income inequality."[27] What had been an equalising force began to work in the opposite direction. This trend has not continued, however. According to Jeff Larrimore, changes in the correlation of the earnings of husbands and wives are no longer operating to increase inequality.[28]

In the immediate postwar period in the US, then, the labour-market changes worked to reduce household income inequality (similar forces were operating in other OECD countries). The next step in the Guide to household income is to add nonlabour income, which consists of three major components: capital income, private transfers, and state transfers. In the case of capital income, there has been much discussion of the trends in wealth distribution in the US, not least on account of the different sources: some data relate to individuals, such as the estate-based estimates, other data relate to tax units (investment-income–based estimates), or to households (survey-based estimates), and still others to wider family units (as in the rich lists). It seems clear, however, that after the Second World War wealth in the US was less unequally distributed than it had been in the 1920s: according to the estate-based estimates, the share of the top 1 per cent in the 1920s was in excess of one-third (36 per cent averaged from 1920 to 1929), whereas in the 1950s it was under one quarter (24 per cent averaged over the 1950s).[29] But there was little apparent further downward trend in the top wealth share over the postwar decades, and to this degree capital income did not contribute to offsetting the rise in earnings dispersion.

What prevented a rise in overall inequality in the immediate postwar decades in the US? Government transfers, which grew rapidly, played a major role. Federal expenditure on payments to individuals doubled as a proportion of national income between 1955 and 1970.[30] The growth of transfers, including the maturing of the New Deal (1935) programme for Old-Age, Survivors, and Disability (the last being added in 1954) Insurance, worked to reduce the inequality of household incomes. Karoly and Burtless refer to the "extraordinary growth in unearned income, primarily government transfers." This increase in transfers, coupled with strong growth of average incomes in the earlier postwar decades, contributed to the impressive reduction in the proportion of the population living below the official poverty line, as shown in Figure 1.1. Karoly and Burtless go on to say, however, that after 1969 "gains in nonlabor income were tilted in favor of the well-to-do. Capital income and benefits from private pension plans have climbed faster than cash government transfers targeted to the poor."[31] In this case, the change in the course of events was due, not to social or economic change, but to policy choices.

The final step in the journey from individual earnings to household disposable income involves the other side of the government account: taxation. In the postwar decades, the tax rates continued at a high level in the period 1950 to 1979: the top US tax rate on earned income averaged 75 per cent (whereas that for the next thirty years, 1980 to 2009, averaged 39 per cent). The figures for the Gini coefficient in Figure 1.1 relate to income before tax (as do the top share figures), and therefore do not reflect the impact of the high rates of income tax. Their impact was much debated at the time. According to Joseph Schumpeter, through redistributive taxation "the New Deal was able to expropriate the upper income brackets even before the war" and had effected "a tremendous transfer." On the other hand, Irving Kravis summarised his statistical findings by saying that the "increase in the progressivity of the tax structure has played little if any part in making the income distribution more equal [after 1929]." An intermediate position is that taken by Richard Goode in his review of the income tax for the Brookings Institution, which "neither corroborates the opinion that the income tax is a Draconian measure for redistribution nor justifies writing-off its equalizing effects as inconsequential."[32]

In considering the impact of progressive taxation, it is important to bear in mind that the tax base is as important as the tax rates, and that one reason for the limited effectiveness of high rates is that the base had been eroded. As a result, the "effective tax rate" in the US at this time was considerably less progressive than the nominal tax rate.[33] (The nominal rate is the percentage of total income paid in taxes according to the tax schedule; the effective tax rate expresses the taxes actually paid, allowing for reduced rates on certain items of income, as a proportion of an extended definition of income, including tax-exempt income, such as interest on state and local government securities.) Moreover, we should note that the impact can be evaluated only by comparing the disposable incomes with the gross incomes that would have obtained if there had been no income tax in existence. This counterfactual is not easy to establish, since it requires us to predict the changes in behaviour that are induced by the tax. Opponents of high rates of income tax argue that gross incomes would have been larger in the absence of the high top tax rates, since people would have worked longer and harder. This is an issue that I take up later.

The end result of this process was that, while the top decile of earnings in the US rose steadily relative to the median during the immediate postwar decades, this increase in earnings dispersion was not translated into increased overall income inequality, as measured by the Gini coefficient. There was also a salient fall in the share of the top 1 per cent. More unequal rewards in the labour market did not translate into greater inequality of incomes. That this did not happen was due in part to the expansion of social transfers and in part to the increased labour-market participation of women acting in an equalising direction. These forces counteracting the rise in wage dispersion did not apply in the final quarter of the twentieth century.

Lowering Inequality in Postwar Europe

In the US, as we have just seen, overall income inequality as measured by the Gini coefficient was much the same at the end of the 1970s as in the late 1940s; in contrast, a number of European countries saw a major decline in overall inequality in the immediate postwar decades. In this section, I describe this reduction in inequality and how it was achieved. Circumstances at that time were different, but the postwar experience provides valuable lessons for us today.

The Postwar Decades in Europe: Two Questions

In the UK, overall inequality measured by the Gini coefficient fell by some 3 percentage points in the 1970s (from 1972 to 1977), meeting the criterion for salience, but the reductions were more marked, and of longer duration, in other European countries. Figure 2.2 shows the time paths of overall inequality and the top income shares for three countries in Scandinavia. We should focus on the time paths, not the levels, since

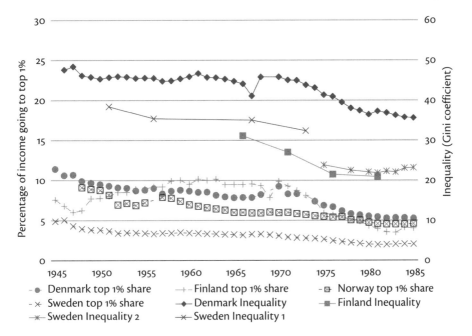

FIGURE 2.2: Inequality in Scandinavia in the post–Second World War decades

Share of gross income going to top 1% (left axis) and inequality (right axis), in post–Second World War period.

the estimates are not necessarily comparable across countries (we cannot conclude that Denmark is more unequal than the other countries). The time paths all show marked reductions from the mid-1960s to the end of the 1980s, typified by Finland, where the Gini coefficient fell from 31 per cent in 1966 to 21 per cent in 1980. In Denmark, the fall was similarly of the order of 10 percentage points. In Sweden, piecing together the two series, the total fall since the 1950s was 8 percentage points. The experience of Continental Europe is illustrated in Figure 2.3. In Germany, the fall was smaller—4 percentage points—and confined to the 1960s. In France and the Netherlands, there was a fall of 8 percentage points in the 1960s and 1970s. In Italy the total fall was 10 percentage points. In the UK, the fall was more limited, but there was a decline of 3 percentage point from 1972 to 1977.

Who was gaining and who was losing? Some countries demonstrated

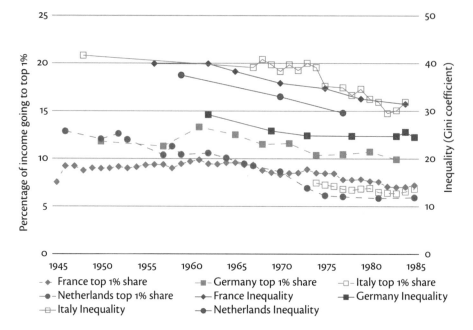

FIGURE 2.3: Inequality in Continental Europe in the post–Second World War decades

Share of gross income going to top 1% (left axis) and inequality (right axis), in post–Second World War period.

an evident improvement in terms of helping those with the lowest in-comes. In France, the proportion of the population living in households with incomes below 60 per cent of the median (the current EU indicator of financial poverty) fell from 18 per cent in 1970 to 14 per cent in 1990. In Finland, the proportion fell from 21 per cent in 1971 to 13 per cent in 1985.[34] In Germany and Italy, however, there was little sign of declining poverty, and for a number of other countries the necessary evidence is not available. For top incomes we know more, and the shares of the top 1 per cent are shown in Figures 2.2 and 2.3 (in each case the dashed lines in the lower part of the graph). In the case of Scandinavia, we can see that the top shares fell from being in a range of 7–9 per cent in the early 1950s to closer to 4–5 per cent in the early 1980s. In Norway and Sweden, the fall was relatively gradual, whereas in Denmark and Finland, the fall was concentrated in the 1970s, in the latter case coming after a rise in the 1950s. In France, the share of the top 1 per cent is described by Piketty as "fairly stable," and the decline does indeed fall just short of the salience criterion: from 9.9 per cent in 1961 to 7.0 per cent in 1983.[35] The fall in Germany is of a similar order of magnitude. In the Netherlands, the fall was larger, the share being halved between the early 1950s and the 1980s. Equally, in the UK the share of the top 1 per cent halved: from 12 per cent in 1949 to 6 per cent at the end of the 1970s.

Thus in the immediate postwar decades income inequality fell in a number of European countries. Two questions follow from this fact. How was the reduction in inequality from 1945 to the 1970s achieved? Why did the process of equalisation end in the 1980s? To provide answers, we can again follow the steps set out in the Guide to household income (Figure 1.5), in this case working in reverse order.

Reducing Inequality: The Welfare State and Progressive Taxation

The first, obvious factor in explaining the fall in inequality in postwar Europe is that this was a period during which the welfare state and social provision expanded, financed at least in part by progressive income taxation. The maturing of state pensions reduced the extent of poverty among older people, and the extension of social transfers to other groups, such as people with disabilities, widened the effectiveness of the social safety net. At the same time, demographic developments, notably the ageing of the population, were increasing the need for social protection. As the size of the dependent population increased, so the distribution of market incomes (earnings, self-employment income, rent, dividends, interest, and private pensions and other private transfers) became more unequal. More people had zero earnings because they had left the labour force. There was, in effect, a race between expanding provision and burgeoning need.

The evidence from household surveys in different European countries suggests that, in this race, the welfare state held its own for a significant period, but then it was unable to keep up. The regular official studies in the UK of the impact of taxes and benefits show a steady rise from 1961 onwards in the inequality of incomes from market sources: the Gini coefficient for market income by the end of the 1970s was some 5 percentage points higher. In contrast, the Gini coefficient for final income, arrived at by adding cash transfers and benefits in kind and subtracting direct and indirect taxes, shows no upward trend from 1961 to the mid-1980s. The "difference," or the arithmetic contribution of taxes and transfers, rose to offset the rise in market inequality; in the 1970s post-tax inequality fell. (This is, again, a purely arithmetic calculation; the market incomes could well have been different in the absence of the state transfers and taxes.) Taxes, and particularly cash transfers, allowed the welfare state to more than hold its own.[36]

So why did it end? After 1984, the UK story is quite different. Inequality in market income continued to rise, but the contribution from taxes and transfers moved in the opposite direction, causing inequality in post-tax income to rise more sharply. Figure 1.2 showed how sharply inequality rose in the UK in the second half of the 1980s. Between 1984 and 1990, the redistributive contribution of taxes and transfers towards reducing the Gini coefficient fell by 8 percentage points. This reflected policy decisions such as the change in up-rating for state pensions, which meant that the basic pension for a single person fell by nearly one-fifth relative to average take-home pay in the second half of the 1980s, and the scaling back of unemployment insurance. Although some of the ground was later made up, it remains the case that the redistributive "difference" is 6 percentage points below the amount that would be required, given the evolution of market income, to return the Gini coefficient for disposable income to its pre-1984 level.

Evidence from West Germany similarly shows that initially the inequality of market income widened substantially but that this development was not accompanied by an equivalent rise in inequality of disposable income. To quote Richard Hauser, "The German tax and transfer system reduces the inequality of market income quite considerably . . . the German social security system, despite the increasingly unfavourable conditions, largely reached its goals from 1973 to 1993."[37] In Finland, the experience was different in that market income inequality fell in the 1960s and the first half of the 1970s, but similar in that the "difference" was rising. As a result, inequality in disposable income fell by twice the amount of the fall in market income Gini coefficient. This trend continued through the 1980s, but in Finland, as in the other countries, there was then a reversal: "During the deepest recession . . . in the 1990s, income inequality did not change, since redistribution of cash transfers compensated the growing inequality of factor incomes. After the recession . . . income inequality has increased, because redistribution of cash transfers has declined, while factor income inequality has continued to grow."[38]

These country case studies illustrate the role played by the welfare state in reducing income inequality and in preventing any rise in market income inequality from feeding into inequality in disposable income. The immediate postwar decades were a success for the European welfare states. But in each case, too, the race was eventually lost, and more generally there has been an unwinding of redistributive policies in OECD countries, with serious adverse distributional consequences. The OECD Secretary-General in his introduction to the 2011 report *Divided We Stand* spelled out that "from the mid-1990s to 2005, the reduced redistributive capacity of tax-benefit systems was sometimes the main source of widening household-income gaps."[39] Michael Förster and István Tóth summarised the position as follows: "The redistributive power of the welfare state was weakened in the period between the mid-1990s to mid-2000s. While in the period between mid-1980s and mid-1990s the share of increased market income inequality offset by taxes and transfers was measured at the level of almost 60%, this share has declined to around 20% by the mid-2000s."[40] The OECD report stresses the role of cash transfers and "the importance of spending levels for inequality outcomes." The key element is less the level of benefits than the proportion of people eligible for transfers. The coverage of unemployment benefits, for example, fell between 1995 and 2005 in Austria, Belgium, the Czech Republic, Denmark, Estonia, Finland, Hungary, Italy, the Netherlands, Poland, Slovakia, Switzerland, Sweden, the UK, and the US. In causing the fall in coverage, "tighter eligibility rules played a role, as did the sizeable increase in the proportion of non-standard workers."[41]

So we have an answer to the two questions posed earlier. In the immediate postwar decades, the welfare state was ahead in the race to keep up with widening inequality of market incomes, but since the 1980s it has failed to do so—often as a result of explicit policy decisions to cut back on benefits and on coverage.

Reducing Inequality and the Share of Wages

The postwar reduction in inequality in Europe was not, however, solely achieved by redistribution. Both wage and capital incomes were—at times—becoming less unequally distributed. Our investigation into how this happened considers the following ways in which these components of income might contribute to reduced inequality:

» the share of wages in total income increases;
» capital income becomes less unequally distributed;
» wage income becomes less unequally distributed

In each case, we need to bear in mind that these three different elements are inter-related and that the effect of a change in one element depends on the others: for example, the impact of a rise in the share of wages depends on how unequally wages are distributed. (There is also a fourth element: the extent to which the same people do well on both wages and capital income. I return to this in the next chapter.)

For many years the share of wages in national income was regarded as one of the core variables in economics. Economists held strong views on the subject, many regarding the share of wages as one of life's constants. One of my teachers at Cambridge, Nicholas Kaldor, observed in 1957 that "the share of wages and the share of profits in the national income has shown a remarkable constancy in 'developed' capitalist economies of the United States and the United Kingdom since the second half of the nineteenth century," and this was later labelled a "stylized fact."[42] In the postwar period, however, there was evidence that the wage share was *increasing*. In his 1969 study of seventeen countries, Klaus Heidensohn found that over the period 1948 to 1963 there had been a "rising trend of labour's relative share in a large number of countries."[43] The labour share rose in Austria, Canada, and Denmark (all by 5 percentage points), in Finland

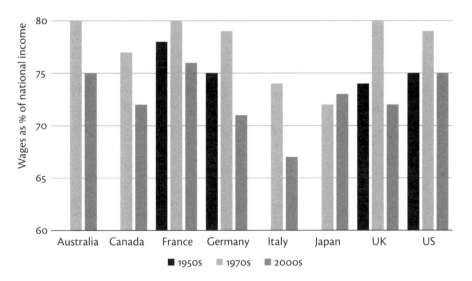

FIGURE 2.4: Share of wages (ten-year averages), selected world countries, 1950s to 2000s

The share of wages in national income was 80% in Australia when averaged over the ten years 1970 to 1979.

and Ireland (both by 6 points), in Belgium and the Netherlands (by 7 points), and by more than 10 percentage points in Norway and Sweden. Figure 2.4 shows the ten-year averages for 1950 and 1970 assembled by Thomas Piketty and Gabriel Zucman. It allows us to compare the average labour shares for 1950–1959 with those of 1970–1979. The increases are smaller, but they show the labour share as rising by 4 percentage points or more in West Germany, the UK, and the US. The Piketty-Zucman data equally show that the rise was subsequently reversed: in all cases apart from Japan there was a fall in the wage share from the 1970s to the 2000s. As summarised by Piketty, "the available data indicate that capital's share of income increased in most rich countries between 1970 and 2010."[44] The rise is not limited to rich countries. Loukas Karabarbounis and Brent Neiman find that, out of fifty-nine countries for which they have adequate data for years between 1975 and 2012, forty-two countries showed a downward trend in the share of labour. Their estimate of the global share of labour in corporate income exhibited a fall over that period of 5 percentage points.[45]

Does a rise (fall) in the wage share mean that the distribution of income becomes less (more) unequal? In the world envisaged by classical economists, the answer was "yes." They assumed that most of the population—the workers—had no income from wealth, and that the rest—the capitalists and landlords—lived off their income from rents, dividends, and profits. When the nineteenth-century English economist (and Member of Parliament) David Ricardo said that "the principal problem in Political Economy" was to determine how "the produce of the earth" was divided among rent, profit, and wages, he envisioned three separate social classes, each with its specific source of income.[46] Today, in contrast, we can make no such clear identification. People may receive income from all three sources. A person may have wages but also receive interest on savings and benefit from owning a house. Indeed, housing has seen dramatic changes. A hundred years ago many people were tenants and houses were typically owned by landlords. In England and Wales in 1918, 77 per cent of households rented their accommodations; by 1981 the proportion had fallen to 42 per cent, and, with the rise of social housing, the proportion renting from private landlords was only 11 per cent.[47]

In a class society, as in Ricardian England, an increase of 1 percentage point in the share of wages would have reduced the Gini coefficient by 1 percentage point.[48] Today, when the links between classes of income and the distribution among persons are less clear-cut, the expected reduction in the Gini coefficient is smaller. Nonetheless, the impact of a change in the wage share may still be substantial. Daniele Checchi and Cecilia Garcia Peñalosa, in a study of sixteen OECD countries over the period 1970 to 1996, estimated that a 1 percentage point rise in the wage share is associated with a 0.7 percentage point reduction in the Gini coefficient.[49] On this basis, a 5 percentage point increase in the labour share would be associated with a salient 3.5 percentage point reduction in the Gini coefficient. One mechanism that reduced inequality in the postwar decades appears, therefore, to have been the rising share of wages in national income, a rise that was subsequently reversed.

Reducing Inequality: Sharing Capital

At the same time, the distribution of capital income was becoming less unequal. Evidence on the personal distribution of wealth (both capital and land) is less readily available on an internationally comparable basis than is the case for income, but Jesper Roine and Daniel Waldenström have assembled a long-run series for the share of the top 1 per cent in ten countries.[50] Their figures show large reductions in top wealth shares. In France, the share of the top 1 per cent in total personal wealth fell between 1950 and 1980 by one-third, from 33 per cent to 22 per cent. In Denmark, the share fell by the same proportion between 1945 and 1975. In Sweden, the fall was even larger: from 38 per cent in 1945 to 17 per cent in 1975, and in the UK the fall between 1950 and 1975 was 17 percentage points.[51]

This decline in top wealth shares has reduced the share of capital income accruing to the top income groups and increased the share received by the bottom 99 per cent. But this has not been a simple transfer. Wealthy people have not simply handed over share certificates. In the UK, one major explanation for the rising share of the bottom 99 per cent has been the rise in owner-occupation. When politicians talk of Britain becoming a "property-owning democracy," they often mean property in the sense of housing. This is, however, a rather special asset, generating a return in the form of imputed income. Other forms of popular wealth, such as savings and bank accounts or pension funds, are held via financial institutions. The latter hold the share certificates. One consequence is that part of the capital income now accrues to the financial-services sector that manages these funds. There is a wedge between the rate of return to capital and the income received by savers. The growth of popular wealth has contributed to the increased "financialization" of the economy. (This in turn has implications for the separation of beneficial ownership and control, to which I will return.)

Has the downward trend in top wealth shares continued or has it been subsequently reversed? The series assembled by Roine and Waldenström show that the share of the top 1 per cent in total personal wealth between the early 1980s and the 2000s rose from 22 per cent to 24.4 per cent in France and increased by 2 percentage points in the UK and by 1.1 per cent in Sweden. These are small changes by the standards of the previous decades, and we need to be cautious in drawing conclusions about any upturn in wealth concentration.[52] Rather, we can conclude that the trend to less wealth concentration came to an end—which is still, of course, a significant departure from what happened in the immediate postwar decades.

Reducing Inequality: Wages and Labour-Market Institutions

Widening of the wage distribution dates back in the US to the 1950s, and the same is true in the UK and in France. The top decile rose in both countries from the mid-1950s to the mid-1960s. This is the period to the left of the first vertical line in Figure 2.5. However, in Europe but not in the US, earnings dispersion began to narrow after the mid-1960s—shown in the middle section of Figure 2.5.

The late 1960s and 1970s were a tumultuous period for European labour markets. After the widespread civil unrest in France in May 1968, earnings differences were narrowed in that country, but the May 1968 effect was not limited to France. According to Christopher Erickson and Andrea Ichino, "during the 1970s, Italy experienced an impressive compression of wage differentials." A major element in this compression was the Scala Mobile (SM), a negotiated agreement between workers and employers to link wages to increases in the cost of living. Writing in 1979, Ignacio Visco, now governor of the Bank of Italy, noted that there was a "marked tendency for the range of earnings to become narrower." The role of collective bargaining was important in the Nordic countries. The data assembled for Sweden by Magnus Gustavsson show the quintile ratio for men as falling from 1968 to 1976. As he notes, the period coincided with the heyday of the "solidarity wage policy" followed by the major trade union confederation, Landsorganisationen (LO). Tor Eriksson and Markus Jäntti found in Finland that "earnings inequality dropped dramatically between 1971 and 1975, and continued to decrease until 1985."[53] In the UK, as Figure 2.5 shows, the top decile fell. At the same time, the bottom decile rose by one-fifth relative to the median between 1968 and 1977, and together these developments narrowed the ratio of the top decile to the bottom decile to an extent that, applying the estimates of the relation of this variable to the Gini coefficient in the study by Checchi

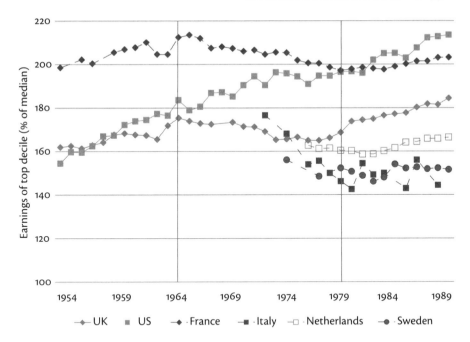

FIGURE 2.5: Earnings dispersion in US and Europe, 1954–1990

This graph shows the earnings of the top decile (the person 10% from the top) relative to the median (the person in the middle) of the earnings distribution for full-time workers.

and Garcia Peñalosa cited earlier, they could account for a fall in the Gini coefficient for overall income inequality of between 4 and 7 percentage points.[54]

An important factor in securing the reduction in earnings dispersion was collective bargaining by trade unions on behalf of their members and government intervention in the labour market. Government influenced the wage distribution via minimum wage legislation (although not in all countries: a national minimum wage was not introduced in the UK until 1999). Piketty says that the change in direction in France was "the result of breaks in the wages policy of the state, and notably in policy towards the minimum wage."[55] In the Netherlands, the minimum wage was raised substantially in 1974, and the government followed a policy of narrowing differentials.[56] To this we must add the contribution made to reducing overall inequality by the reduction in earnings differentials by gender. In a number of countries, equal pay legislation took effect during this period, and we sometimes lose sight of what has been achieved: in the UK, the gender wage gap was more than halved. There was also regulation of wages by collective action. A striking example in the UK is the case of soccer, where until 1961 there was a maximum weekly wage of £20 (which was around average earnings in the country). This is a far cry from today's free market, where footballers in the UK can earn more than 500 times average earnings.

Reduction in earnings dispersion from the mid-1960s to the late 1970s was also the goal of another instrument, now largely forgotten in Anglo-Saxon countries: national incomes policies. These were in origin macroeconomic policies, but negotiations between the social partners (employers and trade unions) meant that they came to have distinct distributional elements. In Norway in 1989, the agreement negotiated between the trade union federation and the employer organisation allowed for a uniform increase of 3 kronor per hour (with a supplement in export industries). In the United Kingdom, the 1973 Stage Two incomes policy under the Conservative government had a progressive formula for pay increases of £1 plus 4 per cent and an absolute limit on individual pay increases. Under Labour's "Attack on Inflation" in 1975, the pay rise allowed under incomes policy legislation was a flat £6 per week, with no increases for those earning above a certain amount. Incomes policy is now typically regarded as an anachronism. The Wikipedia entry introduces a distinctly dramatic historical note: "Incomes policies have often been resorted to during wartime. During the French Revolution, 'The Law of the Maximum' imposed price controls (by penalty of death) in an unsuccessful attempt to curb inflation."[57] But these policies have a contemporary relevance. As discussed in later chapters, I believe that we need to hold a "national conversation" about the development of incomes, as part of a strengthening of the role of social partners.

The Two Questions Answered

The two questions posed at the beginning of this section were: why did inequality fall in Europe in the immediate postwar decades, and why has there been an upward turn in inequality since 1980? There is much more that could be said, but the main factors identified as candidates for explaining the period of falling European income inequality are—as summarised in the middle column of Table 2.1—the welfare state and the expansion of transfers, the rising share of wages, the reduced concentration of personal wealth, and the reduced dispersion of earnings as a result of government intervention and collective bargaining. And the main reason that equalisation came to an end appears to be—see the final column in Table 2.1—that these factors have gone into reverse (welfare-state cutbacks, declining share of wages, and rising earnings dispersion) or come to an end (the redistribution of wealth).

An important factor in answering the second question that we have not discussed—indeed some readers may regard it as the elephant in the room—is the rise in unemployment.[58] The single most obvious feature distinguishing the recent decades from those after the Second World War is the level of unemployment. In the early 1960s, it was the US that had a problem of unemployment. The unemployment rate as a percentage of the total labour force averaged 4.8 per cent over the period 1960 to 1973 in the US, compared with 2.0 per cent in France, 1.9 per cent in the UK, and 0.8 per cent in Germany. Indeed, in many OECD countries unemployment was very low. One prime minister of New Zealand claimed to know personally all the unemployed in his country; this may well have been true, since according to International Labour Organisation (ILO) statistics, in 1955 there were only fifty-five unemployed people in his country.[59] All this was to change. By the period 1990 to 1995, the average unemployment rate in the US was 6.4 per cent, compared with 10.7 per cent in France, 8.6 per cent in the UK, and 7.1 per cent in Germany. The US still had a problem of unemployment—or so it seems to someone who began studying economics when UK unemployment was 1.4 per cent—but it had been joined, and indeed overtaken, by Europe.[60]

How large is the elephant? How much has higher unemployment contributed to higher inequality? The relationship is a complex one. We have to trace through the steps from the market incomes of individuals to the disposable income of households—following the Guide to household income. Moving from the distribution of individual wages to the distribution of market incomes including unemployed workers as well as employed workers has the effect of increasing the degree of inequality, and rising unemployment widens the gap.[61] Adding those who are not in the labour force, so that the entire population of working age is covered,

TABLE 2.1. *Mechanisms leading to change in inequality*

Mechanism	Postwar decades up to end of 1970s	Period since 1980s
Dispersion of wages	Dispersion of wages has at times been reduced, reflecting collective bargaining and government intervention in the labour market.	In many OECD countries there has been a widening at the top of the earnings distribution.
Unemployment and population not in the labour force	Rising proportion not in labour force with ageing population led to rising inequality of market income, offset by social transfers.	Persistent high unemployment.
Share of wages in national income	Tendency for the share of wages to rise, leading to reduction in overall income inequality.	Tendency for the share of wages to fall.
Concentration of capital income (profits and rents)	Substantial decline in top wealth shares, but need to take account of the implications of growth of "popular wealth."	Decline in top wealth shares appears to have come to an end.
Share of transfer income	Redistributive social transfers more than offset rising inequality of market income.	Scaling back of redistributive social transfers.
Impact of progressive direct taxation	Progressive income tax moderated impact of rising top earnings.	Top income tax rates have been substantially cut.

means that the extent of inequality depends on the employment rate, which has been increasing and operating in the opposite direction.[62] The next step is that of aggregating individual incomes to arrive at household incomes, where we have to take account of the joint distribution of unemployment within households. If all unemployed men were married to employed professional women, then we would be less concerned about the income consequences of unemployment. It is for this reason that attention has focused on jobless households. In moving from market incomes to disposable incomes, we have to allow for the response of state transfer payments to unemployment. Where there is full coverage of unemployment insurance, and a generous replacement rate, then the rise in inequality may be less. If, as we shall see to be the case in Chapter 8, social protection is much less complete, unemployment may indeed be associated with financial hardship. Finally, we have to bear in mind that the evidence about inequality largely relates to annual incomes, and that people may be unemployed for only part of the year. To this extent the measured effect is attenuated and the degree of hardship understated.

From this account, it is clear that the relationship between unemployment and inequality is an intricate one, requiring careful examination, and that no simple statement can be made about the quantitative contribution of unemployment to the higher income inequality post-1980.[63] Nonetheless, involuntary unemployment is of concern in its own right, and for this reason alone it receives considerable attention in what follows. Unemployment, and attendant job precariousness, are themselves sources of inequality. A person rejected by the labour market is suffering a form of social exclusion, and even if full income replacement were to allow his or her standard of living to be maintained during unemployment, the individual's circumstances would have worsened. Above all, it is a matter of agency and a sense of powerlessness.[64] Nearly twenty years ago, Amartya Sen ended an article with the statement, "It is amazing that so much unemployment is so easily tolerated in contemporary Europe."[65] It remains amazing today.

Latin America in the Twenty-First Century

The postwar decades in Europe were a period of falling inequality, but this was not a unique episode. We should not lose sight of the fact that there have been other—more recent—periods when inequality has declined. An important example is Latin America in the 2000s. Admittedly, the region's decline in overall inequality and poverty came after a period in the 1980s and 1990s of rising inequality, but its experience shows that a reduction in inequality is attainable.

The remarkable decline in seven Latin American countries is illustrated in Figure 2.6, where the solid lines show the path of the Gini coefficient of overall inequality and the dashed lines show the relative poverty rate, defined as the proportion of the population below 50 per cent of median household equivalised income.[66] Between 2001 (2000 in Chile and Mexico) and 2011 (2010 in Mexico), the Gini coefficient fell by 5 percentage points in Chile, 6 points in Brazil, 7 in Mexico, and 9 points in Argentina. In El Salvador the fall was 6 percentage points between 2004 and 2012. There were major changes and they were not confined to the countries shown. Facundo Alvaredo and Leonardo Gasparini in their study of nineteen Latin American countries find that, whereas only around one-quarter of the countries exhibited a fall in the Gini coefficient in the 1990s, there was a reduction in inequality in almost all of these countries in the 2000s.[67] There was considerable commonality of experience among these countries, although Alvaredo and Gasparini qualify the conclusion by pointing out that incomes at the top of the distribution may not be adequately covered in the household surveys. Andrea Cornia notes, in his analysis of recent distributive changes in Latin America, that "given the scarcity of information on capital incomes and the income of the 'working rich' in household surveys [it is not possible] to establish formally whether the distributive changes . . . concern also the top percentiles of the income distribution."[68] Tax data, an alternative source, although one that is also subject to understatement of top incomes, provide a warning. The estimates of Alvaredo and Gasparini for Argentina show the share of the top 1 per cent in total gross income as rising in the first part of the 2000s and then falling, so that by 2007 it is back close to the 2000 figure. The share of the top 1 per cent in Colombia rose from 17 per cent to 21 per cent between 2000 and 2010.

With the qualification that we have insufficient information about incomes at the top, we see in Latin America an episode of falling inequality that extends over a wide range of countries. In seeking to explain the fall in inequality, Nora Lustig, Luis Lopez-Calva, and Eduardo Ortiz-

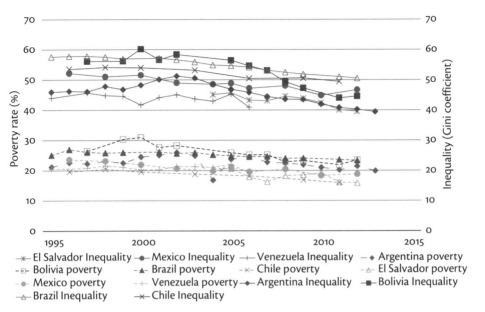

FIGURE 2.6: Recent declines in inequality and poverty in Latin America

This graph shows recent declines in both overall inequality (right axis), measured by the Gini coefficient (per cent), and the percentage of individuals living in poverty (left axis). In 1995 in Brazil the Gini coefficient was 58%, and 25% were living in poverty.

Juarez begin by noting that "there is no clear link between the decline in inequality and economic growth. Inequality has declined in countries which have experienced rapid economic growth, such as Chile, Panama and Peru, and in countries with low-growth spells, such as Brazil and Mexico. Nor is there a link between falling inequality and the orientation of political regimes. Inequality has declined in countries governed by leftist regimes, such as Argentina, Bolivia, Brazil, Chile and Venezuela, and in countries governed by centrist and center-right parties, such as Mexico and Peru."[69] Rather, they suggest, the fall was brought about by a reduction in the wage premium for more educated workers, and by progressive government transfers. Summarising the evidence from studies of Brazil, Alvaredo and Gasparini note in addition that the substantial increase in the minimum wage was an "important force behind the fall in household income inequality, given that the minimum wage sets the floor for both unskilled workers' earnings and for social security benefits." This increase was coupled with "the rapid expansion in the coverage of government cash transfers targeted to the poor, mainly a transfer to the elderly and disabled (Benefício de Prestação Continuada) and Brazil's signature conditional cash transfer program Bolsa Família."[70] In the region as a whole, there was, especially in the upper-middle-income countries, an expansion of social assistance, which—in contrast to the existing social insurance—"worked through the introduction of a set of institutions with a different rationale, institutionalization, and financing." This description is given by Armando Barrientos, who goes on to explain that the "stagnation of social insurance funds in Latin America is associated with the changes in the employment relationship brought about by the new conditions in liberalized labour markets."[71]

To sum up, in Latin America, as in the postwar decades in Europe, inequality reduction was achieved by a combination of changes in market incomes and expanded redistribution.

Where Are We Now?

In the case of Latin America, we have brought the subject up-to-date. Where are we now with respect to the OECD countries discussed earlier in the chapter? As we have seen, the factors that led to the earlier fall in income inequality in Europe have been reversed or come to an end. Where does this leave us?

The short answer is that in many, although not all, OECD countries income inequality is higher today than in 1980. There has been a distinct "turn" towards greater inequality. The rise in inequality has not been confined to the US and the UK, as may be seen from Figure 2.7, which shows the change in the Gini coefficient of overall inequality since 1980.[72] The increases in the UK and the US may have been among the highest, but there are several OECD countries in which the coefficient is higher now than in 1980 by the 3 percentage points that I have taken as a criterion for salience. The graph provides support for the OECD summary of "the big picture: inequality on the rise in most OECD countries."[73] At the same time, it reminds us that there are countries like France where overall inequality was not higher at the end of the 2000s than it had been thirty

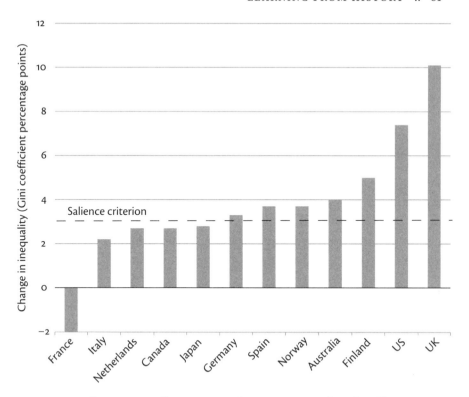

FIGURE 2.7: Change in overall income inequality since 1980 in selected world countries

The graph shows the change in percentage points in the Gini coefficient of overall inequality between 1980 and the end of the 2000s. The Gini coefficient in the UK was higher at the end of the period by just over 10 percentage points.

years earlier: the Gini coefficient has increased from 28.9 per cent in 2004 to 30.6 per cent in 2011, but this still leaves it 2 percentage points below its 1979 value before François Mitterrand came to power.

In seeking to learn from history, we invariably encounter question marks. Of these, the most important concerns the extent to which the world has changed, rendering the conclusions drawn from one period irrelevant today. How far, for example, are the experiences of Europe in the postwar period generalisable to the twenty-first century? In the next chapter, I explore some of the ways in which the economic context has changed and how this affects the design of policies for equality.

Chapter 3 ::

The Economics of Inequality

Economists are often accused of being behind the curve. It is said that their models too often ignore the way the world is changing before our eyes, and that they are too absorbed in professional concerns. As I shall argue, there are valid criticisms to be made of contemporary economics, but credit should be given to the economists who have focused on rising inequality and identified a number of contributing factors, including:

» globalisation
» technological change (information and communications technology)
» growth of financial services
» changing pay norms
» reduced role of trade unions
» scaling back of the redistributive tax-and-transfer policy

The list is impressive, and all these elements feature at some point in the book.[1] In identifying these mechanisms, however, we risk creating the impression that inequality is rising on account of forces outside our control. It is far from obvious that these factors are beyond our influence or that they are exogenous to the economic and social system. Globalisation is the result of decisions taken by international organisations, by national governments, by corporations, and by individuals as workers and consumers. The direction of technological change is the product of decisions by firms, researchers, and governments. The financial sector may have grown to meet the demands of an ageing population in need of financial instruments that provide for retirement, but the form it has taken and the regulation of the industry have been subject to political and economic choices.

We need, therefore, to probe further, and to ask where the key decisions are located. It is my belief that the rise in inequality can in many

82

cases be traced directly or indirectly to changes in the balance of power. If that is correct, then measures to reduce inequality can be successful only if countervailing power is brought to bear. But this is to get ahead of the story, which opens with the now standard textbook account of how rising inequality is due to the forces of globalisation and technological change.

The Textbook Story of Globalisation and Technology

How are globalisation and technological progress redrawing the distributional map? In 1975, Jan Tinbergen, the joint first winner of the Nobel Prize in Economics, famously described a "race" between increased demand for educated workers and the expansion of the educated population.[2] Today, this account has considerable resonance, with the increase in demand for educated workers being driven by the contemporary forces of globalisation and technological change.

In the globalisation version of the "race," advanced economies face increased competition from countries where wages of unskilled workers are lower. Industries that rely heavily on unskilled workers find it increasingly difficult to compete, and jobs are lost or outsourced to lower-wage countries. The other side of the coin is increased demand for higher-educated workers as the balance of production shifts towards high-skill sectors. The story is told in terms of two groups of workers—skilled and unskilled—where it is assumed that all workers in a group are paid the same. This is evidently not the case in reality, but the assumption makes the story simpler to tell. It means that wage differences are represented just by the ratio of the skilled wage to the unskilled wage. The excess of the skilled wage over the unskilled wage is typically referred to as the "wage premium." The hypothesis is that demand shifts in relative terms towards skilled workers, and hence, since demand outstrips supply, the premium for skilled workers rises.

This "supply and demand" explanation of widening earnings differentials can be found in every first-year economics textbook, but what is important is what lies behind supply and demand. In the case of globalisation, what lies behind is the standard international trade model (usually referred to as the Heckscher-Ohlin model after the two Swedish economists Eli Heckscher and Bertil Ohlin), according to which the classes of workers, skilled and unskilled, are employed in two perfectly competitive economies, each with two sectors of production. "Perfectly competitive" means that everyone takes prices as given—there is no market power— an assumption with which I later take issue. One of the sectors in each economy produces an advanced manufacturing good or service that uses skilled labour relatively intensively; the other sector has a more basic product that uses unskilled labour relatively intensively. (There is no capital at this stage of the story.) Typically, OECD countries export the advanced good and import the basic good. Goods and services may be traded freely on international markets, and there are assumed to be no transportation costs. Labour is not mobile across countries, but it can move freely across sectors within a country. There are at any time fixed numbers of skilled and unskilled workers.

The assumptions made in this economic model are quite restrictive, but within this framework international trade economists have been able to demonstrate some powerful conclusions. Under certain further assumptions, there is a unique relation between the relative prices of the two goods and the relative wage rates of skilled and unskilled workers. (Only relative prices are explained.) The higher the wage premium for skilled workers, the higher the relative price of the good that relies heavily on skilled labour. And, importantly for the analysis of income distribution, the reverse is true. The higher the relative price of the good that relies heavily on skilled labour, the higher the wage premium for skilled workers. From this we may deduce that, if globalisation has meant that a country can import basic manufactured goods more cheaply, paid for by exporting more valuable high-tech services, then the skilled wage rises relative to the unskilled wage. The market-clearing wage ratio tilts against unskilled workers.

The technology version of the "race" is based on the view that technological progress is biased in favour of skilled workers—the skill-biased technical change hypothesis. It is argued that the advances in information and communication technologies (ICT) have displaced low-skilled workers and created demand for those with better education. The theory, in its simplest form, is expressed in terms of technological progress augmenting the productivity of the two types of labour, which combine as factors of production to produce national output. Technological progress is assumed to be skill-biased in that it augments the productivity of skilled workers more than that of unskilled workers. As a result of ICT, skilled workers can now get through, say, twice as much work, while unskilled workers are no more productive. Again, we have to go through the analysis carefully. Is it obvious that technological progress increases the demand for skilled workers? The answer is "no." We have to make a further assumption for this to be true. The reason for hesitation is that, while the technological change makes a unit of work cheaper to the employer, he or she also gets twice as many work units from any given worker. It all depends on how many more units the employer wants to buy as a result of the cheaper unit price. This in turn depends on how easy it is to substitute skilled labour for unskilled, and this is measured by economists in terms of *the elasticity of substitution between the two factors*.[3] If the elasticity is greater than 1, then it is relatively easy to substitute skilled workers for unskilled, and the relative demand for skilled workers increases. If the elasticity is less than 1, then the employer wishes to rebalance the labour force in the opposite direction, demanding more unskilled workers. (When the elasticity is 1, then the factor bias in technological progress cannot be distinguished.) The ability of the technological change theory to explain the widening earnings dispersion depends, therefore, on the elasticity of substitution being greater than 1.[4]

So far, I have described two reasons that the demand for skilled workers may be increasing, but we need to consider as well what happens to supply. The usual response is that willingness to pursue further education is governed by the wage premium for skilled workers, which generates the return on the investment made in the costs of education and in the earnings forgone during the period of schooling. In the simplest form, acquiring the necessary qualification means postponing entry into the labour force, so that—in this "human capital" model—earnings when qualified have to be higher by just the amount required to give the same present value of earnings over the lifetime, discounted at the ruling interest rate.[5] If the wage of higher-educated workers rises, to make the yield on the investment higher than the required amount, we can expect the supply to increase. We then have to trace out the dynamic process. If the forces of globalisation and skill-biased technological change continue to operate, then both supply and demand rise, and the gap between them continues to exist, the size of the gap depending on the speed of response of supply.

From this we can draw two policy conclusions. One policy conclusion follows immediately from this analysis. Raising the skill level of a country's labour force renders that country more able to benefit from globalisation. There will be more gainers and fewer losers. A country with a highly skilled labour force may indeed be fully specialised in the production of the advanced product or service. In that case, it can only benefit from globalisation, since it is able to import the intermediate good at a lower relative price. This conclusion appears to be fully in line with the strategy adopted by the European Union, and other advanced countries, of prioritizing investment in education: "equipping people with the right skills for the jobs of today and tomorrow" being one of the Europe 2020 initiatives. It is important to note, however, that we have elided "skill" and "education." Nearly all empirical studies in the US are of the college–high school wage premium, whereas "skill" is a broader concept and not necessarily perfectly aligned with education. When interviewed by the *New York Times,* the senior vice president for People Operations at Google is reported as saying "that GPAs [grades] are worthless as a criterion for hiring [and that] the proportion of people without any college education at Google has increased over time."[6] Noncognitive skills, such as motivation, empathy, and self-control, may be as important as the cognitive skills measured in educational tests.

The second policy conclusion is less commonly noted. The size of the wage premium required for investment in human capital depends on the ruling rate of interest. This is evidently the case where students, or the parents of students, are borrowing from a bank or a loan agency to pay for education. The same applies where parents are using their own savings to support their children through college, since the parents' money is being tied up in this way rather than being invested. The cost to them is the rate of return that they could earn on their savings. There is, therefore, a crucial link between the labour market and the capital market. It is certainly possible that one reason for the rise in the college wage premium in the 1980s was the increase in the real rate of interest at that time. The increase raised the cost of borrowing to finance the period of education, and hence required a larger wage premium. (This has ceased to be the case in recent years, but other costs of education have increased, notably, in the case of the UK, as a result of increased student fees and the withdrawal of studentship support.) In seeking measures to reverse the rise in inequality, we must consider the links between educational decisions and the capital market. We cannot just look at the labour market.

The Economics of Technological Change

So far, as in much of the economics literature, technological change has been discussed as if it were exogenous—determined by the gods. Some accounts even refer to it as "manna from heaven." Yet most technological advance reflects decisions that are made by, among others, scientists, research managers, businessmen, investors, governments, and consumers. And these decisions are influenced by economic considerations that make technical change endogenous; that is, determined from within the economic and social system. Many years ago, the Oxford economist and early Nobel Prize–winner Sir John Hicks observed that "a change in the relative prices of the factors of production is itself a spur to invention, and to invention of a particular kind—directed to economizing the use of a factor which has become relatively expensive."[7] Such motivation was explored by economists in the 1960s who developed theories of induced innovation, in which firms *choose* the degree of bias in technological change. Firms select from a menu of opportunities so as to achieve the fastest rate of cost reduction. What does this imply? Does it mean that the current period of technological change biased in favour of skilled workers will come to an end? As skilled workers become even more expensive, do firms seek ways of replacing them? The answer is "not necessarily," since—as we saw earlier—while skilled workers are becoming more expensive, the cost per unit of skilled work is falling, since the workers are becoming more productive. As discussed earlier, the outcome depends on how easily one kind of worker can be substituted for another, in other words, on the elasticity of substitution. With the assumption that skilled and unskilled workers are relatively substitutable, the long-run outcome is that cost-minimising firms end up concentrating on skill-biased technological progress. It is not the case that the market on its own operates in such a way as to necessarily reverse the bias in favour of skilled workers and hence return the economy to its previous distribution of income.[8]

Decisions by businesses about innovation have to be forward-looking. Today's choices have long-run consequences. Such consequences were emphasised in another economics article from the 1960s by Joseph Stiglitz and myself.[9] We took a different approach to technological change, based not on augmenting the productive capacity of particular workers but on techniques of production. Technical progress is, we argued, often *localised* to particular techniques, or production activities. It makes workers more productive, not in general terms, but in a specific production process, such as a highly capital-intensive steel mill. It is then important to look ahead and ask which techniques of production we would like to see in operation in the future. Moreover, the activity approach offers a richer possible account of the relation between technical progress and the distribution of pay. It has similarities to the "job task" approach, developed by David Autor and colleagues, where "a task is a unit of work activity that produces output."[10] By allowing technological change to affect differentially not only different tasks but also the capacity of workers of different skills to undertake these tasks and the productivity of capital in the tasks, they argue that there has been a displacement of medium-skill workers by machines in the conduct of routine or codifiable tasks. There has been a "hollowing out" of jobs in the middle of the distribution.

Choices matter not only when technical advances come about through research and development, but also when they result from learning by doing. By utilizing a particular method of production, firms learn how to do it better, and the costs of production continually fall. Kenneth Arrow, Nobel Prize–winner from Stanford University who introduced the term "learning by doing" into economics, referred to evidence on the number of hours required to produce an aircraft body, where the US Air Force planned on this basis: "To produce the Nth airframe of a given type, counting from the inception of production, the amount of labor required is proportional to $N^{1/3}$."[11] Steven Chu, another Nobel Prize–winner from Stanford and former US Energy Secretary, gives the example of the construction of nuclear power plants: "South Korea has built 10 plants exactly the same and the 10th plant was only 60 per cent of the cost of the original one."[12] Where technical advance is associated with particular techniques of production, the possibilities open to future generations depend on choices not just about research but also about which goods and services to produce and how they are produced. Today's production decisions have long-term consequences. Focusing on the distributional dimension, we can see that the choices made today with regard to productive activities have implications for the wages and incomes of future generations of workers. It is therefore important that these decisions be made, not by default, but consciously, and by a broad set of stakeholders.

Market Forces and Social Context

In the supply-and-demand analysis of the textbook story, your wage is determined by your contribution to output, and by nothing else. If trade or technology changes, rendering your skills less valuable, then your income falls (even if you pay less for the imported products your family buys and the PC become cheaper every year). In this section, I argue that market forces, while undoubtedly potent, allow considerable room for other determinants, and—more fundamentally—that markets operate within a social context that influences the resulting distribution of income.

The Labour Market as a Social Institution

Apart from spelling "labour" differently, the title of this section is the same as that of a 1990 book by Robert Solow, who opens by pointing out that the dominant tradition "especially in macroeconomics, holds that in nearly all respects the labor market is just like other markets."[13] That is true of the supply-and-demand model described above, which treats the labour market in the same way as the market for milk. The market for milk is typically a simple matter. We know where the dairy or the supermarket shelf is located, and we are pretty sure what is contained in the bottle. However, in Solow's words, "common sense, on the other hand, seems to take it for granted that there is something special about labor as a commodity." The labour market is indeed quite different from the market for milk. Workers have to search for jobs; employers have to search for workers. Neither is sure what they are getting, and the relationship, once entered into, is in most cases less easily ended than simply going to a different supermarket. Taking a job is more than a cash transaction, and therefore the social context is of greater importance. In particular, as Solow says, the labour market "cannot be understood without taking account of the fact that participants, on both sides, have well-developed notions of what is fair and what is not."

That labour-market matching is costly has long been understood. Eric Newby in his account of the last days of trading under sail before the Second World War describes vividly the problems faced by seamen in finding a ship that was in commission, and by the masters of those ships in finding suitable crew.[14] Only more recently have economists developed theoretical models of the process. In these "search" models of the labour market, frictions in the market mean that, while prospectively competition may drive down the expected value of filling a job vacancy to the cost of its creation, in the event the actual matching of a worker to a vacancy creates a positive surplus or rent. The worker offered a job has a degree of negotiating power, since, if he or she rejects the job offer, the employer has to return to the pool with the risk that no match can be secured. The magnitude of the risk, and hence the worker's leverage, depend on the tightness of the labour market; the worker's leverage also depends on the cost of remaining unemployed. The key point, however, is that supply and demand do not fully determine the market wage; they only place bounds on the wage, allowing scope for bargaining about the division of the surplus. In the words of Peter Diamond, Nobel Prize–winner from MIT, "having come together, the firm and worker have a joint surplus . . . there is a wage that makes the worker indifferent between taking this job and waiting for his next job opportunity. There is a wage that makes the firm indifferent between hiring this worker and waiting for the next available worker. The bargaining problem is to agree on a wage between these two limits."[15]

The division of the surplus—and hence the wage—is influenced by the relative bargaining power of the two parties, but there is room for other factors to enter the determination of pay, including appeal to norms of equitable payment, which may in turn be embodied in custom and practice. Such factors are often presented as an alternative to economic explanations. Sir Henry Phelps Brown opens his book *The Inequality of*

Pay by contrasting the economist's approach with that of the sociologist. The former sees people as engaged in rational, impersonal transactions; the latter sees them as interacting members of a social entity.[16] The two approaches are, however, not in competition but better seen as complementary. Wages are influenced by two sets of forces. Supply and demand determine a range of possible pay, and the social conventions determine the location within that range—the extent of pay dispersion depends on both elements. Put more precisely, the introduction of a notion of fairness or of social norms provides a route to removing indeterminacy when in the labour market; to quote Bentley MacLeod and James Malcomson, "individual incentives are not by themselves generally sufficient to determine a unique equilibrium."[17]

Observance of social norms may be consistent with individual rationality, and social codes may enter directly into economic behaviour via their implications for the reputation of workers and of employers. Suppose, for instance, that there is a pay norm that limits the extent to which, within a group of equally qualified workers, individual earnings increase with actual productivity. To make it concrete, suppose further that, where this code is followed, people are paid a fraction (less than unity) of their productivity plus a uniform amount. Truman Bewley refers to such a practice as "wage flattening," and in his interview study in the United States, he found "ample evidence that pay differentials often do not fully reflect differences in productivity."[18] Such a pay policy involves a degree of redistribution, and lower-productivity workers can be expected to subscribe to the pay norm. But other workers also accept it, even if they could increase their own pay by breaking the norm. Those who believe in the norm know that deviating from it would bring a loss of reputation. Of course, the loss of reputation from departing from the social code depends on the proportion believing in the social code, which is undermined if people cease to observe it. Employers, too, are concerned with their reputations. They may also believe that a workforce governed by social norms can attract more engaged and committed—and hence more productive—workers. For these reasons, companies embody principles of equity in their pay and employment policies.[19]

In such a situation, there may be more than one possible market outcome. At any one time, a society may have relatively modest pay differentials supported by strong adherence to a norm of fair pay, or it may have large differentials and a low degree of conformity to a social code. An intermediate situation, with some people conforming and others rejecting the code, is unstable, since deviations lead to a spiralling away. An exogenous shock may switch the society from one outcome to another. The society may move from a situation with a high level of conformity to the pay norm, and hence relatively low wage differentials, to one where a much larger proportion of workers are paid on an individualised basis. The same process may occur at the level of individual sectors. Universities in the UK provide an illustration. When, in 1971, I got a job at the University of Essex, there was a professorial pay scale with (as I remember) five points. There was little scope for negotiation, and one ascended the scale after a number of years' service. Today, in the typical UK university, professorial pay spans a wide range and places on the scale are determined by individual bargaining.

With this kind of dynamic process, a period of movement in one direction might suddenly be reversed. Such a "shock" could result from a change in the political climate, perhaps influenced by events in other countries, causing a reduction in the degree of worker support for a redistributive pay norm. Or there might be a shift on the side of employers. The weight attached to reputation depends on the extent to which employers look to the future. If businesses come to discount future profits more heavily, then correspondingly less weight is attached to the benefits in terms of reputation from adhering to pay norms. It is indeed plausible that the rate of discount of firms has increased on account of increased emphasis on shareholder value. In this way, developments in the capital market impinge on the pay distribution. A further consideration is that, in the past, governments have sought to influence pay levels and relativities through public-sector employment, and this leverage has been attenuated in recent decades as a result of privatisation. The aggregate behaviour of employers has shifted on account of the transfer of state enterprises to private shareholders. As a result, we observe a move towards a more spread-out distribution.

In sum, once we recognise that market forces provide only bounds on the possible labour-market outcomes, we see that there is scope for notions of fairness, and that by bringing these to bear we can change the distribution of pay. But this is not just a matter for individual negotiation, and I turn now to collective action.

Trade Unions and Collective Bargaining

There is general agreement that the widening of the pay distribution has coincided with a decline in the role of trade unions and of collective bargaining. The graph in the OECD report *Divided We Stand* shows that in every OECD country apart from Spain the rate of trade union membership was lower in 2008 than in 1980.[20] But there is considerable debate about the extent of unions' influence on pay differentials. On the one hand, Stephen Nickell and Richard Layard conclude that "most of the gross features of unemployment and wage distributions across the OECD in recent years seem explicable by supply and demand shifts and the role required of special institutional features such as unions and minimum wages is correspondingly minimal."[21] On the other hand, Jelle Visser concludes that "one consistent finding is that collective bargaining . . . compresses the distribution of earnings relative to market pay-setting."[22] The differences surface within studies that have sought to determine how far reduced trade union membership has been responsible for widening wage dispersion. In a study of Canada, the UK, and the US, David Card, Thomas Lemieux, and Craig Riddell find that the substantial decline in the unionisation rate "explains a significant fraction of the growth in wage inequality in the United States and United Kingdom," although this conclusion applies to men, whereas "the modest decline in union coverage among women had little impact on female wage inequality," and their conclusions do not carry over to Canada, where there was little change in wage inequality despite a drop in male union coverage.[23] As with other items on the list set out at the beginning of the chapter, the fall in union influence appears to be part, but only part, of the explanation.

The decline in union power owes much to political events. In this context, we cannot lose sight of the long and often violent history of the establishment of the legal right to organise. Nor can we ignore the extent to which union activities now are governed by a legal framework that has become increasingly hostile, the trend of recent decades having been to scale back the rights of workers. In the UK, the Trade Union Congress believes that today "UK trade unions members have fewer rights to take industrial action than in 1906 when the current system of industrial action law was introduced. Those participating in lawful industrial action remain vulnerable to dismissal and victimisation."[24] But the decline may also be related to what is happening in the economy. In Chapter 5, I discuss the changing nature of employment, but we should note the possibility of a direct link with the textbook story of skill-biased technological change considered earlier in this chapter. In an insightful article that seeks to model labour-market institutions, Daron Acemoglu, Philippe Aghion, and Giovanni Violante have argued that the decline in unionisation is the result of the bias in technical change towards skilled workers. Technological change biased towards skilled workers undermines the coalition between them and unskilled workers that provides the basis for union bargaining power, and the consequent decline in unionisation amplifies the rise in wage dispersion.[25]

One evident problem with empirical attempts to identify the impact of trade unions on the wage distribution is the difficulty in encapsulating their bargaining strength in quantitative indicators. The standard measure employed is that of trade union membership, but the Eurofound report on trade union membership 2003–2008 opens with the warning that "trade union membership figures are a difficult subject area . . . [it is a] field featuring numerous methodological and conceptual problems."[26] There are issues with how trade unions and union membership are defined and how the data are gathered. There is an evident difference between membership and the more extensive concept of coverage, especially in countries such as France and Spain. The impact of collective bargaining depends crucially on the institutional structure, which varies considerably across countries, and cannot be adequately captured by a single macroeconomic variable such as trade union density. An important dimension is the degree of wage-setting centralisation, where over time more countries show a decrease than show an increase; this could have both direct and indirect implications for the distribution of earnings. According to Michael Förster and István Tóth, "centralised bargaining improves the bargaining position of workers; it may help broadening norms of distributive justice."[27]

Capital and Monopoly Power

The recent book by Thomas Piketty is entitled *Capital in the Twenty-First Century*, but in fact it is about both "wealth" and "capital," and it is important to keep them distinct. Wealth is now quite widely distributed, but much of the wealth that people own conveys little or no control over the productive activities of the economy beyond their own front door. It is true that owner-occupiers control the assets that generate housing services, but the fact that they invest part of their pension savings in a hedge fund that holds rented properties conveys no control over those houses or apartments. Decisions about how the tenants are treated are in the hands of the managers. In the same way, the wealth held via institutional investors provides much of the share capital of quoted companies, but the savers have no say in the decisions of those companies. The application of capital in productive activities is different from the beneficial ownership of wealth.

The Share of Profits

It is *capital* that is relevant when we consider the macroeconomic distribution of income. As we saw in the previous chapter, one of the elements contributing to the reduction in inequality in the postwar period was the rise in the share of wage income in national income. This has now been reversed: it is the share of profits that has risen in recent decades.

In considering the rising share of profits, the natural starting point, common to macroeconomists of most schools, is the aggregate production function, where national output is determined by the stock of capital and the size of the labour force.[28] This is the centrepiece of the Solow model of economic growth, which shows that an economy develops over time as the capital stock and labour force increase (in this discussion I assume that the economy is closed, so that there is no capital or labour from abroad, and no exports or imports). What happens if, over time, the stock of capital increases and the labour force remains unchanged? In the case of a perfectly competitive economy, where the rate of return to capital is equal to the marginal productivity of capital, a rise in the stock of capital per worker is associated with a decline in the rate of return. The impact on the share of profits therefore depends on the size of this decline, and this in turn is governed by how easy it is to absorb the additional capital per worker. Again, therefore, it turns out that the impact on the distribution of income depends on the elasticity of substitution—in this case, the elasticity of substitution between capital and labour (earlier in the chapter it was the substitution between skilled and unskilled workers). If it is easy to substitute capital for labour, and the elasticity of substitution is greater than 1, then there is a modest fall in the rate of return and the profit share rises as the capital per worker increases. If the elasticity is less than 1, then the profit share falls.[29]

Establishing what happens to the profits share seems to be a matter of determining the elasticity of substitution between capital and labour. There appears in this respect to be a measure of agreement among economists: "The vast majority of existing estimates indicate a short-run elasticity of substitution significantly less than one," to quote Daron Acemoglu and James Robinson. The review by Robert Chirinko of thirty-one studies in the US concludes that "the weight of the evidence suggests that [the gross elasticity of substitution] lies in the range between 0.40 and 0.60."[30] If that is the case, a rise in capital per worker would lead to a decline, not a rise, in the profit share. But matters are never that simple. The change over time in the profits share depends not only on the rate of capital accumulation but also on the nature of technological change. Technological advances may be biased in favour of capital in just the same way as we discussed earlier in relation to skilled and unskilled labour. For instance, Alfonso Arpaia, Esther Pérez, and Karl Pichelmann conclude that "most of the declining pattern in labour shares in nine EU15 Member States is governed by capital deepening [that is, more capital per worker] in conjunction with capital-augmenting technical progress and labour substitution across skill categories."[31] If that is the case, then we have to ask the same questions as earlier about the determinants of the direction of technological developments.

In the long run, the elasticity of substitution is undoubtedly greater than in the short run, and, more generally, the past may not be a good guide to the future. We need to think more adventurously about the aggregate production function. One interesting possibility has been suggested by Lawrence Summers, Harvard economist and former US Secretary of the Treasury. Capital can be seen as playing two roles: directly via the first argument of the production function, but also indirectly insofar as it supplements human labour.[32] The supplementation may be thought of in terms of the use of robots, but may take many different forms. The production function is such that capital is always employed in the first use, but it may or may not be used to supplement labour. The condition under which robots, or other forms of automation, are used to supplement human labour depends, as we would expect, on the relative costs of labour and capital. There is a critical value of the ratio of the wage to the cost of capital at which the use of robots becomes economical.[33]

This formulation may be seen as a metaphor, but there is an underlying reality. In their study of the future susceptibility to computerisation of US jobs, Carl Benedikt Frey and Michael Osborne conclude that 47 per cent of all US jobs are in the high-risk category, meaning that these occupations are potentially automatable in coming decades. The classification by Frey and Osborne goes beyond the routine/nonroutine division cited earlier or the manual/cognitive division used in earlier studies and considers the specific bottlenecks to computerisation. The high-risk jobs are located particularly in office and administration, sales, and service categories. At low-risk were jobs in health care, education, education/legal/community service/arts, and the media. Not surprisingly, these require particular human skills such as social perceptiveness, negotiation, persuasion, and originality.[34]

We can therefore tell a story of macroeconomic development where initially the Solow model applies. In this context, a rising capital-labour ratio leads to rising wages and a falling rate of return. The capital share rises only if the elasticity of substitution is greater than 1. Beyond a certain point, however, the wage/rate of return ratio reaches the critical value, and robots begin to displace human labour. We then see further growth in the economy, as capital per head rises, but the wage/rate of return ratio remains unchanged. The capital share rises, independent of the elasticity of substitution. In this way, the standard model of economic growth can be modified in a simple way, without making any assumptions about elasticities, to highlight a central distributional dilemma: that the benefits from growth now increasingly accrue through rising profits. The dilemma was indeed stressed some fifty years ago by my teacher James Meade in his book *Efficiency, Equality and the Ownership of Property,* where he argued with considerable prescience that automation would lead to rising inequality.[35] At the time, this was questioned. In his book review, Paul Samuelson asked "does not the boy cry Wolf?" adding that in the US, "no one has yet found in our copious statistics a deterioration in the wage share."[36] At the time (1965) Samuelson was right, but, as we have seen (Figure 2.4), the wage share is now falling. Viewed some half-century later, in this clash of Nobel Prize–winners, Meade seems to have been vindicated in alerting us to the importance of capital and its ownership.

Companies and Market Power

One important class of economic actors has so far played only a walk-on role: firms, companies, and enterprises. In part, this is because attention has focused on the labour market, where firms appeared as employers, with no account being taken of their activities as sellers of products and services. Yet it is the price of these products that determines the purchasing power of wages and other incomes. Trade unions may negotiate higher wages, but these may simply result in higher prices, with no increase for workers in their share of the value of aggregate output. In part, firms have been kept in the background because they have been assumed to be *perfectly competitive;* that is, it has been assumed that they take as given the price at which they can sell their output. This, however, is far from the case in the modern economy, where firms have considerable market power and can determine their own pricing policies. Few of them are pure monopolists, since they face competition, but they know that how much they can sell depends on the price they set: they are *monopolistically competitive.*

Recognition of market power changes the story. The assumption that firms act perfectly competitively is not an innocuous simplification; it may be a highly misleading point of departure. As observed by the Polish economist Michael Kalecki, "perfect competition—when its real nature, that of a handy model, is forgotten—becomes a dangerous myth." In his article titled "Class Struggle and the Distribution of National Income," Kalecki argues that "under perfect competition the share of wages certainly will not change when wage rates alter. However, an oligopolistic market structure, excess capacities, and mark-up pricing are the basis for a successful wage bargain. The more powerful the trade unions are, the more they will be able to restrain the mark-ups and thereby to increase the share of wages in national income."[37] Going beyond the original analysis of Kalecki, and combining today's understanding of the behaviour of monopolistically competitive firms with bargaining in the labour market, we can see that greater worker power does indeed reduce the extent to which firms exploit their market power in the pricing of their products.[38]

To understand fully these interconnections, we have to look at the *general equilibrium* of the economy. For many purposes, it is sufficient to look only at part of the economy, or "partial equilibrium," as in the market for milk, but to investigate the distribution of income we need to bring together the labour and capital markets (as already noted) with the product markets. We must look at the economy as a whole. In determining the general equilibrium of such a market economy, people play several different roles, and the outcome depends both on what they bring to the different markets and on the power that derives from their position in the market. There is today much anxiety about the positional power of large multinational corporations, but this is not new. A concern with the dominance of modern corporations led John Kenneth Galbraith, in his 1952 book *American Capitalism,* to explore the notion of the "countervailing power" of workers and consumer groups.[39] Rebalancing power in the economy is one of the elements in the proposals set out in Part Two.

Macroeconomics and People

In this book, my concern is with what happens to individuals and their families. Such a concern may at times seem far removed from those of economic policy-makers who talk in terms of macroeconomic aggregates such as national income or GDP. And it is the latter—the macroeconomic numbers—that tend to dominate the news bulletins and policy debates.

The two are related, however, and the level of output and the growth of the economy are important determinants of what happens to individual people. So too are the return to capital and to skill, with which this chapter has so far been largely concerned. We need to connect the dots between macroeconomics and the distribution of income.

From National Income to Household Income

Connecting the dots is not easy. If we were to try to explain the standard GDP figures to our noneconomist neighbour, it would be difficult to make a link between these numbers in the national accounts and those that he or she may submit to the income tax authorities. Studying the national accounts is like entering a maze. We depart from some recognisable landmarks—see Figure 3.1—like wages and salaries (although even these are not straightforward, since they include employer contributions for social security and for private benefits, and so are not identical to the amount received in the pay packet). But then we have to find our way through the institutions that stand between the productive economy and the household sector.

The largest intervening institution is the state, which we have already encountered, since households pay taxes and receive transfers, which appeared in Figure 1.5 (and are shown in Figure 3.1 with dashed lines). But the state also plays other important roles that affect the degree of inequality. Two are particularly relevant here. The first is that, as discussed in Chapter 1, the state in many countries provides a substantial quantity of services that are individually consumed, such as health and education. The extent and allocation of these services potentially have significant distributional consequences. A given distribution of money income has a different significance in a country where there is universal health care free at the point of access. We have only to contrast the UK and the US in this respect. Second, as we know all too well, the state issues debt. Interest on the national debt is paid to, among others, households, forming part of their income, shown by a solid line in Figure 3.1. We tend to hear less these days about the asset side of the balance sheet of the state. The state does, however, own assets, which are a counterbalance to the national debt. These include assets directly controlled by the state such as roads,

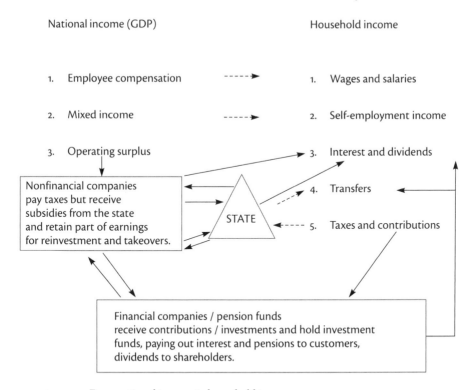

FIGURE 3.1: From national income to household income

schools, and government buildings, but in most countries they also include the state ownership of shares in companies. For example, in 2013,
the state of Lower Saxony in Germany held a substantial stake in the
Volkswagen Group, with 20 per cent of the voting rights.

(Nonfinancial) companies are the second intervening institution. Part
of company profit is paid out to households as dividends and interest, but
part is retained for reinvestment or acquisitions. If the latter pays off, then
these retained corporate earnings will lead to higher future dividends. To
the extent that such an increase is anticipated by the stock market, the
share price rises: the higher future dividends are capitalised immediately
in higher share prices. As we have seen, the adoption of a comprehensive
definition of income points to the inclusion of accrued capital gains and
losses in household income. At the same time, it is clear that this is an
indirect and uncertain mechanism. There are arrows going both ways be-

tween the company sector and the state: companies benefit from state subsidies, and they pay corporation and other taxes. Not shown are the flows abroad. In today's globalised economy, a major stake in the company sector may be owned by overseas investors. In the case of the UK, the 2012 survey of the beneficial ownership of UK ordinary shares showed that over half were owned by "rest of the world" investors (up from under one-third in 1998—a striking indicator of the way the world is changing).[40]

The picture is further complicated by the existence of the third set of intervening institutions, labelled "financial services," where this includes pension funds and life assurance (insurance) companies. These bodies are major holders of company shares. Of the domestically owned shares, two-thirds were in the hands of the financial services sector, with the shares directly owned by individuals constituting only a little over one-fifth. For the greater part of corporate income, there is then an additional lack of clarity as to the link with household income. Where, for instance, pension funds accumulate the returns on their investments in order to meet future pension obligations, then the actual payment may be long deferred. In considering in later chapters the implications of a rising share of capital income, we look at the difference between the overall rate of return and the amount that finds its way into the bank accounts of small savers.

Implications for the Analysis

From this brief guide to the path from national accounts to household incomes, there are two general lessons to be drawn. The first is that the two cannot be equated. Total household income is considerably less than total national income (GDP). A significant part of national income is absorbed by the intervening institutions. The state requires resources to provide public administration, defence, and public goods. Companies retain profits for investment. Looking to the future, we can see that the growth of household incomes may be less than the growth rate of GDP. GDP has to go toward maintaining infrastructure, mitigating climate change, investing in education, and providing for an ageing population. In some countries, and under some governments, the responsibility for meeting these needs may be transferred to the private sector, but the real burden remains in the form of a reduction in the income available for discretionary household spending (the income available after paying for private health care or education). Either way, the expectation for the future is one of slower growth in household spendable income than we have seen in the past.

The second lesson is that total household income, and its distribution, depend not only on macroeconomic factors but also on what Andrea Brandolini has called "entitlement rules," which can be defined as "the mechanism regulating the appropriation of the output of the economy, or . . . as the 'filter' between the production and its distribution among people."[41] Such rules may be quite specific, as in the case of the bankruptcy of a firm, where there is a priority order for claims on the remaining assets, or in the case of a pension fund, where there are provisions for dividing the accrued income between existing and future pensioners. The entitlements may be rather general, as with the expectation that an unemployed worker is entitled to state support. The important point is that these entitlement rules are the product of social and economic interaction that we need to investigate in order to understand the distribution of income. Put differently, two countries with the same macroeconomic conditions may exhibit quite different degrees of income inequality because of differences in the entitlement rules. Changes in the entitlement rules can be a means of reducing inequality in the incomes that reach households after passing through the intervening institutions.

Entitlement refers both to the receipt of income and to the right to a say in its disposition. The economy has to be seen, not only as a pattern of income flows, but also in terms of the location of control. The issue was, unwittingly, revealed in a speech of the British Chancellor of the Exchequer, George Osborne, addressing the 2014 Conservative Party Conference, when he said that "in a modern global economy where people can move their investment from one country to another at the touch of a button and companies can relocate jobs overnight—the economics of high taxation are a thing of the past." Whether or not he is right on the scope for higher taxation is a subject taken up in Chapter 7, but his statement is revealing in the acknowledgement that, in Britain today, the key decisions on jobs are being taken by companies, not by the workers or the consumers or the local governments where the companies are located or even by central government. This underlines the need to distinguish between ownership and control. Ownership of wealth in Britain, as in other advanced countries, has been transformed over the past century. In the days when there was a small capitalist class, ownership was concentrated; today ownership is much less unequally distributed. This change in ownership, however, has not brought with it an equalisation of economic power. Home ownership, which constitutes much of the wealth of the majority of the population, does not carry control over jobs or investments. The wealth invested in pension plans does not give the owners a say in where their money is employed. There is now an important distinction between wealth and capital. The power of capital is exercised by the fund managers, not by the beneficial owners.

The locus of decision-making will be of considerable significance when I come in Part Two to the proposals for the reduction of inequality, but first I explore in more detail the links with the earlier analysis of wages and capital income.

From Categories of Worker to Individual Incomes

Much of the earlier analysis of wages was framed in terms of categories of worker (skilled and unskilled), but this takes us only so far in understanding the role of wages in influencing household income inequality. For this, we have to consider individual incomes.[42] The distinction between college-educated and less-educated workers divides the labour force into two very broad groups. In the US in 2013, 44 per cent of those aged 25 to 64 had a college degree.[43] For other countries, the World Bank table for the proportion of the labour force with tertiary education shows figures close to 40 per cent in Belgium, Cyprus, Estonia, Finland, Ireland, Lithuania, Luxembourg, Norway, and the UK.[44] Educational qualifications alone are not sufficient to explain the more finely graduated pattern that we observe when we look at individual earnings. What we need to explain are the differences in earnings among those with the same qualifications: the within-group component.

For a richer account of the earnings distribution, we need to go beyond a single statistic such as the college wage premium or the ratio of

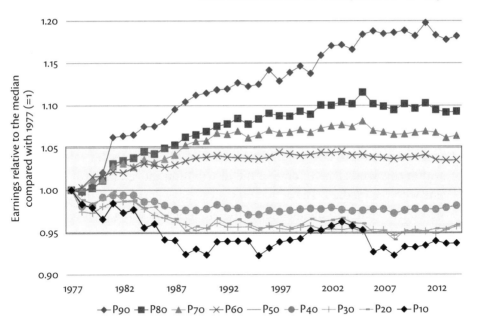

FIGURE 3.2: Change in earnings in the UK since 1977

This graph shows how the earnings of full-time employees in the UK have changed since 1977. Data points represent comparisons of different earnings groups with the median earnings (earnings of the person in the middle of the distribution), indexed such that 1977 = 1.0. The graph shows that the relative earnings of people in the top half of the earnings distribution (P90, P80, P70, P60) have grown between 1977 and 2014, while the relative earnings of people in the bottom half (P40, P30, P20, P10) have fallen.

skilled to unskilled wages. We need to look at the distribution as a whole, as is illustrated for the case of the UK by Figure 3.2. In constructing this figure, I have started with the nine deciles of the earnings distribution. The deciles, denoted by P10, P20, and so on, mark the division of the (full-time) labour force into tenths when ranked according to their earnings. The person in the middle is the median (P50), and earnings are expressed relative to the median, so that P50 = 1. I have then calculated the changes in these percentiles by expressing them relative to their values in 1977, so that a value of 1.1 in Figure 3.2 means that the decile has risen by 10 per cent more than the median. All start at 1.0, and the median (shown by the dashed line) remains there by definition. There is no reason for the other deciles to remain in order when expressed in this way. For example, P20 lies above P30 in some years. This means not that the person at the second decile earns more than the person at the third decile (which would be a contradiction in terms), but that the second decile of earnings has closed the gap. But in general they do remain in order.

The shaded part of Figure 3.2 shows the range where earnings did not change, relative to the median by more than 5 per cent. It is striking that over the period of nearly forty years, five of the nine deciles remained within this band. The middle of the distribution moved more or less in line with the median. The action was at the tails. Earnings at the bottom decile fell relative to the median in the 1980s. There was a brief recovery around the millennium, but that ground has now been lost. The most striking change, however, is above the median. The higher we look in the distribution, the more likely we are to find that the deciles have improved their position relative to the median. The earnings of the person one-fifth from the top (P80) rose by some 10 per cent relative to the median, and the top decile (P90) rose by some 20 per cent relative to the median. There has been an "upward tilt" in the earnings distribution. Looking within the top 10 per cent (those above the top decile), we find that the differences become even more marked. If we imagine an earnings "parade," with everyone lined up in increasing order of their earnings, then the gradient has become a great deal steeper at the top. In the late 1970s in the UK, people in the top 10 per cent looking upwards would have seen those above them earning on average some 30 per cent more; by 2003 the average advantage had increased to 56 per cent. Put a different way, a person at the top decile in 1977 would have needed an increase of 67 per cent in his or her earnings to reach the top percentile; in 2003 he or she would have needed an increase of 128 per cent.[45]

This upward tilt in the upper earnings distribution is not confined to the UK. The situation in the US has been graphically described by Jacob Hacker and Paul Pierson: "American inequality is not mainly about the gap between the well educated and the rest, or indeed about educational gaps in general. It is about the extraordinarily rapid pulling away of the very top. Those at the top are often highly educated, but so too are those just below them who have been left behind. Put another way, the distribution of educational gains over the last twenty-five years—who finishes college or gains advanced degrees—has been much broader than the distribution of economic gains. Only a very small slice of the new educational elite has entered the new economic elite."[46] Fanning-out in this way has happened quite widely—although not universally—in OECD countries, which explains why attention has focused so much on top incomes.[47]

Top Incomes

The tilt in the earnings distribution has propelled top earners into the top 1 per cent of all income recipients. Top earners have caught up with, or overtaken, those living off capital income. Rentiers clipping their dividend coupons have been replaced by hedge fund managers, CEOs, and footballers (who are no longer restricted to £20 a week!). There has indeed been a substantial change in the composition of top incomes. In the UK, the contribution of investment income to the income of the top 1 per cent has fallen from 41 per cent in 1949 to 13 per cent in 2000.[48] Thomas Piketty and Emmanuel Saez, when looking at the top 0.5 per cent in the US, found that capital income (excluding capital gains) "made about 55% of total income in the 1920s, 35% in the 1950s-60s, and 15% in the 1990s."[49] Jon Bakija, Adam Cole, and Bradley T. Heim classified taxpayers in the top 0.1 per cent in the US in 2004 according to occupation and found that 41 per cent were executives, managers or supervisors in the nonfinance sector, and that a further 18 per cent were in financial professions.[50]

It is therefore not surprising that attention has focused on earned incomes at the top. Here we have a variation on the trade and technology story adapted to the top of the pyramid in the form of the "superstar" explanation. A hundred years ago, Alfred Marshall, professor of Political Economy in Cambridge, described how top performers were able to demand high payments to a degree that depends on the size of the market served. The size of the market in turn depends on technology. He saw then the significance of "the development of new facilities for communication, by which men, who have once attained a commanding position, are enabled to apply their constructive or speculative genius to undertakings vaster, and extending over a wider area, than ever before." In the case of the arts, he observed that "there was never a time at which moderately good oil paintings sold more cheaply than now and at which first rate paintings sold so dearly."[51] The earnings gradient has become tilted in favour of superstars. It is not just communication; it is also globalisation that has extended the scale of the market.

The upward tilt in top earnings has been further accentuated by a second mechanism described earlier in this chapter: the switch between regimes where pay is largely governed by pay scales to regimes where pay becomes largely determined on the basis of individual performance. In the US, the rise in the top decile has been accompanied by increased performance-related pay, as has been documented by Thomas Lemieux, W. Bentley MacLeod, and Daniel Parent, who find that "most of the impact of performance pay on the growth in inequality is concentrated at the top end of the distribution."[52] The expansion of top managerial pay may also be related to the reduced top rates of income tax. When tax rates were high, executives allocated little energy to negotiating higher remuneration, deriving their satisfaction more from the scale of operations of the business or its rate of growth. The sizeable cuts that have been made in top tax rates in recent decades, however, have led managers to redirect their efforts towards securing better remuneration: "the sharp fall in true tax rates on very high incomes may have stimulated the rise in executive pay since the recipients capture so much more of any rise in compensation."[53]

Political forces played an important role too. In their study "Winner-Take-All Politics," Hacker and Pierson document the way in which organised interest groups in the US have lobbied to secure changes in the regulatory framework, in accounting standards, and in tax rules. They quote the former head of the Securities and Exchange Commission (SEC), Arthur Levitt, as describing how "groups representing Wall Street firms, mutual fund companies, accounting firms, or corporate managers would quickly set about to defeat even minor threats. Individual investors, with no organized labor or trade association to represent their views in Washington, never knew what hit them."[54] There could hardly be a clearer statement of the need for countervailing power.

Focus on top earnings should not lead us to ignore income from capital. Investment income is a smaller fraction of the income of the top 1 per cent than in the past, but its significance should not be overlooked, particularly if it has become more closely aligned with earned income. The joint distribution of earned and capital incomes is actually an aspect that is rarely given explicit consideration. Yet it is important to know whether the same people are at the top of both distributions. Imagine that we ask the population first to line up along one side of a room in increasing order of their earned income, and then to go to the other side of the room and line up in increasing order of their capital income. Will they be in the same order? How much will they cross over? In the Ricardian class model, the crossing is complete: the capitalists come top in one case (capital income) and bottom in the other (earned income). We have to ask what happens today. Has a negative correlation in the nineteenth century been replaced today by a zero association, with no connection? Or is there a perfect correlation, so that people cross straight over?

The evidence for the US on the pattern of crossing is interesting. In 1980, the degree of association was not strong: of those in the top 1 per cent of capital income, only 17 per cent were in the top 1 per cent for labour income.[55] By 2000, however, the proportion had increased from 17 per cent to 27 per cent, and over one-half of those in the top 1 per cent by capital income were in the top 10 per cent of earners. Looked at the other way around, the overlap in 2000 is greater: of those in the top 1 per cent of labour income, nearly two-thirds (63 per cent) were in the top 10 per cent of capital income receivers. There is more commonality. A third of a century ago, John Kay and Mervyn King described, in the case of the UK, the hypothetical position of a senior executive with a large corporation who had saved a quarter of his after-tax earnings: "Feeling . . . that he has been unusually fortunate in his career and unusually thrifty . . . he may be somewhat surprised to discover that there are in Britain at least 100,000 people richer than he is."[56] Today, it is easier to accumulate wealth as a top earner.[57]

A Summing-Up So Far

Thus far I have described the challenge taken on in this book. I have examined the reasons for concern about inequality, evidence about its extent, and the economics of inequality, with the aim of identifying in the next part of the book a set of concrete measures that could be taken to bring about a distinct reduction in economic inequality.

In the past there have been significant periods when inequality has fallen. These include not just exceptional wartime periods but also the postwar decades in Europe and the recent decade in Latin America. While today's world is different in key respects, there are lessons that we can learn from history. Experience suggests that a fall in inequality has come about through a combination of reduced inequality of market incomes and more effective redistribution, and this is the basis for the proposals made here.

Market incomes are not just driven by exogenous forces over which we have no control. A reduction in market income inequality is possible. We need to explore the determinants of technological change, to see how it can be harnessed to improve the life chances of workers and consumers. In a market economy, supply and demand influence the outcome but leave space for other mechanisms; we need, therefore, to examine the wider social context in which markets operate. In Chapters 4 and 5, I consider these issues in relation to technological change and employment.

Attention in Chapters 2 and 3 has largely focused on widening wage dispersion, but it is important to investigate the role of capital income as well as labour income, and the relation between them. Measures to secure a fairer distribution of wealth are the subject of Chapter 6, but we must bear in mind that the ownership of wealth does not necessarily convey control over capital. We need to identify the locus of decision-making as it affects the incomes and lives of individuals, as well as the balance of power—between individuals and between groups in society. Issues of power are most transparent in the field of politics. The government can have a significant influence on market incomes, and it therefore plays an important role in Chapters 4 to 6, but its impact is most direct in the case of redistributive taxation (Chapter 7) and the provision of social security (Chapter 8).

PROPOSALS FOR ACTION

Part Two makes concrete proposals that would, in my judgement, achieve a significant reduction in inequality. Some of these proposals are developed by concrete reference to the UK, but I believe that the underlying approach has much wider resonance and is applicable in a wide range of countries. A number of the proposals involve the classic measures of progressive taxation and social protection, and I can already hear critics dismissing them as either boringly familiar or wildly utopian. I do indeed set out proposals for "taxing and spending" in Chapters 7 and 8, but one of the main themes of the book is the importance of measures to render less unequal the incomes people receive before government taxes and transfers. Today's high level of inequality can be effectively reduced only by tackling inequality in the marketplace. It is therefore with the economic forces driving market incomes from work and from capital that I begin in Chapters 4 to 6.

Chapter 4 ::

Technological Change and Countervailing Power

In Chapter 3, I described a simple economic story of how capital accumulation and technological change can combine to explain the development of the macroeconomic distribution over recent decades. There is growth in the economy as capital per head rises, but the share of capital in national income increases, limiting the benefit to wage-earners. This story was told in the specific terms of the development of robot technology: a race between the greater capacities of unaided capital (robots) and the productivity of workers. For many observers, robots are more than a metaphor: they are already winning. An article in the *Economist* gave the example of driverless cars and asserted that "a taxi driver will be a rarity in many places by the 2030s or 2040s. That sounds like bad news for journalists who rely on that most reliable source of local knowledge and prejudice."[1] But the invention of robot technology, and technological progress more generally, did not come about by chance: they reflected conscious decisions to make such an investment. We need to start, therefore, by asking how such decisions are made. This leads naturally to the question, Who makes the decisions? as well as to issues of countervailing power.

The Direction of Technological Change

Let us assume initially that the decision is made commercially. Investment in the development of new robotic technology (continuing the robot metaphor) is undertaken by firms, either those specialising in the production of capital goods which they then sell to firms producing final output for consumption, or by vertically integrated firms that develop their own technology in-house. A car manufacturer, for example, is contemplating investing in the robotisation of its paint-spraying plant. On the face of it, this seems like a desirable investment, since it means that humans will no longer be exposed to the hazards of chemicals and a higher-quality product can be achieved. For the workers in charge of the operation and maintenance of the robots, the new paint shops will offer more skilled jobs, requiring a higher level of education. Initially, the new process will involve more employment, as experimentation is required and the robots require frequent manual intervention to deal with break-downs, but in time there will be a substantial reduction in the total work force. The consequent savings on the wage bill will be the return on the initial investment. In deciding whether to embark on this new technology, the firm weighs the future savings against the cost of the current investment. The outcome depends on the time horizon of the firm, so that the investment is more likely to take place if the firm takes a long-term view of profits. There are other considerations too, such as the fact that robots do not go on strike. With a smaller labour force and more mechanised production, the firm will have greater control and less need to negotiate with trade unions.

The picture described above is in many respects a benign one, demonstrating the benefits to be had from technological advances, with unpleasant and hazardous work being eliminated. It sounds like the world that Keynes forecast in his 1930 essay "Economic Possibilities for Our Grandchildren," in which he predicted increased leisure and resolution of the "economic problem."[2] Can we not therefore leave the market economy to make the decisions? Three problems immediately present themselves. The first is distributional. Whose grandchildren are enjoying the increased leisure? Keynes refers to the "problem of labour absorption" as "the growing-pains of over-rapid changes," but we have seen that there are long-run consequences in terms of the shares of national income. We have to consider who receives capital income, and the case for fairer shares of wealth. In a roundtable discussion organised by McKinsey titled "Automation, Jobs, and the Future of Work," Laura Tyson, chair of the Council of Economic Advisers under President Clinton, concluded that the key question is "who owns the robots."[3]

The second problem with the market outcome does not arise in the paint shop case but does in the *Economist* example of the driverless taxi: the fact that an important element in the final product is provided by human contact. This problem does not feature in the case of the paint shop because painting is an intermediate part of the process, and the purchaser of the car is unaware whether robots or humans performed that task. But the taxi ride is a final service. The taxi driver is in effect supplying a joint product: the trip from airport to hotel, and a summary of local opinion. Sometimes, the passenger may prefer to do without the latter, but in many other cases the service is a valued if not essential part of the process. Human interaction may provide reassurance that the product meets the consumer needs or vital information as to how to use the product. Medicines dispensed via automatic boxes would not provide the guidance of the pharmacist on the proper use of the drugs. Delivery of meals on wheels to the housebound by drone would not provide the human contact that for many of the recipients is an essential part of the service.

In effect, the human-service element adds to the relative productivity of people vis-à-vis capital. But this assumes that the human service continues to be supplied. Here, joint supply is a problem, since there is no theorem in economics that ensures that the market determines the right mix of product and human service where the two elements cannot be unbundled. We cannot guarantee that there will be two queues of taxis, one with a driver and one driverless, allowing consumers to signal their separate demands for the human-service element. There is a parallel with geographical location. As the American economist Harold Hotelling showed in the 1920s, there is no reason to suppose that market forces produce the right location of sellers. Imagine that there are two ice cream vendors on a beach (each selling the same ice cream). If there is a uniform density of potential buyers along the beach, then profit-maximising sellers would locate next to each other in the middle of the beach. Both in effect offer the same product. But to minimise the total distance walked by buyers, we want them to spread out. It would be better if each seller located a quarter of the way along the beach, but that outcome would not be sustainable as a market solution, since each would gain customers, given the position of the other seller, by moving towards the centre.

In this way, both consumers and workers have a strong interest in the choice of goods and services to be supplied and, notably, the extent to which there is a human-service element. If firms go for a highly mechanised mode of supply, such as delivery by drones, then this decision has implications for wages and employment. The same is true where the demand takes the form of public purchasing. When requesting bids for services that are contracted out, the government—national or local—can determine the weight to be attached to the human-service element. Emphasis placed on minimising the cost of provision, with little or no weight on maintaining the nature of the service, drives suppliers towards automation. Put in more immediate terms, if the effect of austerity programmes that cut public budgets is to downplay these elements of service, then these budget cuts are contributing to switching income from workers to capital.

The third problem of technological innovation is that decisions today may have consequences stretching far into the future. In the previous chapter I referred to learning by doing. Replacing people by automation today makes it likely that more people will be so replaced in the future, as firms gain in experience. Today's choice of mode of production affects the choices open to us tomorrow. Experience with robots leads us off on a path where they, increasingly, over time, replace humans, the trade-off becoming increasingly favourable. But we could have taken an alternative path where the human-service element was emphasised and the skills of people were increasingly developed. We have therefore to consider the implications of today's production decisions for where we would like to end up in the future. Here, the motives of the firm, giving priority to the specific interests of its shareholders, may not be aligned with the wider interests of society, and we need to consider the role of countervailing power, taken up later in this chapter. First, though, I examine the key role of the state.

The State as Investor in Technological Progress

Public policy can play a significant role in influencing the nature of technological change and hence the future direction of market incomes. This leads to the first of the recommendations as to how the rise in inequality could be reversed:

Proposal 1: The direction of technological change should be an explicit concern of policy-makers, encouraging innovation in a form that increases the employability of workers and emphasises the human dimension of service provision.

It is not enough to say that rising inequality is due to technological forces outside our control. The government can influence the path taken. What is more, this influence is exercised by departments of the government that are not typically associated with issues of social justice. A government that is seeking to reduce inequality has to involve the whole cabinet of ministers.

The first means to this end is through the financing of scientific research. The key role of government funding is illustrated by the example of the iPhone in the US, which depended "on seven or eight fundamental scientific and technological breakthroughs, such as GPS, multi-touch screens, LCD displays, lithium-ion batteries, and cellular networks. . . . They all came from research supported by the federal government . . . Apple deserves credit for the final product, but it depends on government-sponsored research."[4] The Apple story has been investigated in depth by Mariana Mazzucato in her book *The Entrepreneurial State.* In the case of touch-screens, for example, she identifies the role of government-funded research laboratories: "E. A. Johnson, considered the inventor of capacitive touch-screens, published his first studies in the 1960s while working at Royal Radar Establishment [a British government agency] . . . One of the first notable developments of the touch-screen was at the European Organization for Nuclear Research (CERN) . . . Samuel Hurst's invention of resistive touch-screens . . . came right after leaving Oak Ridge National Laboratory." In the case of Giant magnetoresistance, which underlies hard drives, "what started as two separate and independent academic, State-funded and -supported research projects in physics in Germany and France culminated in one of the most successful technology breakthroughs in recent years."[5]

The account just given may suggest a linear process, where basic research is funded by the state and the translation of Nobel Prize–winning research into products is the responsibility of the private sector. However, the state, and society as a whole, have a strong interest in—and engagement in—the translation stage. This is not a question of the state's "picking winners" but a matter of recognising the potential influence of government decisions at many phases of a complex process. We may live in a market economy, but the government impinges in many ways on technological innovation. To quote Mazzucato, "it is important to recognize the 'collective' character of innovation. Different types of firms (large and small), different types of finance and different types of State policies, institutions and departments interact sometimes in unpredictable ways."[6] This in turn has policy implications, as has been stressed by Steven Johnson: "If we think that innovation comes out of collaborative networks, then we want to support different policies and organizational forms: less rigid patent laws, open standards, employee participation in stock plans, cross-disciplinary connections." He draws this conclusion from examining a number of major innovations, including the light bulb, and goes on to say that "the lightbulb shines light on more than just our bedside reading; it helps us see more clearly the way new ideas come into being, and how to cultivate them as a society."[7]

In this context, when making decisions supporting innovation—whether concerned with financing, licensing, regulating, purchasing, or educating—the government should explicitly consider the distributional implications. It is not evident that this happens at present. When the US Defense Advanced Research Projects Agency (DARPA) launched its Grand Challenge prize competition for autonomous vehicles in 2004, an explicit goal of the project was for the US military to provide such driverless vehicles for one-third of its ground forces by 2015. But were the wider consequences outside the military—for taxi-drivers and others—considered? Were plans made to encourage the redeployment of the human drivers who would no longer be required? Did the European-based Euroka consortium in the same field consider the distributional issues when launching PROMETHEUS (Programme for a European Traffic System with Highest Efficiency and Unprecedented Safety)? The fact that "efficiency" is picked out in its title suggests that "equity" was not at the forefront. When President George W. Bush announced in 2006 the American Competitiveness Initiative, doubling US spending on innovation-enabling research, the policy paper stated that "research pays off for our economy." But did any journalist ask him "for whom?"[8] There are important choices to be made regarding the direction of research in which society as a whole has a strong interest.

Public Employment and Technological Change

The direction of technological change has so far been discussed in terms of the enhancement of the productivity of capital or labour, but there is also an important issue concerning the bias in terms of *sectors of the economy*. Such a bias arises in an acute form in what is known as the Baumol effect, after the US economist William J. Baumol, who argued that productivity grows faster in certain sectors than in others, and that in some sectors there was no scope for producing more output per person.[9] The classic example of the latter is that of a string quartet, but the Baumol effect has been taken to apply particularly to the public sector, where slower productivity growth has been taken to imply that the relative cost of public services, such as health care, education, and public administration, rises over time, creating fiscal problems. In its starkest form, if a person can either teach a class or build a car, and technical progress means that he or she can build two cars in place of one, then the relative cost of education is doubled if wages rise in line with productivity in manufacturing.

Does this mean that, as our societies get richer through technical advances, we should devote fewer resources to the public services that are being left behind? Should public employment be cut? Some people have drawn this conclusion, but it does not follow. Baumol himself is careful to point out that, as we get richer, we can also attach more value to the public services.[10] In value terms, the productivity of the public service depends both on the activity (teaching a class or treating back pain) and on the value attached to that activity. To give a concrete example, the back pain treatment may well mean that the hospital patient can return to work sooner. The fact that the worker is more productive in the job (say, building cars) to which he or she returns implies that the gain from the back pain treatment in terms of extra output is now larger. The volume of public service activity is the same, but its value is greater.

How does this relate to the earlier discussion? There I stressed that the direction of technological change was not exogenous but subject to influence and reflected decisions consciously taken. One dimension of these decisions is the choice of sectors in which to seek technological advance. The government should not, therefore, accept the Baumol effect as predetermined; rather, it should seek to raise the productivity of workers in these labour-intensive sectors. Decisions about investment in new technology should be based on the claims of different sectors, where those of the public sector have to be represented by the government. Policy-makers should take account of the rising future value of public services that results from the progress made in the economy as a whole. Current decision-makers, and the electorate who vote for them, need to be forward-looking. We tend to think of investment in terms of infrastructure like roads or airports, but equally—or more—important is investment in human capital. I shall later stress the role of cash transfers to families with children (Child Benefit), but these need to be combined with investment in services and facilities for children, including early-childhood education and care, school meal programmes, and after-school youth programmes, in addition to improving the quality of formal education. As I have argued, considerations of intergenerational equity, and a lower rate of growth of living standards, mean that we should discount the future less heavily; this should be reflected in a higher valuation being placed on the work of those who facilitate human capital investment.[11]

A higher valuation should, for different reasons, be placed on improving public administration. The achievement of an equitable society depends to a considerable degree on the effectiveness of the public administration and the quality of its dealings with citizens. Repressive administration may be cheaper, but a fair society needs to ensure that its operations—in the fields of taxation, public spending, regulation, and legislation—are just, transparent, and accepted. This requires resources. Moreover, as societies become richer, so too they become more demanding in their standards. The proposals advanced involve significant changes in government activity—just as the New Deal in the US in the 1930s required new institutions—and necessarily require investment in new methods. This applies particularly to the proposal in the next chapter for guaranteed employment, where its efficacy in achieving social justice depends on the programme not being captured by clientelist interests. A trained and independent administrative service is required. The potential role of new technology in improving the efficiency of government has been widely recognised. What I am urging is the importance of the equity dimension. In balancing the cost savings from technological advances against the loss of human contact, the government should safeguard the position of those who are disadvantaged, not just materially but also in their relation with new technologies. Economic inequality is often aligned with differences in access to, use of, or knowledge of information and communication technologies. For middle-class taxpayers, filing a tax return on-line may be a time-saving operation, but for a person who has just become unemployed, applying for benefits on-line may be a worrisome challenge. Those facing difficulties are the ones most in need of an administration with a human face.

Countervailing Power

It is a truism that there are many actors in the economy and their interests may differ. The same person may play different roles, even conflicting ones. As a worker, he or she may be pleased to see improved remuneration but concerned if it leads to higher prices in the shops and to a smaller increase in the pension fund. In this section, I consider the power exercised by different actors by virtue of their position and their role in economic decision-making. I include decisions not only about the direction of technological change, on which this chapter has so far focused, but also more broadly about the distribution of the gains from economic growth.

The Balance of Market Power

In *American Capitalism,* Galbraith observes that "for the businessman and political philosopher . . . the appeal of the competitive model was its solution of the problem of power." Where firms and consumers are unable to influence the prices in the market, then their power is indeed limited. But once we leave the hypothetical world of perfect competition, we have to ask how decision-makers exercise their market power. This applies to the labour market, where there may be bargaining between employers and workers (and unions) over money wages and employment; the product market, where firms set prices above the marginal cost of production and determine the range of products supplied (and consumers rarely exercise collective power); and the capital market, where firms may face financial institutions with market power determining the availability and cost of finance. As Galbraith underlined, economists had from the 1930s recognised in the "monopolistic competition revolution" the need to model markets where firms had a degree power intermediate between the poles of pure monopoly and of perfect competition. Firms face competition but are price-makers. Understanding their behaviour has greatly advanced as a result of the game-theoretic analyses of recent decades, a success signalled by the award of the 2014 Nobel Prize in Economics to the French economist Jean Tirole for his contribution to "the science of taming powerful firms."

How does this relate to inequality? Here, as elsewhere in the book, I am not seeking a transcendental solution. I shall not discuss the ultimate question of the socially just allocation of power. Rather, I start from the pragmatic concern that current levels of inequality are too high and that this outcome in part reflects the fact that the balance of power is weighted against consumers and workers. Many share, perhaps with qualifications, the concern embodied in the Nobel 2014 citation that powerful firms need to be tamed. This applies both to producers and—since the financial crisis—to financial institutions, since behind the notion that "banks were too big to be allowed to fail" was also the realisation that they were too powerful for this to happen. I therefore consider how power could be transferred in the direction of empowering consumers and restoring the legal position of trade unions—without attempting to resolve the issue of the ideal balance. It is the direction of movement that is my focus here.

Can a shift in the balance of power be achieved through a change in the motivation of businesses to take greater account of their social responsibilities? For organisations that are not controlled by shareholders, the goals can indeed be set more broadly: "Power should . . . be made responsible to those it affects. The ultimate criteria in the organization of work should be human dignity and service to others instead of solely economic performance. We feel mutual responsibility must permeate the whole community of work and be upheld by democratic participation and the principle of trusteeship" (Constitution of the Scott Bader Commonwealth, a multinational chemical company).[12] What about the more usual shareholder-controlled firms? One route is for firms to take a longer-term view, which may indirectly have distributional consequences. As suggested in the previous chapter, it may be that corporations have become more short-term in their objectives, and this may be one explanation of changing patterns of pay and the upward tilt in managerial remuneration. Milton Friedman famously wrote in the *New York Times* in 1970 that "the social responsibility of business is to increase its profits," but the crucial issue is the specification of the time horizon.[13] Business operates within a legal and political framework, and its long-term viability (and hence profits) may depend on exercising a degree of restraint in seeking short-term gain. If that is the case, then shareholders, particularly institutional investors, could clearly exercise their influence in favour of a longer-term perspective. However, we have to recognise the increasingly globalised nature of share ownership. As we saw earlier, over half of UK ordinary shares are owned by "rest of the world" investors. The notion of "social responsibility" applies to a particular society, and it is not clear that overseas shareholders have a long-term commitment to the country in which they are investing.

Different ways of embodying social responsibilities within the objectives of the firm were discussed in the 1970s by Kenneth Arrow, who lists legal regulation (discussed below), taxation (discussed in later chapters), legal liability in the civil courts (not evidently relevant here), and ethical codes (a generally understood definition of appropriate behaviour). As he says, the last of these may be "a strange possibility for an economist to raise," but he goes on to point out that "a great deal of economic life depends for its viability on a certain limited degree of ethical commitment."[14] He discusses the conditions under which ethical codes may be established and conditions under which they are likely to be sustainable. His emphasis is on the contribution that ethical codes can make to economic efficiency. Here my interest is that the existence of such a code can lead to a different economic outcome, with more egalitarian distributional consequences. In the next chapter, I make a concrete proposal for a pay code. I agree with Arrow that "one must not expect miraculous transformations in human behavior," but I believe that voluntary action has a significant role to play. And there are straws in the wind indicating that the climate may be more favourable than when Arrow wrote forty years ago: for example, the MBA Oath, originating with graduates of the Harvard Business School Class of 2009, which is a voluntary pledge for grad-

uating MBAs and current MBAs to "create value responsibly and ethi-
cally."[15]

Competition Policy

Legal intervention to limit the exercise of monopoly power in the product market is longstanding. In the US, according to Jonathan Baker, the
"Supreme Court has awarded the anti-trust statutes near-constitutional
status."[16] Equally there has been controversy about the purpose of such
legislation since the 1890 Sherman Anti-Trust Act. One of the most influential participants in this debate, Robert Bork, argued in 1978 that "anti-
trust policy cannot be made rational until we are able to give a firm answer to one question: What is the point of the law—what are its goals?"[17]
The answer that he gave, and which has subsequently come to dominate
Supreme Court decisions, is that the objective should be consumer welfare, interpreted as economic efficiency.

In ruling out distributional considerations, the post-1980s chapter of
antitrust law in the US was departing from the earlier approach of the
Supreme Court and indeed from the rhetoric of the 1890 Congress that
passed the Sherman Act. Whatever the true motives of Senator Sherman,
he certainly cited distributional concerns: "The popular mind is agitated
with problems that may disturb social order, and among them none is
more threatening than the inequality of condition of wealth, and opportunity that has grown within a single generation out of the concentration
of capital into vast combinations to control production and trade to break
down competition."[18] In his celebrated 1945 judgment in the Alcoa case,
Judge Learned Hand gave the opinion that "among the purposes of Congress in 1890 was a desire to put an end to great aggregations of capital
because of the helplessness of the individual before them."[19]

The proposition being made here is that competition policy should
embody explicit distributional concerns. It recognises that consumer
welfare is an aggregation of individual interests that are diverse and that
can be combined only by some process of weighting the circumstances of
different groups. An example may make this concrete. As noted in Chapter 1, one source of inequality is lack of access to goods or to services. We
have seen in this chapter that the market cannot be relied upon to supply

the range of products desired by consumers. This has a distributional dimension. Where there is inequality, and a limited number of suppliers, firms may not supply the lower-quality goods that are sought by poorer families, and these families are therefore excluded. The cheaper cuts of meat may no longer be on the shop counters; products may be packaged in sizes that are too large. Of course, competition policy cannot micromanage the contents of supermarkets, but it can influence how firms situate themselves in the market.[20] The viability of small local shops depends on how the large firms are regulated. Setting access prices for rival suppliers may have consequences downstream for the products available to consumers. Regulatory bodies need to be aware of the implications of competition policy for different income groups. Paradoxically, measures to prevent monopoly may reduce services, as when banks are required by competition authorities to divest branches and the banks decide to close those in poorer neighbourhoods.[21]

In recommending that competition policy concern itself with distributional issues, I am flying in the face not just of the US Supreme Court but also of the economics literature that questions whether regulatory policy is well suited to distributional objectives. I may indeed find myself classed with the "charlatans" identified by Henry Simons, the Chicago economist, in his book *Economic Policy for a Free Society,* in which he writes that "it is urgently necessary for us to quit confusing measures for regulating relative prices and wages with devices for diminishing inequality. One difference between competent economists and charlatans is that, at this point, the former sometimes discipline their sentimentality with a little reflection on the mechanics of an exchange economy." I owe this quotation to James Tobin, who goes on to say that "this answer rarely satisfies the intelligent egalitarian layman [who] knows that there are pragmatic limits on the redistributive use of taxation and cash transfers."[22] In this, I am on the side of the layman. I fully understand that actions by competition authorities cannot achieve fine-tuned redistribution. There are, however, distinct limits to what can be achieved by second-best taxes and transfers, and, if we wish to make a significant reduction in inequality, there has to be recourse to a whole range of measures that have a—less than perfectly targeted—equalising impact. All forms of distributional intervention are less than ideal.

The Legal Framework and Trade Unions

Reviewing Thomas Piketty's book *Capital in the Twenty-First Century* from a lawyer's perspective, Shi-Ling Hsu starts with the observation that "Piketty, his supporters, and his critics are all missing a huge piece of the puzzle: the role of law in distributing wealth. That wars and recessions wreak havoc on capital investments is intuitive enough. But in times of peace and prosperity, the legal mechanisms by which the rich accumulate, consolidate, and increase their wealth remains a black box in this discussion."[23] He goes on to argue that a capital-friendly bias inheres in US legal rules and institutions. He is mostly concerned with antitrust (as just discussed) and regulation, but the same issue arises with regard to the legislation concerning trade unions.

It is hard today to remember how much the climate has changed with regard to trade unions, particularly in the US and the UK. In the US, overall membership of trade unions has declined from its peak in the 1950s, and it is low in the private sector. According to Joseph Stiglitz, "the most obvious societal change [is] the decline of unions from 20.1 percent of wage- and salary-earning U.S. workers in 1980 to 11.9 percent in 2010. This has created an imbalance of economic power and a political vacuum."[24] John T. Addison, Claus Schnabel, and Joachim Wagner refer to the "parlous state" of German unions, with membership in West Germany having fallen from 33 per cent in 1980 to 22 per cent in 2004.[25]

In terms of influence, the change in the UK has been dramatic. In the 1950s Ben Roberts, a professor of industrial relations at the London School of Economics, wrote that "whichever party is in power, the trade unions are consulted about every measure that affects them. They are represented on no fewer than sixty government committees and have access to ministers at almost any time they desire."[26] This has long ago ceased to be the case, and if one refers to "social partners," people in Britain are more likely to think of a dating agency than the representatives of labour and management. The decline in the influence of trade unions cannot be separated from the sustained period in the 1980s during which the Conservative government passed legislation limiting their activities. Table 4.1 lists a succession of laws enacted between 1980 and 1993 that reduced the autonomy of trade unions in the UK and the legitimacy of industrial action. The end result of the legislation is that unions are considerably weakened in their legal status and protection.

It is therefore not surprising that in 2006 the UK Trade Union Congress proposed a new Trade Union Freedom Bill, the significance of the date being that it marked the centenary of the 1906 Trade Disputes Act, which had been a watershed in trade union legislation, providing immunity against damages. The "freedom" embodied in the proposed bill is to allow workers to engage in industrial action as a last resort. The proposed bill would provide protection from dismissal for workers taking part in official industrial action, simplification of the regulations which restrict the ability of unions to organise industrial action where a clear majority of members have voted in support, and redefinition of what constitutes a trade dispute. It seems to me that there is a strong case for a new and more secure legal framework for trade union activity, along the lines described above. This does not mean a return to the pre-1980 situation: for example, the requirement of secret ballots (see Table 4.1) seems a reasonable one.

The proposal is put forward with the UK specifically in mind, but all countries need to consider the appropriate balance of power in the twenty-first-century labour market. The result of such consideration may be to leave the present structure unchanged, or even to limit union powers. I recognise that the pendulum has not swung so far against unions in other countries, and that there are concerns that unions have contributed to the creation of two-tier labour markets by protecting their members at the expense of outsiders, but it seems unlikely that the right outcome is for trade unions to be completely sidelined.[27]

In addition to the proposal of a new legal framework, there is the issue of the engagement of UK trade unions in the making of social policy. Colin Crouch drew attention in 2000 to the "total absence of the unions" from discussions of the reform of the welfare state and observed that this seemed to be peculiar to Britain, unlike, for example, continental European countries, where unions have a formal role in schemes for pensions, sickness insurance, and unemployment benefits.[28] With a government more willing to consult on the design of policy, there would be a good

TABLE 4.1. *Major trade union legislation in the UK, 1980–1993*

Employment Act 1980	provided a right for members not to be unreasonably excluded or expelled from a trade union; limited employees' right against unfair dismissal; narrowed the immunity for lawful picketing; considerably reduced the immunity for secondary industrial action; required 80 per cent vote to legalise closed shops. Enabled trade unions and employers to obtain government funds for ballots.
Employment Act 1982	narrowed the definition of a trade dispute and prohibited union- and recognition-only clauses in contracts and the informal practice of such arrangements; extended the 80 per cent ballot rule to all closed shops every 5 years; and allowed employers to obtain injunctions against unions and to sue unions for damages.
Trade Union Act 1984	required trade unions to hold secret ballots in the election of their principal executive committees and on the continuance (as well as establishment) of their political funds; withdrew the immunities from official industrial action which had not been the subject of a valid vote.
Public Order Act 1986	introduced new offences related to picketing.
Employment Act 1988	provided an unqualified right to dissociate (refuse to be a union member). Gave trade union members the right to challenge industrial action that had not been validly balloted, and prevented unions from disciplining members who did not support industrial action, even if approved by ballot. Provided for the appointment of a Commissioner for the Rights of Trade Union Members to assist members in litigation against unions.
Employment Act 1990	removed the last remaining legal protection for the closed shop; brought unofficial action under similar legal control as official action; and removed immunity from all forms of secondary industrial action.
Trade Union Reform and Employment Rights Act 1993	imposed further obligations on trade unions when they conduct ballots which are required by statute. Introduced new procedures which unions must follow before industrial action can lawfully be called, including giving advance notice to relevant employers. Allowed individuals to seek an order to halt allegedly unlawful industrial action, regardless of whether they have suffered loss, with assistance from the Commissioner for Protection against Unlawful Industrial Action where the action is organised by a union. Extended the restrictions on union autonomy introduced by the Employment Act of 1988 by allowing unions to exclude or expel individuals from membership only on grounds specified in the legislation. Accorded the Certification Officer extensive powers of investigation in relation to unions' financial affairs and subjects unions to additional reporting requirements.

Source: Eurofound website, http://www.eurofound.europa.eu/emire/UNITED%20KINGDOM and Institute for Employment Rights, *A Chronology of Labour Law 1979–2008,* http://www.ier.org.uk/resources/chronology-labour-law-1979–2008.

case for establishing in the UK a "Social and Economic Council" that could address longer-term issues of reform—such as those proposed in the chapters to come. Lessons could be learned from bodies in other countries, such as the Dutch Sociaal-Economische Raad (Social and Economic Council), founded in 1950, which represents the social partners— trade unions and employers' organisations—and has an active role in policy development. It is indeed striking that the UK is among the minority of EU member states that does not have such a body: there are twenty-two in the EU (two in the case of Belgium). The existing bodies vary in their effectiveness, and in at least one case (Italy) the council has been recently abolished. It would be in line with my proposal for the UK that all countries with such bodies review their role and powers and, if necessary, strengthen them.

The constitution of the Social and Economic Council could take the form of existing bodies, but I envisage it as multipartite, including nongovernmental bodies and consumer groups, as well as the standard three parties of employers, unions, and government. In Chapter 1, I stressed the horizontal dimensions of inequality, and it is important that the council should be representative in terms of gender, ethnicity, and generations. There should, for example, be involvement of those who are outside the labour market, particularly the young, who are currently excluded. In the chapters that follow, I suggest a number of items that should be on the agenda for the envisaged Social and Economic Council, but they should be empowered to report to parliament on new legislation covering the labour market, the regulation of business and social protection, the determination of the minimum wage, and measures affecting levels and uprating of benefits.[29]

> Proposal 2: Public policy should aim at a proper balance of power among stakeholders, and to this end should (a) introduce an explicitly distributional dimension into competition policy; (b) ensure a legal framework that allows trade unions to represent workers on level terms; and (c) establish, where it does not already exist, a Social and Economic Council involving the social partners and other nongovernmental bodies.

The extent to which these measures involve radical change varies from country to country. For the UK, they would involve a substantial new legislation; for other countries, they would require only limited amendments. For member states of the EU, there is an important EU dimension, but what I am proposing is highly complementary to policies that are already central to the Union, notably the promotion of competition and the development of the role of the social partners.

Chapter 5

Employment and Pay in the Future

This chapter is concerned with the role of employment and earnings in reducing inequality. As we have seen, in the immediate postwar decades when inequality fell in Europe, unemployment rates were low: an unemployment rate of 1 per cent was not unknown (see Figure 5.1 for the UK). There is a distinct difference between the period 1945 to the mid-1970s and the forty years since then. The post-1975 period has been much more like the interwar years of high unemployment. Surely, then, one obvious route to reducing inequality and poverty is to tackle unemployment. After all, most political leaders agree on the need to create jobs. "Jobs," indeed, were the first on the list of desiderata in the title of the election manifesto of Jean-Claude Juncker, president of the European Commission in 2014.[1] However, the world of work has changed since the 1950s, and not only because of the technological advances discussed in the previous chapter. I argue here that the nature of employment is changing, and that the regular full-time job is increasingly being replaced by various forms of non-standard employment and by people engaged in a "portfolio" of activities. The changing nature of employment has consequences for the design of social protection that I discuss later in Chapter 8. For now I am concerned with the implications of the changes for the goal of full-employment policy. I argue that we need radical action to make progress towards this goal, which has eluded most OECD countries since the 1970s, and I go on to make the case for state-guaranteed employment. That said, employment on its own is not enough. Being in work does not ensure escape from poverty. This is why "pay" features in the title of this chapter.

The Changing Nature of Employment

The standard model of employment in economics is, often implicitly, that of a regular full-time job. People are either working or they are not. It is a

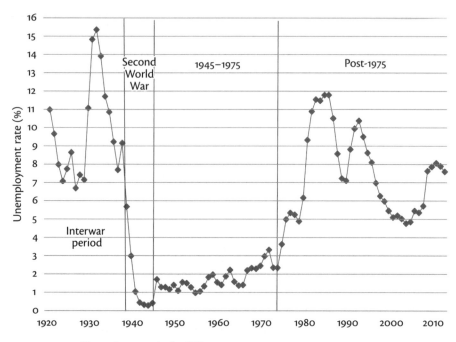

FIGURE 5.1: Unemployment in the UK, 1921–2013

(0,1) phenomenon, the aim of employment policy being to move people from 0 to 1. European Commission President Juncker refers to "jobs." The first of the headline targets in the Europe 2020 Agenda is that 75 per cent of those aged 20–64 should be employed.

Such a focus on "jobs" would appear rather strange to people from earlier periods of our history. Before the Industrial Revolution, people often had a mix of part-time employment and self-employment, a pattern that characterised many rural societies until recently. In past centuries, the concepts of "unemployment" and "retirement" had little meaning. The title *L'invention du chômage* (The Invention of Unemployment), adopted by Robert Salais, Nicolas Baverez, and Bénédicte Reynaud for their study of unemployment in France, reminds us that unemployment is a relatively recent concept.[2] As described by Michael Piore in his review of their book, "the modern concept of unemployment derives from one particular employment relationship, that of the large, permanent manufacturing establishment [which] involves a radical separation in time and in space from family and leisure time activity."[3] As the economy industrialised and the population became more urbanised, employment became all or nothing. The same observation is made about retirement by Leslie Hannah in *Inventing Retirement*, where he argues that "for a proper understanding of this largely new phenomenon, we have to look at the employment relationship."[4] Retirement as a discrete event was not a feature of the earlier pre-industrial economy, where "as the medieval independent worker became old, he worked less and produced less, but he went on working as long as he could produce something."[5]

Nonstandard Work in the Twenty-First Century

In the twentieth century, employment in OECD countries was largely characterised by regular jobs, but the twenty-first century is witnessing a significant return to what is now regarded as nonstandard employment. Part-time work is the most common. When I asked my granddaughter the name of her new teacher, she told me that it was Mrs. A on Mondays to Wednesdays and Mrs. B. on Thursdays and Fridays. There are many forms of nonstandard work. Kees Le Blansch, Guido Muller, and Patricia Wijntuin describe nonstandard workers as including, in addition to part-timers, "those on fixed term contracts . . . homeworkers [and] those in a large number of other arrangements, such as seasonal work, casual work, telework, family work, or self-employment. The main characteristic common to such groups is that their working arrangements differ from those of the 'typical employee' (an imaginary person working full-time on an indefinite contract)."[6] The difference in working arrangements includes in some cases not being paid. In the UK there has been rapid growth in unpaid internships, where young people work for free in the hope of later securing entry to a paid position, and in the number of people on zero-hours contracts, where they are considered employed but have no guaranteed hours and may earn nothing in a week.

Nonstandard work is on the increase. In the words of Günther Schmid, "the last decades have seen an erosion of the traditionally defined 'standard employment relationship' through part-time work, fixed-term contracts, temp-agency work and self-employment."[7] The OECD in

its *Employment Outlook 2014* described the "surge in the use of temporary contracts in a number of OECD countries over the last twenty-five
years" and devoted a whole chapter to "non-regular employment."[8] The
McKinsey Global Institute 2012 paper *Help Wanted: The Future of Work
in Advanced Economies* found that "managing employees and contract
workers across the Internet, companies now have the ability to make labor more of a variable cost, rather than a fixed one, by engaging workers
on an as-needed basis. Across the OECD . . . nations, part-time and temporary employment among prime-age workers has risen 1.5 to 2 times as
fast as total employment since 1990. . . . In our own surveys of US employers, more than one third say they plan to increase use of contingent
labor and part-time workers in the years ahead, and we see a range of
new intermediaries emerging to supply high-skill talent for short-term
assignments." They went on to say that "the jobs that will be created in
the future are increasingly unlike those of the past."[9]

The extent of nonstandard work varies between countries. The Netherlands, for example, is well known as topping the league for part-time
employment, and the nonstandard employment rate is also high in the
Nordic countries. In the UK, the proportion of those engaged in nonstandard employment, defined to include part-time work, self-employment,
and fixed-term contracts, is around one-quarter, and it would be higher if
zero-hours contracts and unpaid internships were added. "Even in family
centered or so-called conservative employment systems like Austria, Belgium, France, Germany, Italy, Spain and Portugal," nonstandard employment is increasing, according to Schmid.[10] His study showed that in the
majority (sixteen) of the twenty-four EU member states covered, the nonstandard employment rate increased between 1998 and 2008, and in only
four (the Baltic states and Romania) was there a decrease. In Germany
there was a decline in standard employment in the twenty-year period
from 1985 to 2005 from 42 to 37 per cent of the working-age population,
at a time when the labour-force participation rate increased from 68 to
76 per cent.[11] There is a gender dimension to nonstandard work. Part-
time work is much more common among women in many EU member
states. In 2011, according to the report *Benchmarking Working Europe
2012,* "nine countries have at least every third woman in part-time employment . . . with shares of more than 40% [in] the UK, Austria, Bel-

gium, Germany, and the Netherlands (76.4%). The Netherlands is the only country that has a substantial share of men in part-time work."[12] The European Commission concluded in its *Employment and Social Developments in Europe 2013* report that part-time work is "one of the main factors leading to lower full-time equivalent employment rates for women compared with men."[13] Among those in full-time work, a pattern of multiple activities is spreading. It is becoming more common that employment is fractional: people are holding portfolios of activities, offering to their employers "slivers of time." In the Euro area (17) the number of people in the Labour Force Survey reporting second jobs rose from 3.7 million in 2000 to 5.1 million in 2013.[14] On the day I wrote this, the *Guardian* newspaper carried a profile of a prospective parliamentary candidate who is a support worker for a mental health charity, cares for a disabled man, works for another charity, and is a local councillor.[15]

It is therefore increasingly misleading to talk in terms of people having, or not having, a job. Work is not simply a (0,1) activity. The twenty-first-century labour market is more complex, and this has implications for how we think about employment as a route out of poverty and full employment as a means of assisting us on the way to less inequality.

Full Employment and Guaranteed Work

These changes in the labour market have immediate consequences for the setting of employment targets and for the goal of reducing unemployment. In the US, the Federal Reserve Board has a statutory mandate from Congress to promote "maximum employment," but this needs to be reinterpreted to take account of people holding a portfolio of activities who cannot easily be labelled as "employed" or "unemployed." In the European context, Andrea Brandolini and Eliana Viviano have argued that we need to reconsider the EU employment target. It is not sufficient to simply adopt a headcount measure: people with jobs. They propose, instead, a measure of work intensity defined on the basis of the months of employment and hours worked per month.[16]

Equally, the goal of reducing unemployment becomes more complicated than in the immediate postwar decades when people in OECD countries either had a job or did not. We have seen this during the economic crisis. Most eyes have been on the unemployment figures and on employment rates, but many of the new jobs have been part-time. How this is viewed depends on whether or not part-time work is voluntary. As put by the International Labour Organisation, "there is a fundamental distinction to be made between voluntary and involuntary part-time employment: whether people deliberately choose to work part time or accept reduced hours of work simply because they cannot find full-time employment. In the latter case, part-time work becomes a form of underemployment."[17] In the former case, the level of unemployment is overstated by the current statistics, which, like the employment target, need to be expressed in full-time equivalents. In the case of people who want to work more but cannot find full-time jobs, the level of unemployment is understated because it fails to include the hidden unemployment represented by people whose current work falls short of their desired level. The evidence presented by the European Commission shows that in 2012 part-time work was "involuntary" in a relatively small proportion of cases in Austria (10 per cent), Germany (17 per cent), and Denmark (18 per cent), but averaged 29 per cent over the Euro Area and exceeded 50 per cent in Greece, Italy, Romania, and Spain.[18] To this must be added those who are working in internships and other forms of unpaid work, while seeking paid employment.

The goal with regard to full employment has therefore to be approached in a more nuanced way to reflect the changing nature of the labour market. But it also needs to be made explicit. At the moment, the policy ambitions are stated in a general way—in sharp contrast to the quite explicit objectives that have been adopted by central banks in more than twenty countries with regard to inflation. In the case of inflation, the UK has a precise quantitative target. If the target is missed by more than 1 percentage point, the governor of the Bank of England must write an open letter to the Chancellor of the Exchequer explaining the reasons inflation has departed from this range and the actions that the bank proposes to take. However, neither the governor of the Bank of England nor the Chancellor of the Exchequer has any such responsibility for explaining high unemployment (presumably no letter would be required to explain low unemployment).

One reason for there being no comparable unemployment target is that there is a degree of ambiguity about the goal itself. Indeed, we have to ask why the US Congress is seeking "maximum employment." Why is it better to increase the number of sixty-four-year-olds stacking super-market shelves? To pursue this further, we have to distinguish between intrinsic and instrumental reasons for seeking to increase employment. The instrumental reason is that with which I began the chapter: that employment is the principal route for individuals and their families to escape poverty and for societies to return to lower levels of inequality. How far this is in fact the case is a subject to which I turn below. The intrinsic reasons are less straightforward. Why should governments seek to raise the level of employment above that determined in the market? If sixty-four-year-olds in Europe decide that they would prefer to spend time looking after their grandchildren (or their ninety-year-old parents), rather than in paid work, should this be regarded as a failure? In welfare economic terms, it may be that the government wishes to over-ride individual preferences. Applying the concept introduced by Richard Musgrave, employment may have the quality of a "merit good," like education or health, where the government attributes greater value than that attached by private citizens.[19] Or, on a welfare basis, the case for intervention may be made on the grounds of market failure. However, the most obvious evidence of market failure—the absence of balance between supply and demand—is the existence of involuntary unemployment, and this suggests that the goal should be the minimisation of involuntary unemployment.

For these reasons, I believe that the labour-market goal should be stated, not in terms of maximising employment, but in terms of minimising involuntary unemployment, where this is measured in a way that reflects the new features of the twenty-first-century labour market. We should count as partially unemployed people who have lost paid work that is only part of their job portfolio. And the goal should be stated explicitly, not in the form of a bland commitment to full employment without a specific reference point. What should the goal be? Here I immediately recognise that the ability of a government to attain any specified level of unemployment depends on the macroeconomic circumstances, and the degree to which its attainment is consistent with other goals, such as the UK inflation target described above. I am not seeking to predict the outcome of such a balancing exercise. Rather, I am asking about the extent of our ambition. What is the employment counterpart of the 2 per cent inflation rate? One possible point of reference is the level of unemployment achieved in the immediate postwar decades (see Figure 5.1). On this basis, a target unemployment rate of 2 per cent would not seem over-ambitious. It would certainly shift the dial. Googling "UK unemployment" at the time I write leads to the *Trading Economics* website with a graph where the vertical axis starts at 5.5 per cent. The 2 per cent target would be off the radar. In fact, we would have to go back to the historical series from 1971 to find a graph that *starts* at 2 per cent. The espousal of a target for unemployment would push the issue up the agenda. When the unemployment figures are published, the question to be asked would be, not just whether they rise or fall, but how they relate to the 2 per cent target.

Guaranteed Work

There will no doubt be readers who respond to the proposal of an unemployment target by objecting that talk of "shifting the dial" is simply empty rhetoric, just as much cheap talk as affirming a commitment to full employment. My own view is that explicit goals are important, and that changing the discourse is a step on the road to achieving the ambition. I do, however, accept that the key question is how this is to be achieved. For this reason, I combine the setting of an explicit target with a second element—the proposal that the government should act as an employer of last resort.

> Proposal 3: The government should adopt an explicit target for preventing and reducing unemployment and underpin this ambition by offering guaranteed public employment at the minimum wage to those who seek it.

Public employment has formed part of active labour-market programmes in a number of countries. In the United States, there is a long history. The Works Progress Administration (WPA) formed a major part of the New Deal and between 1935 and 1943 financed some eight million jobs. Much of the budget went to public infrastructure projects, including more than a third on roads and public buildings. As part of the War on Poverty in the 1960s, the administration developed a Public Employment Program that was forecast to be able to create 4.3 million jobs.[20] This was not implemented, but much smaller-scale job programmes were introduced, increasingly directed at disadvantaged workers, brought together in the Comprehensive Employment and Training Act of 1973. Under President Carter, a general public employment programme was approved by Congress under the Humphrey-Hawkins Full Employment and Balanced Growth Act of 1978, authorising the federal government to create a "reservoir of public employment." This, too, was not put into effect, and with the election of President Reagan, who "adamantly opposed direct job creation efforts," the idea of large-scale public-service employment vanished.[21]

US history demonstrates that, even though Reagan brought the discussion to an end, the idea of public-service employment in the form of a jobs guarantee was at one time taken seriously in that country. In Europe, too, there have been steps in this direction. As described by Robert Haveman in the 1970s, "the Dutch took seriously the right-to-work mandate of the United Nations Universal Declaration of Human Rights" and established a Social Employment Programme that, at the time, accounted for 1.5 per cent of total employment.[22] There are today programmes of at least limited public job creation (for example, providing sheltered employment) in a number of European countries. Figure 5.2 shows the expenditure reported by Eurostat on such programmes as a percentage of Gross Domestic Product in 2010, ranging from one-third of 1 per cent in Belgium (which would correspond in the UK of 2014 to some £5.5 billion) through one-fifth of 1 per cent in France and 0.05 per cent in Germany (which would correspond to £0.75 billion in the UK) to very little in Italy and the UK. German spending is almost exactly the same, relative to national income, as the projected cost of US economist Hyman Minsky's proposal in the 1980s to tackle chronic unemployment by reviving the New Deal Works Progress Administration.[23] The largest public-employment programme in the world has been the Mahatma Gandhi National Rural Employment Guarantee Scheme in India, which guaran-

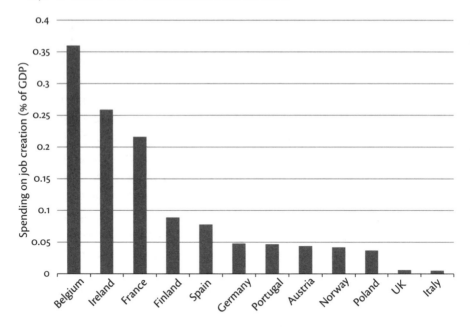

FIGURE 5.2: Expenditure on direct job creation in UK and Europe, 2010

This graph shows each country's expenditure on direct job-creation programmes as a share of GDP, in 2010 (UK data are from 2008).

tees 100 days of public-sector employment per year to all rural house-holds, although it has been criticised by the Indian government elected in 2014 and may well be modified.

The proposal made here is that individuals seeking employment, and meeting the qualifications (see below), are guaranteed a position for a minimum number of hours per week (say, thirty-five hours) paid at the minimum wage working for a public body or an approved non-profit-making institution. Applying for guaranteed public employment under this scheme would be voluntary, and failure to apply would not have any implications for benefit receipt (under existing social transfers or under the participation income proposed in Chapter 8). Several key elements of this proposal need to be spelled out. To begin with, in focusing on "jobs," it is open to the criticism that I am failing to take account of the changing nature of employment described earlier. This is a good point, and it raises

particular issues when we come to the inter-relation with social protection. Indeed, the changing nature of employment is one reason I propose
a radical alternative to existing forms of social protection.

For the present, I concentrate on the job guarantee itself, and the way
that it would operate given the growth of nonstandard employment and
the rise in the number of people holding portfolios of activities. From the
side of the worker, the fact that the scheme is voluntary means that the
person could add hours of public employment to the portfolio according
to their availability. From the side of the public employer, however, there
would have to be restrictions on the total number of hours offered to the
worker and on the conditions of availability. In the case of workers who
are partially unemployed, the number of total hours offered would take
account of their existing employment, so that a person holding a job for
twenty-five hours at XYZ Manufacturing would be guaranteed ten hours
a week employment in the public sector. In order to make effective use of
public-sector workers, their availability would have to be established in
advance. The job at XYZ could not be a zero-hours contract; it would not
be possible for the employer to decide each week how many hours were
offered.[24] A contract between the government department administering
the scheme and the individual would be required; it could not involve
just the employing body and the individual. A description of the US Public Employment Program (PEP) under consideration as part of the 1960s
War on Poverty suggested that "a hospital orderly, for example, would be
paid by the hospital, and need not even know that he was a PEP person,"
but this would not be possible in the scheme proposed here (since he
might have another job that took him over thirty-five hours).[25] Administration of the scheme would involve a degree of complexity, but one inevitable consequence of our more complicated lives is that we cannot rely
on simple categorisations, and this increases the cost of operating social
institutions (as discussed in the previous chapter).

Another important element is the definition of "qualifying" individuals in a world of international labour mobility. This raises issues of great
political sensitivity, not least within the European Union. It would be
possible for the European Union as a whole to offer a guarantee to all the
citizens of the Union, but if a single member state were to act alone, it
would have to do so while observing the principle of the free movement

of labour. This treaty provision allows people "to stay in a Member State for the purpose of employment in accordance with the provisions governing the employment of nationals of that State." Here, the UK job guarantee could be introduced initially for the long-term unemployed: those who have been registered as unemployed in the UK for twelve months or more, who are available for work full-time or part-time, and who had previously been employed in the UK, paying National Insurance Contributions, for at least twelve months. It would be available to all—nationals or non-nationals—who met these conditions. At a subsequent stage, a more extensive scheme could cover those who had been unemployed for less than twelve months, but who had previously been in UK employment prior to becoming unemployed. In this case again, eligibility would be conditional on National Insurance Contributions having been paid. In this way, the contribution condition would ensure that the guarantee is offered only to those with a continuing attachment to the UK labour force. I have not referred specifically to the position of young people, but the proposal made here could complement, or be combined with, the EU Youth Guarantee, which aims to ensure that all young people under the age of twenty-five receive an offer of a job, apprenticeship, training, or continued education.[26]

Critics of the proposal that the government act as an employer of last resort are naturally concerned that the government would compete with the private sector and crowd out private employment. There are grounds for that concern. In their review of the US experience, David Ellwood and Elisabeth Welty conclude that "public service employment done wrong can be wasteful, inefficient, displacing, and counter-productive." But they immediately go on to say that "public service employment done carefully seems to be able to increase employment, keep displacement near 25 per cent, and produce genuinely valuable output."[27] And it should be remembered that some crowding out is desirable. If the option of a job on a public-sector employment programme means that people leave insecure private-sector jobs on zero-hours contracts, or causes the employers of the latter to convert them into regular jobs, then this is a positive outcome.

What jobs would be undertaken by those on the employment-guarantee scheme, and would they be productive? My answer in part follows from the discussion in the previous chapter of the value to be placed on public services. In a number of countries cuts in public spending have reduced the availability of public services, and these have been only partially replaced by private purchase of services. There is, therefore, immediate scope for employing people in the fields where services have been withdrawn: child care, preschool education, schools, youth services, the health service, care for the elderly, meals on wheels, library services, and police support activities. I do not, however, see the creation of guaranteed jobs as an emergency programme; it is not a return to the Works Progress Administration. Rather, I believe that the programme should be developed carefully over time to provide employment that is meaningful and not simply a stop-gap. For the same reason, evaluation of the programme should not be based solely on the subsequent labour-market success of participants. The 2000 review by the US Department of Labor found that "for the most part, early efforts to address the problem of long-term unemployment through public service employment programs have proved unsuccessful. Participants seldom learned marketable skills and rarely moved on to jobs in the private sector."[28] However, the second sentence reveals that the judgement is being reached from a particular perspective: the extent to which the programmes provided a stepping stone to future employment. This is important, but the immediate concern here is with the impact on workers while they are on the programme. Moreover, the focus on "marketable skills" takes a narrow view of what is being sought. A key element of the job guarantee is that its adoption would change the relationship of the individual to the economy. It has intrinsic value, being a clear signal of inclusion. As argued by Lane Kenworthy, "by guaranteeing a job to anyone who wants but cannot find one, such a policy would affirm the value of work."[29] The proposal sends the message that "no one is too small to fail."

But would the job guarantee reduce inequality? In particular, would reduced unemployment make a major contribution to the combatting of poverty? In brief, the answer is that it would and that it would not, as well summarised by the European Commission: "Non-working adults taking up a job have one chance in two to leave poverty."[30] The basis for this statement is shown in Figure 5.3, which gives the proportions in each EU country of people who took a job between 2008 and 2009 and who had

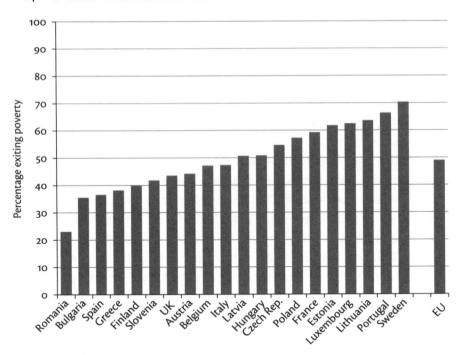

FIGURE 5.3: Proportion exiting poverty after taking up a job in EU countries, 2008–2009

This graph shows what happened to unemployed people between ages 18 and 59 who took up a job between 2008 and 2009. The bars show the percentage of the people taking up a job who exited from poverty. About half (EU average) the people who became employed remained in poverty.

thereby risen above the poverty threshold. In some countries, such as Sweden, Portugal, and the Baltic republics, the rate of exit from poverty was 60 per cent or higher, but in others, such as Spain, Greece, Romania, and Bulgaria, the rate was below 40 per cent. Escape from poverty requires that the job pay enough to support the household at or above the poverty line. In-work poverty is, however, a serious problem; according to Ive Marx and Gerlinde Verbist, "as many as a quarter to a third of working-age Europeans living in poverty are actually already in work."[31] As a result, there is no simple relation between national employment rates and the incidence of poverty. To quote the OECD, "the fact that many of the 'poor' hold jobs, at least for some part of the year, goes a long way towards explaining the lack of a significant cross-country association between relative poverty [and] employment rates."[32]

We need, therefore, to do something about pay.

Ethical Pay Policies

Does this mean intervening in the market determination of pay? Yes. I argued earlier that the forces of supply and demand are important, but they only set bounds on what can be paid for a particular piece of work. It is not the case that we are all paid in precise relation to our marginal product—no more and no less. To a considerable degree the market outcome is currently the result of the bargaining power of different participants. If people take zero-hours jobs with no guarantee of pay, it is because they are powerless in the labour market. As noted, we need to take steps to ensure a fairer balance between the parties to such bargains, increasing the countervailing power of consumers and workers. But I believe that we should go further. We can make progress towards less inequality only if we establish a society-wide approach to earnings determination. We need a national policy towards pay, a policy that recognises the bounds placed by supply and demand in a globalised economy, but which does not let incomes be determined purely by market forces.

What does this mean? A good starting point is provided by the often-quoted figures of the share that the top 1 per cent has secured of the total real income growth in recent years. It is indeed the latter figure—the overall growth of incomes—that should be the starting point for a "national conversation" involving all stakeholders that could ideally take place at the Social and Economic Council. In planning what is possible, we need to start from the prospective future growth. In past incomes-policy negotiations, this was typically assumed to be equal to the expected growth of productivity. Today, we cannot expect household incomes to rise as fast as total output, for reasons that I discussed earlier, such as the demands arising from the ageing of the population and climate change. This makes it all the more urgent that we hold a conversation to consider how the growth can be fairly distributed. To initiate such a conversation, I place on the agenda the case for the next proposal:

Proposal 4: There should be a national pay policy, consisting of two elements: a statutory minimum wage set at a living wage, and a code of practice for pay above the minimum, agreed as part of a "national conversation" involving the Social and Economic Council.

The Minimum Wage

The first element in the pay policy is a statutory minimum wage, which most OECD countries have already adopted. The idea of the minimum wage has a long history; in 1906, Winston Churchill stated in the House of Commons that "it is a national evil that any class of Her Majesty's subjects should receive less than a living wage in return for their utmost exertions . . . where you have what we call sweated trades, you have no organisation, no parity of bargaining, the good employer is undercut by the bad . . . where these conditions prevail you have not a condition of progress, but a condition of progressive degeneration."[33]

The key question, however, is the level at which the minimum wage is set. This raises issues of principle, which I explore in the UK context, but which have undoubted relevance to other countries, like Germany, where a statutory minimum wage was approved for the first time in July 2014. As may be seen from Figure 5.4, according to the comparisons made in the ILO Global Wage Report 2012/13, the UK national minimum wage as a proportion of median earnings is around the middle of the range for OECD countries. In considering the different levels, we should bear in mind that even the highest—that for France—is below the low-pay threshold of two-thirds of median earnings that has been applied in publications by the OECD and other bodies.[34]

At what level should the minimum wage be set? The UK national minimum wage (NMW) is determined on the advice of the Low Pay Commission, whose measured reports since the introduction of the statutory minimum in April 1999 have done much to facilitate its wide acceptance and political support. But reading the reports, one is struck by how much the commission's attention is focused on the labour market rather than on the implications for the distribution of income. Its key measure is the "bite" of the NMW, which is the ratio of the NMW hourly rate to median hourly earnings. Focus on the labour market is of course

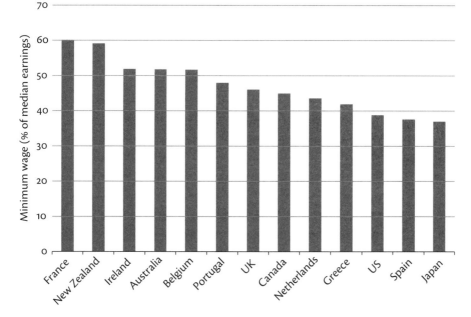

FIGURE 5.4: Minimum wages in OECD countries, 2010

This graph shows the minimum wage in each country as a percentage of that country's median full-time earnings in 2010. The figures include holiday pay in the Netherlands, and 13th- and 14th-month salaries in Portugal and Spain.

quite understandable in that one important consideration of a minimum wage is its effect on employment—which I discuss in Chapter 9—but this underlines the fact that, from an income-distributional perspective, the relevant variable is not hourly earnings but weekly, or monthly, earnings, which depend on the hours worked. Moreover, the implications for family living standards depend on the household circumstances and on the operation of the tax-and-benefit system. These factors have been emphasised by the independent Living Wage Commission, chaired by Archbishop John Sentamu. In effect, the living wage is calculated by tracing through the implications of individual earnings, assuming a specified number of hours, for the level of household disposable income. As we have seen in the Guide to household income, this is a relatively complex process, since we have to consider the earnings of all family members, other sources of income, and the impact of the tax-benefit system. But only by going through this process can we see what a given hourly wage implies in terms of living standards. Or, putting the process in reverse, we can see what should be the target for the hourly NMW.

Underlying the definition of the UK living wage is the research of the Centre for Research in Social Policy at the University of Loughborough, which, together with the Social Policy Research Unit at the University of York, developed a Minimum Income Standard, based on detailed budgets derived from a "social consensus about what people need to make ends meet."[35] On the basis of the Minimum Income Standard, we arrive at a necessary hourly wage (called the Reference Rate) by averaging across family types. There is, however, a further twist in the story: the independent Living Wage Commission then applies a "cap," "so that the rate does not rise at an unrealistic pace that employers are unable to keep up with."[36] The end result is a recommended living wage (outside London) that is some 20 per cent higher than the actual UK national minimum wage but also some 20 per cent lower than the figure that came out of the "uncapped" calculations. It should be noted that, if the cap had not been applied, the figure for the UK minimum wage would have reached 66 per cent of the median, in line with the OECD low-pay threshold.

Does this provide the basis for setting a target for the minimum wage —in the UK or elsewhere? Does the Minimum Income Standard provide a foundation for defining a low-pay standard? Doubts must arise. If we examine the details of the wage requirement derived from the Minimum Income Standard, we see that it varies across family types from 67 per cent of the Reference Rate for couples with no children (for them it is below the NMW) to more than double for single parents with three or more children (who would have had to earn well above the median). What is more, the wage requirement depends on the other elements that enter the determination of household disposable income, notably capital income and social transfers. The minimum wage cannot do all the work on its own.

Where does this leave us? There is evident pressure for the minimum wage in the UK to be increased as a proportion of median earnings—to increase its "bite." The Low Pay Commission in its 2014 report refers to the "start of a new phase—of bigger increases than in recent years."[37] The living wage campaign has enjoyed considerable success in terms of the voluntary participation of employers, and the proposal made here is that the national minimum wage should be raised to this level. Whether we should go further and move towards the higher level that comes out of the "uncapped" calculations can be judged only as part of an overall policy for incomes, where this encompasses capital income and social transfers.

Code of Practice for Pay and Employment

The UK national minimum wage is statutory, enforced by law; the living wage is voluntary with employers who agree to pay the wage being accredited by the Living Wage Foundation, a charitable organisation. An increasing number of UK employers are participating—a notable signatory being Chelsea Football Club—and I now consider how far the principle of a voluntary code of practice can be extended to pay above the minimum. As stressed throughout the book, issues of social justice apply to the distribution as a whole, from bottom to top.

Much of the current interest in a pay code stems from the explosion of pay at the top of the distribution that has taken place in many countries in recent decades. In the UK, the top decile of earnings in the 1970s was two-thirds higher than the median; today it is double. The top percentile used to earn three times the median but today earns five times.[38] The marked widening of the pay gap has led to pressure for limits on the range of pay. In Switzerland in 2013, a public referendum took place on whether executive pay should be limited to no more than twelve times the lowest pay in the company. The proposal was defeated, but as many as 35 per cent of Swiss voters supported it. In the UK, the independent High Pay Centre has been campaigning for a maximum pay ratio, which "would recognise the important principle that all workers should share in a company's success and that gaps between those at the top and low and middle earners cannot just get wider and wider."[39] Such a pay policy is, for example, in force in the employee-owned company John Lewis, where the highest-paid director is not allowed to be paid more than 75 times the average salary, although both the size of the multiple (75) and the application to the average salary are rather different from the Swiss proposal.

Other companies follow a similar policy with different ratios. The TSB bank, for instance, is adopting a pay policy with a multiple of 65. A striking contrast in terms of multiple is the policy of the fair trade organisation, Traidcraft, which "does not expect the best paid member of staff to be paid more than six times the full time equivalent salary of the lowest paid member of the UK staff."[40] If the lowest-paid member of staff were on the minimum wage, this would limit the top salary to some £80,000 a year. As this example illustrates, the adoption of a pay limit may well reflect the ethos of the organisation. In Spain, the Mondragon cooperatives limit executive pay to no more than 6.5 times that of the lowest-paid worker.

The operation of a pay limit within a single company or organisation poses a number of problems. These led the UK government–commissioned Review of Fair Pay in the Public Sector, conducted by Will Hutton, to conclude that the introduction of a limiting public-sector pay multiple, in which no manager could earn more than twenty times the lowest-paid person in the organisation, would not be "helpful as the core of a fair pay system in the public sector."[41] Such a multiple of 20 would, in 2011, have limited top civil servant pay to some £225,000 per year. This hardly appears restrictive. However, the review, while favouring the publication of pay multiples, did not support a pay limit. Among the problems evoked were the variation across public bodies depending on the nature of their labour force, and the incentive offered to management to remove low-paid staff from their payroll (for example, by outsourcing). The second of these objections could be overcome by basing the lower limit on the minimum wage. This would have the merit of greater transparency, though it would have the side effect that improvements in the minimum wage would generate increases in the maximum permissible top salaries.

The adoption of a pay limit in the public sector alone would mean that employment at the top of the public service would become less financially rewarding in relative terms, raising the question as to how far, apart from through moral suasion, the private sector too could be induced to espouse a pay code containing limits on the range of pay. Three avenues suggest themselves. The first is to make use of the state's market power as a purchaser of goods and services. The adoption of a pay code could be a precondition for eligibility to supply goods or services to public bodies. The second is to embody a compulsory reporting element, so that the relevant pay multiples would be readily publicly available. The third is via corporate governance. The existence of a state-promoted pay code would strengthen the hands of those on remuneration committees who were concerned about excessive executive pay. Some, including the High Pay Centre, would go further and propose a new Companies Act, requiring company directors to have "equal regard for the interests of all stakeholders—including employees, customers, partners and suppliers and wider society, as well as shareholders."[42] Such a move would be in line with the steps towards greater countervailing power considered in the previous chapter.

The principles of a pay code should govern the spread of pay between top and bottom, but the code should also be concerned with whether people are being paid equally for work of equal value. This is an increasingly relevant issue as pay has become more individualised and as societies and workplaces have become more demographically diverse. A firm may be an equal-opportunity employer in terms of hiring, but how far does this translate into equal ex post rewards? Consideration of the fairness of existing pay policy should probe issues such as the gender, ethnic, and age distribution of pay. Why, for example, in the UK does only 1 in 6 of the top 1 per cent of incomes go to a woman? Why has the gender gap ceased to narrow? In 1970 earnings at the top decile for women were some 57 per cent of those for men in the equivalent position in the male distribution. The ratio rose substantially in the 1970s, notably when the Equal Pay Act came fully into effect. The ratio continued to rise until the early 1990s, but then the improvement stalled. In the last twenty years there has been virtually no gain.[43] There has been much discussion of "women in the board room" and, in the EU, "gender mainstreaming," but progress in terms of narrowing the pay gap at the top has been glacially slow.

A National Conversation

In proposing a voluntary pay code, I am deliberately not suggesting a return to statutory intervention in the determination of pay relativities, as was the case with certain income policies pursued in the 1960s and 1970s (such as the wage and price controls introduced by President Nixon in 1971 or the prices and incomes policies in the UK). Voluntary agreement is harder to achieve but, once in place, is more likely than statutory controls to be sustained in the face of changes in government. Progress is indeed unlikely to be possible unless there is a broad base of public support.

What in my view is needed is a "national conversation" about the distribution of income, considering the wider question of the distribution of the gains from a growing economy, and the extent to which those in the middle and below are being left behind. Such a conversation should embody an ethical approach to pay, as discussed in this chapter, but also the determination of benefit levels and capital incomes, which are the subject of the chapters that follow. All of these represent claims on the national income. At present, these different types of income tend to be considered in different fora, whereas they should form part of the same discussion. In short, on the agenda for the first meeting of the Social and Economic Council should be an analysis of the prospects for income growth and how this can be shared fairly.

Chapter 6 ::

Capital Shared

In the economic analysis of the causes of inequality, I emphasised the role of capital income and the need to reconsider the balance of ownership. I assumed there, and continue to assume here, that the economy is organised as a form of market capitalism, with the greater part of economic activity carried out by private businesses that employ workers and sell their goods and services in open markets. I have also argued that, in considering the role of capital, it is necessary to keep distinct the beneficial ownership of wealth and the control conveyed by capital over economic decisions. A person with a defined-contribution pension fund is indirectly the beneficiary from the dividends paid on shares in the ABC Corporation owned by that fund, but has no say in the decisions made by the ABC Corporation. He or she cannot replace the management or vote for or against a takeover. Both beneficial ownership and control are important.

Debate about wealth tends to focus on large fortunes at the top, but the redistribution of wealth is as much about the encouragement of small savings at the bottom as it is about the restriction of excesses at the top. Historically, the decline in the share of the top 1 per cent in total personal wealth in OECD countries has come about not only because of estate and other taxes on the rich but also because of the expansion of "popular" holdings, notably, but not exclusively, of housing wealth. This can be seen for the UK in Figure 6.1A, which shows the real wealth, adjusted to 2000 in terms of consumer prices, of the top 1 per cent and the bottom 99 per cent from 1923 to 2000. The real value of the wealth of the top 1 per cent rose in the interwar period but fell back to the 1923 level after the Second World War. (It should of course be remembered that these were not necessarily the same people or even their descendants). Their *share*, however, was much influenced by the faster rise from 1923 to 1937 in the real value of the wealth of the bottom 99 per cent, and by the fact that

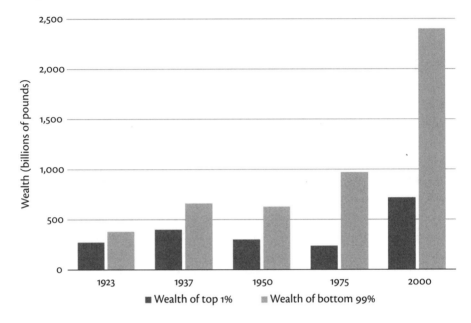

FIGURE 6.1A: Wealth of top 1% and bottom 99% in real terms, UK, 1923–2000

This graph shows changes in the total personal wealth (including real estate) of the top 1% and the bottom 99% in the UK between 1923 and 2000. Wealth values are adjusted to 2000 prices; see Figure Sources for details.

this popular wealth was reduced much less after the Second World War. Moreover, in the immediate decades after the Second World War, the real value of the wealth of the top 1 per cent continued to decline, whereas that of the bottom 99 per cent rose substantially. The latter was important. If the real wealth of the bottom 99 per cent had stayed at its 1950 level, then the share of the top 1 per cent would have fallen by only 5 percentage points, whereas the actual fall was 12.5 percentage points. Over the second half of the twentieth century as a whole, the wealth of the bottom 99 per cent quadrupled: some £600 billion in 1950 had become £2,400 billion by 2000. In considering these numbers, we should bear in mind that they do not include the value of private or state pensions, which also greatly increased over this fifty-year period.

The absolute levels of wealth are shown in another way in Figure 6.1B, where the wealth of each group is expressed as a ratio to national income.

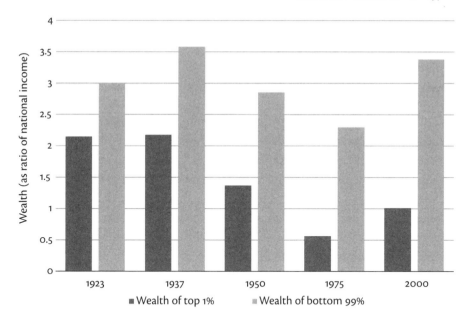

FIGURE 6.1B: Wealth of top 1% and bottom 99% compared to national income, UK, 1923–2000

This graph shows total personal wealth in relation to economic growth by showing wealth as a fraction of national income. For example, in 1923, wealth of the top 1% was more than twice (2.1) the national income; in 1975, wealth of the top 1% was about half (0.5) the national income.

This measures the capacity of real wealth to keep up with the growth of the economy. Growth occurs because the population is bigger; there are more people in the top 1 per cent. It occurs because income per person is increasing on account of capital accumulation and technical progress. Over the interwar period, the rise in the real wealth of the top 1 per cent was sufficient to maintain the ratio to national income, but from 1937 to 1975 the ratio fell from twice national income to one-half. The ratio for the bottom 99 per cent also fell, but less. Then since 1975, the ratios have risen, with that for the top 1 per cent increased from half national income to around national income, and that of the bottom 99 per cent from 2.25 to 3.25 times national income.

In the next chapter I consider the taxation of those in the top 1 per cent and above. In this chapter, my focus is on pre-redistribution wealth-holding.

The Drivers of Wealth Accumulation

In *Capital in the Twenty-First Century,* Thomas Piketty identifies the key mechanism governing the distribution of wealth as the difference between the rate of return on capital (denoted by r) and the rate of growth of the economy (denoted by g). Such has been the impact of his book that these symbols have entered the public arena: there are even $r > g$ T-shirts! When the rate of return is high relative to the rate of growth, then wealth can increase faster than national income through accumulation; or, put differently, savings out of capital income do not need to be so high in order to keep up with national income. What happens to the distribution of wealth depends on r and g at the individual level. I come to r in a moment, but I start with g.

For the individual, keeping up in terms of wealth over a lifetime depends on the growth of overall incomes, but if we are taking the long view and considering generations, then it depends also on the extent to which wealth is divided among a larger number of people in each successive generation. For purposes of discussion, I assume that wealth passes down through the generations, not sideways nor skipping generations nor passing totally outside the family. I also leave out the complications introduced by the combining of wealth via marriage. If families practise primogeniture, passing wealth on each time to a single member of the next generation (typically the oldest son), then the total would be unaffected. There would be no erosion of wealth. Where the total population is growing (one source of the rise in national income), the additional, younger children get nothing. In fact, in a growing population, the wealthy inheritors find that they are a smaller percentage of the new larger population, and in this sense concentration increases. This is what happens with strict primogeniture, but even in eighteenth-century England, primogeniture was only partially the rule; younger sons also shared in the wealth. In Jane Austen's *Mansfield Park,* Edmund Bertram, the second son of wealthy Sir Thomas Bertram, cannot become rector of the local parish and draw its associated income after he takes holy orders on account of his older brother's profligacy and debts; otherwise, he could have expected to enjoy this start in life. Outside England and Wales, many countries do not allow the same freedom of bequest. Under the legal system in Scotland, a testator is not free to divide his or her estate in an unrestricted manner. In France "reserved parts" of an estate are guaranteed to specified classes of heirs. The amount restricted in this way depends on the family circumstances: for example, with one child the reserved part is one-half the estate; with two children, it is two-thirds; and with three or more children it is three-quarters. In France and many other countries, one cannot leave all one's wealth to a donkey sanctuary.

In cases where the total estate is divided among the children of the next generation, the amount inherited necessarily depends on the size of the family (this is the individual-level dimension of growth, the g term). Indeed, even where all families are the same size, the effect of division is, other things the same, to cut down large wealth-holdings, and this is speeded up where the population is growing faster. When richer families have more children, inequality is reduced: to quote my former teacher James Meade, "if the rich had more children than the poor, the large properties would fall in relative size as they become more and more widely dispersed and the smaller would grow in relative size as they become more and more concentrated on a smaller number of children."[1] Or it may be the other way around. Josiah Wedgwood, who wrote a thesis in economics before becoming managing director of his family's pottery business, studied the pattern of inheritance among rich men: "The average upper middle-class family is only *two-thirds* of the size of the average working-class family. Hence, in the absence of modifications introduced by marriage, fresh accumulations, and taxation, the distribution of property would be likely to become more and more unequal."[2] More recently, Geoffrey Brennan, Gordon Menzies, and Michael Munge have argued that historically there was a positive relationship between family size and resources, but that this situation began to change towards the end of the eighteenth century. This has led to the present negative relationship, with better-off families having fewer children and hence accentuating the tendency towards greater inequality.[3]

The transmission of wealth is further influenced by marriage, where the consequences depend on who marries whom, and on the frequency of divorce and remarriage. To the extent that marriage involves the pooling of assets (and liabilities) it is in itself an equalising device. But this effect is smaller to the extent that there is assortative mating: that is, wealthy people tend to marry equally wealthy people. In the case of earnings, Christine Schwartz summarises the situation for the US as follows: "Before the late 1970s, the relationship between husbands' and wives' earnings was negative, with high-earning husbands tending to have low-earning wives, whereas from the 1980s on, the relationship has been positive and increasing, with high-earning husbands tending to have high-earning wives."[4] On the basis of evidence on family incomes from Germany and the UK, John Ermisch, Marco Francesconi, and Thomas Siedler conclude that "assortative mating appears to be a major factor in the intergenerational transmission of economic status."[5] Earnings and income are not the same as wealth, but in their study of parental wealth in the US, Kerwin Charles, Erik Hurst, and Alexandra Killewald examine the spousal correlation (albeit based on the reporting of parental wealth by children, with the attendant issues of measurement error). They find that the correlation of spouse's wealth is around 0.4, which, as they note, is similar in magnitude to the estimated intergenerational correlation of wealth.[6] To the extent that, as this suggests, people tend to marry in the same wealth class, there is less of a tendency towards wealth equalisation.

These forces operating via the factor g are full of human interest and may well explain part of the evolution of the distribution of wealth, but they do not really point to possible policy proposals. For these, we have to turn to the r side of the balance.

Rates of Return and Portfolios

Many readers of Piketty's *Capital in the Twenty-First Century* responded with puzzlement to the book's emphasis on the rate of return exceeding the rate of growth. While borrowers from pay-day lenders may recognise high interest rates as a problem, small savers at the time the book appeared were earning little or nothing on their savings. Interest rates were very low (0.15 per cent per year on my bank account), which meant that in real terms, with prices rising at some 2 per cent per year in the UK, their rate of return on these savings was negative.

It is not surprising that readers of Piketty were puzzled. We need to distinguish different rates of return. The return on capital—the factor price generated by the production side of the economy—is not the same as the return to individual households in the form of investment income. As we saw in Chapter 3, there are claims on the operating profits of companies in addition to the interest on bonds and the dividends on shares that the companies pay to households. These claims include taxation, and, where enterprises are owned publicly, the profit goes directly to the state. A significant part of company profit is retained for reinvestment. There are important intermediaries, such as banks, pension funds, and investment funds, that stand between the company sector and the household sector. Part of the return on capital is absorbed by these and other institutions in the financial-services sector.

The implications for the distribution of wealth depend on how that wealth is invested. For owner-occupiers in the bottom 99 per cent, their most valuable asset is likely to be their home, and increased housing wealth has been a major reason for the rise in popular wealth. This has been particularly the case during the booms in house prices that occurred in a number of countries, such as the US, between the mid-1990s and the mid-2000s. In the UK, according to Francesca Bastagli and John Hills, "changes in total wealth between 1995 and 2005 were heavily affected by changes in housing wealth. Over the period, house prices increased greatly, at least doubling in real terms."[7] Housing wealth is less unequally distributed than wealth as a whole, but the returns on this asset class have not benefitted the minority who are not owner-occupiers. According to the estimates of Bastagli and Hills, median net housing wealth per household increased from £27,000 in 1995 to £102,000 in 2005 (at 2005 prices) in Great Britain. The Gini coefficient for housing wealth fell from 65 per cent in 1995 to 56 per cent in 2005.[8] This is an impressive fall, but it still leaves the coefficient very high—much higher than for disposable income. This reflects the fact that the net housing wealth at the bottom decile in Britain is close to zero. Social tenants (those in public housing) and private tenants were left behind by the housing property boom. Indeed, they have been adversely affected by rising rents.

The British experience is of general interest in that the UK is not alone in having a high proportion of owner-occupiers. The Eurosystem Household Finance and Consumption Survey shows that, although in Austria and Germany owner-occupiers are in a minority (44 and 48 per cent, respectively), on average across the countries covered owner-occupiers make up 60 per cent of residents, and in Spain and Slovakia, they are over 80 per cent.[9] The UK has also experimented with a major programme of asset redistribution—the Right to Buy programme—the scale of which does not seem to have been fully appreciated. Right to Buy, introduced in 1980 by the Conservative government, allowed tenants of social housing to buy their properties at heavily discounted prices. The sale of council houses to sitting tenants by local authorities was not new, but the programme was greatly expanded with the express intention of increasing the proportion of owner-occupation. The discount, which had averaged 27 per cent under previous legislation, rose to 42 per cent in 1981–1984, reaching 50 per cent in 1993–1995. By 2003, 2.8 million dwellings had been sold under Right to Buy, and the sales had generated £36.8 billion in Great Britain.[10] These are large numbers. To quote John Hills and Howard Glennerster, "the accumulated value of the property wealth these discounts represent is considerable . . . Such a 'gift from the state' was large in any terms. It represented 3–4 per cent of all household wealth."[11] In 2010/12 terms, this amounts to £200 billion.

The transfer of wealth from the state to households under the UK Right to Buy programme had the effect of raising the share of wealth of the bottom 99 per cent, but at the cost of accentuating the differences within that group. This in turn has wider implications for inequality. The 2010 report by Regeneris Consulting and Oxford Economics found that "access to good schools, locations with low levels of environmental pollution, good transport and other public infrastructure is priced into the housing market. As average house prices have risen relative to incomes, largely because of lack of supply, so less wealthy families find themselves increasingly priced out of the more advantageous locations. This makes relative poverty matter even more than before for life chances and for access to opportunities whether for education, health or employment." The report goes on to note that "housing assets are also very unevenly distributed across generations. . . . In terms of housing wealth per capita for instance, those over the age of 65 hold more than ten times the amount of those under 45, while those in the 45 to 65 age group hold nearly eight times the amount of those under 45."[12]

Measures that would contribute to reducing these differences between owner-occupiers and tenants, in the UK and in other countries, include the expansion of house-building and the provision of more social housing. But there are two further measures that are part of proposals made in later chapters. In Chapter 7, I discuss the major changes in local taxation made by Britain's Conservative government a quarter of a century ago. The move from a domestic rating system, with taxes broadly related to property values, to the more regressive Council Tax reduced the local taxes on higher-value properties. This was capitalised in higher house prices (since the local taxes were lower, people were willing to pay more for the houses) and contributed to the housing price boom. The proposal in Chapter 7 is for the UK to return to a proportional tax on property values, raising the tax paid on more valuable houses and flats. This too is likely to be capitalised, lowering house prices. Such a measure will impact the distribution of wealth though in a progressive direction.

The second policy proposal, discussed in Chapter 8, relates to state pensions. This subject may appear to be quite unconnected to the housing market, but there is a clear link. In the UK, the impact of successive policy measures to scale back state pensions, and to transfer responsibility for provision for retirement to individuals, has led many people to search for appropriate alternative assets. The fact that interest paid on mortgages taken out to finance acquisition of rental properties is deductible against the income received, coupled with changes in tenancy law favouring landlords, has led to buy-to-let becoming an attractive option, adding further fuel to the boom in house prices. It is my hope that the measures proposed in Chapter 8 to strengthen social protection in retirement will serve to reduce the buy-to-let demand and hence reduce the upward pressure on house prices.

Savers and the Financial-Services Sector

Small savers not investing in property are largely investing in financial assets and in pensions. In both cases, they are dependent on financial services, a sector of the economy that has expanded greatly in recent decades. Paying for these financial services is a major factor creating the wedge between the rate of return on capital and the rate received by savers. In some cases, the wedge is explicit. If the savings are held in a unit trust, then there is an annual management charge levied as a percentage of the value of the fund, for example, 0.75 per cent per year in an actively managed fund. There may in addition be fees for auditing or paying the trustees. There are similar fee structures for defined-contribution pension schemes, where the fees reduce the pension ultimately paid. In their study of defined-contribution workplace pensions in the UK, the Office of Fair Trading highlighted the role of the "charges the scheme member has to pay—including charges paid for the administration of the scheme and for investment management services. Small differences in the level of scheme charges can make a significant difference to the value of a member's accumulated savings at retirement. For instance, a 0.5 per cent Annual Management Charge (AMC) over an employee's working life can reduce the overall value of a scheme member's retirement savings by around 11 per cent, whereas a one per cent AMC can reduce retirement savings by around 21 per cent."[13] In defined-benefit schemes—which in most countries are becoming increasingly rare in the private sector—the pension paid on retirement is related to final or average salary. In that case, the rate of return is of immediate concern to the pension fund trustees and to the employer, but not directly to the saver. But the charges levied by the fund managers may still adversely impact savers via increased contributions or scaled-down pension benefits, and may in part have been responsible for withdrawal of employers (both private and public) from this form of pension provision.

But what exactly is the output of the financial-services sector? Savers undoubtedly wonder for what exactly they—as a group—are paying, since performance of fund managers seems to be measured in relative rather than absolute terms. If one investment fund is outperforming another through picking the right shares, is not another fund losing on the other side of the transaction? What makes it a positive-sum rather than a zero-sum business? These are good questions, and the measurement of the output of the financial-services industry has indeed proved a conundrum for national accountants. In the case of the car industry, we observe the incomes earned and the output produced: cars coming out of the factory gates. In the case of financial services, we observe the incomes but not much of the output. In some cases, the output can be identified, as when banks, for example, charge a fee for particular services, such as safekeeping your documents or arranging a loan. But in other cases, the payment is made implicitly. By keeping a balance in one's account, one is in effect paying for the bank services of handling payments. By "in effect" I mean that one is forgoing interest that could have been earned if the money had been held elsewhere (or else that one is receiving a lower rate of interest on the account). If the bank pays 0.5 per cent on current account balances, whereas the savings bank would have paid 2 per cent, then the forgone interest is 1.5 per cent. This kind of consideration underlies the treatment in the United Nations System of National Accounts (SNA). The SNA, an internationally agreed standard set of measurements for economic activity, now contains an item titled "Financial Intermediation Services Indirectly Measured," or FISIM: "The difference between interest calculated at the reference rate and interest actually paid to depositors and charged to borrowers is a financial intermediation service charge indirectly measured."[14] The SNA treatment of financial-sector activity provides a statistical answer but does not resolve the more general question as to the nature of its value added. What are savers getting? John Kay, economist and *Financial Times* columnist, asks in his book *Other People's Money* why financial services are so profitable: "Common sense suggests that if a closed circle of people continuously exchange bits of paper with each other, the total value of these bits of paper will not change much, if at all. If some members of that closed circle make extraordinary profits, these profits can only be made at the expense of other members of the same circle." He goes on to conclude that not much is wrong with the commonsense view.[15]

One source of extraordinary profits has been the high interest rates charged on certain forms of lending, notably by pay-day lenders. Searching a UK rate-comparison site on 2 January 2015, I found only one rate for short-term loans of less than 1,000 per cent (the annual percentage rate). The one lower rate was 154 per cent. This value of r is clearly greater than g. The same applies—at more modest levels—to the rates of interest charged on credit cards. On the same day, the most common annual rate on the comparison site was 18.9 per cent. This brings me to the question of debt.

Debt is much discussed in relation to the macroeconomy, but the distributional impact warrants more attention. The reason the share in total wealth of the bottom groups is so small has a lot to do with negative entries. When he described the distribution of income as a parade, with people's height represented according to their incomes, Jan Pen pointed out that at the beginning of the parade some people are walking upside down, since they have negative incomes (for example, owing to a loss in their business).[16] When we look at net wealth (assets minus liabilities), we see many more upside-down people. Edward Wolff, analysing data from the US Survey of Consumer Finances (SCF) conducted by the Federal Reserve Board, found that 18.6 per cent of US households in 2007 had zero or negative net worth and that the share of the bottom 40 per cent of households in total net worth was effectively zero (0.2 per cent).[17] Debt, of course, comes in many different varieties. A major part of household debt is borrowing for home ownership, secured on the property. The interest rates paid in this case are rather different from those cited for pay-day lending. The report on the 2013 US SCF found the typical interest rate for a thirty-year mortgage to be 3.5 per cent (the figure for credit cards was 11.9 per cent).[18] In this case, of course, there is an asset to counterbalance the mortgage, and only in situations of "negative equity" is there a risk of negative overall net worth. But credit not secured by residential property is also important, and some forms have been growing rapidly. The 2013 US SCF found that "the level of education loan debt held by U.S. families had increased dramatically over the past decade" and that "about 24 percent of young families' education debt is held by those making less than $30,000."[19] Concerns for the implications of this development are echoed in quite a number of other countries.

The two issues just evoked—astronomical rates of interest charged to pay-day borrowers and the rising extent of education loan debt—are signs that the whole question of the terms on which households can borrow needs careful examination. Policy-makers have focused on access to lending for businesses, but households potentially face even greater problems, and the distributional consequences may be serious. For this reason, I suggest:

> *Idea to pursue: a thoroughgoing review of the access of households to the credit market for borrowing not secured on housing.*

In the meantime, these considerations provide motivation for the proposal below for a minimum inheritance.

Realistic Returns for Small Savers

In 2014, setting out his Political Guidelines for the new European Commission, President Jean-Claude Juncker declared, "I am a strong believer in the social market economy. It is not compatible with the social market economy that during a crisis, ship-owners and speculators become even richer, while pensioners can no longer support themselves."[20] One of the major reasons pensioners are no longer able to support themselves is the low return on their savings. In the same month that *Capital in the Twenty-First Century* was published in English, the IMF's *World Economic Outlook* depicted the widening gap since 2001 (in the US) between the real return on equity and the real interest rate: "Real interest rates worldwide have declined substantially since the 1980s and are now in slightly negative territory."[21] In the UK the real rate has indeed become negative, as shown for two types of savings (fixed-rate bonds and instant-access accounts) in Figure 6.2, and has remained essentially so for a number of years. Unless savers are adding to their investments out of new savings, their wealth held in these forms has been going backwards.

For financial assets in general, the wedge between the rate of return (Piketty's *r*) and the return actually received by the small saver is the source of income for the financial-services industry, which is itself highly unequally distributed and has contributed markedly to the rise in top income shares. Here, though, I am concerned with the implications for small savers and the disequalising impact of the *differences in r*. As James Meade notes, "the rate of return on property is much lower for small properties than for large properties."[22] What then can be done to rebalance the economy in favour of small savers? How can the return on their savings be brought closer to the rate of return on capital? Market competition has not secured this outcome. The Office of Fair Trading study cited above concluded that "competition alone cannot be relied upon to drive value for money for all savers in the DC [Defined Contribution] workplace pension market." One mechanism is regulation, as with the imposition of maximum management fees for pension providers. The UK government is pursuing this approach, having announced a cap of 0.75 per cent on management charges for pension funds. However, competition by state financial institutions is a more direct route to ensuring an adequate return. For this reason, I recommend the following:

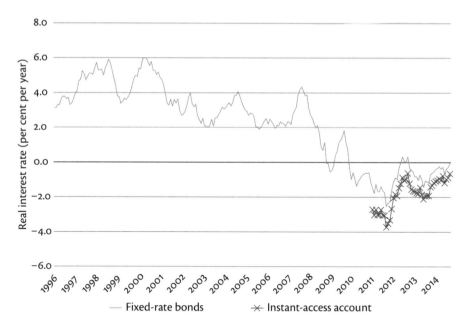

FIGURE 6.2: Interest rates in the UK, 1996–2014

The graph shows changes in the real interest rate (the nominal interest rate adjusted for inflation) for fixed-rate bonds and instant-access accounts from 1996 to 2014. Rates reported are from January 1 of the year.

> Proposal 5: The government should offer via national savings bonds a guaranteed positive real rate of interest on savings, with a maximum holding per person.

This is not a radical idea. Inflation-indexed bonds were issued by the Commonwealth of Massachusetts in 1780 during the Revolutionary War.[23] For small savers, index-linked savings certificates have in the past been offered by the governments in Ireland, the UK, and other countries. Originally known in the UK as "Granny Bonds," since they were initially limited to those over retirement age, National Savings Index-Linked Savings Certificates were available until 2011. Not only did they guarantee the purchasing power of your savings, but they paid interest at 1 per cent per annum, so you were gaining in real terms. As may be seen from Figure 6.2, their reintroduction with such a return would represent a major improvement for small savers over what has been available since that time.

What rate should be guaranteed to small savers? This would be an obvious question to be placed on the agenda of the Social and Economic Council proposed in the previous chapter. In seeking an answer, we may note that in the past the real rate offered in the UK has been as high as 1.35 per cent. This could be taken as corresponding to the medium-term expected rate of real growth of household incomes per head (averaged to smooth out cyclical fluctuations), allowing for the fact that, as argued earlier, household incomes cannot be expected to grow as fast as national income. If in this way the real rate of interest for small savers can be guaranteed to match the rate of growth, then their savings will not fall behind.

But how do they get started?

Inheritance for All

In 1797 Thomas Paine, the philosopher and revolutionary, set out in his *Agrarian Justice* a scheme "to create a national fund, out of which there shall be paid to every person, when arrived at the age of twenty-one years, the sum of fifteen pounds sterling, as a compensation in part, for the loss of his or her natural inheritance, by the introduction of the system of landed property."[24] According to the estimates of Peter Lindert and Jeffrey Williamson, fifteen pounds would have represented around half of the annual earnings of a farm labourer in England and Wales in 1797.[25]

The modern counterpart of the proposal by Paine is to be found in schemes for asset-based egalitarianism, as proposed in the US by Bruce Ackerman and Anne Alstott. They argue that every American citizen has the right to share in the wealth accumulated by preceding generations, and that "a single innovation once proposed by Thomas Paine can achieve what a thousand lesser policies have failed to accomplish."[26] In the UK in the 1960s, Cedric Sandford had proposed a "negative capital tax" payable on adulthood, and in my 1972 book *Unequal Shares,* I put forward the idea of a universal capital payment as part of the state pension.[27] Sandford's proposal was developed by Julian Le Grand in the form of a start-up grant for young people.[28] This idea took root and was implemented by the UK government in 2003 as the Child Trust Fund. The government started off the fund with a £250 voucher for each child born on or after 1 September 2002, with a further payment for families below a means-tested threshold. Parents could contribute to the fund, which accumulated until the child reached the age of eighteen. The resulting sum would depend both on the parental addition and on the way in which it was invested by the parents. On reaching adulthood, the person could withdraw the money with no restrictions on use. The scheme was abandoned by the Coalition government in 2010.

Inheritance is typically seen as one of the mechanisms by which the wealthy are able to preserve their position at the top of the distribution, but there is nothing intrinsically wrong with inheritance. The problem is that inheritance is highly unequal. If everyone inherited the same amount, the playing field would be level. A step in this direction is to ensure that everyone receives a minimum inheritance; hence the following proposal:

> Proposal 6: There should be a capital endowment (minimum inheritance) paid to all at adulthood.

The proposal needs to be fleshed out. Several key questions arise. When should it be paid? How should it be phased in? Who would be eligible? How large should it be? How should it be financed? What restrictions, if any, should be imposed on its use?

The Capital Endowment

First, when should it be paid? In the course of the book, I have referred to the intergenerational distribution of income and to the risk of growing inequality between generations if the rate of growth of average household incomes is slower in the future than we had expected in the past. This consideration points to the use of the minimum inheritance as a means of redressing the generational balance. I therefore discuss it in terms of a payment on reaching adulthood, stepping back from my 1972 proposal that it be paid on retirement. To quote Bob Dylan, "I was so much older then/I'm younger than that now." There remains the issue of phasing-in the minimum inheritance. There would be an evident injustice in hand-ing a large sum to those born after 1 September 2002 and leaving those born on 31 August 2002 or earlier with nothing. This in turn is related to the definition of eligibility. No one should be able to arrive in the UK for the first time on their eighteenth birthday and be able to claim the minimum inheritance. For this reason, I propose that the eligibility be attached to the past receipt of the Child Benefit: a person qualifying for x years of Child Benefit since the initial date would be entitled to $x/18$ of the minimum inheritance.[29] This would allow a natural build-up over time.

What should be the size of the minimum inheritance and how would it be funded? The US proposal by Ackerman and Alstott envisaged (in 1997) a payment of $80,000 financed by a 2 per cent tax on personal wealth. The proposed sum was around double the median family annual income at the time, and a great deal larger than the likely pay-out from the UK Child Trust Fund if it had been allowed to continue. In his proposal for the UK, Le Grand argued, citing in support Alfred Doolittle from *Pygmalion,* that too small a sum is more likely to be misused, and his proposal (in 2006) was for £10,000.[30] (Alfred Doolittle said that, if given £5, he would have "just one good spree," but if it were £10, then "it makes a man prudent-like.") Le Grand proposes that this should be financed by increasing inheritance taxation. In the next chapter, I propose moving to a lifetime capital receipts tax, and that the revenue should be allocated to the financing of the capital endowment. While there are arguments against hypothecation of tax receipts in general, here there is a good case for making a link between the tax-and-benefit sides of the equation. With some three-quarters of a million people reaching the age of eighteen each year in the UK, the existing inheritance tax revenue would finance a capital endowment closer to £5,000 than £10,000, so that—in order to meet the Doolittle objection—the revenue from the new tax would have to be higher.

I do not consider here whether restrictions should be imposed on the use of the minimum inheritance. Clearly any such restrictions would add significantly to the administrative cost, but a case can be made for imposing a degree of "prudence." The obvious restriction is to investment in education or training. It is not, however, possible to treat this adequately without entering into the whole question of student fees. At the same time, there are grounds for not restricting the endowment to formal education and allowing, for example, its use to finance an apprenticeship. Other possible "permitted uses" could include down payments on houses or flats, or the establishment of a small business.

National Wealth and a Sovereign Wealth Fund

From individual wealth, I turn to the national wealth—the wealth that the citizens of a country own collectively. National wealth is a neglected part of the distributional story. Indeed, while there is much debate about public finances, little is said about the assets side of the account. The fiscal issue is typically presented in terms of debt and deficits. In order to reduce the national debt, governments have to run surpluses. Tax revenue has to exceed state outlays (and the debt interest paid) by an amount sufficient to allow debt to be redeemed. Many years ago, President Eisenhower said, "I do not feel that any amount can be properly called a 'surplus' as long as the nation is in debt. I prefer to think of such an item as 'reduction on our children's inherited mortgage.'"[31]

The president was wrong, however, to concentrate solely on the national debt, since, in addition to passing on the national debt, we also pass on to our children:

» state pension liabilities;
» public infrastructure and real wealth; and
» public financial assets.

The key point is that we should look at the full balance sheet of the public sector, not just the national debt. In part this makes the picture more gloomy, since we have to add to the national debt the obligation to pay future state pensions. The value of already-accumulated state pension rights in most OECD countries is substantial. On the other hand, on the plus side of the balance sheet are the public assets, both real and financial. The former was well illustrated by President Eisenhower himself when, in his next, and last, State of the Union Address, he recorded proudly that he had been responsible for the interstate highway system and many other major public investments. The children and grandchildren of those he addressed in 1961 are driving along those roads today. These assets

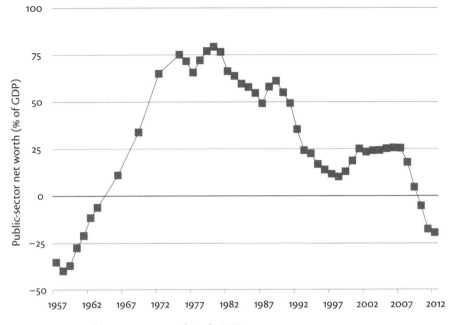

FIGURE 6.3: Public-sector net worth in the UK, 1957–2012

The net worth (assets minus liabilities) of the UK public sector has changed relative to GDP. Declines after 1979 are partially due to asset transfers, including sales of council housing to residents and privatisation of public corporations (e.g., British Telecom, British Gas).

may be difficult to value, but they should clearly enter the determination of the net worth of the state.

It is important to look at the full balance sheet, and for every country it would be good to have statistics such as those shown for the UK in Figure 6.3. The graph shows the ratio of the net worth of the public sector expressed relative to the size of the national income. (The figures do not take account of state pension liabilities.) There are several distinct phases. In 1957, the national debt exceeded the value of state assets, to an amount equal to around one-third of national income. Over time, the net worth position improved, becoming positive in the early 1960s. The improvement continued up to the late 1970s, by which time the public net worth amounted to some three-quarters of national income. After 1979, however, the net worth of the state declined. In effect, the state transferred title in much of its real assets to individual households. As we have seen, the Right to Buy programme of council house sales at discounted prices amounted to a massive transfer of assets, as did the substantial discounts involved in the privatisation of public corporations such as British Telecom and British Gas.[32] By 1997, the public-sector net worth was not much above zero. There was some recovery in the first years of the Labour government, but then a fall from 2007, which continued under the Coalition government.

In my view, we should be focusing on the overall net worth of the state, not just on the national debt. The proper objective of fiscal policy should be a return to a situation where the state has a significant positive net worth. Of course the reduction of the national debt would contribute to this end, but it is only one side of the equation. The other side is the accumulation of state assets. By holding capital and by sharing in the fruits of technological developments, the state can use the resulting revenue to promote a less unequal society. This is all the more important, given the earlier analysis of the economic forces driving the distribution of income. To the question, who owns the robots? the answer should be that, in part, they belong to us all.

A Sovereign Wealth Fund

In some countries, the accumulation of state assets has taken the form of a *sovereign wealth fund,* which is a state-owned investment fund. Such funds have a long history. In 1854, the Texas Permanent School Fund was created with a $2 million appropriation by the Texas Legislature expressly for the benefit of the public schools of Texas. The later Constitution of 1876 stipulated that certain lands and proceeds from the sale of these lands should constitute part of the fund. There is a similar fund for the Texas state university system. The more recent sovereign wealth funds established in a variety of countries are much larger, as shown in Figure 6.4, where the assets under management are expressed relative to GDP. In many cases, these funds are financed out of oil revenues, but one should also note the presence of China and Singapore.

One of the most recent sovereign wealth funds is that established in France in 2008, Le Fonds stratégique d'investissement (Structural Invest-

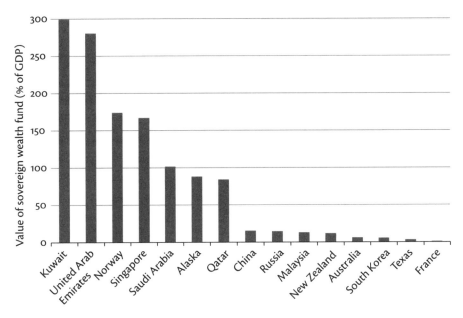

FIGURE 6.4: Sovereign wealth funds compared with GDP, worldwide, 2013

Sovereign wealth funds (state-owned investment funds) are often, but not always, financed out of oil revenues. This graph shows the value of the assets under management in sovereign wealth funds, relative to GDP, in 2013.

ment Fund). It forms part of a longer history: the fund comes under the jurisdiction of the Caisse des Dépôts that was founded in 1816. The fund is answerable to Parliament and is a long-term investor in the service of the public interest. This is a model that other countries could follow:

> Proposal 7: A public Investment Authority should be created, operating a sovereign wealth fund with the aim of building up the net worth of the state by holding investments in companies and in property.

In the same year the Structural Investment Fund was established in France, the UK did in fact set up the UK Financial Investments, a company responsible for managing the investments made by the government in the recapitalisation of banks (and the investment in UK Asset Resolution). The total value of the assets depends on the share prices and the extent of the shareholding retained. (On 31 March 2014, it was some £40 billion.) The policy of the UK Coalition government has been to sell these assets (and to continue with the privatisation of other state assets, such as the Royal Mail), but—in line with my focus on the asset side of the account—I believe that the policy should be reversed. The state should be seeking to build up its net worth by enlarging its holdings of shares in companies and of property. Put differently, the net worth of the state is a measure of what we pass on to future generations, and the establishment of a sovereign wealth fund is a vehicle for achieving intergenerational equity.

In the case of Norway, the sovereign wealth fund was established to ensure that the benefits from North Sea oil production accrued, not just to the current generation, but also to future generations. There is a rule limiting annual spending to 4 per cent, on average, of the fund. Norway is not the only country to have benefitted from North Sea oil, and it is an interesting piece of conjectural history to ask what would have happened if the UK had created such a fund in 1968 and had spent only the real return (that is, had accumulated not only the government revenues but also sufficient revenue from the fund income to maintain its purchasing power). Norway's spending out of the fund has been broadly equal to the real return in recent years.[33] Figure 6.5 shows how the existence of the fund would have changed the picture for state net worth shown earlier in Figure 6.3 (the new line is the dashed one). The accumulated fund would be very considerable (some £350 billion, or about 60 per cent of the Norwegian fund). The UK is a larger country, so the fund is smaller as a percentage of national income, but it would have provided a useful cushion. The net worth of the state in 2012 would have been positive rather than negative. What might have been if my generation had voted for fiscal prudence rather than for tax cuts!

Is the proposal for a sovereign wealth fund simply nationalisation by the back door? Here it is essential to distinguish between two different dimensions: the "control" dimension of state enterprises, where the government—central or local—can directly influence enterprise policy, and the "beneficial ownership" dimension. These can be separated. The state can retain, via a privileged share, control over an enterprise, while allowing private shareholders to receive the bulk of the profits. Or, conversely, it can own a sizeable shareholding, benefiting fiscally, without exercising

FIGURE 6.5: Public-sector net worth and hypothetical sovereign wealth fund, UK, 1957–2012

The solid line shows the value of the UK public sector relative to GDP. The dashed line shows how the value of the UK public sector would have increased (relative to GDP) if a sovereign wealth fund had been established in 1968 and only real income spent. See Figure Sources for calculation of government revenue from oil and gas.

a controlling influence on the policies of the enterprise. It is the latter—benefit but not control—that I am primarily advocating. In the UK case, the government (in 2014) owned some 80 per cent of the Royal Bank of Scotland, so that in theory at least, the benefit and control interests coincided, but it would be quite possible for the proposed UK Investment Authority to take minority holdings in a wide range of companies, drawing the income but not taking control. It would be natural, for example, for the authority to acquire holdings in companies that have benefitted from state-supported research, as discussed in Chapter 4. My proposal is far from new. Thirty years ago, James Meade urged the raising of tax revenue "to acquire for the public the unencumbered rights to a share of profits in enterprise whose management could be left entirely in private hands. . . . the receipt of income from the state ownership of shares in private enterprise would provide for the government a lasting net revenue which could contribute towards the costs of a social dividend [here the Participation Income discussed in Chapter 8]."[34]

The formal creation of a sovereign wealth fund would not represent a return to the nationalisations of the last century. At the same time, I am not advocating a totally passive Investment Authority. Its investments should be guided by ethical criteria covering the fields in which companies are active and by its sensitivity to its wider social responsibilities, such as its pay policy. This is underlined by the fact that one of the non-UK sovereign wealth funds cited earlier is reported to have made significant purchases of blocks of flats in London, attracted by the opportunity of capital appreciation. If the UK Investment Authority were to make such an investment, it is to be hoped that it would have regard to the wider social impact in terms of the provision of housing as well as the immediate short-run profit. In the same way, it would provide a source of funding for infrastructure investment and for climate change mitigation. This would be a natural accompaniment to its role in securing a fairer distribution between generations.

Chapter 7 ::

Progressive Taxation

Higher taxes at the top? If one reason for the widening income gap is that top income tax rates have been cut, then should we return to a more progressive rate schedule? In this chapter, I put forward a set of proposals for a more progressive structure of the personal income tax; for the preferential treatment of earned income; for radical reform of inheritance taxation; for the modernisation of property taxation (Council Tax in the UK); for the revival of the idea of an annual wealth tax; and for global taxation. In *The Importance of Being Earnest,* the governess, Miss Prism, says that her charge may omit the chapter in her economics textbook on the fall of the rupee as being "too sensational"; I am not sure what she would have made of the present chapter, but it covers a lot of ground.

In terms of the overall structure of taxation, the proposals raise the tax collected on income, capital, and wealth transfers—the reverse of the recent tendency to raise taxes on consumption (VAT) and on earned income (social security contributions). The proposals are a means of distributing more fairly the cost of financing the operation of the government and of raising additional tax revenue in order to finance redistribution.

Restoring Progressive Income Taxation

Figure 7.1 is an updated version of a graph that I suggested ten years ago for the dust jacket of the first of the two volumes edited by Thomas Piketty and myself on top incomes. It depicts for the UK the changes over time in two variables: (a) the share of the top 0.1 per cent in total gross income over the last hundred years and (b) the top rate of personal income tax. More accurately, the latter shows how much a person paying the top rate of income tax retains out of an extra £1 of earned income, what I refer to here as the "marginal retention rate." With a top tax rate of

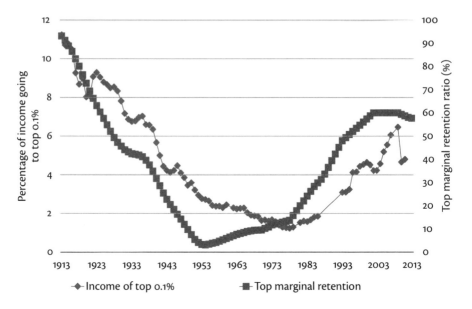

FIGURE 7.1: Income share and after-tax retention rate of top earners in the UK, 1913–2013

The diamonds (using left axis) show the share of total gross income that goes to the top 0.1% (the top 10% of the top 1%) of income recipients. In 2011, for example, their income share was 4.8%, meaning they received 48 times their proportional share of income. The line of squares (using right axis) shows the marginal retention rate, or how much a person paying the highest tax rate keeps out of each additional £1 earned—almost 60% in the 2000s; less than 10% in the 1960s. Marginal tax rates are averaged over 15 years.

45 per cent, that person retains 55 per cent. The retention rates are averaged over the past fifteen years, so as to smooth out the jumps in tax rates and to reflect the presumption that today's top shares are influenced by tax rates in the past. This presumption assumes that the causality runs from tax rates to top shares, but of course the causality may run the other way. Top shares today may influence tax rates today and in the future. The striking feature of Figure 7.1 is that both curves exhibit a similar V pattern. They are not identical, and the trough comes earlier for the retention curve, but the shapes of the curves are suggestive. In considering the picture, it is important to remember that the share of income is the share in *gross* income; we would obviously expect the share of *net* income to follow the retention rate.[1] This kind of graph has appeared on Occupy Movement placards, and, at a more academic level, the relation between

top taxes and the shares of top income groups has been the subject of much analysis.

The reduction in top tax rates in the UK was particularly sharp under the Thatcher government, which on taking office in 1979 reduced the top rate on earned income from 83 per cent to 60 per cent. Then, in 1988, when Nigel Lawson was Chancellor of the Exchequer, the top income tax rate was reduced further, to 40 per cent. This announcement in the Budget Speech was greeted with loud cheers from Conservative MPs, one of whom was quoted as saying that he did not have enough zeroes on his calculator to work out how much tax he was saving! (My own reaction is described in Chapter 11.) In this dramatic change in tax policy, the UK was not alone. In the US, the top rate has similarly been halved: from 70 per cent in 1980 to 35 per cent, raising the marginal retention rate from 30 per cent to 65 per cent. These two countries are extreme cases, as is illustrated in Figure 7.2, which shows the change in the top income shares (measured in percentage points, so that the value of 2 on the vertical axis means that the share has moved from, say, 6 per cent to 8 per cent) and the change in the top marginal retention rates.[2] In each case, the change is measured by comparing the average for the five years 1960 to 1964 with the average for the years 2005 to 2009. Some countries made little or no change in the top tax rates over the period, such as Denmark (slight rise in tax rate), Germany, Spain, and Switzerland. In others, the changes were less drastic than in the US and UK but were nonetheless substantial, as in Canada, Japan, and Norway.

The two diagrams are suggestive: the increases in the proportion of income retained, as a result of cutting top tax rates, seem to be associated with rises in the top share of gross income. It is immediately evident, however, that a simple comparison of two series—either cross-country or across time—does not allow us to draw any conclusions about the causal relationship between tax rates and income shares. Across countries, there are other factors that may have influenced the evolution of top shares. Some countries may have become more integrated in the global economy, with the consequences that their top shares have increased but they have also had to cut tax rates to attract workers. The causal mechanism is in this case not from taxes to top shares but from globalisation to each of the variables separately. Over time, within a country, still other factors

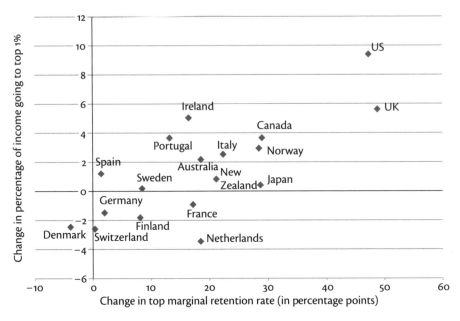

FIGURE 7.2: Change in top income shares and tax rates of top 1% in selected world countries, 1960s to 2000s

This graph shows changes in the share of income going to the top 1% of income recipients and in the after-tax retention rate for top earnings from the 1960s (1960–1964) to the 2000s (2005–2009). See Figure Sources for specific dates. For each country, the change in the share of total gross income that goes to the top 1% is shown on the vertical axis. Countries above the 0 line have a higher proportion of total income going to the top 1% in 2005–2009 than in 1960–1964; countries below the 0 line have proportionally less income going to the top 1% in this 45-year span. The horizontal axis shows how much more top earners keep after taxes (the top marginal retention rate; see Fig. 7.1 and text) in the 2000s compared with the 1960s. The further to the right on the graph a country is, the greater the increase in the after-tax retention rate (i.e., the greater the reduction in the tax rate) over this 45-year span.

might influence both shares and taxes. Conservative/Republican/Liberal governments are more likely to impose lower taxes than are Labour/Democrat/Socialist governments, but the same governments may take other actions that lead to rising top income shares, such as the adoption of privatisation programmes. This was certainly the case in the 1980s with the Thatcher government in the UK and President Reagan in the

US. Moreover, the picture is further complicated by the fact that changes in government, and anticipated changes, may lead to changes in the recorded income shares that do not correspond to changes in the underlying incomes from production. The identification of low taxes with conservative governments may cause businesses to distribute more dividend income to shareholders during the conservative term of office, to avoid the tax increases expected when a left-wing government wins the election. In such cases the income tax data record a rise in top shares in personal income at a time of low taxes, whereas there may have been no change in the underlying profits (the difference being retained earnings—see Figure 3.1).

Estimating the Effects of Top Tax Rates

The approach widely adopted in economic studies to holding other things constant is described as "difference in differences." The essence is simple. The change (first difference) in top shares when the top tax rate is increased is compared (second difference) with the change for other groups not affected. In a randomised trial, the latter would be a control group. This was the case with the early studies of the effects of marginal tax rates in the negative income tax experiments in the US in the late 1960s and early 1970s. The negative income tax, described further in the next chapter, involves making payments to people below the tax threshold, with the payment tapered as their income approaches the threshold. In this way, they are subject to a marginal rate of withdrawal equivalent to a tax, as well as being made better off. In the negative income tax experiments, the payments were made to some families (the experimental group) and not to others (the control group). These pioneering uses of the field experimentation approach in economics underline one of the themes of this book: that we need to consider the distribution as a whole. Issues of high marginal tax rates arise at the bottom as well as at the top of the income scale.

Although it is entertaining to contemplate the reactions at the top of the income scale to an announcement that the government is about to carry out field experiments, offering reduced tax rates to top earners selected randomly in cities in New Jersey or in Clacton-on-Sea, such undertakings seem unlikely. We must therefore rely on "natural experiments," in which we can identify a group that is not affected by the tax change but is otherwise comparable. Michael Brewer, Emmanuel Saez, and Andrew Shephard, writing about the UK, argue that the changes in the top marginal tax rate have essentially affected the top 1 per cent, and that the next 4 per cent can therefore be taken as a control group.[3] Thus in considering the impact of the 1988 budget, when the top tax rate went from 60 to 40 per cent, they look not just at the change in the share of the top 1 per cent between 1986 and 1989 but also at how this change differed from that experienced by the next 4 per cent. From this information they obtain a difference in differences estimate of the response of gross incomes to the top tax rate. They express this response in terms of an "elasticity," which they estimate to be 0.46 (the precision of this estimate is discussed below). What does such an elasticity mean? It implies that if the retention rate goes up by 10 per cent (that is, taxes are cut), then the gross income rises by 4.6 per cent. Put in reverse, a fall in the retention rate of 10 per cent causes the gross income to fall by 4.6 per cent. (It should be noted that these numbers refer to percentages, which should not be confused with percentage point changes: a 10 per cent rise in a retention rate takes it from, say, 50 per cent to 55 per cent.)

These apparently abstruse calculations are relevant to the debate, since they provide an answer to the question, will a rise in top tax rates lead to more revenue? For if a fall in the retention rate causes a fall in gross income, the tax base is smaller. Balancing the two elements—the gain from raising the tax rate and the loss from the smaller tax base—Brewer, Saez, and Shephard conclude that the revenue-maximising top tax rate would be 56.6 per cent.[4] On the face of it, this indicates that there is room to increase the UK top tax rate from its present 45 per cent. However, their calculation of the marginal retention rate is more extensive than that described above, in that they take account of social security contributions by employers and employees, and of value-added tax payable when the income is spent. What is being calculated is the total amount of consumption that can be financed from £1 paid out by the employer. When they allow for these other taxes, they arrive at a revenue-maximising income tax rate of 40 per cent.

These research findings were factored into the influential review of UK taxation carried out by the Institute for Fiscal Studies and chaired by

Sir James Mirrlees. The conclusions of the Mirrlees Review in turn influenced the UK Chancellor of the Exchequer, George Osborne, when he announced that the top income tax rate in the UK would be cut from 50 per cent to 45 per cent beginning in 2013: "The direct cost is only £100 million a year. Indeed HMRC [the UK tax agency] calculates that the loss of other tax revenues may even cancel that out. In other words, it . . . may raise nothing at all."[5]

The Argument Re-examined

I believe that the UK should move in the opposite direction—increasing the top tax rate to 65 per cent—and that similar arguments apply in other countries. Why, though, am I flying in the face of evidence that the revenue-maximising top tax rate is 40 per cent?

The first reason is that there is considerable uncertainty surrounding the estimate of the taxable elasticity. The study by Brewer, Saez, and Shephard is one of many that attempt to estimate the relevant elasticity, and the authors themselves stress that "as our estimate of the elasticity is tentative, so is the estimated optimal top tax rate."[6] The report of the Mirrlees Review states clearly that "there is no escaping the uncertainty around the estimate of a 40% revenue-maximising income tax rate."[7] There is a considerable margin of error. In statistical terms, the 95 per cent confidence interval around the estimated elasticity of 0.47 is sufficiently wide that, combined with the earlier assumptions about other taxes entering the calculation, the revenue-maximising tax rate on the top range could be as low as 24 per cent or as high as 62 per cent. Seen this way, the conclusion is less definite: the views of most politicians could be encompassed.

The second reason for taking a different view is that I am not convinced by the arithmetic that took the Mirrlees Review calculation of the top tax rate from 56.6 per cent down to 40 per cent. Here the assumptions all go in the direction of maximising the other taxes paid and hence minimising the room for income tax increases. Suppose that we make the alternative assumptions that the marginal earnings come from self-employment, or that people are paid via a company, so that the full rate of social security contributions is not payable? The top-rate taxpayers may well not spend all their income on goods taxed under VAT. Suppose that they save their extra income or spend it abroad? Then the confidence interval for the revenue-maximising tax rate runs from 46 per cent to 74 per cent.

The third reason concerns the assumption underlying the difference in differences estimate of the key elasticity parameter and goes to the heart of the approach adopted by economists to the analysis of individual behaviour. The elasticity used in the optimal tax calculation is estimated on the assumption that there is no interdependence between the incomes of different people. It is based on the changes in the incomes of those affected by the tax cut (the top 1 per cent) relative to the incomes of those in the next 4 per cent whose tax circumstances have not changed, assuming that this latter group receives the same income as in the absence of the tax change. However, there may be spillover effects. If a cut in taxes causes the top 1 per cent to increase their incomes through increased entrepreneurial effort, and this generates employment for others, then the revenue effect should include in addition the taxes collected on these new employees. This would justify a lower tax rate. It seems to me, however, that the interdependence is more likely to be in the opposite direction: that the increase in income of the top 1 per cent resulting from the tax cut comes at the expence of other taxpayers. In terms of entrepreneurial activities, they may be fishing in the same pool, and the increased income at the top means less opportunity for others.

A specific example of negative spillovers is provided by managerial remuneration. In the past, with high marginal tax rates, top business executives saw little benefit from negotiating higher pay. Instead, they may have sought untaxed fringe benefits or indulged in wasteful corporate spending, but they may also have favoured ploughing back profits into securing faster expansion of their firms. Cuts in top tax rates in the 1980s meant that they switched their effort back to increasing their remuneration or bonuses, and the bill for this has been met by the shareholders. So against the increase in managerial pay has to be set the smaller amount paid out to shareholders, which—if in the form of lower dividends—means lower tax revenue. This is a concrete example of the bargaining effect that has been identified by Thomas Piketty, Emmanuel Saez, and Stefanie Stantcheva, who show that, when this factor is taken into account, there is a significantly higher revenue-maximising top tax rate—specifically, 83 per cent in place of the 56.6 per cent with which we began.[8]

Finally, I believe that a wider view should be taken of social objectives, going beyond revenue maximisation. This could take us far afield, but here I want to bring in just one consideration that is so far missing: the concept of "fairness" as applied to taxation. A frequent complaint about taxation is that it is not "fair." Tax rates are not just a matter of incentives: the change in take-home pay as a consequence of an increase in earnings is also judged in terms of intrinsic fairness. Fairness involves a perceptible link between effort and reward: people deserve to keep at least a reasonable portion of what they earn through increased hours or increased responsibility or a second job. This has been dramatised in terms of the "poverty trap," according to which people on low incomes are unable to improve their situation because an increase in their earnings causes them not just to pay more tax but also to lose income-related benefits. On the addition to their income, they are facing a high implicit marginal rate of tax. It is the *marginal* rate of tax because it applies to the additional income; this is not the same as the *average* rate of tax that is the total tax divided by the total income. The objections to the poverty trap are not only that it discourages work (and savings) but also that it allows people to keep little out of their extra earnings. It is unfair.

Such fairness concerns apply quite generally; they relate not just to the poverty trap but to the whole range of incomes. A maximum fair marginal tax rate—in terms of what people keep as a result of extra effort—should be the same for everyone. Applying this principle suggests a quite different criterion for the top tax rate: that the marginal rate at the top of the income distribution should be the same as that applied at the bottom of the scale. In the UK, the government is introducing the new Universal Credit (an income-tested transfer programme for low-income households) with the stated intention of limiting the withdrawal rate to 65 per cent.

The Proposal for Income Tax Rates

These considerations, notably the last, lead me to propose a top personal income tax rate for the UK of 65 per cent. This would represent a considerable increase on the current (2015) top rate of 45 per cent, but it is not high by historical standards. The UK has had a top income tax rate of 65 per cent or higher for nearly half the past 100 years, and for more than half of those years we have had a Conservative prime minister. The specific rate of 65 per cent may not be directly applicable to other countries, but similar factors are relevant. The same applies to the design of the schedule leading up to the top income tax rate. Here we need to consider the purpose of high marginal rates. For many years, high marginal tax rates on high incomes were seen as a hallmark of a progressive tax policy. However, the mathematical analysis of tax design initiated by William Vickrey and James Mirrlees brought out that, if policy-makers are concerned with the distribution of after-tax income, then the purpose of high marginal tax rates is to raise the *average* tax rate paid by people on higher incomes.[9] The average tax rate for a person is the ratio of total tax paid to total income, and it depends not on the marginal tax rate he or she faces but on the marginal tax rates lower down the scale. This means that, to increase the average tax rate on the well-off, marginal tax rates have to rise lower down the income scale. For the specific case of the UK, the marginal tax rates proposed in Chapter 11 start at 25 per cent (20 per cent on earned income), and rise by steps of 10 per cent until reaching 65 per cent.

> Proposal 8: We should return to a more progressive rate structure for the personal income tax, with marginal rates of tax increasing by ranges of taxable income, up to a top rate of 65 per cent, accompanied by a broadening of the tax base.

As described below, in the case of the UK the base broadening would encompass removal of the investor reliefs listed on the next page and the levying of National Insurance Contributions (NIC) on employers' contributions to private pensions.

Broadening of the Tax Base

Almost invariably, reports on tax reform, in whatever country, call for a broadening of the tax base and criticise governments for "charging more and more on less and less." The narrowing of the tax base comes about as successive governments introduce tax concessions that depart from any principled definition of income, and these barnacles on the fiscal hull prove remarkably tenacious. These concessions are typically "tax expenditures," being equivalent in budgetary terms to cash outlays. A government can, for example, either pay a cash child benefit of Y per child or it can allow taxpayers to deduct a specified amount, Z, from their taxable income. If they pay tax at the rate of 25 per cent on any extra income earned, then the two systems have the same financial consequences where 25 per cent of Z is equal to Y. But the former appears as government spending and the latter as a reduction of tax revenue. Tax expenditures are benefits delivered through the tax system. What is more, they are benefits that increase in value with the marginal tax rate, and hence with taxable income. For a person with a marginal tax rate of 50 per cent, the deduction of Z from taxable income is worth 50 per cent of Z. This led Stanley S. Surrey, onetime assistant secretary of the US Treasury, to call such benefits "upside-down assistance."[10]

In the UK, the list of tax expenditures includes the following: the Enterprise Investment Scheme intended to encourage investment in small unquoted companies; Enterprise Management Incentives, providing a tax advantage to help small companies reward employees with share options valued up to £250,000; Share Incentive Plans, allowing the purchase of shares out of income free of income tax and National Insurance Contributions; and Venture Capital Trusts relief, providing a subsidy for the purchase of newly issued shares by these trusts up to a maximum of £200,000. Here I am proposing to widen the base for the personal income tax, abolishing the above-named investor privileges for both income tax and National Insurance Contributions, whose cost in 2013–2014 is estimated at £795 million.[11]

A major tax expenditure in the UK concerns private provision for pensions. The Mirrlees Committee categorises the different tax treatments of pensions and other savings in terms such as EET and TTE that appear mysterious, but which help clarify the essential issues. T is for Taxed and E is for Exempt. Under the income tax, the current position is that contributions to private pensions by both employees and employers are not included in taxable income; they are exempt (denoted by the first E; if they had been included in taxable income then it would be T). The contributions are accumulated in a fund where income (including capital gains) is tax-free, which gives the second E. The pension in payment is then taxed (T), although since there is an exemption for a 25 per cent lump sum, it should perhaps be a lower case (t). Although it is operated under the UK *income* tax, the present tax treatment corresponds to an *expenditure* tax, since tax is paid only when the money is finally in the hands of the saver. It may be contrasted with the (TTE) treatment of "ordinary" savings where a person saves out of taxed income (T), pays tax on the interest and dividends (T), and can then spend the money with no further taxation (E), or with the (TEE) treatment of "privileged" savings such as cash ISAs (Individual Savings Accounts), where the interest is tax exempt.

The treatment of savings via private pensions on an expenditure tax basis is welcomed by those who espouse the expenditure tax as a matter of principle, but those of us who remain supporters of income as the basis for personal taxation may reasonably ask whether there is an income tax alternative.[12] At least in the case of defined-contribution pension schemes, where there are individual accounts, it would be possible to operate the TEE treatment currently applied to privileged savings under the income tax. Employees would become liable for income tax on the contributions made both by them and by the employer, but would receive the pension benefits tax free (and the tax would not be levied on the investment income of the pension fund). There would have to be transitional arrangements, allowing the collection of tax on pensions arising from contributions made under the present EET regime. As the ordering of the E's and the T's suggests, moving from an EET to a TEE regime would bring forward tax payments. If the revenue from the tax on contributions were used to build up the funds of the Investment Authority, the switch in tax policy could be seen as a switch of investment funds from private to public hands. The size of the private pension funds would be reduced to the extent that after-tax contributions were smaller, but the fact that the resulting pensions would be tax free means that a smaller amount would need to be accumulated. I make no definite recommendation but raise the issue for discussion:

> *Idea to pursue: examination of the case for an "income-tax-based" treatment of contributions to private pensions, along the lines of present "privileged" savings schemes, which would bring forward the payment of tax.*

Base broadening applies not only to the personal income tax but also to National Insurance Contributions, where there is the added complication that the NIC are paid by both employee and employer. In the UK, there is no exemption from employee's NIC on the contributions they make to private pensions (they are paid out of income on which employee's NIC have been paid), and NIC are charged neither on the income of the pension fund nor on the pension paid. There is a TEE regime for employee contributions, just as has been discussed above for an "income-tax-based" treatment under income tax. However, in the case of employers, no NICs are levied on their contributions to private pensions, and the rest of the NIC treatment is the same, so there is in effect an EEE regime. The absence of NICs at an estimated cost in 2013–2014 of £10.8 billion creates a powerful incentive for contributions to be paid by the employer.[13] In view of this, the proposal made here is to take a partial step towards removing the disparity in the treatment of employee and employer contributions by removing the employer's exemption from NIC on their contributions to pension schemes. Such a move may well be criticised as encouraging employers to scale back pension provision, but the absence of any T seems indefensible, and the Mirrlees Review of taxation recommended the elimination of "the inconsistencies that make employer contributions substantially tax privileged relative to employee contributions."[14]

Earned Income Discount

The rise in the share of capital income has led to calls for higher taxes on capital. I discuss below the taxation of wealth, but first I consider the taxation of income from capital. In the past, investment income in a number of countries has been taxed under the personal income tax at a higher rate than earned income, and the return to such a situation would shift the balance of taxation towards capital income. Until 1984, the UK had an investment income surcharge, which raised the tax rate on investment income by up to 15 percentage points. I would like to go back further in time to the *earned income relief* that used to apply in the UK before 1973–1974. In my view, such a system has a lot to recommend it—in the UK and elsewhere. It differs from an investment income surcharge in maintaining the same top rate (65 per cent) for earned and investment income (which may not be easily distinguished at this level), but allowing a lower marginal tax rate on earnings for an initial band. To achieve this effect, the total tax-free amount would become the personal allowance *plus* an *Earned Income Discount,* which would be, say, 20 per cent of earnings.

(Earned income includes self-employment and pension income.) This means, for example, that with a tax threshold of £8,000, a person with only earned income would not pay tax until his or her earnings reached £10,000. On earnings above this level, the tax rate would be 80 per cent of that levied on non-earned income. Unlike the earned income relief, the Earned Income Discount would restrict the tax reduction to those on middle and low earnings by gradually withdrawing the discount once a specified level of earnings was reached. If the rate of withdrawal were to be 40 per cent (twice the rate at which the discount accumulates), then the additional tax-free amount would fall to zero at 1.5 times the specified earnings level. For people with higher total earnings, the income tax payable would be the same as if they received investment income. In the range of earnings where the discount is being withdrawn, the effective marginal tax rate would rise: for example, with a rate of withdrawal of 40 per cent, a tax rate of 25 per cent would become 35 per cent.

The proposed Earned Income Discount resembles the Earned Income Tax Credit (EITC) in force in the US. (The EITC was enacted in the US in 1975, just a couple of years after the UK abandoned the earned income relief.) However, the proposal for an Earned Income Discount differs in that there is no refundable element, and it is not linked to family status. The reasons for these departures are explained in the next chapter; the proposal has to be seen in conjunction with the other measures advocated here. The purpose of the Earned Income Discount is to ensure that the introduction of the progressive tax structure does not raise the tax rate on low levels of earnings (and pensions), a benefit that should not be extended to all levels of earnings. It provides modest help to low earners without conveying the benefit to those with investment income. In both respects, it differs from introducing a new lower income tax band, which benefits both higher earners and those with investment income.

Proposal 9: The government should introduce into the personal income tax an Earned Income Discount, limited to the first band of earnings.

Taxing Inheritance and Property

Wealth can be taxed either on a periodic basis, as with an annual wealth tax, or on its transmission, as with taxes payable on a person's estate when he or she dies, but also including transfers between living persons, known as *gifts inter vivos*. I begin by considering taxes when wealth is transmitted, a subject about which there are strong views. Some people are keen to abolish estate taxes, and legislation was indeed passed in the US repealing the tax for the year 2010 (it was later reinstated). Others believe that, with the growth of inheritance, wealth-transfer taxation should be contributing more to the government budget.

Taxing Wealth Transfers

In the UK today, the revenue from the Inheritance Tax (IHT) is modest. In 2013–2014 it represented some 2 per cent of the amount collected in income tax; fifty years earlier, the figure had been 9 per cent.[15] Of course, such a decline might simply reflect the fact that inheritance is a less important feature of our society than was once the case. If the 1795 tax on powdered wigs were still in force today, we would expect the revenue to be small. However, as Piketty's research for France has shown, inheritance has returned as a potent force. In France, the annual wealth transmitted was some 20 to 25 per cent of national income in the nineteenth century, but fell to around 2.5 per cent in 1950. Since 1950, however, it has risen and was around 20 per cent of national income in 2010.[16] In the UK, the rise has been less marked, but it has still taken inherited wealth from 4.8 per cent of national income in 1977 to 8.2 per cent in 2006.[17]

More effective taxation of wealth transfers in the UK could be achieved either through converting IHT into a lifetime capital receipts tax or by abolishing IHT and taxing inheritances received under the personal income tax. The latter has a number of attractions, not least that it could be presented in terms of abolishing a whole tax. Integration with the income tax was indeed proposed in Canada in the 1960s by the Carter Commission as part of its plan for reforming the tax system: gifts and inheritances should be "taxed as income to the donee, on the same footing as such various receipts as wage and salary income, dividend payments, royalties, and other familiar components of taxable income, without allowing at the same time any deduction of the amounts transferred from the donor's taxable income."[18] The last qualification is an important one. The transfer is not meant to be deductible for the giver. If it were, then the revenue consequences could well be negative, and in any event the tax charge should be a tax on the *use* of income. Of course, there would have to be averaging provisions to allow for the lumpy nature of capital receipts. In the UK income tax, there are provisions for authors and artists who have fluctuating profits to average their profits for successive tax years, since they would otherwise pay a large amount of tax in a good year and little or no tax in a bad year. For inheritances a longer period of averaging would be required. Otherwise, people inheriting houses worth, say, £250,000, would find themselves paying up to 65 per cent in tax (under the schedule proposed earlier in this chapter) even if this is the only amount they ever inherit. But if the receipt were to be averaged over a period such as ten years, then the integration with the income tax would begin to approach the lifetime cumulation period.

My own preference is for a lifetime capital receipts tax, replacing the Inheritance Tax. The idea of such a tax is not revolutionary; it was proposed more than 100 years ago by John Stuart Mill: there should be "a heavy graduated succession duty on all inheritances exceeding [a] minimum amount, which is sufficient to aid but not supersede personal exertion."[19] Under such a tax, every legacy or gift received by a person would be recorded from the date of initiation of the tax, and the tax payable determined by the sum received to date. The tax would include all gifts inter vivos above an additional modest annual exemption. Transfers between spouses or persons in civil partnerships would not be taxed. To give an example, a person receives £50,000 from an aunt's estate in the first year. Suppose that this is below the threshold (set, say, at £100,000 per person), in which case no tax is payable. Five years later, the person receives a further bequest of £80,000. This takes the total to £130,000, which is £30,000 above the threshold, so that tax is due on £30,000 at, say, a rate of 20 per cent. An uncle then gives the same person £20,000. Tax is payable on the entire gift. If the uncle had instead made the gift to the person's brother, and the brother had not previously had any inheritance (or gift), then no tax would have been payable.

> Proposal 10: Receipts of inheritance and gifts inter vivos should be taxed under a progressive lifetime capital receipts tax.

In designing a lifetime capital receipts tax, the UK can clearly learn from the experience on the other side of the Irish Sea with the Capital Acquisitions Tax introduced in the Republic of Ireland in the 1970s. This comprises taxes on gifts and inheritances and a tax applied to discretionary trusts. An important issue is the extent of reliefs provided for farms and businesses; under the present UK Inheritance Tax, the cost of these reliefs in 2013–2014 is estimated at £800 million.[20] Robin Boadway, Emma Chamberlain, and Carl Emmerson describe the existing reliefs as "rather unsatisfactory and arbitrary in effect. These reliefs should be better targeted."[21] They cite the Irish experience and their limitation of reliefs to working farmers. The Irish tax threshold depends on the relationship with the donor, as in the old UK Legacy and Succession Duties (abolished in 1949). No such provision is envisaged here, and it certainly seems unlikely that any new UK legislation will follow the Irish model in having a "Favourite nephew/niece relief"!

In Chapter 6 I proposed that the revenue from the lifetime capital receipts tax in the UK be allocated to the payment of the minimum inheritance for all. (The overall budget balance for all proposals, as applied to the UK, is considered in Chapter 11.) The revenue from the existing Inheritance Tax, coupled with a substantial reduction in the business and agricultural reliefs, could finance a capital endowment of some £5,000 for all when they reach the age of eighteen. The revenue from the proposed new lifetime tax is not readily predicted. The base would be broadened in that gifts inter vivos would be covered in full (at present gifts are exempt if the donor lives for at least seven years after making the gift, and rates are reduced when the donor lives between three and seven years). On the other hand, the tax is levied on the amount received, which is at the discretion of the testator. A rich person could in principle pass on all of his or her estate without the recipients being liable, if they are all below the threshold. The choice of the threshold and rate structure would have to balance these considerations. However, I suggest that, in place of the present single-rate system, where Inheritance Tax becomes payable at the single rate of 40 per cent once the threshold is passed, there should be a graduated structure of rates, similar to that proposed earlier for the personal income tax, although in the case of inherited wealth there may be grounds for a top marginal rate exceeding 65 per cent.

The present forms of inheritance taxation are unpopular, and the aim of my proposal is to shift the mind-set with which the tax is approached.

The key element in the proposal is that people are taxed on the amount received rather than the amount left, as happens under the current system. A tax on giving would be converted into a tax on receiving. (The same would be true if receipts were taxed under the income tax.) With a progressive rate structure, this switch would provide a direct incentive to spread wealth more widely. People could pass on their wealth tax free if it were transferred to people who have received little so far in lifetime receipts. In this way, it could contribute to reducing both gender inequality and inequality across generations. Most important, the new tax would be patently directed at seeking to secure a more level playing field and thus contributing to reducing inequality of opportunity—a goal that, as discussed in Chapter 1, enjoys wide support.

Taxation of Owner-Occupied Housing Property and Reform of the Council Tax

I turn now to the local taxation of property. This is not a promising topic. In his lectures *The History of Local Rates in England* delivered at the London School of Economics in 1895, shortly after the foundation of that institution, Edwin Cannan admitted freely that "it would be absurd to study a subject so dry, not to say so odious, as local rates except with a view to practical aims. We do not study such subjects from a love of truth in the abstract or to while away a wet Sunday afternoon, but because . . . we hope we may learn something."[22] Taking the UK experience as a case study, we can indeed learn a lot about fiscal redistribution and how reform can (and cannot) be put into effect. The local taxation of property in the UK has in fact had a particularly chequered—and dramatic—history.

For many years, local government in the UK was financed, as far as domestic taxpayers were concerned, from "domestic rates" that were, in broad terms, related to property values. The Conservative government in the 1980s decided to replace this system with a radically different one: a flat-rate charge, officially called the Community Charge, but which popularly became known as the "poll tax." The highly regressive tax provoked widespread opposition and taxpayer resistance. There were riots in British cities. In time, the prime minister resigned and her successor announced that the poll tax would be abandoned. In its place came the

Council Tax, introduced in 1993, charged on occupiers of domestic property in Great Britain (Northern Ireland continues to have domestic rates). In England and Scotland, houses are placed into one of eight bands (the lowest being A and the highest H) according to the estimated market value on 1 April 1991.[23] The overall level of Council Tax is set locally, but the ratios between the amounts charged for each band are set centrally. These ratios embody a regressive structure. Houses at the start of band H were (in 1991) worth 4.7 times those at the start of band D, but were taxed at only twice as much. The adoption of a regressive structure has been justified on the grounds that the new local tax is based on the benefit principle in contrast to the earlier domestic rating system, which was closer to being based on ability to pay. These two principles of taxation—benefit and ability to pay—are quite different. The former implies that taxes should be related to the benefits received from government spending; the latter implies that taxes should be related to income, wealth, or other measures of capacity to pay. The switch to a benefit principle for local taxes in the UK is now largely forgotten, no doubt because the earlier version—the poll tax—was even more regressive. But the shift to the Council Tax undoubtedly contributed to rendering the after-tax income distribution more unequal than if the tax had been levied on the obvious benchmark of proportionality with property values.

A proportional tax on property values—rather than a regressive tax—is applied in many countries. Most local governments in the US impose a property tax, and this is typically based on a constant tax rate applied to a specified proportion of the market value of the property. The case for a proportional tax on property value in the UK is made in the report of the Mirrlees Review of taxation, where it is estimated that a tax of 0.6 per cent on current property values would have been revenue-neutral in 2009–2010. This, the report argued, should be accompanied by revaluation: "The absurdity of the status quo becomes ever more apparent. Any property tax requires regular revaluations, and this process should begin as soon as possible."[24] Updating their analysis to 2014–2015, the tax rate becomes 0.54 per cent, on the basis of an average Council Tax bill of £1,468 and an average house price of £271,000.[25] Figure 7.3 shows the difference in tax paid by the occupants of houses of differing value, compared with those paid under the Council Tax in 2014–2015. As may be seen, there is a considerable difference for houses valued at £500,000 and more. The comedian Griff Rhys Jones has drawn attention to the sums involved. Apparently, his house in London's Fitzroy Square is valued at £7 million (way off Figure 7.3 to the right), on which the proportional tax at 0.54 per cent would be some £38,000. This is indeed a large sum, and in the case of valuable properties there should be provision for payment in the form of an equity participation in the value of the house. Such a provision would help, for example, pensioners living in a valuable house who have a relatively small cash income. Of course, the change in local taxation would decrease the value of many large houses: the burden of the tax increase would thus fall on current owners rather than on those who subsequently buy the house at a lower price. (Economists refer to this as the "capitalisation" of tax changes.) It also seems clear that the present Council Tax payment on the £7 million seven-bedroom house in central London of £2,640.96, some 0.04 per cent of the property valuation, is remarkably low.[26] Put differently, the proposed level of taxation at 0.54 per cent is a lot lower than that under the earlier domestic rating system: at the start of the 1970s domestic rates were on average rather more than 1 per cent of property values.[27]

The difference between the two curves in Figure 7.3 illustrates the point made earlier about the regressive nature of the change made in local taxation when the UK moved first to the poll tax and then to the Council Tax, from the earlier domestic rating system that had been broadly of a proportional character. This shift in local taxation was one of the elements defining the "Inequality Turn" of the 1980s. The switch to a benefit principle, from a tax linked to ability to pay, was a move towards greater inequality. If our aim is to secure a less unequal society, then a clear contribution can be made by moving the UK local public finances back to taxing according to a principle that gives more weight to social justice.

> Proposal 11: There should be a proportional, or progressive, property tax based on up-to-date property assessments.

In the UK context, the specific proposal made is that the Council Tax should become a single-rate, revenue-neutral property tax based on revalued property assessments, with the possibility of paying, where the

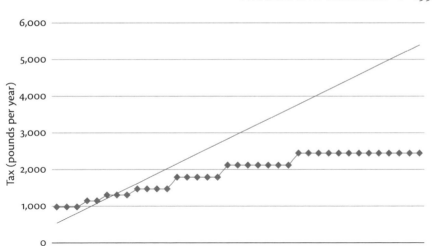

FIGURE 7.3: Property tax (Council Tax vs. proposed proportional) in the UK, 2014–2015

This graph shows the Council Tax currently paid by property owners and the tax that property owners would pay with a 0.54 property tax rate. A person living in a house valued at £2 million pays at present Council Tax of less than £3,000 per year; with the proposed proportional property tax, the payment would be £10,800.

sums are substantial, in the form of an equity stake in the value of the house.

An Annual Wealth Tax

I turn now to the annual wealth tax, which is getting renewed attention in a number of countries. This idea was examined in the UK in the 1970s but not pursued by the then Labour government. In his autobiography, the Chancellor of the Exchequer at the time, Denis Healey, drew the lesson that "you should never commit yourself in Opposition to new taxes unless you have a very good idea how they will operate in practice. We had committed ourselves to a Wealth Tax; but in five years I found it impossible to draft one which would yield enough revenue to be worth the administrative cost and the political hassle."[28] However, times have changed, and according to Martin Weale, there are "reasons for thinking that the 1970s arguments might have been presented rather differently in the current circumstances. . . . One suspects that the 1970s Labour government would have been put off less easily than they were thirty years ago."[29]

Among the reasons for considering an annual wealth tax more favourably in the UK today than forty years ago are the much higher level of income inequality and the rise in the ratio of personal wealth to Gross Domestic Product. There have been major changes in this ratio over the postwar period. In the immediate postwar decades the ratio fell, but from the early 1980s it began to rise again, and personal wealth in the 2000s was some five times Gross Domestic Product. What caused the increase? Have the British, like the Chinese, had a soaring savings ratio? It is true that the household savings ratio increased from the 1950s to the 1970s, but it reached no more than 14 per cent, and then it declined: "The share of their income that households saved fell steadily over much of the period 1995 to 2007."[30] According to Ehsan Khoman and Martin Weale, "it is clear that saving by households has played little role in the accumulation of household wealth."[31] Their assessment is that the rise in personal wealth was driven by asset price rises, noting that over the period house prices had risen at a rate of 3 per cent per year faster than gross disposable income, that bond prices had risen as interest rates fell, and that share prices had risen by 4.7 per cent per year in real terms. In the previous chapter, we saw how households in the UK have benefitted since 1980 from the sales of state-owned housing (council houses) at discounted prices, and we have similarly seen the privatisation of public companies. As discussed in the previous chapter, these represent a significant transfer, having reduced considerably the net worth of the public sector.

To the extent that the increase in wealth is due to asset revaluations, there is a case that "given the source of the wealth, a more stringent capital gains tax might be more appropriate than a wealth tax."[32] However, after the event, this would be like bolting the proverbial stable door. There are therefore grounds for re-examining the possibility of introducing an annual wealth tax in the UK. In such a re-examination, it would be necessary to take account of other ways in which circumstances have changed since the 1970s with regard to the globalisation of the economy.

One important question is the extent to which national governments could effectively collect such a tax, without collective action at the EU level and stronger agreements on information exchange. There are lessons to be learned from the French experience with the Impôt de Solidarité sur la Fortune (France's annual wealth tax), regarded by Piketty as only a mixed success.[33] He favours a global wealth tax, to which I turn in the next section.

To sum up:
Idea to pursue: a re-examination of the case for an annual wealth tax and the prerequisites for its successful introduction.

Global Taxation and a Minimum Tax for Corporations

In the penultimate chapter of *Capital in the Twenty-First Century,* Piketty argues that we need new instruments to reduce inequality. He says that "the ideal tool would be a progressive global tax on capital, coupled with a very high level of international financial transparency."[34] He gives the example of taking a regional step in this direction and setting, in a European context, a tax threshold of €1 million, with a tax rate of 1 per cent on wealth between €1 million and €5 million, and of 2 per cent on wealth above this amount, estimating that this would bring in revenue equivalent to 2 per cent of national income. Oxfam has called for a global tax on wealth, setting the threshold higher at $1 billion and the tax rate at 1.5 per cent, which it estimates would raise $74 billion worldwide.[35]

Such a global tax is described by Piketty as "utopian," requiring "a very high and no doubt unrealistic level of international cooperation."[36] It is not, however, unimaginable that the existing steps towards tackling harmful international tax practices, under the auspices of OECD (discussed further in Chapter 10), may lead to the creation of a World Tax Administration. Such a WTA could start by creating a "global tax regime" for personal taxpayers. In a presentation to the Landau Working Group on New International Financial Contributions in 2004, I suggested the establishment of a status of global taxpayer, which would allow individuals to apply to opt out of the national (and subnational) taxes on income, capital gains, and wealth by entering a global tax regime.[37] Combining this idea with that of a global tax on capital, the entry price could be set at a minimum net worth (at least $1 billion), with a minimum tax payment based on a progressive wealth tax. Participation would depend on an agreed valuation of net worth, which would be made public knowledge. As suggested by Piketty, the kind of net worth tax schedule described above would typically involve significantly higher tax payments: "in France, the United States, and all other countries we have studied, the largest incomes declared on income tax returns are generally no more than a few tens of millions of euros or dollars."[38] Proceeds would, in my proposal, be shared among the country of tax residence, other participating countries, and the financing of development and global public goods.

Participation in the global tax regime would be voluntary on both sides. As we have seen, this proposal is expected to yield higher tax receipts, but why—if that is the case—should any taxpayer take part? How can it be a positive-sum game? There are, in fact, definite advantages to the taxpayer in that he or she has to deal with only one tax authority, and the regime would create greater certainty about the tax liabilities. In addition, as we have seen with the *Forbes List,* the *Sunday Times Rich List,* and similar public rankings, appearing in this company carries with it a certain prestige.

Taxing Multinational Corporations

"Company X pays only £y million Corporation Tax on sales of £y billion" has been a recurring recent headline. There is much concern about the failure of multinationals to pay taxes in countries where they have large sales, shifting their profits to countries where the Corporation Tax is lower. Does this matter? According to one view, the Corporation Tax is simply a form of withholding on the income tax due from individual shareholders and bondholders. If that were the sole function, then the small amount paid would not be a matter for concern, provided that the owners of Company X shares, and the bondholders, paid the full amount of income tax in their country of tax residence. If all the shares and bonds are held by foreigners, then no tax is due, even where Company X has massive sales in the home country.

Such a response is not, however, likely to satisfy those concerned with tax justice, and for good reason. The rationale for the tax on corporations is not simply that they act as a collecting agent for the personal income tax but also that corporate status conveys privileges, particularly that of limited liability. The Corporation Tax is a levy on the resulting benefits and a source of revenue to finance redistribution. In their public finance textbook, Richard and Peggy Musgrave describe the situation well; the corporation is "a legal entity with an existence of its own, a powerful factor in economic and social decision-making . . . being a separate entity, the corporation also has a separate taxable capacity."[39] They immediately go on to dismiss this view, but it is one that has considerable appeal, even more so today in the age of multinationals than when they wrote in 1989. More generally, corporations benefit from the infrastructure of the countries in which they sell: the physical assets, such as roads, the legal structure, and the administrative apparatus of the state. A payment of 0.1 per cent of sales may not be regarded as sufficient to cover this contribution to the company's profitability.

What can be done to ensure that corporations with extensive economic presence in a country are making a more reasonable contribution to its public finances? The US tax authorities were faced with an analogous issue for income taxation in the 1960s. As described by George Break and Joseph Pechman, "stimulated by the dramatic revelation in early 1969 [that twenty-one persons] with income of over $1 million paid no federal income tax at all, Congress added to the tax law a feature that may become an important means of controlling excessive tax avoidance."[40] This feature was the "minimum tax," which for both persons and corporations limits the tax advantage that can be received from certain tax exemptions. Break and Pechman go on to say that "the minimum tax is regarded by many as a weak and inadequate attack on tax privileges," but it has continued to play a significant role in the US tax system. It does suggest one route forward to reduce the extent to which corporations use tax shelters to minimise their tax liability. In addition to steps being taken to restrict the activities of tax havens, it would be possible to set a national minimum tax that would limit the tax relief that was available on interest paid and other deductions. The minimum could be defined in terms of company earnings before interest, tax, depreciation, and amortisation. Corporations would then be required to pay the greater of the regular tax or the alternative minimum tax. Or the minimum tax could be based on the value of sales within the tax jurisdiction. The companies accused of not paying Corporation Tax to the countries where they operate have always argued that they meet all their tax obligations under the fiscal law; this suggests that we need to change the law, and the introduction of an alternative minimum tax is one way that this could be done.

Ideas to pursue: A global tax regime for personal taxpayers, based on total wealth, and a minimum tax for corporations.

Chapter 8 ::

Social Security for All

The welfare state has in the past played a major role in reducing inequality. It is the primary vehicle by which our societies seek to ensure a minimum level of resources for all members. One reason for rising inequality in recent decades has been the scaling back of social protection at a time when needs are growing, not shrinking. Ive Marx, Brian Nolan, and Javier Olivera conclude in their review of antipoverty policy in rich countries that "no advanced economy achieved a low level of inequality and/ or relative income poverty with a low level of social spending, regardless of how well that country performed on other dimensions that matter for poverty."[1] I see it as an essential part of the proposals made for reducing inequality that the additional tax revenue raised by the measures described in Chapter 7 be employed in part to finance an expansion of spending on social protection.

How should such additional money be spent? In part, it is a matter of reversing the cuts made in the past in a number of countries. In the UK the sharp rise in overall income inequality in the second half of the 1980s coincided with a substantial cut in the level of social security benefits. The basic state pension was reduced, relative to average net take-home pay, by around one-fifth, which not only increased the income gap between pensioners and the working population but also widened the difference between relatively fortunate pensioners with private occupational pensions and those dependent solely on the state pension.[2] Reversing such decisions, and those made more recently during austerity measures, is one key step towards returning to the lower levels of inequality successfully achieved in the past.

Increasing benefit rates is not, however, enough. We also need to seize the opportunity to reconsider the structure of the welfare state. Many countries have made significant changes to social benefits in recent decades, particularly reducing coverage and increasing the degree of income-testing. These developments were often intended to improve the degree of targeting, increasing the proportion of benefit payments that went to those at the bottom of the income distribution, but in the event they contributed to increasing inequality—although this has not been sufficiently recognised. Errors of one kind—making unjustified payments—may have been reduced, but errors in the opposite direction—failure to reach those in need—were increased. In my view, we shall make progress towards tackling poverty only if we adopt a different approach.

We need to reconsider the welfare state for the obvious reason that the world is changing. We saw in the case of Latin America that the new social transfer programmes associated with declining inequality and poverty operated outside the traditional social insurance system, which had not kept pace with the evolving labour market. I argued in Chapter 5 that OECD countries need to come to terms with a changing labour market, and that this evidently requires change in a social insurance system that was designed on the basis of people holding single, full-time jobs. I begin, therefore, with the structure of social transfers—an issue of concern to all countries.

The Design of Social Security

I once planned a paper whose title contained no words: "SI vs SA vs BI." Its purpose was to contrast the three main forms of social security: social insurance (SI), social assistance (SA), and basic income (BI). In most countries, the system of income maintenance contains all three elements, and some people receive help under all three types of system. But the balance among the different programmes is important, and that balance has changed over time.

The key features of the three forms are summarised in Table 8.1, where the essential differences are highlighted. It should be noted that not all benefits fit into the classification: disability benefits are an important class that is missing. Readers are no doubt familiar with social insurance and social assistance, but the idea of a basic income needs some explanation. BI is a payment made to all citizens, regardless of their labour-market status, financed by general taxation. Such an idea may sound outlandish, but it is in fact closely related to the personal exemption in the income tax. Under most personal income tax regimes, no tax is paid until income reaches a certain threshold. When the income tax was introduced in the UK in 1799, no tax was payable on incomes below £100 a year. At that time, if a person's income passed £100, he or she paid tax on all of the income, but that has since been replaced by a system in which tax is paid only on the excess of income over the threshold. This means that the threshold is of interest to all taxpayers. If the tax rate is 30 per cent, then a £100 threshold saves the taxpayer £30 of tax. But the threshold is worth less to people below the tax threshold: a person with £50 income is only saved from paying £15 of tax. This led to proposals that the tax threshold be replaced by a uniform cash credit, with all income being subject to tax. Such a cash credit is a basic income, and it was proposed in the United States under the title of a "negative income tax" separately by two American Nobel Prize–winners with contrasting political views: Milton Friedman (monetarist and advisor to President Reagan) and James Tobin (Keynesian and advisor to President Kennedy). The tax becomes negative in the sense that people below the threshold would be receiving a payment rather than paying tax.

Over time, the balance between the different types of social transfer has changed, as is illustrated for the case of the UK in Figure 8.1. The share going to SI (National Insurance) has shrunk from nearly three-quarters (72 per cent) to under one-half. The share fell initially as a result of an increase in social assistance under the Conservative government of the early 1970s, including the introduction of an income-tested benefit for families with children (Family Income Supplement, later Family Credit), widely regarded as an unsatisfactory alternative to the Conservatives' 1970 election promise to raise family allowances. The 1974–1979 Labour government raised family allowances, converting them and the child tax allowances into the present Child Benefit, which is a basic income for children. The bulk of the fall in the share of social insurance took place under the subsequent Conservative government from 62 per cent in 1979 to 49 per cent in 1997. The Labour government of 1997 to 2010 initially raised the Child Benefit, but overall income-tested benefits were expanded to reach 44 per cent, reflecting the growth of tax credits. The latest innovation, under the Coalition government, is the Universal Credit.

TABLE 8.1. *Essential differences between forms of social security*

	Social insurance (SI)	Social assistance (SA) / tax credits	Basic income (BI)
Entitlement	On basis of contributions	On basis of current resources (income and assets)	Citizenship (?)[a]
Eligibility condition	Depends on labour-market status	Depends on labour-market status	Independent of labour-market status
Unit of assessment	Individual (possibly with extra payments for dependents)	Family unit (or household)	Individual
Finance	Largely by contributions	General taxation	General taxation

a. The reasons for inserting a question mark regarding entitlement to a basic income are discussed below in text.

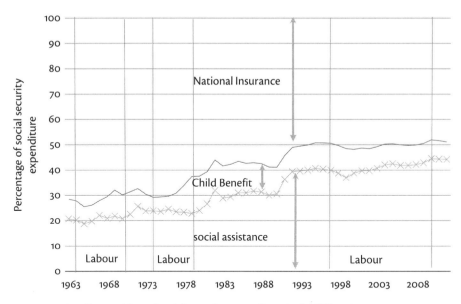

FIGURE 8.1: Composition of social security expenditure in the UK, 1963–2012

This graph shows the proportion of the total social security expenditure of the UK going to National Insurance, Child Benefit, and social assistance. Time periods not marked Labour had a Conservative government, except after 2010, when there was a Coalition government of Conservatives and Liberal Democrats.

Greater use is now made of income-testing. I can understand the short-term appeal of such a move, but in my judgement this is the wrong direction for the long-run.

The Twin Failures of Means-Testing

There are two major reasons that means-testing is the wrong approach. The first arises from the effects of the high marginal tax rates created by the withdrawal of income-tested benefits, coupled with the existing rates of income tax and social security contributions. A situation is created where a person can do little to raise the take-home pay of the family by increasing gross earnings. In the UK the resulting poverty trap has been illustrated by the calculations made by the Mirrlees Committee: "Once annual earnings have reached £6,420 [equivalent to twenty-two hours a week at the national minimum wage], entitlement to tax credits begins to fall, and this increases the [marginal tax rate] by 39 percentage points to 70% . . . For a family with two children and a full-time earner, the 70% [falls back to 31%] once gross annual earnings reach £28,150." The latter would be equivalent to working forty hours a week at an hourly rate close to 2.5 times the national minimum wage, which demonstrates that a wide band of earnings was affected.[3] Since that time, the benefit system has changed for people receiving the Universal Credit, but the withdrawal rate applied to net earnings is 65 per cent. For a person subject as well to income tax and employee National Insurance Contributions, the cumulative marginal tax rate is 76.2 per cent. There is still a poverty trap.

In the past, the impact of high marginal tax rates lower down the scale was dismissed on the grounds that many people had little discretion about their working hours or intensity of work. However, even if that were true in the past, it has become less so in a labour market where there is greater fluidity. The growth of self-employment is just one reason for attaching greater weight to the possible disincentive effects of income-testing. This is reinforced by further considerations. The example described above assumed a single earner in the family, but more typical today are two-earner couples, and the high marginal tax rates apply to both, doubling the potential disincentive. What is more, as discussed in the previous chapter, marginal tax rates are not just a matter of incentives: the change in take-home pay as a consequence of an increase in earnings is also judged in terms of its intrinsic fairness. Fairness involves a perceptible link between effort and reward: people deserve to keep at least a reasonable portion of what they earn through increased hours or taking increased responsibility or a second job.

The second reason for concern about the growth of income-testing is that not everyone who is entitled to benefits claims them. Unlike the SI benefits and Child Benefit, income-tested benefits have frequently failed to achieve close to 100 per cent coverage. A significant minority of those entitled have failed to claim. The report *The Social Situation in the European Union 2008* concluded that "non-take-up of benefits appears to be widespread," citing evidence from Austria, Denmark, Finland, France, Germany, Greece, and Portugal.[4] The review by Manos Matsaganis, Alari Paulus, and Holly Sutherland for Europe reports claim rates, for a variety of different means-tested benefits, ranging from 72–81 per cent in the

Netherlands and 72 per cent in Portugal, to 65–67 per cent in France, 50–60 per cent in Finland, down to 44 per cent in Austria, 33 per cent in Germany, and 30 per cent in Ireland.[5] In the US, the official study of the Earned Income Tax Credit found that the claim rate in 2005 was 75 per cent.[6] In Britain failure to collect benefits was one of the important findings of the book *The Poor and the Poorest* that caused such a stir in 1965 and led to the establishment of the Child Poverty Action Group.[7] The take-up rate has improved since then, but in 2010–2011 the central estimate of take-up for the UK Child Tax Credit in terms of numbers was 83 per cent. This meant that a significant number (1.2 million families) of those eligible were not benefitting from the programme.[8] Nonclaiming continues despite the efforts at the national and local levels to publicise benefits.

Persistence of unclaimed benefits raises serious questions about an antipoverty strategy that relies on means-tested schemes. It is possible that failure to claim arises from misunderstanding. People may have previously been rejected and believe themselves to be ineligible, whereas the eligibility conditions or their own circumstances have changed in a way that renders them entitled. But non-take-up arises on account of shortcomings that are intrinsic to the means-testing approach. First, the inherent complexity of income-testing creates barriers to claiming. Anyone with experience of welfare knows that complicated form-filling spells trouble, particularly for those with limited literacy (including computer literacy). The form required for Child Tax Credit in the UK in 2013 was ten pages long, and the accompanying notes were eighteen pages. A claim required information about the applicant's employer and registration information from the childcare provider. Assembling the relevant information and completing the form require time, and time is a scarce resource. Non-take-up may be a rational response to the circumstances in which families find themselves "time poor."[9] The second intrinsic reason is that receipt of means-tested benefits, as opposed to universal benefits, is stigmatising. This has long been a concern in the UK. When asked in 1824 by the Select Committee on Labourers' Wages whether he had ever applied for an addition to his wages, Thomas Smart, an agricultural worker, replied, "No, I never did. I always try to do without."[10] We live in very different times, but it remains the case that the capacity of a transfer scheme to provide effective income support depends on how that support is viewed by the potential beneficiaries. Here the problem is intensified by the adverse publicity attached to benefit claimants in the media and the negative comments of politicians. If the receipt of benefit is seen as an unfortunate sign of failure, if such benefits are administered in ways inconsistent with twenty-first-century ideas about human dignity, the system is not fit for purpose. Incomplete take-up can be seen as the (sickening) canary in the mine: a warning that the scheme of social protection is seriously flawed.

Conclusion So Far

I should make clear just what I am, and what I am not, saying. I am not arguing that all income-tested transfers are necessarily ineffective. In many countries they play a significant role in reducing the risk and extent of poverty. In the case of the UK, there can be little doubt that, without the expansion of family-income-tested tax credits under the Labour government of 1997 to 2010, the reduction in child poverty would have been less and inequality would have been higher. Means-tested transfers are better than nothing. But I believe that the income-testing approach is flawed, and that, for a sustainable long-term solution, we need to explore the alternative routes of either reformed social insurance or a basic income. This is why William Beveridge, the architect of the postwar welfare state in Britain, saw social insurance as the cornerstone of his Plan, with benefits provided "as a right" without any test of means, stressing the "strength of popular objection to any kind of means test."[11] But before coming to social insurance, I consider the basic income alternative.

The Key Role of Child Benefit

A basic income does indeed exist in many countries in that a payment for all children, without reference to the family's labour-market status or resources, is a basic income for children. In my view, a substantial Child Benefit is central to any programme to reduce inequality. In making this case, I am not arguing for the superiority of cash transfers over services. I believe that Child Benefit is complementary with investment in infrastructure and services that aid children; improvements in cash transfers and in benefits in kind should go hand in hand. As the University of Chicago Nobel Prize–winner James Heckman has argued, "the investments we make today in disadvantaged young children promote social mobility, create opportunity and foster a vibrant, healthy and inclusive society and economy."[12] He rightly emphasises the future return on investment in high-quality early childhood programmes. At the same time, we have to consider the current circumstances of children and their families. They also require cash in their hands.

The proposal for Child Benefit is a challenge to countries such as the US that do not have a universal child benefit programme. As Timothy Smeeding and Jane Waldfogel have argued, this challenge is highlighted by a comparison of the child poverty trends in the US and the UK. Figure 8.2 is an updated version of their graph showing the diverging trends in the child poverty rates, measured with a poverty threshold that has constant purchasing power. In the US case, the threshold is the official poverty measure, which in 1998–1999 was some 30 per cent of median income, which is evidently lower than the 50 per cent taken in the case of the UK in their study.[13] It is the changes over time on which we should focus. In contrast to the UK, where child poverty fell sharply in the 1990s, the US has not seen a significant reduction. There have been periods (the Clinton presidency) when child poverty fell in the US, but the overall picture is disappointing. Child poverty in 2013 in the US was one-third higher than in 1969. Existing policies, such as the Earned Income Tax Credit, have not succeeded, and new measures are needed.

Many countries face the challenge of child poverty—see Figure 8.3, which applies the more common relative poverty standard of 60 per cent of the contemporary median income (the difference in definition accounts for the figures for the UK and the US being higher than in Figure 8.2). Half the countries shown had child poverty rates in 2010 of 20 per cent or higher. To meet this challenge, I believe that we have to increase substantially the cash support offered to families with children. What form should this take? Faced with the problem of child poverty, a natural response is to advocate the targeting of benefits to low-income families. However, we have just seen the flaws that undermine the means-testing approach, and to these considerations I add—as explained below—those

FIGURE 8.2: Child poverty rates in the US and UK, 1969–2014

This graph shows the percentage of children (persons under age 18) who live in poverty. For the US, poverty is the official poverty line. For the UK, poverty is defined as 50% of the 1998–1999 median income held constant in real terms.

concerned with generational and gender equity. For these reasons, I believe that the Child Benefit should be paid with respect to all children, regardless of the income of the family. In the UK context, we should eliminate the current ineligibility of families at higher incomes, which has denied Child Benefit to some 700,000 children.[14] At the same time, I do favour the tapering that can be achieved by making Child Benefit taxable. Higher-income families should receive the benefit, but it should be subject to income tax. Where husbands and wives are taxed independently rather than jointly, the Child Benefit should be taxable in the hands of the recipient (typically it is paid to the mother). A Child Benefit that is substantial but taxable, combined with a progressive rate structure as proposed in the previous chapter, is an effective way of ensuring that all families receive some recognition of their family responsibilities but that more is given per child to those on lower incomes. If the income tax rates rise in steps from 25 per cent to 65 per cent, the net Child Benefit

Percentage of children in poverty

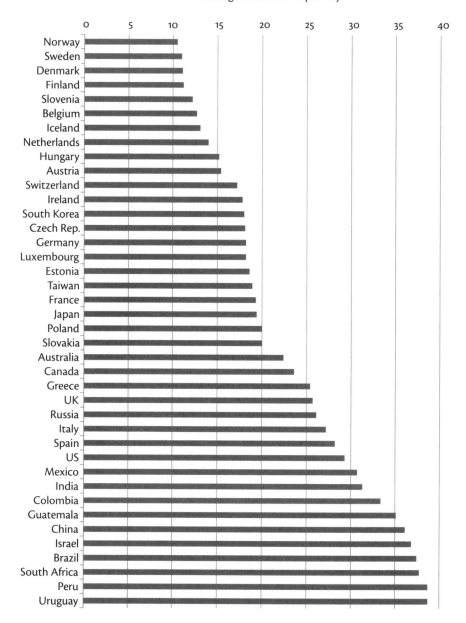

FIGURE 8.3: Child poverty rates in selected countries, c. 2010

This graph shows the percentage of children (persons under age 18) living in poverty. Poverty is defined as 60% of the median equivalised disposable income in each country.

to a rich family is less than half that to a family paying the lowest marginal rate.

The Case for Child Benefit

Advocacy of universal (but taxable) Child Benefit appears to fly in the face of economic advice, which in many countries has favoured income-tested family benefits. In the UK, the Institute for Fiscal Studies proposed an Integrated Family Support scheme targeted via income-testing towards low-income families. Their study was prepared for the review chaired by Sir James Mirrlees, and draws on his highly influential article on the optimal design of income taxation and income maintenance.[15] Income-testing is equivalent to raising the marginal income tax rate, since earning an extra £1 means that a person loses some part of the family benefit, until the benefit is finally extinguished. In this way, the cost is contained and the working poor can be helped without the need for substantially higher taxes on the better-off. The difference between the income-testing strategy and the Child Benefit strategy I have proposed can be represented in terms of where marginal tax rates are highest. With income-testing, marginal tax rates are highest on those with low incomes; with the alternative strategy proposed here, the marginal tax rates are raised on those with middle and upper incomes. (It is important to remember that a higher marginal rate does not imply a higher average rate, and that many people in the middle-income group would be better off.) The Mirrlees formula for an optimal tax scheme indicates that marginal rates should be high either where there are relatively few people or where people are relatively unresponsive to the magnitude of the marginal tax rate. Whether this favours one strategy over the other depends, then, on empirical matters—the distribution of income and the variation in response—but there are certainly empirical studies that find that the labour-supply response falls as one moves up the income scale, implying that the marginal tax rate should rise with the level of income, as with the proposal made here.[16]

There is, moreover, a second crucial difference between the two types of scheme: the Child Benefit strategy would continue to make transfers to families with children at all income levels. This means that we have to consider issues of equity, not just between rich and poor, but also between those with and without children. We have to examine the way in which families with and without children are valued in our society—an issue not discussed in the standard economic analysis. Should we, other things equal, attach a higher value to £1 received by the person with a child than to a person with no children? Some people would say "no," arguing that having children today is a "lifestyle choice" and that the parent should be treated no differently than if he or she made a different choice. For those making such a judgement, the withdrawal of Child Benefit from those with higher incomes would indeed be the distributionally preferred policy, since income would be taken from those who on average were better off. Such a "lifestyle choice" view, however, attaches no weight to the welfare of the child.[17] Many people would regard this as unacceptable. Surely the children should count in their own right in our social judgements. A single person with a child should be counted as two people. The lifestyle choice view runs counter to the widely adopted practice in distributional analyses of adjusting household income for differences in family composition, as discussed in Chapter 1. Children are here today and should count today—as well as being an important part of the future. This is further reinforced by the demands of intergenerational equity. Taken together, these considerations mean that there should be transfers to families with children at all income levels.

The view that "children should count" certainly surfaces in the public debate. In a newspaper article on the reasons that parents are having only one child, a mother in England with an income too high to receive the present Child Benefit said, "We feel that we are being penalised by the government. We don't get any help at all. No child benefit, no working tax credit, no childcare free hours, nothing. We carry this on our own."[18] She might also have made the point that Child Benefit has an important gender dimension. One purpose of social transfers is to offset the labour-market disadvantage faced by many women. When Child Benefit was introduced in the UK, it was a deliberate policy intention to aid women by making the benefit payable to the mother in the first instance. Child Benefit ensures an independent source of income for the mother in a way that cannot be reproduced by an income-tested benefit based on a couple's joint income.

For all these reasons, I believe that Child Benefit, paid with respect to all children, but taxable, and paid at a rate sufficient to make a significant contribution to reducing child poverty, should play an essential role in any strategy to reduce inequality.

Proposal 12: Child Benefit should be paid for all children at a substantial rate and should be taxed as income.

Basic Income

What about adults? They, too, could receive a basic income or, as it is more commonly described today, a citizen's income. In the version often discussed (but not advocated here), the citizen's income would be paid on an individual basis, differentiated possibly by age or disability/health status. It would not be related to labour-market status and would not be conditional on social security contributions (which would be abolished). It would not be related to income, but all income would be taxed under the personal income tax, and personal tax allowances would be abolished. In its pure form, the citizen's income would replace all existing social transfers: there would be no social insurance or means-tested benefits. (Transitional arrangements would of course be required; for example, honouring previously earned pension rights.)

Such an idea has attracted political support. In his 1972 campaign for the US presidency, George McGovern proposed a $1,000 a year demogrant (basic income) financed by a broad-based income tax. The story goes that he made the announcement on the campaign trail, before returning to ask his economic advisor what tax rate would be required. The advisor, James Tobin (referred to earlier), is said to have replied that, if you need an x per cent tax rate to finance the rest of government, then a demogrant equal to y per cent of average income means that the tax rate has to be $(x+y)$.[19] I had promised no equations in the text, but the $(x+y)$ expression does capture well the trade-off faced in designing a basic income. It means that, with a 20 per cent rate of tax needed to finance other government purposes, a flat-tax rate of 33 1/3 per cent would finance a basic income of 13 1/3 per cent of average income, which seems scarcely adequate to replace existing social transfers. Even a 50 per cent flat-tax rate would only finance a basic income set at 30 per cent of the average.

Participation Income

The stark trade-off between basic income and tax rate has led to the search for variations on a simple basic income. I am proposing a version of the citizen's income that differs from that outlined above in two respects. First, it would complement existing social transfers rather than replace them. A retiree receiving a state pension would be paid whichever amount was higher: the pension or the citizen's income. A pensioner who also receives an income-tested pension credit would see no net gain unless the citizen's income was sufficient to reduce the pension credit to zero. In the case of a pensioner couple, the credit would be calculated taking account of the total citizen's income received. The basic income would be paid at the same rate for all adults but embody additions paid with respect to disability or other special circumstances. The participation income would replace all personal tax allowances except for the Earned Income Discount (if introduced under Proposal 9), so that all income would be subject to income tax.

Second, the proposal is for a benefit to be paid on the basis not of citizenship but of "participation," and for this reason it is referred to as a "participation income" (PI). "Participation" would be defined broadly as making a social contribution, which for those of working age could be fulfilled by full- or part-time waged employment or self-employment, by education, training, or an active job search, by home care for infant children or frail elderly people, or by regular voluntary work in a recognised association. There would be provisions for those unable to participate on the grounds of illness or disability. The notion of contribution would be broadened, taking account of the range of activities in which a person is engaged. Reflecting the features of the twenty-first-century labour market described in Chapter 5, the definition of participation would allow for people holding a portfolio of activities over, say, a thirty-five-hour week, and people may qualify for fractions of this period.

The participation condition is controversial. Critics say that an "unconditional" benefit is being replaced by a "conditional" benefit, thus undermining one of the core principles of the approach. To this I reply that, while a basic income is often described as "unconditional," there has to be a qualifying condition. A tourist cannot arrive from abroad and claim the basic income. As it is put on the website of the UK Citizen's Income Trust, what they are proposing is "an unconditional, nonwithdrawable income paid to every individual *as a right of citizenship*" (italics added).[20] We therefore have to compare two conditions: citizenship and participation. After careful consideration, I have come down on the side of the latter. In my view, citizenship on its own is both too extensive and too restrictive to serve as the criterion for paying a basic income. It is too extensive in that it includes all citizens irrespective of their location. The British government cannot be expected to fund transfers to the British diaspora, the size of which (and hence the budgetary cost) cannot readily be estimated. Nor is it likely to be politically acceptable to pay the citizen's income to people who are not subject to the taxes necessary to finance the scheme. It is too restrictive in a European context in that one country cannot exclude the citizens of other EU member states that come to that country to work. According to Article 45 of the Treaty on the Functioning of the European Union, such persons should enjoy "equal treatment with nationals in access to employment, working conditions and all other social and tax advantages." The UK government may seek to reinterpret the last phrase, but it appears to rule out paying working-age benefits only to citizens.

ADMINISTRATION

Critics are right to say that the operation of a participation income would involve an administrative process and that the criteria would require careful specification, particularly with regard to people who cross borders. Jurgen De Wispelaere and Lindsay Stirton, in their article "The Public Administration Case against Participation Income," argue that the administration faces a trilemma: "The first horn of the trilemma consists of the requirement that PI must remain substantively inclusive . . . [The second horn] is that recipients must satisfy a genuine participation requirement . . . the third horn is made up of . . . the economic and human costs associated with administrability. The trilemma arises because PI can only avoid two of the three horns simultaneously."[21] The application of the category decisions does indeed raise important issues of the burden of proof, the degree of intrusiveness, the interpretation of different activities in a multicultural society, and the location of power in the beneficiary-administrator relationship. I believe, however, that if we avoid the first two horns, the third is less damaging than suggested. To begin with, certain of the eligibility tests are already part of the benefit administrative system, such as, in the UK, caring responsibilities determining whether or not a Job-Seeker's Allowance (JSA) claimant can restrict the hours of availability for work, and engagement in voluntary work determining whether a person can delay taking up a job offer. Compared to the present means-tested schemes, the PI would involve category decisions but not the assessment of income and assets, which adds further complexity to the administration. In making only category decisions, the PI *is* simpler than the current means-tested programmes, and if we can reduce dependence on the latter then administrative resources can be reallocated to the PI programme. More important, I revert to a theme of Chapter 4: that the state should invest in better social administration, recognising that this requires a higher labour input, and emphasising the quality of service rather than simply measuring cost efficiency. It is also important to note that the PI would significantly reduce the number of people receiving means-tested benefits. Of course, a similar argument can be made for social insurance, and readers should be reminded that I am offering the PI as an alternative to reformed social insurance.

The first horn of the trilemma cannot be totally avoided. A universal income is, I have argued, a chimera. Any actual scheme would involve a condition of eligibility and hence the risk of exclusion. Who then would be excluded from the PI? The criteria would exclude those who devoted their lives to pure leisure. The Belgian philosopher Philippe Van Parijs has written a famous article titled "Why Surfers Should Be Fed: The Liberal Case for an Unconditional Basic Income." In advocating the participation income, I am adopting the opposite position. I agree with John Rawls, who said that "those who surf all day off Malibu must find a way to support themselves and would not be entitled to public funds."[22] In reality, relatively few people would be excluded (and the costings in Chapter 11 do not seek to identify surfers). The participation condition should, in my view, be interpreted positively. It is an answer to the question, who is eligible for the basic income? The answer conveys a positive message about "reciprocity," a message that is both intrinsically justified and more likely to garner political support.

THE EU COULD TAKE THE INITIATIVE

So far the participation income has been discussed at a national level, but I believe that it should also be on the agenda for the European Union. Launching an EU initiative for a participation income would be a bold political move. Proposing such an initiative would appear to fly in the face of decades of EU failure to make progress on social security harmonisation. There is, however, a distinctive feature of the participation income: it offers a new form of social security. There would be no imposition of an existing national model. The EU would be breaking new ground.

The first step that the EU could take would be to establish a basic income for children. An EU-mandated Child Benefit would require countries to add to the existing level of child-contingent support the amount required to reach the EU-specified level. (Where national schemes already provide more than the EU-specified amount, no action would be required.) The level of child-contingent support would be calculated in terms of incomes after all transfers but before income tax. (This means that UK Child Benefit would not have to be increased to raise the net of tax payment to families in the 65 per cent income tax band!) It would, under the subsidiarity provisions, be administered and financed by each member state. Such a programme—refined in its details—would allow the EU to invest in its future and contribute to intergenerational equity. Moreover, where the child basic income is paid in the first instance to the mother, the scheme would contribute to redressing the present gender inequality. At what level should the EU-wide basic income for children be set? A natural benchmark is the EU at-risk-of-poverty threshold of 60 per cent of the median, which with the modified OECD equivalence scale of 0.3 for a child would imply a target of 18 per cent of median equivalised income in each member state for each child. Child Benefit for the eldest child in the UK is currently around 7 per cent, and for younger children it is less than 5 per cent. The EU target would therefore involve a substantial increase, as has been proposed above.

The impact of an EU basic income for children, and its contribution to reducing child poverty in Europe, were investigated by Horacio Levy, Christine Luetz, and Holly Sutherland using the EUROMOD tax-benefit

SOCIAL SECURITY FOR ALL :: 223

simulation model (described in more detail in Chapter 11) that makes use of household survey data at that date covering the EU15. They consider different levels of the EU minimum Child Benefit expressed relative to the national median, financed by a flat tax on income at the same rate in all countries. This implies intercountry redistribution, since countries differ in the number of children in the population and in the generosity of their existing child support. The proposal made in this book does not envisage such redistribution: it would operate strictly under subsidiarity.[23] The first interesting conclusion from their study concerns the tax rate required, which—despite the difference in assumption—throws light on the feasibility of the proposal made here. For a Child Benefit at 10 per cent of national median income, the flat tax would be 0.52 per cent, rising to 2.35 per cent for a benefit set at 20 per cent of the median. Would these measures produce a salient reduction in child poverty? The 10 per cent benefit is estimated by Levy, Luetz, and Sutherland to reduce EU15 child poverty from 19.2 to 17.8, and the 20 per cent benefit would lower it further to 13.5 per cent. A reduction of more than 5 percentage points is indeed salient. The reduction exceeds 4 percentage points in all except Belgium, Denmark, Germany, and the UK. From these findings, I deduce that achieving a salient reduction in child poverty requires a significant outlay, but it can be accomplished. Further consideration of the method of financing is necessary, since the results show that the scheme as studied could push some families *into* poverty as a result of the flat tax, and this warns that a more progressive source of funding should be sought.

> Proposal 13: A participation income should be introduced at the national level, complementing existing social protection, with the prospect of an EU-wide child basic income.

The Renewal of Social Insurance

If social assistance is to be superceded, the principal alternative to basic income is a renewed and reinvigorated system of social insurance. This would involve two key ingredients: (a) the restoration of social insurance programmes to their previous role and (b) their adaptation to the labour market of the twenty-first century. In my first book in 1969 on the reform of social security in the UK, I referred to the proposals made there as a "Back to Beveridge" plan, and the same phrase may be appropriate today, in that it would represent a return to the insurance principle and the rejection of income-testing as the main determinant of social protection. It also embodies the aim of providing aid to families with children in the form of Child Benefit that was an essential element in the Beveridge Plan. But Beveridge himself would have moved with the times, and we have to take account of the new forms of employment which are developing today and which cause us to reconsider the relation between income maintenance and the labour market.

The need for reforms of social insurance varies from country to country, according to their institutional structure and specific circumstances. It is, nonetheless, not sufficient to remain at the level of generalities: concrete proposals are necessary. I therefore take the UK as a case study. In so doing, I am conscious that this may appear insular to readers in other countries and reflect the history of its particular welfare state. Indeed, the first element is a return to the Beveridge Plan. A new state pension has already been enacted, effective in April 2016, intended to provide a guaranteed flat-rate SI pension for all, set at a level substantially (about 25 per cent) higher than the current basic state pension. The amount received depends on the number of qualifying years (years for which the National Insurance contribution conditions are satisfied), the maximum being reached after thirty-five years. In the interim period before the scheme is fully mature, the government will calculate for those reaching the state pension age a "summary figure" of all the state pension entitlements accrued to that date. The new pension entitlement will then be a function of this summary figure and the qualifying years accrued after April 2016, so that a person reaching pension age x years after April 2016 receives the summary figure plus $x/35$ times the new state pension.

The new state pension offers both simplification and, in time, a significant improvement in the pension. The build-up will, however, be slow, and there is no change in the position of the thirteen million existing pensioners. In view of this, I propose that there should be an immediate increase in the state pension to the "New Amount," taken as a 25 per cent increase, with the increase taking the form of a "Minimum Pension Guarantee." For those already retired, this would involve increasing the state pension to fill the gap between the New Amount and the sum of the existing state pension and any occupational pension in payment. So a person with no other pension income would have the full 25 per cent increase, but a person with £20 pension from a former employer would receive that amount less £20. For those retiring, there would be a calculation of the state entitlement plus the occupational pension, taking account of the withdrawal (then or earlier) from pension savings that had enjoyed income tax relief. In this way, the proposed Minimum Pension Guarantee would apply a "pension test" but not an income test.[24] The Minimum Pension Guarantee would provide particular help to those currently eligible for but not claiming pension credit, which is the means-tested addition to the basic state pension. The official estimates show that in 2009–2010 between 32 and 38 per cent of those entitled to the credit were not claiming it. The scheme was therefore failing to help one-third of entitled pensioners—or between 1.2 and 1.6 million people.

The same gains accrue from raising other National Insurance benefit rates, where there is a strong case for a significant up-rating. Peter Kenway has made an interesting comparison between the thirty years from 1948 to 1978, when the real value of National Insurance Unemployment Benefit (now Jobseeker's Allowance) rose in line with the real value of consumption per head (both increased by some 75 per cent) and the thirty years from 1978 to 2008 when the real value of consumption per head more than doubled but the real value of unemployment benefit remained around its 1978 level.[25] This echoes the division of the postwar period found for European countries in Chapter 2, when the immediate postwar decades were characterised by falling or stable overall inequality, whereas the post-1980 period saw a reversal and rising inequality. Figure 8.4 shows the dramatic difference between the two periods in a different way: unemployment benefit expressed as a proportion of average household consumption expenditure per head.[26] At the beginning of the postwar period, the National Insurance unemployment benefit for a single person was some 40 per cent of average consumption, and this relationship was maintained until the early 1980s. Since then, the insurance benefit received by the unemployed has failed to keep up with rising incomes, and it is now less than one-quarter of average consumption expenditure per head. Another way of expressing the change is that in 1948 unem-

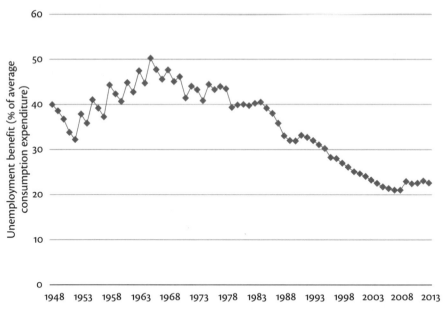

FIGURE 8.4: Unemployment benefit relative to average consumption expenditure in the UK, 1948–2013

This graph shows the standard unemployment benefit of a single person aged over 25, as a percentage of the average household consumption expenditure per head, in the UK from 1948 to 2013.

ployment benefit was equal to the retirement pension; parity was main-tained until the 1970s, after which unemployment benefit fell behind, and today it is 64 per cent of the basic state pension. All this has happened with little debate and to the same extent under Conservative and Labour governments. To quote Kenway, "While the past record of a Labour gov-ernment taking office might have led to the expectation that this policy would be altered, the continuity of the effect within the statistics is testi-mony to the fact that this Labour Government has been perfectly happy to continue with the policy laid down by its predecessor."[27] This was in a period when the poverty rate among workless, unemployed families was close to 70 per cent. For all those out of work, whether unemployed, sick, or on account of disability, improved social insurance offers the promise of a secure source of income that prevents poverty and unacceptable in-equalities.

Benefit Coverage

Raising social insurance benefit rates is only part of the story; we also have to look at benefit coverage. This applies especially to unemployment insurance, which is a key part of any social insurance system. In the US, unemployment compensation, introduced in the 1930s, has served as an important part of antirecessionary policy via the lengthening of the dura-tion of unemployment payments. Most recently in 2008, the Emergency Unemployment Compensation Act and subsequent legislation provided for extended benefits, depending on the state unemployment rate, but this expired at the end of 2013, and Congress failed to renew the legisla-tion. This has led to a decline in the rate of receipt of unemployment in-surance in the US: in August 2014 this rate at 26 percent was one of the lowest in recent decades.[28] The coverage in different OECD countries of unemployment benefits more generally is shown in Figure 8.5. Coverage is defined as the proportion of those who are classified as unemployed ac-cording to the ILO definition who receive benefits (including unemploy-ment assistance as well as unemployment insurance). In some countries, such as Germany and Luxembourg, coverage increased, but in the major-ity of countries the coverage fell between 1995 and 2005. Perhaps more important, coverage in 2005 was below 50 per cent in all of the twenty-four OCED countries apart from Austria, Belgium, Denmark, Finland, and Germany. In ten of the twenty-four countries the coverage was less than one-third.

The fact that many unemployed people do not receive unemploy-ment benefit comes as a surprise to many, as does the fact that the un-employed account for only a small fraction of total welfare spending. In 2014–2015 spending in the UK on benefits for the unemployed was less than 4 per cent of the cost of social security and tax credits, and, as John Hills observes, is "a tenth of the proportion most people think goes to un-employed people."[29] In the UK, the reduced coverage of unemployment insurance came about as the result of a successive tightening of the con-

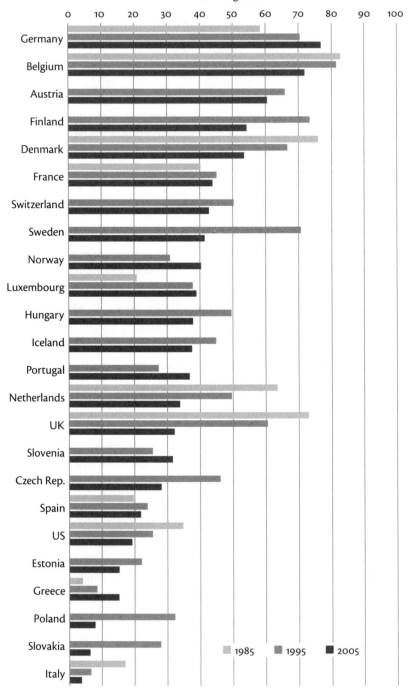

Percentage of unemployed
receiving benefit

ditions of entitlement under the Conservative government in the 1980s. John Micklewright and I listed at least seventeen legislative changes to National Insurance unemployment insurance between 1979 and 1988. Of these, eleven were definitely to the disadvantage of the unemployed, lowering or abolishing benefits and reducing coverage. The changes included more stringent contribution conditions and longer periods of disqualification.[30] The process of tightening continues today.

Contribution Conditions

Many economists would like to do away with social security contributions, replacing them with increased taxes on income. In some respects, this has appeal, since it means that the burden of taxation is shifted from earned income exclusively to income from all sources. I do not, however, support this position for three reasons. The first is that it is possible to treat earned income separately under the income tax, and the shifting of the burden can be achieved through extending the Earned Income Discount that has been proposed on a modest scale above.

The second reason is that, although social security contributions may impinge on the household budget in the same way as income tax, taxpayers may regard them differently.[31] It is a mistake to focus purely on the algebra of the household budget constraint, ignoring the way in which different deductions are perceived, as has been borne out by the literature on behavioural economics. To begin with, there is a voter preference for the implied hypothecation: that the contributions are linked to a spending programme. This is a quite rational response, particularly where there are contribution conditions for receipt of benefits (and I have argued that these conditions can play an important role, particularly where there is between-country mobility). Or it may be that people are misled. In re-

---

FIGURE 8.5: Proportion of unemployed receiving benefit in selected countries, 1985, 1995, 2005

This graph shows the percentage of unemployed people (using ILO definition) who received unemployment benefits (unemployment assistance or unemployment insurance). Values are given for 1985, 1995, and 2005, where available; for some countries the years are slightly different.

gard to the US, the findings of Edward McCaffery and Joel Slemrod suggest that "many smaller taxes [can raise more revenue] with the same psychic discomfort, as fewer larger taxes, because people do not sum them up fully in their minds."[32] If social security contributions and income taxes are, on either ground, perceived differently, then retaining the contributions means that the government can make use of this difference to finance the welfare state with a lesser cost to taxpayers and to the economy.

The third reason for keeping contribution conditions is that they play a positive role in the administration of social transfers and government labour-market policies. Contribution conditions allow social protection to overcome important problems of design. In Chapter 5, we saw their potential role in relation to determining eligibility for guaranteed public employment. Conversely, the fact that people holding these jobs contribute to social insurance means that they would accrue entitlement to insurance-based benefits in the event of subsequent unemployment, and hence this would alleviate the problem of low coverage. The discussion of the administration of the participation income showed that even a radically different form of social protection depends on eligibility conditions, and these are likely to involve an element similar to the current contribution conditions.

Nevertheless, social security contribution conditions need to be adapted to meet the changing nature of work. Such moves have been under way for many years. The present UK conditions are not those of 1948, when postwar National Insurance was introduced. The pensions minister, Steven Webb MP, responsible for the new state pension, has rightly said that it should be paid for years when people have caregiving responsibilities that qualify them for credited contributions: "All years contributing to society whether through paid work or caring responsibilities will be of equal value."[33] The European Union has been at the fore in developing employment rights for part-time and other nonstandard workers, and the social protection system needs to ensure that these are fully matched in the reformed social insurance system. Part-time unemployment is covered in a number of member states: for example, in Austria, Germany, Ireland, and Portugal. In Finland, jobseekers have been entitled to an adjusted unemployment allowance where they are in part-time work through no choice of their own, or if they have income from a small business activity that does not prevent them from accepting other work.[34] The system is thus accommodating "slivers of time." Such steps would not only raise the incomes of families where no benefit is currently received but also avoid the disincentive to return to work embodied in the family means-test—a point to which I return in the next chapter on the economic consequences of the proposals.

To sum up, the social insurance approach, an alternative to the participation income, involves:[35]

> Proposal 14: There should be a renewal of social insurance, raising the level of benefits and extending their coverage.

Our Global Responsibilities

So far I have been concerned with redistribution within countries. I turn now to the role of social transfers in reducing inequality between rich and poor countries. What can be done on a global scale?

At first sight the numbers are too daunting. What can a single country like France, Italy, or the UK do in a world with a population more than 100 times larger than their own? World-wide, progress has been made towards the Millennium Development Goal of reducing extreme poverty, but an estimated 1.2 billion people still live on less than $1.25 a day.[36] Even with this low poverty line, the scale is demanding. But it should not be overstated. It is true that the maximum poverty gap—the amount required to bring everyone up to the poverty line—is an annual $550 billion (1.2 times 365 x $1.25). But in most countries the average shortfall is only a fraction. In India, for example, the World Bank figures show the poverty gap as some 20 per cent of the maximum. If this applies generally, then the total poverty gap is $110 billion. This is a large number, but only some 5 per cent of Gross Domestic Product of France, Italy, or the UK. It is between five and six times the current level of UK Official Development Assistance, which is £12 billion, but the difference is less than an order of magnitude. Put this way, the elimination of extreme poverty appears much more manageable, and—in any case—no one is suggesting that any individual country should solve the world's problem on its own.

Should, then, an individual country such as the UK be increasing development assistance? I should begin by recognising the recent actions of governments that have substantially increased overseas aid as a proportion of national income. Figure 8.6 summarises the history of aid since 1960, where the three lines show aid as a percentage of Gross National Income (GNI) in the UK, the US, and the average for the OECD Development Assistance Committee (DAC, a forum of major aid donors). Overall aid from the DAC in the early 1960s was around 0.5 per cent of GNI. At that time, I believed that this figure was too low, and I supported the campaign to raise aid to 1 per cent of national income. There was wide agreement. As observed by the Canadian economist Harry Johnson in 1967: "It has by now become a generally accepted rule of thumb among writers on aid that the developed countries should contribute a minimum of 1 percent of their national incomes to the less developed countries in the form of aid."[37] Far from being increased, however, aid as a proportion of GNI showed a steady fall, and when the Millennium Goals were under discussion in 2000 the DAC figure was half its 1960 value. Overall DAC aid fell in real terms in the 1990s. The long-term fall was particularly marked for the US, which at the outset was setting the pace (it was President Kennedy, in his Address to the General Assembly in 1961, who launched the proposal that the United Nations designate the 1960s as the "UN Development Decade"). But US aid fell from some 0.6 per cent at that time to only 0.1 per cent at the end of the century. Not only the actual aid but also the target had been reduced below the 1 per cent aspiration. The 1970 UN General Assembly agreed that the goal should be 0.7 per cent of GNI, a figure that in the UK was formally accepted by the 1974 Labour government.

Establishment of the Millennium Development Goals marked a turning point. At the Monterrey Conference in 2002 donor countries agreed that there needed to be a major increase in aid and that there should be concrete efforts to reach the 0.7 per cent target. As may be seen from Figure 8.6, the proportion allocated to aid rose. The Labour government in the UK set in train an expansion of aid with the aim of reaching the 0.7 target. This commitment was taken over by the Coalition government, and the target was reached in 2013, placing the UK alongside Denmark, Luxembourg, Norway, and Sweden in attaining this objective.

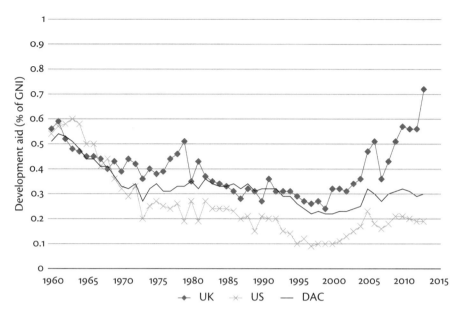

FIGURE 8.6: Development aid expenditures, UK, US, and OECD countries, 1960–2015

This graph shows levels of international development aid given by donor countries, as a percentage of the donor country's Gross National Income (GNI), from 1960 to 2015. Values are shown for the UK, the US, and the DAC (a forum of major aid donors in the OECD). Note that the scale goes from 0% to 1% of GNI.

The Case for Development Aid

Does this mean that, provided the new level is maintained, no further action is needed? Or should we be aiming to raise the bar to 1 per cent (the top of Figure 8.6)?

The case for further global redistribution rests on arguments that in some respects are similar to those for domestic redistribution but are different in others. As discussed in Chapter 1, we can make either an *intrinsic* or an *instrumental* case for transfers. Intrinsically, we can make an ethical case. To quote Harry Johnson again, the "justification of the 1 percent standard is clearly the reasonableness of a contribution of 1 percent of their incomes by the rich to the poor."[38] It is a tenth of a global tithe. To this intrinsic motivation may be added instrumental reasons: that aid has beneficial consequences, such as reducing the pressure to migrate to OECD countries or increasing political stability or reducing the risk of terrorist attacks. This is the line illustrated in the UK by the statement of Jim Murphy when he was Labour spokesman for International Development: "Global altruism won't get us far enough. You've got to have a national interest argument. . . . So the argument goes—'Mrs Smith [aid] money means . . . a safer world.'"[39]

The argument regarding transfers overseas is, however, different in a major respect from those concerned with domestic redistribution. Overseas aid involves actors who are outside the jurisdiction of the donor government. Use of the funds depends on the decisions of the government and others in the country of receipt. Donors have influence but much less control than in the case of within-country redistribution (here too there are limits, but there is a qualitative difference). This has major consequences for the instrumental arguments for aid, since achievement of the objectives, such as increased security, depends crucially on the deployment of the aid. Lack of control has led in turn to questions about the effectiveness of aid. It has been argued that aid may be counterproductive if it is diverted into channels that counteract the original intentions, intensifying within-country inequality. Some studies have argued—with varying degrees of persuasiveness—that there is little relation between the volume of aid and the rate of economic growth, and hence that aid contributes little to closing the gap between rich and poor countries.[40]

Lack of control, on this argument, is a problem; however, it may be better seen as recognition of the twenty-first-century relationship that now links donors and aid recipients. We live in a world with different nation states, each with a substantial degree of autonomy and each with its own cultural background and societal goals. In his critique of aid, Angus Deaton asks, "Who put *us* in charge?" and this is a question that applies to both instrumental and intrinsic arguments for aid.[41] On what basis are we seeking to intervene? In response to this questioning of national responsibility, we need to recast the argument for aid. We have taken over from colonial days the presumption that the purpose of aid is to foster the growth of output. Growth is the yardstick by which aid effectiveness is measured. However, this loses sight of our underlying concern with the current plight of poor individuals and the fragility of their circumstances.

The proverbial statement "Give a man a fish, and you feed him for a day; show him how to catch fish, and you feed him for a lifetime" may have led us to undervalue the importance of the fish today.[42] Channing Arndt, Sam Jones, and Finn Tarp have rightly aimed "to provide a broader assessment of aid effectiveness. While a focus on the effect of aid on macroeconomic growth is necessary, it is not sufficient. . . . Many outcomes are valued independently of their contribution to growth."[43]

The recasting of global justice in terms of national responsibilities has been described by my Nuffield colleague David Miller as a "double-edged sword." He explains that "it may allow richer nations to justify some of the advantages they have . . . but it may also create liabilities." He goes on to say that "to determine the extent of these liabilities . . . we need to use the idea of a global minimum—a set of basic human rights which must be protected for people everywhere regardless of circumstances."[44] In the same way, Arndt, Jones, and Tarp continue the quotation in the previous paragraph by saying that "'merit goods,' such as basic health care and primary education, are viewed as essential human rights and fundamental to the development process. Accordingly, these outcomes should be included."

Setting the case for aid within a framework of national responsibility may appear to give it a conservative turn. In the terms of our discussion in Chapter 1, we are saying that, at a national level, our concern should be with the distribution as a whole ("inequality" as well as "poverty") but that, globally, our concern is limited to securing a basic minimum set of rights. I am not myself convinced that we should limit our global concerns in this way (since I believe that our degree of worldwide interdependence is, while less, not zero), but even if we restrict aid to ensuring a global minimum, it remains a highly challenging task. The sword is indeed double-edged. If we cast the motive for aid as a redistribution of resources in a world where there is deprivation to a degree and on a scale that is not experienced in rich countries, then the present 0.7 per cent of our national income does not appear so generous. Even with considerable leakages, through corruption and diversion of funds, aid "works" if some part at least trickles down to those whose current consumption is so far below that of the typical OECD taxpayer. This is a motive recognised by the large number of people who support charities in this field.

There must be many who believe that "UN cancels food aid to 1.7m Syrian refugees" (as declared in a newspaper headline in December 2014) should never have been allowed to happen.[45]

In the present context, embarking on a programme to reduce inequality within rich countries, we should signal that our concern with unequal distribution is not limited to our national borders. For this reason, I believe that it is opportune for rich countries to return to the target of 1 per cent of Gross National Income. Critics may ask: "Why 1 per cent, why not 2 per cent?" Indeed. We could go further, but here I am concerned with the direction of movement. This is in the spirit of Amartya Sen's *The Idea of Justice*, where he says in the Introduction that, "in contrast with most modern theories of justice, which concentrate on the 'just society', this book is an attempt to investigate realization-based comparisons that focus on the advancement or retreat of justice."[46] The aim is progressive reform rather than transcendental optimality. Moreover, seen from the perspective of the UK, the time is ripe. Underlying much of the recent political debate about the European Union has been an anxiety about the loss of international leadership; here is an excellent opportunity for the UK to exercise leadership, both within the EU and in the world as a whole.

To sum up, I have suggested that our national responsibilities for global redistribution should lead to:

Proposal 15: Rich countries should raise their target for Official Development Assistance to 1 per cent of Gross National Income.

Proposals to Reduce the Extent of Inequality

In Part Two, I have set out fifteen proposals for measures that would, I believe, substantially reduce the extent of inequality:

Proposal 1: The direction of technological change should be an explicit concern of policy-makers, encouraging innovation in a form that increases the employability of workers and emphasises the human dimension of service provision (Chapter 4).

Proposal 2: Public policy should aim at a proper balance of power among stakeholders, and to this end should (a) introduce an explicitly distributional dimension into competition policy; (b) ensure a legal framework that allows trade unions to represent workers on level terms; and (c) establish, where it does not already exist, a Social and Economic Council involving the social partners and other nongovernmental bodies (Chapter 4).

Proposal 3: The government should adopt an explicit target for preventing and reducing unemployment and underpin this ambition by offering guaranteed public employment at the minimum wage to those who seek it (Chapter 5).

Proposal 4: There should be a national pay policy, consisting of two elements: a statutory minimum wage set at a living wage, and a code of practice for pay above the minimum, agreed as part of a "national conversation" involving the Social and Economic Council (Chapter 5).

Proposal 5: The government should offer via national savings bonds a guaranteed positive real rate of interest on savings, with a maximum holding per person (Chapter 6).

Proposal 6: There should be a capital endowment (minimum inheritance) paid to all at adulthood (Chapter 6).

Proposal 7: A public Investment Authority should be created, operating a sovereign wealth fund with the aim of building up the net worth of the state by holding investments in companies and in property (Chapter 6).

Proposal 8: We should return to a more progressive rate structure for the personal income tax, with marginal rates of tax increasing by ranges of taxable income, up to a top rate of 65 per cent, accompanied by a broadening of the tax base (Chapter 7).

Proposal 9: The government should introduce into the personal income tax an Earned Income Discount, limited to the first band of earnings (Chapter 7).

Proposal 10: Receipts of inheritance and gifts inter vivos should be taxed under a progressive lifetime capital receipts tax (Chapter 7).

Proposal 11: There should be a proportional, or progressive, property tax based on up-to-date property assessments (Chapter 7).

Proposal 12: Child Benefit should be paid for all children at a substantial rate and should be taxed as income (Chapter 8).

Proposal 13: A participation income should be introduced at a national level, complementing existing social protection, with the prospect of an EU-wide child basic income (Chapter 8).

Proposal 14 (alternative to 13): There should be a renewal of social insurance, raising the level of benefits and extending their coverage (Chapter 8).

Proposal 15: Rich countries should raise their target for Official Development Assistance to 1 per cent of Gross National Income (Chapter 8).

Alongside these proposals are several possibilities to explore further:

Idea to pursue: a thoroughgoing review of the access of households to the credit market for borrowing not secured on housing.

Idea to pursue: examination of the case for an "income-tax–based" treatment of contributions to private pensions, along the lines of present "privileged" savings schemes, which would bring forward the payment of tax.

Idea to pursue: a re-examination of the case for an annual wealth tax and the prerequisites for its successful introduction.

Idea to pursue: a global tax regime for personal taxpayers, based on total wealth.

Idea to pursue: a minimum tax for corporations.

I have put forward a programme for action. Is it a package? No, in the sense that you need not dismiss all the proposals if you find some elements unacceptable or infeasible. But yes, in two senses. First, there are interdependencies. Some measures will be more effective if accompanied by other parts of the programme. The taxation of benefits is a more effective targeting device when accompanied by a rate structure for the income tax such that the marginal tax rates increase steadily with income, as proposed here. The effective operation of the proposed Social and Economic Council under (4) would be eased if the legal position of trade unions were to be strengthened under (2). Second, there is a confession of our ignorance. While we have a good idea of the mechanisms that have led to rising inequality, we are far from sure about their relative contributions. If we want to make progress, we cannot rely on a sole approach.

But some people will object that "it cannot be done" or that "we cannot afford it." I turn to these objections in the third part of the book.

Part Three

CAN IT BE DONE?

The proposals outlined in this book will no doubt meet mixed reactions. Some readers will welcome the proposals and perhaps even consider them insufficiently radical. Some will reject them out of hand as undesirable or unwarranted. A third group will take them seriously but doubt whether they are feasible. It is towards this third group that the final part of the book is particularly directed. The chapters that follow are intended to meet the criticism that the proposals are too costly in terms of economic efficiency or that they cannot be put into effect by a single country in a global economy. Or, to put it more matter-of-factly, "has the author forgotten about budget deficits?"

Chapter 9 ::

Shrinking the Cake?

The standard objection to proposals such as those described in Part Two is that reduced inequality can be achieved only at the expence of lowering economic output or slowing economic growth. We have to sacrifice efficiency in order to secure greater economic justice.

To this objection, I have two responses. First, the possibility that the cake will be shrunk by the proposals is not a knock-down argument against pursuing them, since a smaller cake more fairly distributed may be preferable to a larger one with present levels of inequality; the two aspects—size and distribution—have to be considered in conjunction. We have to probe further before any conclusion can be reached. Into the balance come *both* the extent of the efficiency loss *and* the way in which we judge gains and losses. Economists are happier discussing the former. For example, there is a large econometric literature on estimating responses to taxation and the magnitude of the losses entailed. In Chapter 7 I examined this issue in relation to the behaviour of top-income recipients. I also addressed the second aspect. I assessed the consequences of top tax rates in terms of their impact on total revenue, where that revenue was—implicitly—assumed to be used to finance transfers to the least well-off. With such a Rawlsian perspective (concern for the least advantaged), an increase in top taxes that generated additional revenue would represent an acceptable trade-off between efficiency and equity. Of course, the proposal to increase the top income tax rate could still be opposed. The opposition could be on the grounds that the prediction of increased revenue is incorrect; or it could be on the grounds that we should be concerned not just with the well-being of the least advantaged but also with the well-being of people higher up the scale. These are two different objections, and it is important to clarify the locus of the debate.

There cannot, therefore, be a blanket rejection on the grounds that the cake would become smaller. Rather, we have to consider the way gains and losses are judged and the nature of the underlying trade-offs. It is on the latter that I principally focus in this chapter. This brings me to the second response: although some of the proposals may lead to a smaller cake, others are efficiency-enhancing. Equity and efficiency may point in the same direction. This does not seem possible in the standard economic model of competitive, fully clearing markets—as is explained below. However, the picture changes once we take account of imperfect competition and markets where supply and demand determine only a range of wages, where there is unemployment, and where there is an important place for institutions. All of these departures from the standard model are active areas of research in economics. Recent Nobel Prizes have rewarded work on industrial organisation, on search in labour markets, and on matching processes. There is an active debate about the role of institutions. But they do not form part of the core of economics. In the early chapters of the standard textbooks, students learn about households and firms engaged in competitive markets where prices equate supply and demand. If I were writing an economics textbook, I would start instead with monopolistically competitive firms with market power, bargaining over wages, in a world where workers are unemployed. I am not writing such a book, but my position influences the answer I give to the question, Can inequality be reduced while enhancing efficiency? If I take a different view from other economists about the consequences of various forms of government intervention, it is in part because I start from a different view as to the working of the economy. The choice of economic model can profoundly affect the conclusions drawn regarding the desirability of policy proposals.

Welfare Economics and the Equity-Efficiency Trade-Off

The view that there is an inevitable trade-off between equity and efficiency is rooted in classical welfare economics. The First Theorem of Welfare Economics states that, under certain conditions, a perfectly competitive market equilibrium is efficient, in the sense that no one can be made better off without making someone else worse off. This is referred to as "Pareto efficiency" after the Italian economist (who is also famous for the discovery of the Pareto curve as a description of the distribution

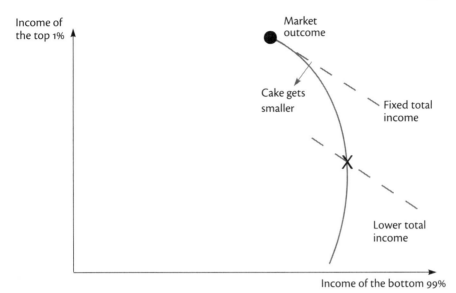

FIGURE 9.1: "The cake gets smaller" argument against redistribution

of income). The efficiency of the market outcome, in the absence of intervention by the government, is a theoretical basis for the "shrinking of the cake" concern about the measures proposed here. This is displayed schematically in Figure 9.1, which shows the position of two groups (the top 1 per cent and the bottom 99 per cent) whose well-being is assumed to be represented by their income. Suppose that the distribution of income at the competitive equilibrium is regarded as too unequal. If the government could carry out costless redistribution, then it could achieve a first-best outcome, shown as moving along the line of "fixed total income." But in reality, it has to employ costly tax-and-transfer instruments, generating the "second-best" frontier shown by the solid line in Figure 9.1.[1] Taxing the top 1 per cent and making transfers to the bottom 99 per cent has a cost: $10 billion of taxes on the top 1 per cent finances only, say, $8 billion of transfers. The situation is that described in terms of the "leaky bucket" in Chapter 1. Total income is reduced. It could even be the case that no transfer is possible since the top 1 per cent reduce their gross income by such an amount that no additional tax revenue is collected. This point is shown as X in Figure 9.1.

Before reaching any conclusions, however, we have to take account of the conditions under which the First Welfare Theorem is valid. The conditions are stringent: (1) households and firms have to act perfectly competitively (taking prices and wages as given); (2) there has to be a full set of markets, equilibrating the supply and demand for all goods and services now and in the future; and (3) there has to be perfect information. Stated this way, it seems clear that these conditions do not apply to actual economies. There are strong elements of monopolistic competition in many markets, firms being price-makers not price-takers. In the labour market, where there is matching of workers and jobs, both workers and employers may bargain over the wage. The theorem assumes that markets clear; in reality there are high levels of unemployment and other signs of market breakdown. There are few markets in which one can buy or sell future goods and services. It is not in general possible, for example, to transact today for the supply of care in ten years' time. Information is not perfect and freely available; rather, it is a valuable commodity for which people are willing to pay.

Once we recognise these features of the real-world economy, then the nature of the argument changes. We cannot presume that a market economy is, by its nature, efficient. Moreover, the position from which we start, when considering measures to reduce inequality, is one in which the government already intervenes in the economy. The proposals would not be introduced into a pristine world without taxes, transfers, regulation, or other instruments of state intervention. Indeed, it is hard to imagine a functioning economy in which there was no government. The question then becomes one of comparing one outcome with another. It becomes quite possible that the size of the cake may be increased through any one, or all, of my fifteen proposals—either to change market incomes (as with the living wage) or to redistribute incomes through taxes and transfers. Each proposal has to be evaluated on its merits.

To make this concrete, let us consider two industries that are much in the public eye: the pharmaceutical industry and the tobacco industry. The pharmaceutical industry has large fixed costs of production, arising from research and development, but relatively low costs of producing the final product. This leads to the market being monopolistically competitive. Firms would not cover their full costs if they charged a price equal to the cost of production, and they use their market power to set prices at a mark-up over production costs to ensure that the firm is profitable. This, however, reduces access to their product, and people, particularly those on low incomes, have to go without medicines. Intervention by the state to subsidise the fixed costs would allow firms to reduce their mark-up while preserving profits, and would make consumers better off. The to-bacco industry also has increasing returns to scale, but in this case the public interest is in reducing consumption. A tax on the fixed costs would raise the mark-up. Once again there are distributional issues, since the rise in cigarette prices would hit those on low incomes especially hard, but if the revenue from the tobacco companies were used to finance so-cial transfers there could be a revenue-neutral policy change that leads to an outcome that is both more efficient and more equitable.

How does this relate to the proposals made here? I am not arguing that all interventions offer gains in both equity and efficiency. In some cases, the proposals for measures to reduce inequality have efficiency costs. People who are being taxed more heavily under the progressive in-come tax may respond by reducing their work effort below the level they would choose if they received the full wage (the efficiency cost arises from the distortion of their choice). Employers faced with higher wage costs as a result of the increased minimum wage may offer fewer jobs. The provision of guaranteed jobs may be administered imperfectly or corruptly by government officials or contractors. But there is no general conclusion that this is the case. Each situation has to be considered on its merits. The combination of the lifetime capital receipts tax and the mini-mum inheritance redistributes endowments in a way that may give peo-ple a start in life that overcomes imperfections in the capital market, such as obstacles to borrowing to set up a business. Increased Child Benefit may mean that children are better fed and more able to concentrate at school. Families no longer facing the poverty trap (as they are floated off means-tested benefits) may invest more in training and provide the skilled workers that employers are currently lacking.

The argument has been cast in a static context—the size of today's cake—but similar considerations apply to the rate of growth over time. Again the effects may go either way. The provision of more generous state pensions may lead people to save less themselves for retirement. Reduced private savings may not be fully offset by increased public savings (where the state scheme is of the pay-as-you-go variety). A lower level of overall savings may lead to a lower level of investment and hence to a lower rate of economic growth. Intervention in these circumstances causes the cake to grow more slowly over time. But the relationship between measures to reduce inequality and the rate of growth may be a positive one. To quote from an IMF paper by Jonathan Ostry, Andrew Berg, and Chara-lambos Tsangarides, "While considerable controversy surrounds these issues . . . equality-enhancing interventions could actually help growth: think of taxes on activities with negative externalities paid mostly by the rich (perhaps excessive risk-taking in the financial sector) or cash transfers aimed at encouraging better attendance at primary schools in developing countries."[2]

There are two approaches to assessing whether the effects are positive or negative. The first is a theoretical examination of the possible impacts; the second is an investigation of the empirical evidence on how comparable measures work in reality. Here I focus on the former. I do so because, after many years of working on the empirical effects of public policy, I have concluded that it is remarkably difficult to shift people's opinions if they are carrying in their heads a theoretical construction that reaches strong conclusions about the impact. In addition, such empirical evidence tends to be country-specific, and I am attempting in this and the next chapter to cover a wide range of countries.

Complementarity between Equity and Efficiency

When I taught a first-year economics course, I encountered a challenge familiar to university teachers: some of the students were starting from scratch and some had studied economics at school. The challenge was to keep the interest of the latter without losing the former. One device I employed was to pose questions to which I then gave answers different from those in school texts. A favourite such question was to ask the students whether "a minimum wage causes unemployment if set above the market wage." The standard response of students when asked about the minimum wage is to draw a demand curve for labour, showing how many workers are taken on by employers at any given wage, where this curve slopes down since employers reduce their labour force as workers become more expensive. Indeed, we saw earlier in the book that there may be a wage sufficiently high that people are replaced by machines. Students then draw a supply curve of labour, showing the number of people seeking employment, where this is assumed to slope upward: the higher the wage, the greater the supply of workers. With a downward-sloping demand curve and an upward-sloping supply curve, there is a single intersection, where supply and demand are in balance. If the minimum wage is set above this level, then demand falls short of supply and there is unemployment.

This is the textbook answer. However, suppose that, over a range of wages, the supply curve bends back, as shown in Figure 9.2. For example, suppose that the supply of labour depends on the length of the working life: moving to the right in Figure 9.2 corresponds to people retiring later. At low wages, people keep on working because they and their families need the money badly. But as the wage rate rises, they are better off and decide that they can afford to stop paid work and stay at home with their grandchildren. The supply of labour curve then bends back. But eventually the wage offered becomes so attractive that people are tempted to stay on at work and the curve resumes its previous upward slope. The crucial point is that there can be more than one intersection of the supply-and-demand curves. There is more than one wage that equates supply and demand. This underlines an often-overlooked point: there may be more than one market outcome. People talk about "what the market determines," but A, B, and C in Figure 9.2 are all possible market outcomes. More precisely, if wages rise (fall) when there is excess demand for workers (unemployment), then the economy could end up at either A or C. (Why do I exclude B?)[3] This in turn means that, if the government imposes a minimum wage, or raises the existing minimum wage, as proposed in Chapter 5, the economy may shift from C to A, as illustrated in Figure 9.2. At the new market outcome, the wage is higher and there is no unemployment. This is not a universal improvement. If the First Welfare Theorem applies, then both A and C are Pareto efficient, and moving from C to A means that some people are worse off (on account of the higher wage; for example, those living off capital income have to raise the wages of their domestic servants), but the initial distribution of market

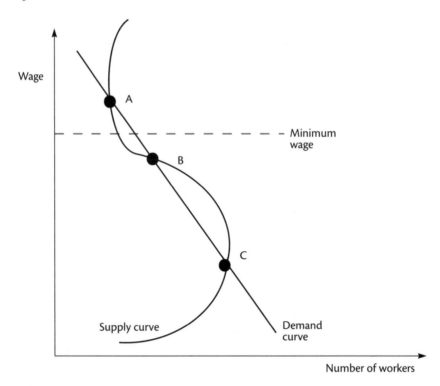

FIGURE 9.2: An alternative view of the impact of a minimum wage

income is different. In Figure 9.1, a different dot would be needed for the market income.

In richer models of the economy, the answers to standard questions may turn out to be different. How is this relevant to thinking about the proposals advanced here? The first example that I take is that of "efficiency wages."

Efficiency Wages and the Minimum Wage

I have proposed a significant rise in the national minimum wage, to which the standard objection is that this will cause a reduction in employment and hence undermine the attempt to return to full employment. Why, opponents will ask, should employers retain workers whose productivity is less than the wage cost? The answer given here, as in the earlier discussion of technological change, is that productivity is not fixed. The productivity of workers can be increased and—the new ingredient—the efficiency of the worker can depend positively on the wage paid. Once employers recognise that by paying more they get greater productivity, they are no longer acting in a perfectly competitive manner: they are acting as wage-setters.

There are several possible reasons for a positive relationship between wages and productivity, as discussed in *Efficiency Wage Models of the Labor Market*, edited by Nobel Prize–winner George Akerlof and Janet Yellen, now chair of the Board of Governors of the Federal Reserve System. Historically, the relationship was understood in terms of calories. Better-paid workers were able to afford more or better food: "The amount of work that the representative laborer can be expected to perform depends on his energy level, his health, his vitality, etc., which in turn depends on his consumption level."[4] In the modern labour market, employees who are better paid may be more highly motivated and loyal to their organisation. The person who placed a sign on his desk saying "pay-related performance" was not just making a joke. The positive link between pay and performance can arise on account of incomplete information. The employer cannot, realistically, fully monitor the work effort of individual members of the labour force. The combination of partial monitoring with the payment of a higher wage can be used to induce workers to choose to work hard, the threat of the loss of the better-paid job acting as an incentive not to "shirk."[5] Paying higher wages may be a device to discourage workers from leaving and thereby involving the employer in recruitment costs. Or the efficiency wage may play a role at the point of entry. At the time of hiring, an employer may lack information about the productivity of individual workers, and offering a higher wage attracts a pool of applicants who privately know themselves to be better qualified than other applicants. In each case, of course, we have to ask whether there are alternatives to paying efficiency wages. There may be alternative contracts, for example, through the payment of wages that rise with seniority.

How is this relevant to the minimum wage? Surely, if it benefits employers to offer higher wages, they will be doing so already. For example, in the analysis based on shirking, the employer offers a wage just sufficient to make sure that workers supply effort, where the amount required as inducement is larger the smaller the amount of monitoring that is undertaken. Suppose that the minimum wage is introduced. To be effective it has to be set above the level chosen by the employer, who then finds that a higher amount has to be paid. The key point, however, is that with an efficiency wage, there is some gain to the employer; the extra wage is not a pure cost. For with the wage set—according to law—at a higher level, the employer can now ensure no shirking with a lower level of monitoring, since the cost to the worker of losing the job is greater (it is also possible that the worker feels more loyalty to the employer). If the level of employment is influenced by both the wage and the cost of monitoring, then there is a counterbalancing force.

As in the simple supply-and-demand model, there may be multiple possible market outcomes, and the minimum wage may cause the economy to shift from a low-wage to a high-wage outcome. This can arise with another version of the efficiency wage story, proposed by George Akerlof on the basis of the sociological literature on labour markets. This views the labour contract in a less confrontational manner, treating it as a form of "gift exchange," where the norms of the workplace are such that workers volunteer greater effort in exchange for being better paid. As discussed earlier in Chapter 3, there may be multiple possible outcomes depending on the extent to which the norms are prevalent. In this situation, the introduction of a minimum wage may cause employers to switch from offering "bad jobs," where work discipline is maintained by monitoring, to offering "good jobs," where effort is ensured by adherence to social norms. Calls for a "high-wage economy" are frequently made by politicians, and this is one route by which it could be achieved.

Institutional Design and Unemployment Insurance

Martin Feldstein, pioneer of research on the economics of social security in the US, once wrote, "I believe that the government never considered that raising the amount and duration of unemployment benefits . . . would encourage layoffs and discourage reemployment."[6] This was not true in Britain. Those who designed welfare states more than a century ago were well aware that social protection had to be carefully designed in order to avoid disincentives. The chief architect of the UK's 1911 legislation for National Insurance (Sir Hubert Llewellyn Smith) drew up a list of fifty-two possible objections to the new scheme that had to be countered, including the increased risk of layoffs and voluntary unemployment.[7] The administrative machinery was explicitly created in such a way as to limit the possible disincentives and—in conjunction with labour exchanges—operated to improve the functioning of the labour market. Much of today's discussion of the welfare state ignores its institutional features, and economists are particularly at fault in this respect. This applies especially to the proposals to raise and extend the coverage of social insurance benefits. All too often, for example, the treatment of unemployment benefit fails to include the conditions under which it is paid. To treat unemployment benefit as "the wage when not working" is to ignore the features that have been introduced precisely to help ensure that social protection works with—rather than against—the grain of economic policy.

The standard economics textbook analysis of unemployment concludes that the payment of unemployment benefit is one of the causes of high unemployment, the argument being that the existence of the safety net leads people to spend longer searching for a job, to turn down job offers, and to be more willing to risk losing their job through shirking. But this analysis is typically based on the assumptions that:

a. benefit is paid irrespective of the reasons for unemployment;
b. there are no contribution conditions related to past employment;
c. there are no conditions on job search or on availability to take up new employment;
d. there is no penalty for the refusal of job offers;
e. benefit is paid for an unlimited duration; and
f. neither eligibility nor the amount of benefit is affected by the other income received by the claimant or members of the household, nor by the level of household assets.

In reality, the institutional details are quite different: these assumptions do not hold. Under the typical unemployment insurance scheme, benefit is paid only to those who lose their employment involuntarily; people are ineligible if they have left their job voluntarily or if they have been dismissed for misconduct. Real-world social insurance is restricted to those satisfying contribution conditions. In order to receive unemployment insurance, claimants must typically have had recent insured employment, and there may be conditions regarding minimum contributions over the working life. Commonly claimants must be able to demonstrate that they are actively engaged in a job search, and that they are available to take up work if it is offered (for example, that they have child-care arrangements in place). Registration with the employment services is a standard condition. Refusal of suitable job offers is grounds for the termination or suspension of benefit. Insurance benefits are typically paid for a limited period.[8]

All of these institutional conditions are familiar to those who have been unemployed, but they are absent from the usual economic analysis. Does this matter? The short answer is "yes." It matters in two respects. First, the real-world conditions under which benefits are paid mean that the key steps in the economic analysis do not follow. For example, the job search model assumes that the unemployed can adopt a "reservation wage strategy," saying that they will only accept a job paying at least X or £Y. However, such a strategy may backfire should the administration enforce the eligibility requirement that no job offer be refused. Or, to take a different example, the "shirking" analysis of job monitoring described above assumes that the fall-back position of the worker dismissed for shirking is the receipt of benefit. The existence of benefit then increases the efficiency wage that has to be paid to induce nonshirking and hence reduces the level of employment. However, dismissal for shirking is likely to be found to violate the "industrial misconduct" rule, in which case the argument breaks down and we cannot conclude that the benefit causes unemployment. Such a conclusion assumes away the very institutional feature that is incorporated to avoid the potential disincentive effects. While enforcement may be less than complete, receipt of unemployment benefit cannot be guaranteed. Equally, the neglect of the contribution conditions means that an important aspect of unemployment insurance is missed in the standard analysis. In the absence of such insurance, the workers would need a higher wage to compensate for the risk, and that higher wage would reduce employment.

Social insurance increases the attractiveness of working in the market economy, rather than in the informal or domestic economy, and helps bind people into participation. When their entitlement to unemployment benefit comes to an end, people may drop out of the labour force entirely. David Card, Raj Chetty, and Andrea Weber observe that this gives a different complexion to the finding that exit from registered unemployment spikes upward in the week when benefits are exhausted. They find, using data for Austria, that job seekers do not wait to return to work until they have used up their benefits; rather, they simply leave the unemployment register when benefits are finished. Their status is reclassified, but there is no change in their actual behaviour. Since the distortionary effects of unemployment insurance (UI) "depend on how UI affects the time spent working, [the spike in unemployment exit] may substantially overstate the degree of moral hazard induced by UI benefits."[9] ("Moral hazard" refers to the disincentive associated with compensation for risk.)

Two elements in my proposals contribute to increasing the effectiveness of income support for the unemployed: the restoration of unemployment insurance and the substantial increase in Child Benefit. How far do these gains in equity come at the expence of efficiency? (Here I am considering only the benefit side of the account, not the effect of the additional contributions or taxes.) In the case of Child Benefit, the payment is independent of labour-market status, and the effect is neutral in terms of decisions about return to work. Child Benefit may have a positive impact, however, in that it would be a secure source of income that continues even if a person were to take and then lose a new job. In view of the uncertainties surrounding benefit claims, this could be a significant factor in encouraging a person to leave unemployment benefit and take a job.

In the case of unemployment insurance, I have explained why the potential for disincentive effects has been overstated and how insurance can play a positive role. There is a further important consideration. Unemployment insurance is paid on an individual basis, whereas means-tested unemployment assistance is paid to the benefit unit and calculated on the basis of the total family income. This means that, in the case of a couple, the receipt of benefit by one partner has potentially serious disincentive effects for the other: there may be little gain to their taking paid work. The improved unemployment insurance proposed here would reduce dependence on means-testing, and the measures would improve the incentives for the partner. Greater reliance on social insurance has in this case positive implications for the size of the cake.

Growth and Pensions

I turn now from the labour market to the impact of the proposals on the capital market, which include the issuing of government securities for small savers guaranteeing a real rate of return that will keep up with incomes, a capital endowment for all, a substantial rise in the state pension, and the accumulation of state wealth in a sovereign wealth fund.

Some of these measures may act as a disincentive to work or to savings. Raising the state pension reduces the need for pensioners to continue working. Supermarkets may find it harder to recruit pensioners to work on their tills or to stack shelves. The improvement in pensions may, as discussed earlier, reduce the savings rate, as both current and prospective pensioners feel less pressure to make provision for the future. Less money may be saved in the form of private pensions. Raising the rate of return may make savings more attractive, but it also reduces the amount that needs to be saved in order to achieve any given standard of living. If people save with a target in mind, then a higher return makes it easier to reach, and they consequently save less. It is also necessary to factor in the capital endowment and examine its incidence. If young people receive a capital sum on reaching adulthood, then one consequence may be that their parents, grandparents, and other relatives feel less need to assist them financially. In turn, this may affect the savings and work behaviour of the older generations, reducing their savings and labour-market participation.

On the other side, there are positive effects from the proposals as far as output and growth are concerned. First, one of the aims of the social insurance reforms/participation income and other measures is to reduce dependence on means-tested benefits. The rise in the state pension will raise some people above the cut-off for, in the UK, pension guarantee credit and savings credit. As noted in Chapter 8, the Minimum Pension Guarantee proposed would impose a test on the total of pension income, but not on savings that were undertaken outside the pension regime. Dependence on means-tested benefits in old age is important because the existence of these benefits discourages savings on account of the high rates of withdrawal: the more people save, the less they receive in transfers. There is a "savings trap." Reducing dependence implies that for more people, saving for old age is worthwhile. We can achieve less poverty and more savings.

The second consideration is less obvious in its effects. It concerns the impact on the capital market and on the decisions of firms regarding long-term investment. In their analyses of economic growth, economists tend to emphasise the role of savings, the assumption being that changes in savings are automatically translated into changes in investment. But this translation depends on the operation of the capital market and on the determinants of the investment plans of firms. Here the proposals for inequality reduction impinge in that they seek to reverse, at least in part, the move towards private pension provision by restoring the key role of the basic state pension. The scaling back of state pensions in recent decades has led to the growth of private pension funds that now hold a large fraction of corporate shares. This in turn has led, paradoxically, to a greater emphasis on short-term profitability. I say "paradoxically" because the pension funds are by definition concerned with long-term savings. It is, however, the nature of competition in this market that the primary concern of fund managers is the immediate investment performance. The objectives of pension funds matter on account of the relationship between ownership and control discussed earlier. The pension funds belong, indirectly, to the current and future pensioners, but control is vested in the fund managers whose time horizons are shorter. It is the fund managers who vote. The renewal of state pensions, to the extent that it reduces reliance on private pensions, may reduce the emphasis on short-term returns and allow firms to invest in expansion and growth.[10] In the same way, the establishment of a state-owned investment fund, holding minority shares in key companies, can also work towards ensuring that investment decisions become less short-term.

The argument of the previous paragraph could appear circuitous, but it underlines the need for an integrated view of the economic and social system. Changes in one part of the policy arena—pension policy—can have implications for industrial policy. For this reason the analysis of inequality has to be centrally engaged with the economic mainstream and not hived off into a separate compartment.

The Proof of the Pudding

In this chapter I have been examining the a priori reasons that the proposals to reduce inequality may or may not affect the size of the cake. I have argued that there is no automatic presumption of a trade-off between equity and efficiency. Once we recognise that the actual economy departs from the perfectly competitive, full-information, fully clearing markets ideal, we are comparing two second-best situations (before and after the proposed reforms), and there are respects in which the reforms may increase rather than decrease efficiency. Shifting away from means-tested benefits may eliminate elements of the poverty trap; strengthening social insurance may increase labour-market attachment; the capital endowment may allow young people to set up their own businesses; the provision of a guaranteed rate of return on savings may reduce uncertainty about people's incomes in retirement. At the same time, there are some respects in which national output may be reduced: for example, more adequate state pensions may allow people to retire earlier. And for some reforms it is hard to evaluate the direction of the effect on economic performance. Should we not therefore look at what actually happens when inequality is lower? As the English expression goes, surely the "proof of the pudding is in the eating"?

In Chapter 1, we saw that some OECD countries in Europe have Gini coefficients of overall income inequality that are 5 percentage points or more lower than in the UK or the US. Do they perform worse? Figure 9.3 shows what we find if, taking a dynamic perspective, we go back a quarter century and examine the growth of GDP from 1990 to 2013 in relation to the initial level of overall inequality.[11] The Gini coefficients at the initial date are for 1990 (or for a close year) and are like those shown in Chapter 1, coming from the same source that is constructed to give figures that are as comparable across countries as possible. (For some countries the inequality data are not available until later, particularly those for Latin America, China, and India.) The growth figures cumulate the annual

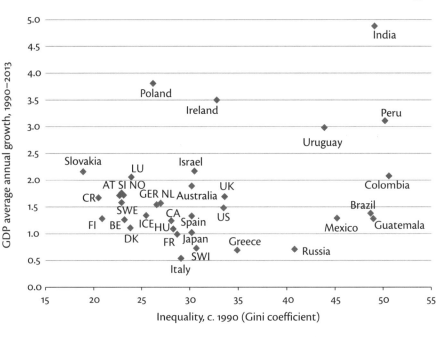

FIGURE 9.3: Inequality (1990) and GDP growth (1990–2013) in selected countries

This graph shows how a country's inequality in c. 1990 (Gini coefficient, in per cent) re-lates to that country's annual average growth in GDP per head, at constant domestic prices, in the period from 1990 to 2013. Country abbreviations: AT Austria, BE Belgium, CA Canada, CR Croatia, DK Denmark, FI Finland, FR France, GER Germany, HU Hungary, ICE Iceland, LU Luxembourg, NL Netherlands, NO Norway, SI Slovenia, SWE Sweden, SWI Switzerland.

growth rates reported in the World Development Indicators assembled by the World Bank and represent the growth in real income per head, al-lowing for domestic inflation.[12]

What do we find? On the right-hand side are countries with high in-equality. This group includes China, which is off the graph in terms of its growth rate, which was in excess of 9 per cent per year. In some cases there was, as in China, a high rate of growth, but in others the growth was more lacklustre. If we look at the countries in the range of Gini coeffi-cients below 35 per cent, we find a wide variety of growth rates. No clear relationship stands out from the data. Growth was rapid in Poland. Growth was rapid in Ireland, even allowing for the recession, although it should be remembered that these figures relate to the domestic product, and the growth rate of national product (allowing for profits going abroad) is slower. The UK and the US averaged growth per head of 1.7 per cent and 1.5 per cent per year, respectively. Some countries had similar growth rates but lower Gini coefficients: lower by 6 percentage points in Germany and more than 10 percentage points in Austria. In both these countries, growth over this period may have benefitted from the expansion of the EU to the East. Finland had a level of inequality similar to that in Austria, but its growth rate was lower at 1.3 per cent per year. However, Finland had been hit economically by the collapse of trade with the former Soviet Union: its GDP per head in the mid-1990s was more than 10 per cent below its 1990 level. There was, moreover, a banking crisis in the early 1990s, in Finland as well as in other Nordic countries (Norway and Sweden). If the growth rates of Finland and Sweden had been calculated from 1995, then they would have been in excess of 2 per cent per year.

In seeking to understand the picture shown in Figure 9.3, we are beginning to tell country-specific stories, and this brings out one serious problem in using such cross-country evidence—in addition to the obvious point that any causality may run in the opposite direction.[13] It is not clear that we are holding constant all the other factors that influence economic performance. One pudding may taste better than another, and we may know that the tastier pudding was made with more brandy. But unless we know all the other ingredients we cannot attribute its superiority to the added alcohol. Of course, with puddings, we can make two that are identical and add more brandy to one. But with economic performance this is not so easy. Earlier I referred to the "difference in difference" approach adopted by economists. In the present context, this would point to seeking to match *changes in inequality* to *changes in performance*. This involves looking at a panel of countries over time. As we have seen, there have been periods in the past when inequality has changed. Indeed, in Europe the last seventy years have seen inequality first falling and then rising. It is not evident that the second period saw a superior economic performance, but we are not holding constant other potential determinants of output and growth, of which there are many. This is a well-recognised problem with cross-country studies of growth. As Steven Durlauf notes, a "problem with the empirical growth literature is the multiplicity of theories. In their 1998 survey of the empirical growth literature, Durlauf and Quah found over 90 different variables that have been proposed . . . since that survey a number of new variables have appeared. Each of these variables is, in my judgment, at least somewhat plausible ex ante as at least a partial determinant of growth. This large number of candidate variables relative to available data is naturally a worry."[14] In the case of a panel of countries, we have to ask which of the relevant variables has changed over the period in question.

The picture drawn in Figure 9.3 can also be criticised because it shows the relation between growth and inequality, when what we want to know is how growth is affected by the instruments used to achieve lower inequality, notably taxes and redistribution. This, as has been emphasised in recent IMF studies, is a different question. It is also a difficult question to answer from panels of cross-country data, as one has to summarise the impact of complex tax-and-benefit systems in a single index (or a small number of indices) of the extent to which they are redistributive. The raw parameters of a tax-and-benefit system are numerous. The simulation of a subset of the proposals made for the UK in Chapter 11 contains thirty-two different parameters, each of which has different potential effects. In the IMF study by Ostry, Berg, and Tsangarides, the extent of use of redistributive fiscal instruments is measured by an overall indicator: the difference between the Gini coefficient for market income and the Gini coefficient for net income.[15] This is similar to the difference studied in Chapter 2, where it was noted that the Gini for market incomes was not necessarily the same as the Gini that would be observed in the absence of the redistributive measures, since the market incomes may well be affected by taxes and benefits—indeed, that is the issue under discussion. Coupled with this specification issue is the need to determine which of the 90+ other variables, referred to above, should be included in the statistical analysis as control variables. The difficulties are well explained by Ostry, Berg, and Tsangarides, who note that "a degree of humility is warranted in defining a baseline specification: not only is there no unanimity in the empirical growth literature on the precise set of controls to be included, in our case the complex set of interrelations among the controls (for example, inequality may impact growth not only through a physical or human capital investment channel but also other channels) complicates the specification issue considerably."[16] Even before starting to consider the availability and quality of the data, we can see that there are many ways in which people could make different choices with regard to the statistical modelling. The conclusions of studies such as that by the IMF (which finds that "redistribution appears generally benign in terms of its impact on growth") must be interpreted in that light.

Summary

The short summary is that there is no smoking gun. It is possible that some of the proposed measures to reduce inequality will have negative effects on the size of the cake—that cannot be ruled out. But there is no general presumption that this will happen, or that the rate of growth will be harmed. The a priori view that there is an inevitable conflict between equity and efficiency is not borne out by an examination of the underlying assumptions. The standard economic analysis of the impact of the welfare state ignores the safeguards that are built into the institutional design of social protection and is typically based on models of economic behaviour that ignore the potential positive contribution of the welfare state to economic performance. Redistribution has to be financed, but the analysis of the effect of higher taxes, like that of higher benefits, is more complex than suggested by simple textbook models. Moreover, the proposals have positive incentive effects. The increased minimum wage could increase labour-market attachment and investment in skills; the proposals to help small savers could encourage wealth accumulation; and the capital endowment would expand the opportunities for young people.

Chapter 10 ::

Globalisation Prevents Action?

In this book I make proposals to reduce inequality in OECD countries. One evident response is to say, "These are fine, but we live in a world that prevents us from pursuing such a path." We might have had such ambitions in the past, but today a fairer distribution of income is a luxury that we cannot afford in a globalised economy, since any country going down that route will cease to be competitive in world markets. Even if the size of the domestic cake is not reduced, we face external constraints. On this view, the welfare state, progressive taxation, the idea of pay policies, and a full employment target are all relegated to history; they have no place in the twenty-first century. There are in fact two related but different versions of this objection to the proposals. The first concerns the capacity of OECD countries as a whole or, more narrowly, the European Union as a whole, to pursue broadly similar policies when faced with competition from the newly industrialising world. The second concerns the scope for single countries to adopt measures of redistribution and enhanced social spending in the face of other OECD countries continuing their current policies unchanged.

These are real concerns, and I take them seriously. It would indeed be foolhardy to dismiss this objection, since we know so little about how the world is going to develop. Had I written this book ten years ago, the prospects for the world economy would have looked very different from those of 2015. There are major forces potentially affecting the world economy—notably climate change and political relations with China and Russia—which I am not competent to assess. Instead, I offer three reasons that I am not totally pessimistic about our economic future. The first is that one of the main elements in the proposed measures—the welfare state—had its European origins in the nineteenth-century period of globalisation. It is therefore puzzling that the present period of globalisation should elicit the opposite response—that we are compelled to dismantle the welfare state rather than, as I have argued here, strengthen it as a response to rising inequality. The form of today's globalisation may be different, but the consequences in terms of jobs and wages are similar. My second reason for optimism is that countries are not simply passive agents in the face of world developments. A central theme of this book is that it is wrong to see today's high inequality as the product of forces over which we have no control, and the same applies to globalisation. The third reason is that I am mildly optimistic about the potential for international cooperation.

The Welfare State in History

Globalisation is not new. The Wikipedia entry reminds us that "the 19th century witnessed the advent of globalization approaching its modern form. Industrialization allowed cheap production of household items using economies of scale, while rapid population growth created sustained demand for commodities."[1] What I would like to stress is that the same period saw the emergence of one of the key institutions—the European welfare state—whose survival is said to be threatened by today's globalisation.

It was the development of the modern employment relationship with the Industrial Revolution that led to pressures for the creation of the key institutions of social protection. Industrial employment meant that many workers came to face a situation where unemployment, sickness, or retirement meant a total loss of earnings. This led towards the end of the nineteenth century, or in the early years of the twentieth century, to the establishment of unemployment insurance, industrial injury benefits, sickness insurance, and old-age pensions. These new schemes underwrote the risks for workers involved in industrial employment where they could find themselves suddenly without means of support, either on account of personal ill-fortune, such as industrial injury, or on account of a general downturn in trade. In Germany, which led the way, there were several motives for the introduction of the Bismarckian system of social insurance. These included the need to preserve political and social stability in the face of the rise of workers' organisations and the spread of socialist ideas. But a significant factor was the need for social protection that arose from the precariousness of employment when Europe was exposed to greater competition in the 1870–1914 period of globalisation.

The origins of the modern welfare state in this earlier pre–First World War period of globalisation should be stressed, since it is sometimes suggested that the welfare state originated in the interwar period. It is true that old-age and survivors insurance in the US began in the 1930s under Franklin Roosevelt, the thirty-second president, not under Theodore Roosevelt, the twenty-sixth president (1901–1909). It is true that spending under the different European social security programmes expanded in the interwar period. But many of the schemes had been set in place before 1914—see Table 10.1.[2] As described by an American observer, there had been a "rapid development of the complex body of legislation towards social insurance in Europe. . . . From the frozen shores of Norway down to the sunny clime of Italy, from the furthest East and up to Spain, all Europe, whether Germanic, Saxon, Latin, or Slav, follows the same path. . . . The movement for social insurance is one of the most important world movements of our times."[3] This was written in 1913.

I emphasise the timing because the introduction of the welfare-state programmes in Europe should be seen as complementary with, rather than in competition with, the achievement of economic goals. In the early days of the European welfare state, social and economic policies were seen as working in the same direction. This view persisted for several decades. When, in the United Kingdom, Beveridge drew up his 1942 plan for postwar social security, he collaborated with Keynes to ensure that macroeconomic and social policy worked together, notably via the role of social transfers in providing automatic stabilisers. In the United States, Moses Abramovitz argued that "the support of income minima, health care, social insurance, and other elements of the welfare state, was . . . a part of the productivity growth process itself."[4]

Only later, in the 1980s and 1990s, did the predominant view shift and come to see social protection as an impediment, rather than as a complement, to economic performance. Unemployment benefits were seen as causing unemployment, and state pay-as-you-go pensions as lowering savings rates and causing a slowing of the growth rate. According to the US Nobel Prize–winning economist James Buchanan, writing in 1998,

TABLE 10.1. *Social security legislation in the period of globalisation before the First World War*

1881	German kaiser Wilhelm I proposed old-age social insurance.
1883	Germany introduced national compulsory health and maternity insurance for industrial workers.
1885	Austria adopted compulsory health insurance.
1889	Germany introduced old-age social insurance.
1891	Denmark introduced noncontributory old-age pension.
1891	Hungary adopted compulsory health insurance.
1895	Finland adopted accident-compensation law.
1898	New Zealand introduced noncontributory old-age pension.
1900	Spain adopted accident-compensation law.
1901	The Netherlands, Greece, and Sweden adopted accident-compensation laws.
1901	Belgium adopted Ghent system of unemployment insurance.
1902	US enacted in Maryland first state workmen's compensation law (declared unconstitutional in 1904).
1905	France introduced government subsidies to voluntary mutual aid associations offering unemployment benefits.
1907	US created first federal employment service.
1908	UK introduced noncontributory pensions.
1909	Norway introduced compulsory sickness insurance programme.
1909	US introduced first federal old-age pension bill in Congress.
1911	UK passed National Insurance Act introducing unemployment insurance and national health insurance.
1911	Italy introduced national compulsory system of insurance for maternity.
1911	US enacted in Wisconsin first workmen's compensation law to be held constitutional.
1913	Sweden introduced universal national pension system.

Source: US Social Security Administration website, detailed chronology of social insurance and social security, http://www.ssa.gov/history/chrono.html.

"the 'social model' that many Europeans hold as superior to the somewhat more limited welfare states elsewhere is not economically viable for the twenty-first century."[5] The view was expressed by international organisations, according to Michel Camdessus, then managing director of the International Monetary Fund: "We see it as extremely important for the future of European economic and monetary union that member countries be flexible enough, that they alleviate the impact on their budgets of regimes of unemployment benefits or social security which are no longer suited to the present world, and are of very high cost."[6]

The Welfare State in the Twenty-First Century

Is it the case that we cannot afford the welfare state in the twenty-first-century global economy? At the core of the position that the welfare state is unaffordable is the argument that globalisation has reduced the tax-raising possibilities of welfare states. On this view, there are limits to the proportion of national income that can be raised as tax revenue. As popularised by the US economist Arthur Laffer, there is a curve linking total tax revenue to the overall tax rate that first rises but then reaches a maximum and begins to fall, a curve that he reputedly drew on a Washington restaurant napkin for President Nixon's staff members Dick Cheney and Donald Rumsfeld, later respectively vice president and secretary for defence. As Laffer himself recognised, the "Laffer curve" is not a new concept, but it is much cited today.[7] The key point is that globalisation and technological change have together shifted the curve downward, so that for any tax rate the government collects less revenue. The maximum of the curve has moved to the left. This happens because the expansion of Internet commerce means that it is more difficult to collect indirect taxes; the development of a global labour market limits the taxation of earned income; and tax competition between countries lowers the receipts from corporate taxation and the taxation of investment income. If countries were previously close to the revenue-maximising tax rate, then they have to cut back, and if they previously believed they had space to expand, then this headroom no longer exists.

All this sounds gloomy. However, the analysis is more complex and the conclusions less evident, even if we accept the premises on which they are based. To begin with, the limit applies to total government spending, and we have to consider the relative merits of cutting different spending categories. Social transfers are a major item, but total size is not a reason to single out a particular category. We need to make comparisons of the cost and benefit from reducing spending by X billion in all government departments. Defence, public infrastructure, research and development, and agriculture and education, for example, all need to be compared with social transfers. A less obvious but important point is that we need to compare direct government expenditures with those made indirectly via the tax system in the form of "tax expenditures" (see Chapter 7). Eliminating tax expenditures raises tax revenue and therefore should be scrutinised with equal intensity. In some OECD countries tax expenditures are substantial: estimates for years in the period 2004–2007 showed them to be around 8 per cent of GDP in the UK, and around 6 to 7 per cent in the US and Canada (they were smaller in Germany, Korea, and the Netherlands).[8]

Tax expenditures are important in the context of the present argument because we have to ask what would happen if the welfare state were cut or not expanded. One answer is that there would be increased private provision. If the state does not help, then individuals have recourse to the private sector. That this happens at present is brought out by the international comparisons made by the OECD of total social spending, adding both private and public. Social expenditures are defined as benefits in cash or kind by public and private institutions provided to individuals or families during circumstances that adversely affect their welfare. They include social security, health benefits, housing benefits, and active labour-market programmes. As is illustrated for 2011 in Figure 10.1, levels of public provision (shown by the hollow bars) vary considerably among OECD countries. In the United States, spending is smaller as a percentage of national income than in most European countries; it is not much higher than in the Czech Republic. However, the US moves way up when we add in private spending to give the total (solid bars). The only country that is higher is France. The contrast with Denmark is instructive: Danish public spending is 3 percentage points higher, and its total spending is 3 percentage points lower, than in the US. This suggests that the needs for social spending are going to be met, and that if we abandon public spending, it will be replaced by private spending.

The significance of this finding is twofold. If private spending on social needs has to rise to offset reduced public spending, then this cost falls either on employers or on households. Where employers face higher costs, this renders them less competitive in the same way that higher employer taxes do. Their outlay on employer health plans enters their location decision in the same manner as employer taxes. Where it is the employee who pays, then the required outlay reduces their take-home pay and is likely to lead to wage demands. The transfer from state to private

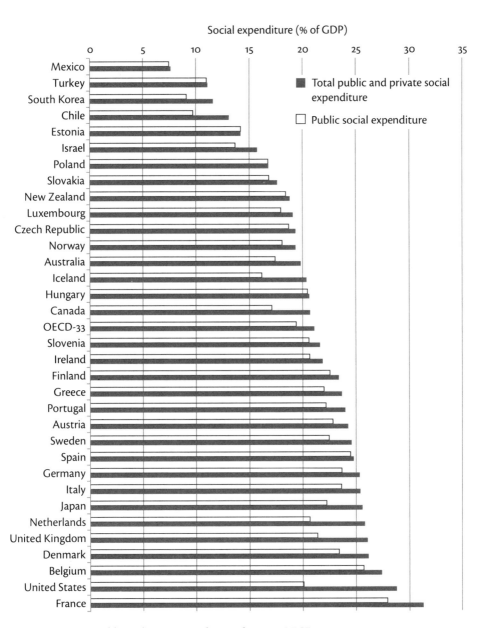

FIGURE 10.1: Public and private social expenditure in OECD countries, 2011

provision changes the economic impact only to the extent that one is more efficient than the other. Second, increased private social spending, such as that on pensions or health care, often entails tax expenditures, affecting the tax side of the account. To this extent, a solution to the fiscal problems of countries in a globalised world will not be achieved by transferring social spending from the public to the private sector.

Can Welfare States Compete Globally?

What are the implications of the budgetary cost? Do higher taxes make our goods more expensive, so that we cannot compete globally? Employers commonly complain that taxes and social charges on employment render their goods and services uncompetitive. The same effect may arise from taxes on employees, which may be passed on in higher employment costs. To take a rather special case, if footballers in the UK Premier League insist on a certain after-tax wage, any rise in top tax rates means that their clubs have to raise their pay, and this is likely to be passed on in higher ticket prices and increased demands for broadcast fees, and so on. This in turn may reduce the number of tourists coming to the UK to watch football and result in Premier League matches losing their television audiences to the Bundesliga, La Liga, and Serie A.

Taxes are not, of course, the only factor driving wage costs. My colleague John Muellbauer has stressed the role of housing costs. The fact that people require large mortgages leads them to bargain for higher wages. Higher salaries are necessary to attract people to London and cities such as Oxford and Cambridge. Actions to reduce house prices, including the reform of Council Tax proposed here, could therefore reduce wage pressure. The provision of public services is also important, and the availability of good schools and health services is a factor working in the same direction.

To the extent that higher taxes raise wage costs, does this make the UK less competitive? I have always been puzzled by the term "national competitiveness." I can understand that a firm may not be competitive, or a university, or even a whole industry, but not a nation. I was therefore relieved a few years ago when Paul Krugman, Nobel Prize–winning international trade theorist, said that "competitiveness is a meaningless word when applied to national economies" and that "not one of the text-books in international economics I have on my shelves contains the word in its index."[9] For a country, unlike a single firm, there is a process of ad-justment to external imbalance. If exports fall and imports rise, then—in-sofar as the exchange rate adjusts to the trading balance—the exchange rate falls, restoring the ability of exporters to sell their goods and services at prices that are comparable with those in export markets. Equally, the fall in the exchange rate renders imported goods more expensive in do-mestic prices and brings their prices into line.

The adjustment may not work, and it is not without cost. It may not work because the exchange rate is driven by other factors, such as capital movements, either short-term or long-term; it may not work because the exchange rate is fixed, as in the Eurozone. For the latter reason, a single country within a currency area may face constraints that are not applica-ble to a country outside the area. That is why it is important to separate the two versions of the question. A single member of the Eurozone may be constrained in a way that does not apply to the Eurozone as a whole. But, at whatever level, adjustment via the exchange rate has a cost, in that the fall reduces the standard of living in the country. The fall in the pound from \$2.80 to \$2.40 in the devaluation of 1967 meant that for an Ameri-can product priced at \$100 people in the UK had to pay £42 rather than £36 (rounding). When Prime Minister Harold Wilson told the country that the pound in their pockets was still worth just as much, he actually prefaced it with the more accurate statement that "from now the pound abroad is worth 14% or so less in terms of other currencies." This is really the crux of the matter. When people talk about "being competitive" they really mean maintaining their national standard of living. In the present context, it means that financing for the welfare state and greater redistri-bution has to be identified. The costs of the programme of proposals have to be met by reductions in the real incomes of better-off groups in the population. In that sense, the problem is no different from that faced do-mestically by a country with fixed total resources.

As I said in the previous chapter, the fact that there are losers as well as gainers is not a decisive argument against redistribution. If govern-ments are serious about reducing inequality, then there have to be trade-offs. These are not easy. As Tawney said in his essay *Equality*, "while inequality is easy, since it demands no more than to float with the current, equality is difficult, for it involves swimming against it . . . it has its price and its burdens."[10] The difficulty takes two forms. At an individual level, it involves "material sacrifice for some"; there has to be acceptance that taxes have to be raised. At a societal level, it means that we have to ask difficult questions. Rather than simply accepting the outcome of the market process, we have to examine what we mean by a "fair" distribution.

Summary

I have argued that the scope for redistributive measures, particularly those involving enhanced social spending, is not as restricted by global competition as has sometimes been suggested. There are constraints, but they do not imply that nothing can be done. This becomes clear when we consider the budget as a whole, taking account of all types of outlay and of total social spending, both public and private. There *is* a fiscal problem, but it is a problem that is within our powers to solve, not one whose outcome is determined purely by external forces.

Globalisation and Control over Our Destiny

A second ground for optimism is that countries are not simply passive in the face of world developments. The extent to which national policy is constrained depends to a significant degree on how countries react to the changing world.

To give a concrete example, there is much discussion in the UK of the consequences for the labour market of the free movement of workers within the European Union, the implication being that the UK is powerless to act. In July 2014, the official Migration Advisory Committee issued a report titled *Migrants in Low-Skilled Work: The Growth of EU and Non-EU Labour in Low-Skilled Jobs and Its Impact on the UK*. The report identified five main themes, and, significantly, the first four related to policies under the control of the UK government. Only the fifth, and last, theme referred to the EU and to the issues raised by EU enlargement to countries with lower wage levels. In relation to the other themes, the committee stated that the "demand for migrant labour is strongly influenced by institutions and public policies not directly related to immigration." They amplified this by saying that "reducing the growth in the reliance on migrant labour in certain occupations will not happen without fundamental changes to the policies and the way these institutions operate. This may include greater labour market regulation in some sectors, more investment in education and training, better wages and conditions in some low waged publicly-funded sector jobs, improved job status and career tracks, a decline in low-waged agency work, and addressing any abuse of zero-hours contracts."[11] This is a set of policies that is within the powers of the UK government—and one that would make a major contribution to reducing inequality.

A second example from the UK makes the same point. It concerns the plight of the long-term tenants of a housing development in London who discovered in 2014 that they were being given two weeks' notice to leave. The housing had been built by a charitable trust in the 1930s with the objective of providing working-class families with affordable private rental accommodations. When it was sold to a real estate management company based in New York, the new owners announced plans for a large rent increase, which would have generated sizeable gains—at the expense of the tenants—for the operators of the real estate investment fund and their investors, which include financial institutions, public and private pension funds, and sovereign wealth funds. The resulting public outcry led to the withdrawal of these plans and placement of the property into a housing trust. The key point is that the problem arose, not so much on account of the globalisation of capital, as from the underlying fact that tenants in the UK lack protection. The same issues would have arisen if the investment fund had been based next door in the City of London. If, as I believe it should be, the government of the UK were concerned about the security of tenants of tenure with respect to their own homes, then it should reenact protective legislation. A visitor from Mars, or even from abroad, might be amazed to learn that in England business tenants enjoy more protection than domestic tenants. The same consideration applies to the tax and other subsidies provided to landlords. As Danny Dorling wrote in *The Guardian,* "overseas property buyers are not the problem: landlord subsidies are."[12]

These examples underline one of the strands that runs through the book—the key distinction between the ownership and the control of wealth. By the appropriate design of domestic institutions, it would be possible for the beneficial ownership of housing to pass to investors outside the country while the control remained in the hands of a body subject to that country's laws and norms regarding its activities. If the policies of the latter body yielded lower returns since they balanced the needs of tenants with the interests of investors, then the investors could sell their holdings, but they could not change the management.

International Agreements and Countervailing Power

Of course, national capacity to act may be restricted by international agreements. This is why there is widespread concern about the Transatlantic Trade and Investment Partnership (TTIP), an agreement under negotiation in 2015 between the EU and the US to remove barriers to market access; and to secure the liberalisation of investment and the restriction of national regulation. The possible implications for national regulation are spelled out in a critical assessment by John Hilary: the aim of TTIP is "to remove regulatory 'barriers' which restrict the potential profits to be made by transnational corporations on both sides of the Atlantic. Yet these 'barriers' are in reality some of our most prized social standards and environmental regulations, such as labour rights, food safety rules (including restrictions on GMOs), regulations on the use of toxic chemicals, digital privacy laws and even new banking safeguards introduced to prevent a repeat of the 2008 financial crisis."[13] A key element in the proposed agreement is the Investor-State Dispute Settlement (ISDS) procedure, which allows corporations to bring cases against national governments, challenging national regulation.

Here I want to focus on the lack of symmetry in the approach to the trade agreement. The ISDS procedure does not allow any rights for governments, trade unions, consumer organisations, or individuals to bring cases against corporations. The aim is to protect investors. A US negotiator made the position clear: "A comprehensive 21st century trade agreement should include appropriate protections for investors." No reference is made to consumers or workers.[14] The EU Commission, in defending the policy, refers to the expected benefits in terms of gain in Gross Domestic Product, but surely this is an occasion in which we should be concerned with the wider objective of adding to the welfare of EU citizens. Some citizens benefit insofar as they are investors, but others are affected in their roles as consumers and workers. Before proceeding along the TTIP path, we should ask what such an agreement would look like if it were drawn up from the standpoint of the interests of consumers and workers. It is clear, for example, that the dispute-settlement procedure should be open to all, and that the adjudication panels should be tripartite with representatives from consumer and worker organisations, as well as from business.

In short, individual governments, and multilateral organisations such as the European Union, are themselves in part responsible for the terms on which they engage with the world economy. They are constrained but not powerless. What is required is that they give prominence to the distributional impact of globalisation and ensure that all stakeholders are represented.

Scope for International Cooperation

My third reason for optimism is founded, despite the concerns expressed with regard to TTIP, in the progress of international cooperation. International organisations have a long history, and in their modern form date back to the nineteenth-century period of globalisation. In 1863, the US instigated an International Postal Congress, leading to the creation of the Universal Postal Union (as it became) in 1874. Among other benefits of this agreement, it abolished any requirement to affix stamps of countries through which the letter passed; the necessary stamps were simply those of the country in which the letter was posted. In fact, we have 150 years of experience with worldwide organisations since the International Telegraph Union was founded in 1865 (it is now the International Telecommunication Union).

In the recent period of globalisation there has been rapid growth in the number and extent of international organisations. Ranjit Lall has described "the dramatic expansion in the number, scope, and resources of IOs [international organisations] in recent decades . . . between 1970 and 2013 the number of intergovernmental organisations (IGOs) increased from 242 to 7,710. . . . During this period, IOs have branched out into diverse issue areas such as environmental protection, finance, and women's rights, supplanting traditional state-based modes of governance in unprecedented ways."[15] This growth is in itself grounds for some degree of optimism.

Tax Competition and Collaboration

Ambitions for international cooperation have increased along with a good deal of fine rhetoric. However, is there any evidence that national governments are more willing to place global concerns above national interests? A crucial area is that of fiscal competition, where countries have competed to attract high-income individuals and corporations either through offering preferential low tax rates or through the operation of a financial system that shelters tax evaders through bank secrecy.

In this field, unlike many other contentious areas of global disagreement, there are indeed signs that progress may be possible. The leakage of information about undisclosed financial holdings, and concerns about the funding of military/political organisations, are leading towards the possible creation of a World Tax Administration, as already evoked in Chapter 8. The long-standing work of the OECD on multilateral tax legislation has developed considerably in recent years. Under OECD auspices, and those of the G20, the Global Forum on Transparency and Exchange of Information for Tax Purposes in OECD and non-OECD economies has been established. Note that the latest classification shows the UK and the US as falling short of complete compliance. They are classified as "largely compliant"; there is more to be done to restrict the activities of tax havens that come under British or US sovereignty. Within the EU, Cyprus and Luxembourg (but see below) are classified as "noncompliant." From this body, with 123 countries as members, and including many of the well-known tax havens, a global tax body may in time emerge.

At the behest of the G20, the OECD Base Erosion and Profit Shifting project has set out a 2014 package of seven measures to meet what the OECD Secretary General described as "a serious risk to tax resources, sovereignty and fair tax systems worldwide." In presenting the proposals, he referred to both the "willingness" of national governments to cooperate and "their need" to do so.[16] This may appear optimistic in the light of the shortfall in compliance just described, but countries are beginning to act with regard to the exchange of information. The passing in the US of the Foreign Account Tax Compliance Act (FATCA) in 2010 was in many respects remarkable. FATCA requires foreign banks to report to the US Treasury Department all accounts and investments held abroad by US citizens or US residents. Moreover, international pressure to conform is beginning to take effect, as is evidenced by the case of Switzerland. In 2013, the Swiss Parliament passed a law allowing cooperation with the US tax authorities, and the attempt to overturn this decision by calling a referendum failed to attract sufficient signatures. Pressure is similarly mounting on corporate tax havens. Following disclosure of corporate tax deals that allowed multinational companies to avoid taxes in other countries, the Luxembourg finance minister announced in November 2014 a distinct change of heart, saying that "the result of the application of today's international, European and national law can sometimes lead to a result where companies are confronted with a very limited tax-rate, or even to a non-taxation. The Luxembourg government, together with most countries around the globe, does not consider this a satisfactory solution. But this problem cannot be solved by one country alone; it needs to be solved by changes in national laws, all the national laws together, or in cooperation with international laws, be it at the European level or at the OECD level."[17]

The European Union

I have been engaged with the European Union ever since the UK joined what was then the European Communities in 1973. Early in the period of UK membership, I was appointed a member of an Expert Group on the financing of the health service. Some member states suspected that the UK National Health Service, financed largely from general taxation, was a possible source of unfair competition with member states whose health costs were borne by charges on employees and employers. This in turn nurtured a suspicion among those on the left of UK politics that the European Union, as it became, was hostile to concerns with egalitarian policies and social justice. At the time, these suspicions were not justified. The year after the UK joined the first European Social Action Programme was adopted. In the discussions of economic and monetary union that took place at the time there was serious advocacy for an EU-wide unemployment benefit. The Marjolin Report stated that "a Community initiative in the unemployment field is particularly opportune, for it will have beneficial effects on the economy and society as a whole. . . . One definite step in this direction might be to prove before public opinion that Community solidarity is a reality."[18] The proposal was subsequently supported by the MacDougall Report: "Apart from the political attractions of bringing the individual citizen into direct contact with the Community, it would have significant redistributive effects and help to cushion temporary setbacks in particular member countries, thereby going a small part of the way towards creating a situation in which monetary union could be sustained."[19] If this prescient advice had been followed, the history of the last few years would have been rather different.

As it was, there followed a period when the European project was dominated by the economic agenda: the internal market and the euro. For those concerned with advancing the social dimension of Europe there has in fact been a succession of highs and lows, as summarised in Figure 10.2. An important step forward was taken by the agreement of the Lisbon Agenda for the first decade of the twenty-first century. In 2001 the Laeken European Council agreed that social performance by member states should be judged according to a set of social indicators, which included the proportion of the population at risk of poverty, income inequality, regional cohesion, the long-term unemployment rate, the proportion in jobless households, and the proportion of early school-leavers. In retrospect, the achievements may appear meager, even allowing for the fact that we were blown off course by the economic crisis. There was also a time, mid-decade, when the Kok Report led to a downgrading of the social objectives in favour of a single-minded focus on jobs and employment. As I have argued earlier, achieving full employment is an important goal, but it does not mean the end of poverty. In the light of this experience, the agenda for the second decade has moved to setting concrete goals. The Europe 2020 strategy has set five headline targets covering employment, research and development spending, action on climate change, education, and poverty/social exclusion. The last of these targets means reducing by at least twenty million the number of people living at

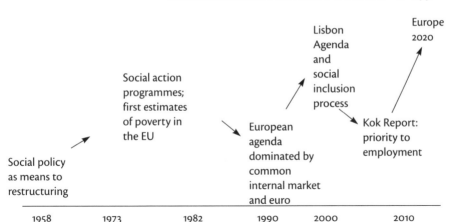

FIGURE 10.2: A brief history of EU social policy

risk of poverty or social exclusion, which would represent a reduction of one-sixth.[20]

The Europe 2020 strategy can be criticised in detail—for the choice of indicators—and in general—for being cheap talk with no political momentum.[21] There are nevertheless positive lessons to be drawn. It is remarkable that the member states, with their very different histories and different political standpoints of the current governments, were able to agree on a set of objectives for the European Union. They established an agreed set of social indicators, and these are now routinely reported by Eurostat. Later, with a different set of governments, and with many more member states, the EU was able to agree on a set of concrete targets. We tend to lose sight of the fact that existing nation states rarely have to be explicit about their national objectives. To what extent can the United States today be said to have a set of agreed national goals? The EU, being a new and evolving political construction, has had to make explicit its ambitions, and these are set firmly in the direction of reducing poverty and inequality.

Summary

Much of this chapter has been concerned with issues that are at heart political rather than economic. Policy has to be made within an economic context, and in the currently globalised world there are many constraints. But I have argued in this chapter that these constraints leave room for choice. It is not the case that "there is no alternative." Countries are themselves partly responsible for the terms on which they engage with the world economy. The impact on the extent of inequality depends on domestic policy, and this is one of the reasons we have seen larger increases of inequality in some countries than in others, even though they are faced with similar external challenges.

National governments are individually more constrained, particularly those in the Eurozone. Action to reduce inequality by countries acting in conjunction is likely to be more effective. For this reason, I believe it is imperative that the EU should prioritise measures to ensure achievement of the Europe 2020 target for reducing poverty and social exclusion. At a world level, the post-2015 Development Summit is of great importance. But the primary locus of policy-making remains national governments, and whether we move in the future towards less inequality is very much under the control of national policy-makers.

Chapter 11 ::

Can We Afford It?

In the US, the Congressional Budget Office (CBO) is legally required to produce estimates of the budgetary cost of legislative proposals approved by the committees of Congress. It gives similar cost estimates for many proposals that are being discussed or debated by members of the House of Representatives or the Senate. This procedure, adopted in the 1970s, imposes an essential discipline. In the same way, I take seriously the impact on the government budget of my proposed measures to reduce inequality. I have emphasised that a significant reduction in inequality requires measures beyond taxes and spending, but the measures designed to affect pre-redistribution incomes themselves have budgetary consequences. A rise in the minimum wage, for example, reduces the cost to the government of in-work, means-tested benefits; it brings in additional social security contributions and raises the receipts under the personal income tax. In the other direction, if enterprises adopt pay limits for their executives, then income tax receipts fall. Taking the measures as a whole, the challenge is to balance the extra outlays against the extra taxes. Critics will say that "the sums do not add up" or that "there is fiscal room to be more ambitious."

This chapter has two objectives: one general and one more specific. The general objective is to describe how economists approach these fiscal issues and to show how research on the modelling of taxes and benefits can inform the public debate. Economic models are often seen as abstract devices, removed from reality, but the tax-benefit models employed in this chapter allow bridges to be built between high-level policy discussion and the implications of policy changes for individuals and their families. Such bridges are essential wherever policy is being discussed, and the approach described would apply to the development of fiscal proposals in any country. The specific goal is to show in the case of the UK how a concrete version of the proposals can be financed and to demonstrate that—in broad terms—the fiscal arithmetic can be made to add up in the context of the UK economy. The calculations are necessarily surrounded by qualifications, but they indicate that the proposals should not be rejected solely on the grounds that "we cannot afford it." As such, the analysis is specific to a particular country and a particular set of circumstances, but the example should be instructive for readers elsewhere as to how governments can afford measures to reduce inequality. They also allow us to investigate the impact of *part* of the package of proposals on the extent of inequality and poverty. It is important to stress that the resulting reduction in inequality is only part of the story; there are other proposals for which we can predict the *direction* of the effect but not quantify its magnitude.

Tax-Benefit Models

The tools available to assess the feasibility and implications of proposals for tax-benefit reform have greatly advanced in recent decades and may be contrasted with the difficulties of policy-making in the past. Just after the Second World War, the idea of a citizen's income, in the form of a social dividend, received considerable support in the UK as an alternative to the Beveridge Plan for social security. As a result, the idea was explored seriously by the Royal Commission on Taxation established at that time. In discussing evidence presented to the commission on the distributional impact of the social dividend, Sir John Hicks expressed surprise at the figuring involved: "It does seem very extraordinary that there are so many pluses in the last column and so few minuses . . . this is essentially a redistributive scheme . . . and, therefore, on balance, somebody must lose for somebody else to gain."[1] The view that supporters presented to the commission was over-optimistic because their calculations were based on macroeconomic aggregates, but, as we have seen, there is a great deal of slippage between these totals and the incomes received by households. The social dividend calculations were not based on the actual circumstances of families in Britain, and therefore ignored this slippage.

Today much more sophisticated calculations can be made of the budgetary cost and of the impact of tax-benefit proposals on individual families, and there has been a great deal of research on the construction of tax-benefit models for this purpose. Progress in the construction of such models has been made possible by the availability of survey and administrative data on individual household incomes and circumstances. In earlier chapters, I described this data revolution. Equally important have been developments in computing. The now widespread use of tax-benefit models can be attributed in part to the enormous advances in computing power. When I first made estimates in the 1960s of the cost of proposals for the reform of social security in Britain (utilising tabulated rather than individual data), I had recourse to the most powerful mainframe computer in Cambridge—mostly used by astronomers at that time. Twenty years later, in 1988, Holly Sutherland and I were able to produce results on the effects on UK incomes of the Lawson Budget using a PC in the Shadow Cabinet Room before the chancellor had completed his speech.[2] Today, Holly directs the EUROMOD project, which has constructed a single tax-benefit model covering twenty-seven members of the European Union, for which results can be obtained in a matter of minutes. As a result of this investment, we can go beyond wishful thinking or "back of the envelope" calculations when considering major reforms of the tax-and-benefit system.

What Is a Tax-Benefit Model?

How do such tax-benefit models work? At heart they follow a pattern like that shown in the Guide to Household Income. For each household interviewed in a representative sample survey, a calculation is made of the different elements of income, including all transfers received, and of the payments made in taxes. These are then added, and multiplied up, to reach a total for the UK population as a whole. This means that, if there are 27,000 households in the survey and 27 million households in the UK, then on average the sample figures are multiplied by 1,000. It is clearly important that the sample be representative. The method requires not that every household stands the same probability of being included but that the probabilities of inclusion are known and can be applied in the form of differential multiplying factors. Surveys are therefore crucial to the modelling. At the same time, we saw in Chapter 2 that household surveys have their limitations. Some people do not live in households;

some people do not agree to take part; some people do not respond fully or honestly to questions. In multiplying up the survey numbers to arrive at estimates for the whole population, we have to take account of differential nonresponse. If, for example, the response rate of those aged sixty-five and over is higher than that for people under sixty-five, then a smaller multiplier is applied to the older group. Otherwise, pensioners would be over-represented.

Tax-benefit models build on the household surveys in that they add the facility to calculate taxes and benefits. Operating on the household data, the models use information on individual and household characteristics, and on market incomes, to calculate benefit entitlements and tax liabilities. In this way, they provide not only a description of the current state of affairs but also much more: parallel calculations both of the current policy impact and of what would happen to household incomes, and to tax revenue and benefit spending, if a policy change were introduced. These parallel calculations, shown in Figure 11.1, tell us whether a particular household gains or loses from the policy change. By adding up the changes for individual households, appropriately weighted, we can see the overall effect on the government budget. In this chapter, the results are based on calculations made by Paola De Agostini, Chrysa Leventi, Iva Tasseva, and Holly Sutherland using the UK component of the EUROMOD model, which employs data from the Family Resources Survey for 2009–2010, updated to the later policy year 2014–2015.[3] It should be noted that the taxes covered do not include indirect taxes, such as VAT or customs duties.

Qualifications

The scheme set out in Figure 11.1 may appear to be a simple matter of arithmetic. Below the surface, however, are problems to be resolved. The first is that the different tax-and-benefit policies have to be modelled, taking account of all the diversity of household circumstances. The exercise is not based on an assumed representative person earning the average wage and living with a partner and two children. The tax-benefit models seek to incorporate all the available information about a family. For the policy-maker, it is essential that the models contain "all human

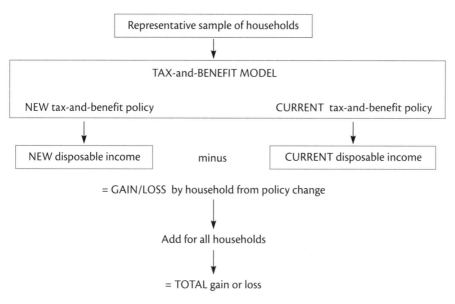

FIGURE 11.1: Calculating who gains and who loses

life"; otherwise there is a serious risk that the introduction of a policy change will produce unexpected results. More than once I have seen a government minister embarrassed by people who were on the losing side of a reform and about whose circumstances the minister had not been warned. Moreover, it is not just family circumstances that are complex; the policies themselves are byzantine. The annual Child Poverty Action Group's *Welfare Benefits and Tax Credit Handbook* now extends to more than 1,700 pages. The description of the variables used in the UK component of EUROMOD runs to 38 pages. Just to give one example, in considering the increase of (newly taxable) Child Benefit, we have to ask whether the increase is to be taken into account in assessing eligibility for means-tested benefits, and, if so, should it be the amount before or after the deduction of income tax?

A second problem is that, since the tax-benefit models are built on individual data, it is possible to compare the calculated taxes and benefits with those recorded in the household survey. Such an exercise can reveal incoherencies in the raw data. The respondent may have been confused in answering the detailed questions. The exercise may reveal limitations in the model: we may lack the information to verify conditions for benefit receipt (such as those related to past contributions). A more worrying explanation is that people may not receive the benefits to which they are entitled. As we saw in Chapter 8, a significant number of people do not claim the means-tested benefits for which they qualify. If it is simply assumed that all households get the benefit to which they are entitled, then the total cost is overestimated and the effectiveness of the benefit system is exaggerated. In the tax-benefit model for the UK employed here, allowance is made for non-take-up. The model makes use of the take-up proportions estimated by the Department of Work and Pensions: for example, 23.5 per cent of those entitled to Pension Credit are assumed not to claim the benefit, and that proportion reaches 51 per cent among those who qualify only for the Savings Credit component.[4] Since one of the primary aims of the policy reforms is to provide help to those who are not receiving the means-tested benefits to which they are entitled, it is essential to take account of non-take-up.

A third issue is that the new policy may induce changes in behaviour. If the income tax is raised, people may work more or less. Increased pensions may cause people to save less. In the calculations made here, and in the typical official costings, it is assumed that no such changes take place. They are therefore less complete than if behavioural responses could be taken into account. The steps necessary to consider behavioural response are, however, far from straightforward. One approach is to consider the impact of the tax-and-benefit parameters on the underlying decisions, such as the choice of hours of work or of retirement age. These decisions have been the subject of a great deal of econometric analysis, producing results of considerable interest, but they have been limited to particular areas of behaviour, notably those concerned with labour supply.[5] Use of these results in a tax-benefit model would therefore cover only a subset of the possible behavioural responses. Moreover, the results are often limited to specific subgroups of the population, and it is not evident that applying partial results would be satisfactory.

A different approach is to consider the gross income that is the result of a range of decisions. How much income people receive depends on which job they choose, on how many hours they work, on their past decisions about education, on how much they have saved, on their asset portfolio, and on other choices. All of these decisions are rolled up in the estimated response of gross income to variations in taxes and benefits. It is therefore not surprising that, as we saw in Chapter 7, there can be a wide margin of error around the estimated responses. What is more, in order to interpret the distributional impact, we have to unravel the underlying determinants. The footballer example illustrates the problem. If his gross pay remains unchanged in the face of an increase in the rate of income tax, then the footballer would bear the reduction in income, and the simple tax-benefit model calculation would be correct. On the other hand, if the footballer were to be paid on a net basis, then the cost of any increase in income taxation would fall on the club and be passed on to spectators in one form or another. It would then be necessary to trace the distributional implications, and this is not easily done.

For these reasons, official costings tend to be on the "no-behavioural-change basis" followed here. In the US, the Congressional Budget Office discusses the issue from a macroeconomic perspective: "CBO's cost estimates generally do not reflect changes in behavior that would affect total output in the economy, such as any changes in the labor supply or private investment resulting from changes in fiscal policy." The CBO adopts the convention of not incorporating behavioural effects in part because the estimates of the effects "are highly uncertain."[6] But even if there were a high degree of certainty about the size of the estimated effect, there remain serious problems of interpretation.

UK Proposals and Their Cost

I turn now to the cost of the proposals in the specific context of the UK in 2014–2015. There are fifteen proposals, and they are treated in three categories. The first category consists of those which do not enter the budgetary calculations since the cost is likely to be negligible or depends on further policy decisions. The second and third categories are both included in the budgetary package, but in the former case only a total figure enters, whereas for the third category there is a full distributional analysis based on the tax-benefit model.

The first category consists of those proposals for which the budgetary cost is hard to determine or is likely to be negligible, and so they are not included in the cost estimates. Strengthening of the role of the social partners, or the redirection of scientific research, may have consequences for tax receipts and transfer spending, but these are not easy to quantify and may be either positive or negative. In these cases, however, the final sum is likely to be small compared to the billions that arise under other proposals. For this reason I have shown these as "negligible" in the summary Table 11.1. In the case of the sovereign wealth fund (Proposal 7), the cost refers only to the operation of the fund. New investment in the fund would require the government to run a corresponding budget surplus, and this does not enter the present calculations. In the case of the guaranteed return to small savers, the forecasting of the cost depends on the future path of interest rates, and I have not attempted to estimate the extent to which this will add to borrowing costs.

The remaining eleven proposals all enter the budgetary package, as indicated in Table 11.1. Of these, Proposal 11 (Council Tax reform) is by assumption revenue-neutral. The capital endowment (Proposal 6) is to be financed by the reformed Inheritance Tax (Proposal 10), so that the cost to the rest of the budget is that arising from the transfer of the current Inheritance Tax revenue (taken to be £3.5 billion in 2014–2015). The cost of the guarantee of employment to the unemployed has been estimated on the basis of paying the living wage for a thirty-five-hour week for fifty-two weeks. This net cost calculation allows for the saving on the Job-seeker's Allowance and other means-tested benefits resulting from the return to employment, for the increased amount of Child Tax Credit to which the recipients would be entitled, and the income tax and National Insurance Contributions that would be payable. With some allowance for administrative costs, the net cost could be in the region of £6.5 billion. (Here, as elsewhere, no account is taken of changes in the amounts paid in indirect taxes.) With the national pay policy, to the extent that this leads to moderation of top pay, there will be a reduction in income tax and National Insurance Contribution receipts (including employer contributions). In the opposite direction, the raising of the national minimum wage to the level of the living wage has the effect of increasing these receipts. Although the latter is fully specified, the former is not, and, in the absence of any firm basis to make revenue estimates, I simply assume that the two components broadly cancel. The final proposal—increasing ODA to 1 per cent of Gross National Income—would cost some £4.5 billion in 2014–2015 terms.

TABLE 11.1. *Analysis of fifteen proposals for the UK*

Proposal	Budgetary cost (2014–2015 terms)	Distributional analysis
1. Direction of technological change	Negligible	
2. Competition policy, strengthening of social partners and Social and Economic Council	Negligible	
3. Unemployment target and guaranteed public employment	*Budgetary package*	
4. National pay policy and increase in minimum wage	*Budgetary package*	
5. Guaranteed return for small savers	Not easily predicted	
6. Capital endowment	*Budgetary package*	
7. UK Investment Authority	Negligible	
8. More progressive income tax structure	*Budgetary package*	Yes
9. Earned Income Discount	*Budgetary package*	Yes
10. Lifetime capital receipts tax	*Budgetary package*	
11. Replace Council Tax by property tax	Revenue-neutral	
12. Child Benefit	*Budgetary package*	Yes
13. Participation income	*Budgetary package*	Yes
14. Social insurance	*Budgetary package*	Yes
15. Overseas aid	*Budgetary package*	

Taken together, these different elements require, therefore, additional revenue equal to £14.5 billion. Against this may be set the extra revenue from the base broadening for income tax and National Insurance Contributions described in Chapter 7 (this is not included in the tax-benefit calculations). On the basis of the official costing of tax expenditures this would represent £11.6 billion in 2013–2014 terms, but with the more progressive rate structure proposed the additional revenue is likely to be significantly higher. Taking all these elements together, I work on the basis that, for overall budget neutrality, the remaining measures should generate a surplus of some £2.5 billion. I need hardly draw attention to the highly approximate nature of this calculation.

The third category of proposals consists of those for which distributional estimates are made using the tax-benefit model—those marked "Yes" in the final column of Table 11.1. This yields not only more accurate budgetary calculations but also estimates of the impact on the extent of inequality and poverty. It should be emphasised that the distributional results relate only to this subset of proposals. They cover only five out of the fifteen measures proposed.

Detailing the Five Proposals

The five proposals covered by the tax-benefit modelling need to be spelled out in more detail:

A) Proposal 8 for income tax:

» A more progressive rate structure for the personal income tax, with an initial rate of 25 per cent on taxable income (income in excess of the tax threshold), followed by 35 per cent when taxable income reaches £35,000 a year; by 45 per cent when taxable income reaches £55,000; by 55 per cent when taxable income reaches £100,000; and with a top rate of 65 per cent on taxable income above £200,000.

» National Insurance Contribution rates unchanged but upper-earnings limit (Class 1 for employees and Class 4 for the self-employed) raised to £55,000 per year.

» Abolition of the current withdrawal of the personal allowance at higher incomes.

» Retention of the additional age allowance, blind person's allowance, 10 per cent savings rate, but abolition of married couple's allowance.

B) Proposal 9 for Earned Income Discount

» Discount of 20 per cent on earned income (including self-employment and pension income); discount to be withdrawn when earned income reaches £23,333 by subtracting 40 per cent of earnings above this level, so that the discount is extinguished at £35,000.

» Personal income tax threshold reduced from £10,000 to £8,000 per year; with discount at 20 per cent; this leaves effective threshold unchanged where all income is earned (since 20 per cent of £10,000 plus £8,000 gives a total tax-free amount of £10,000).

C) Proposal 12 for Child Benefit

» Reinstatement of Child Benefit at higher incomes, so that it is paid for all children, but Child Benefit taxable in the hands of the person in the couple with the lowest taxable income.

» Child Benefit to be paid at £40 per week per child (eligibility defined as at present).
» Entitlement to Child Tax Credit and to child components of Housing Benefit and Council Tax Benefit to be reduced by decreasing child and family premiums by the amount of the increase in Child Benefit over the current rate (£20.50 a week for the first child and £13.55 a week for subsequent children).

At this point, there are two alternatives:
EITHER

D) Proposal 13 for participation income

» Introduction of a PI paid to all adults, defined as those aged sixteen and over (excluding those sixteen to eighteen if enrolled in secondary education and not married).[7]
» The PI paid on an individual basis with account taken of the individual National Insurance benefits, so that if T denotes the state pension paid to a person then that person receives the higher of PI and T; in the former case, T continues to be paid, but there is a PI equal to (PI-T).
» The PI received by individuals is taken into account in the calculation of the income-tested benefits received.
» Income tax threshold and National Insurance Contribution Primary Threshold set to zero.

OR

E) Proposal 14 for social Insurance

» National Insurance State Pension (basic pension and additional state pensions) raised by 25 per cent.
» Contributory Job-seeker's Allowance raised to £113.10 per week (level of existing basic retirement pension); contributory ESA and Bereavement Allowance increased by 25 per cent.
» A larger increase in Child Benefit than under Proposal 12 below, with a premium of £50 a week for the first child (making the total payment £90 a week for the first child), and an additional £20 a week for second and subsequent children (making the total payment per child £60 a week); these would be taxable as under Proposal 12.

In all cases, the benefit cap applied by the Coalition government (limiting the amount that can be paid to people aged sixteen to sixty-four) would be removed.

Budgetary Cost

The first step is to calculate the net budgetary cost. This may appear straightforward, but the calculation has to take account of the interaction between the different elements. For example, we cannot simply look at how many people are in each income range and how much more tax they pay, and add these up. The tax paid affects the entitlement to income-tested benefits that are based on income after taxes. The more tax paid, the more the benefit to which taxpayers are entitled. The increase in spending on means-tested benefits has to be subtracted from the increase in income tax receipts. This is why we need a tax-benefit model that incorporates the complex tax-and-benefit rules and the diverse range of household circumstances.

The move to a more progressive income tax combined with the Earned Income Discount (steps A and B) raises the net revenue by some £31.0 billion in 2014–2015 terms. This a substantial increase in income tax receipts—about one-fifth. Allowing for the extra revenue required on balance for other items in the package, this means that the spending proposals in the package can cost £28.5 billion.

The spending proposals in the package have in common an increase in Child Benefit. Raising the Child Benefit to £40 a week for all children has a large apparent gross cost (some £16 billion), but making it taxable and taking account of the *increase* when calculating entitlement to income-tested benefits reduces the net cost substantially. In calculating the cost, it has been assumed that Proposal 8 is in force; that is, the calculations are cumulative.[8] At this point, for those childless readers who are regarding £40 a week as an eye-watering amount, I should remind them that it has become taxable. For those on the initial tax band, the increase is indeed substantial: the after-tax weekly amount is £30, compared with the present rate of £20.50 for the first child and £13.55 for all other children. The net benefit is tapered as income rises. For those on the 55 per cent tax band, the after-tax benefit is £18. Moreover, it should be remembered that the cost of a child embodied in the EU poverty threshold for

2013 was some £55.00 a week, and the Minimum Income Standard (discussed earlier in relation to the living wage) allowance for an additional child is £90 a week or more.

After this increase in Child Benefit, £22.9 billion would be available for the remaining spending items in the package. This can be used in one of two ways, where the measures outlined above have been designed to yield the required surplus of £2.5 billion (when rounded). The first route is via the participation income, which is additional to the existing system, so that modelling using the tax-benefit model is essential. The amount of PI that can be paid while securing the £2.5 billion surplus is £3,110 per person per year, which is comfortably more than the value (£2,500) of the current tax threshold at the initial tax rate of 25 per cent. (As noted in Chapter 8, when making the calculations the participation condition has not been imposed; to this extent the cost is overstated.) The payment of £60 a week per person provides a point of departure. If, as has often been proposed by the supporters of a citizen's income, there is a higher tax rate, then the PI can be higher: there is a trade-off between the PI level and tax rates levied under Proposal 8. If all income tax rates, except the top rate of 65 per cent, were to be increased by 5 percentage points, the PI could be raised to £4,061, or nearly £80 a week per person.

The second—alternative—route is that of renewed social insurance. The proposals described above cost a small amount (some £250 million) more than the permitted total cost as part of the package. It should be noted that the modelling does not cover two elements of the proposals made in Chapter 8 (as may be seen from the description of E above). The increase in state pension is assumed to be paid to all pensioners, rather than in the form of a Minimum Pension Guarantee. The cost is to this extent greater than would be the case with the guarantee proposal. In the opposite direction, the model does not take account of the proposed extensions of entitlement to social insurance, such as that involving extension of Contributory Job-seeker's Allowance. This causes the cost to be understated.

Impact of (Part of) the Proposals

We have therefore a set of proposals for which the—broadbrush—numbers add up, in the sense that they are revenue-neutral relative to current policies. For five of the proposals, we can use the tax-benefit model to investigate the impact on inequality and poverty. These proposals are 8 (progressive income tax), 9 (Earned Income Discount), 12 (Child Benefit) and 13 (participation income), or 14 (social insurance). In looking at the results, we must remember that there are ten other proposals that together are likely to have a significant effect in reducing income inequality. (The net cost of these proposals is, however, taken into account.)

Earlier in the book I suggested that a salient reduction in overall inequality, as measured by the Gini coefficient, would be a 3 percentage point reduction, taking the present value of 32.1 per cent (as calculated in the EUROMOD model) to 29.1 per cent or below. A salient reduction in the number living in poverty would, equally, be a 3 percentage point reduction, from the present level of 16.0 per cent (again the EUROMOD figure). The last of these would be closely in line with the one-sixth target of the Europe 2020 strategy (which would take the figure to 13.3 per cent).

The first step—the income tax reforms of Proposal 8 and the Earned Income Discount of Proposal 9—is estimated to reduce the Gini coefficient from 32.1 to 30.4 per cent, which takes us more than half way to a salient reduction. It should be emphasised that these are estimates. There is a margin of error (95 per cent confidence interval) around the decrease of 1.7 percentage points, which is some 0.2 percentage points. The Child Benefit reform is directed at securing fairness between families with and without children, and it is not therefore surprising that there is only a small reduction in the Gini coefficient to 30.2 per cent. The final step depends on which route is chosen. With the PI and the same tax rates, the Gini coefficient is reduced to 28.2 per cent. (This, and the figures given below, relate to the total effect of all proposed measures for which calculations are made: A, B, C, and D in this case.) With all tax rates increased by 5 percentage points, going from 30 per cent up to 60 per cent, but leaving the top rate at 65 per cent (remember that it is average, not marginal, rates that matter from the point of view of redistribution), the Gini coefficient would be reduced to 26.6 per cent. With the reform of social insurance, the combined effect of A, B, C, and E is that the Gini coefficient is reduced to 29.4 per cent. This falls a little short of the 3 per cent salience criterion, whereas the combined set of measures including the PI scheme, even with the lower tax rates, comfortably passes this test. With higher tax rates, the combined measures achieve a 5.5 percentage point reduction.

Effects on Poverty

As far as the overall poverty rate is concerned, the first step—the income tax reforms and the Earned Income Discount—has a modest effect, and combined with the Child Benefit reform the poverty rate is only reduced from 16.0 to 15.6 per cent. It should be noted that, when making these policy changes, the poverty threshold is kept unchanged; the median income changes but the threshold (60 per cent of the median) remains at the level set by the baseline median. The small impact reflects the fact that those families currently on means-tested benefits derive little benefit, although a not insignificant number (328,000) are floated off dependence on tax credits and other means-tested benefits. Those gaining most are the families entitled to, but not currently claiming, means-tested benefits. These families are among those who are currently the worst off. The final step depends again on which route is chosen. With the reform of social insurance, the poverty rate is reduced to 13.9 per cent (again, this is the combined effect of all the measures, in this case A, B, C, and E). With the PI and the same tax rates, the poverty rate is reduced to 12.1 per cent. With all tax rates increased by 5 percentage points (but leaving the top rate at 65 per cent) the poverty rate would be reduced to 10.4 per cent, with a margin of error from 10.0 to 10.9 per cent. Importantly, the proposals would reduce not only the extent but also the depth of poverty. The depth is measured by the poverty gap, which shows the average shortfall as a percentage of the poverty threshold. In the baseline situation, the gap is 4.7 per cent, but this is more than halved to 2.2 per cent among those remaining below the poverty line. The PI version of the reforms therefore not only ensures that the UK meets the Europe 2020 target (with the social insurance version, the target is nearly met) but also provides considerable assistance to people still below the poverty line.

Child poverty is significantly reduced. The reform of social insurance (measures A, B, C, and E) reduces the child poverty rate from 16.8 per cent to 14.6 per cent, and the poverty gap for children from 4.6 per cent to 3.7 per cent, the latter showing that there is substantial gain to those remaining below the poverty line. With the PI and the same tax rates, the poverty rate is reduced to 13.4 per cent. With all tax rates increased by 5 percentage points (but leaving the top rate at 65 per cent) the poverty rate would be reduced to 12.1 per cent—that is, nearly 5 percentage points— and the poverty gap would be more than halved.

Overall Distributional Effect

The income schedule proposed here may appear to involve worryingly high tax rates, but it is important to distinguish, as stressed earlier, between the *marginal* tax rates, which were the focus of attention, and the *average* tax rates. It is the latter that determine how much of income goes in tax. The average rate rises much less steeply. For example, with the tax schedule studied here, the marginal income tax rate reaches 45 per cent when total income is £63,000, but the average income tax rate does not reach 45 per cent until income is over £200,000. It should also be remembered that the purpose of the Earned Income Discount is to ensure that the introduction of the progressive tax structure does not raise the tax rate on low levels of earnings (and pensions), while not extending this benefit to all levels of earnings. It provides help to low earners without conveying the benefit to those with investment income. In both respects, it differs from introducing a new lower income tax band, which benefits both higher earners and those with investment income.

The impact of the two versions of the proposals (PI and SI), in each case combined with Proposals 8, 9, and 12, is shown in Figure 11.2 in terms of the proportions gaining or losing by more than 5 per cent in each tenth of the income distribution, ranked by household equivalised disposable income. So "1" indicates the lowest tenth and shows that there were mostly gainers but some losers. There are in fact more of both groups for the PI scheme, with 72 per cent gaining but 10 per cent losing. The latter figure is a reason for concern; at the same time, the losers may be helped by other proposed measures not covered by the calculations. For example, retired people with modest investment income would be paying more tax as a result of the reduction in the threshold, but they are likely to benefit from the proposal designed to raise the return to small savers.

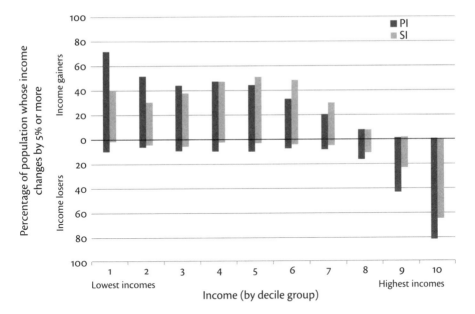

FIGURE 11.2: Effects of proposed PI and SI programmes on income, by income level

This graph shows the effects on income of the proposed participation income (PI) and social insurance (SI); see Proposals 13 and 14 in the text for details. In each case, they are combined with Proposals 8, 9, and 12. The effects vary with income; here the population is divided into tenths (decile groups), with Group 1 the lowest-income (bottom 10%) households and Group 10 the highest-income (top 10%) households. In each income group, some percentage of households will gain more than 5% of their income (part of bar above 0) and some percentage will lose more than 5% of their income (part of bar below 0). Note that under both the proposed PI and the proposed SI, lower-income households tend to gain income, whereas higher-income households tend to lose income. Although the results relate to only five out of the fifteen proposals made in this book, they generate the £2.5 billion required to cover the net cost of the other parts of the budgetary package.

Overall, the participation income is more redistributive, and the proportion gaining in excess of 5 per cent falls more regularly with income than with the social insurance alternative. With the latter, the proportion of gainers is actually higher in the middle of the distribution. The majority (52 per cent) of those in the bottom half of the distribution gain 5 per cent or more with the PI; with the SI scheme the proportion is 41 per cent—still an impressive figure. If the level of the PI were increased, along with higher tax rates, the proportion in the bottom half gaining

5 per cent or more would rise to 62 per cent. Substantial redistribution is possible.

Qualifications

In considering the impact on inequality described above, we must remember that the estimated reduction is the result of only part of the proposals made here. Indeed, there are additional fiscal measures under Proposal 8 that have not been modelled and which tend to lower the extent of inequality: for example, the removal of tax privileges for investors, the benefit from which is likely to accrue largely to those in the upper ranges. Moreover, the results quoted above have to be seen in the light of the limitations of the underlying tax-benefit model. Rich though the data are, and much more securely based though the calculations may be than earlier methods of figuring, the results are surrounded by "health warnings," as Paola De Agostini and Holly Sutherland emphasise in their description of the model. In particular, they note that "high income people, self-employment earnings and investment income are generally underrepresented, possibly due to higher survey non-response by the types of people concerned, and under reporting of such sources of income, particularly by high income respondents."[9] The results are therefore likely to understate the additional revenue raised by the increased top rates of income tax.

The most serious qualification is that the calculations make no allowance for changes in gross incomes induced by the tax-and-benefit changes. In the case of the top tax rate increases, this may cause the revenue to be overstated. However, there are other elements in the package that work towards increasing gross incomes. The strategy adopted is based on reducing dependence on means-testing, which has failed to reach all of those entitled, which has led to great complexity, and which has given many people severe disincentives to work and to save. The SI scheme would cut the number of people living in households receiving means-tested benefits from 22.3 million to 18.1 million. The PI scheme would reduce the number of people living in households receiving means-tested benefits by substantially more, to 17.1 million, or to 15.4 million with the increased tax rates. It would reduce expenditure on means-tested benefits from £63.2 billion to £40.8 billion, or £35.9 billion with increased taxes. These are large reductions: 5 million, or as many as 7 million, people would be floated off means-tested benefits. This scaling back of tax credits and other means-tested benefits would reduce the number of people facing high marginal tax rates. On top of this, it would reduce administrative costs and ease the lives of many people.

Summary

In brief, these calculations suggest that a revenue-neutral version of the proposals could achieve a salient reduction in overall inequality, in overall poverty, and in child poverty. With a Gini coefficient reduced from 32 per cent to around 28 per cent, the UK would be on the way to becoming more like a middle-of-the-road OECD country, rather than keeping company with high-inequality countries such as the US. The proposals could reduce significantly the number of people living in families dependent on means-tested benefits. The UK government has chosen to go down the route of Universal Credit, preserving means-testing, but here I have shown that there are alternatives.

But this would only be a step towards lower inequality. The calculations provide a warning of the limits of what can be achieved by conventional redistribution through taxes and benefits. They underline the importance of the proposals that seek to render incomes less unequal before taxes and transfers. Securing full employment, with a fairer distribution of pay, and a more egalitarian ownership of capital are essential elements in any strategy to reduce inequality.

The Way Forward

This book has been written in an attempt to answer the question, If we wish to reduce the extent of inequality, how can this be done? There are many reasons to tackle inequality. If we reduce inequality of economic outcomes, then this contributes to securing the equality of opportunity that is seen as a key feature of a modern democratic society. Social evils, such as crime and ill-health, are attributed to the highly unequal nature of societies today. These provide an instrumental reason for seeking to achieve lower levels of poverty and inequality, as does the fear that extremes of inequality are incompatible with a functioning democracy. And there are those, like me, who believe that the present levels of economic inequality are intrinsically inconsistent with the conception of a good society. Whatever the reason for concern, the question remains— how can a significant reduction in inequality be achieved?

The aim is to outline ways forward, not the final destination. I have not sought to describe an ultimately desirable state of our society; this book is not an exercise in utopianism. Rather, it indicates directions of movement for those who are concerned with reducing inequality. And it starts from the current state of society. Woodrow Wilson, in his first Inaugural Address as US president in 1913, said that "we shall deal with our economic system as it is and as it may be modified, not as it might be if we had a clean sheet of paper to write upon."[1]

The steps to be taken depend on the reasons that societies are so unequal and why inequality has risen in recent decades. Just why has there been an "Inequality Turn" in the years since 1980? In seeking to apply the tools of economics to answer this question, I have stressed the need to place distributional issues at the heart of the analysis. This is not a fashionable position among economists, but one that is, I believe, essential, not only to provide an understanding of inequality but also to explain the working of the economy and to tackle the major policy challenges facing us today. It makes little sense to posit that the world consists of identical people with the same resources and interests if we are confronting problems of restoring fiscal balance, of ageing populations, of climate change, or of international imbalances. Consideration of the distributional dimension is necessary if we are to relate the big numbers of economic policy—such as GDP—to the real-life experience of individual citizens.

The approach adopted in this book differs from that of much of mainstream economics in placing distributional issues centre stage. It emphasises the following:

» In order to understand inequality, we need to examine all aspects of our societies, both today and how they developed in the past.
» The historical record is better interpreted in terms of episodes, rather than long-run trends, and we can learn from the periods during which inequality has been reduced.
» Moves towards a lesser extent of inequality are achieved through changes in market incomes, as well as through taxes and spending.
» The sources of rising inequality are to be found in both capital and labour markets; it is not just a matter of an increased premium on educational qualifications.
» Market power plays an important role, and we need to investigate the locus of decision-making and the scope for countervailing power.
» The world is changing in significant respects, notably in the nature of employment and in the relation between wealth (as a source of income) and capital (as a source of control).

Crucially, I do not accept that rising inequality is inevitable: it is not solely the product of forces outside our control. There are steps that can be taken by governments, acting individually or collectively, by firms, by trade unions and consumer organisations, and by us as individuals to reduce the present levels of inequality.

The Proposals

As explained at the outset, I have not discussed investment in education and training, which I regard as important and complementary to the measures proposed here. Rather, I have focused on proposals that have been less widely canvassed and that are more radical. The fifteen proposals are summarised below:

PROPOSAL 1: The direction of technological change should be an explicit concern of policy-makers, encouraging innovation in a form that increases the employability of workers, emphasising the human dimension of service provision.

PROPOSAL 2: Public policy should aim at a proper balance of power among stakeholders, and to this end should (a) introduce an explicitly distributional dimension into competition policy, (b) ensure a legal framework that allows trade unions to represent workers on level terms, and (c) establish, where it does not already exist, a Social and Economic Council involving the social partners and other nongovernmental bodies.

PROPOSAL 3: The government should adopt an explicit target for preventing and reducing unemployment and underpin this ambition by offering guaranteed public employment at the minimum wage to those who seek it.

PROPOSAL 4: There should be a national pay policy, consisting of two elements: a statutory minimum wage set at a living wage, and a code of practice for pay above the minimum, agreed as part of a "national conversation" involving the Social and Economic Council.

PROPOSAL 5: The government should offer via national savings bonds a guaranteed positive real rate of interest on savings, with a maximum holding per person.

PROPOSAL 6: There should be a capital endowment (minimum inheritance) paid to all at adulthood.

PROPOSAL 7: A public Investment Authority should be created, operating a sovereign wealth fund with the aim of building up the net worth of the state by holding investments in companies and in property.

PROPOSAL 8: We should return to a more progressive rate structure for the personal income tax, with marginal rates of tax increasing by ranges of taxable income, up to a top rate of 65 per cent, accompanied by a broadening of the tax base.

PROPOSAL 9: The government should introduce into the personal income tax an Earned Income Discount, limited to the first band of earnings.

PROPOSAL 10: Receipts of inheritance and gifts inter vivos should be taxed under a progressive lifetime capital receipts tax.

PROPOSAL 11: There should be a proportional, or progressive, property tax based on up-to-date property assessments.

PROPOSAL 12: Child Benefit should be paid for all children at a substantial rate and should be taxed as income.

PROPOSAL 13: A participation income should be introduced at a national level, complementing existing social protection, with the prospect of an EU-wide child basic income.

PROPOSAL 14 (alternative to 13): There should be a renewal of social insurance, raising the level of benefits and extending their coverage.

PROPOSAL 15: Rich countries should raise their target for Official Development Assistance to 1 per cent of Gross National Income.

Alongside these proposals are:

Idea to pursue: a thoroughgoing review of the access of households to the credit market for borrowing not secured on housing.

Idea to pursue: examination of the case for an "income-tax-based" treatment of contributions to private pensions, along the lines of present "privileged" savings schemes, which would bring forward the payment of tax.

Idea to pursue: a re-examination of the case for an annual wealth tax and the prerequisites for its successful introduction.

Idea to pursue: a global tax regime for personal taxpayers, based on total wealth.

Idea to pursue: a minimum tax for corporations.

The proposals are set out in a way that should apply quite widely to different countries, even if some are specifically designed with the UK in mind (and some of the measures, such as those on social insurance, would simply bring the UK into line with its neighbours). A substantial role for Child Benefit, for example, should in my view be the cornerstone of redistributive policy in all countries, including the US, where such a measure might ensure that it was genuinely the case that "no child is left behind." I have proposed that a universal Child Benefit income could be enacted at the level of the EU, ensuring that all children in the EU are guaranteed a basic start in life.

The proposals are bold, but bold measures are required if, as in the case of the UK, we are to return to the levels of inequality before the "Inequality Turn" in 1980. To get back to the time when the UK was ranked in the middle of OECD countries and not among those at the high end of inequality, it is not enough to tinker with existing instruments of economic and social policy. Major reforms are required, engaging all areas of economic and social life. In the past, governments in the UK have taken bold moves. The Conservative government espoused a policy of selling local authority housing to tenants that cost some £200 billion in current terms. The 1997 Labour government introduced the national minimum wage. In some cases, policy was "over-bold," such as the Conservative Poll Tax, but this left in its wake the Council Tax, which represented a major shift in the principle of local taxation from ability to pay to the regressive benefit principle.

How to Make Progress

There has to be an appetite for action, and this requires political leadership. The inter-relation between inequality and politics is crucial. A major instrumental reason for concern about economic inequality is that concentrations of wealth and income convey political power and influence. Mark Hanna, US senator in the nineteenth century, famously remarked that "there are two things that are important in politics. The first is money and I can't remember what the second one is." The post-1980 rise in income inequality has reinforced the opposition to redistribution and strengthened support for economic policies, such as market liberalisation, that contribute to inequality: a cumulative process is in operation. Readers may feel that I have devoted too little attention to politics. This is not because I discount in any way the significance of the inequality/politics nexus. Rather, my aim has been to focus on one particular way in which the political message has been couched. This is the corrosive view that there is nothing that can be done: that there is no alternative to the present high levels of inequality. I reject this view. There have been periods in the past, not just in wartime, when significant reductions in inequality and poverty were achieved. The twenty-first century is different, notably in the nature of the labour market and in the globalisation of the economy, but we can learn from history when looking to the future.

One important lesson is that action needs to be taken across the whole range of government. Policy to combat inequality and poverty cannot be delegated to one ministry, or to one directorate of the European Commission, or to one agency of the United Nations. In the specific context of the UK, I have proposed the establishment of a Social and Economic Council, which could assume this overarching role. In other countries where such institutions exist, rather than abolishing them (as in Italy in 2014), governments need to reconsider their constitution and powers. In my view, such a body requires a wide membership, representing all stakeholders and ensuring that the interests of all—workers, consumers, nongovernmental organisations, as well as corporate organisations—are taken fully into account. This body can initiate the much-needed "national conversation" about national goals—such as setting a target for unemployment. But it also requires power. It must be able to call ministers to account for their actions in pursuing the agenda of reducing inequality and combating poverty. It must have access to the head of government and it must report to the legislature.

The book has discussed at length what can be done by national governments, and much of the "heavy lifting" will fall to them. Action does not, however, concern only national government. The approach adopted is relevant to all levels of government from local to multinational and worldwide—from Oxford City Council to the European Union and the World Bank. In some cases, action may be most appropriate at the local level, such as the role of local governments in developing employment in their local economy and in regeneration projects. In some cases, such as the global tax regime, action is possible only with intergovernmental agreement.

The reader may feel that, in emphasising the role of government action, I have not learned the lesson from history that many government initiatives end in abject failure, and it is therefore hopeless to embark on a further ambitious programme. To this counsel of despair, I have three responses. The first is that one of the factors (not the only one) underlying the reduction of inequality in the past has been successful government intervention. Such intervention included the social programmes created in the decades after the Second World War, equal pay legislation, the extension of education, and the operation of progressive capital and income taxation. These measures were not perfect, but they certainly had an effect. The second response is that an important reason for failure of government programmes has been a lack of prior planning and consultation. The ground needs to be prepared by spelling out proposals in detail and by public debate. I have stressed the importance of institutional detail in understanding current policy, and in the same way the ideas set out in this book need to be translated into concrete proposals for legislation and action. This process will no doubt lead to improvements in their form and content. I should emphasise that I am not wedded to the details set out in Chapters 4 to 8 and would welcome constructive amendments (although I should be less enthusiastic about "watering down"!).

The final response is that I have not suggested, and do not believe, that governments are the sole audience for this book. It is individuals who will ultimately determine whether the proposals set out here are implemented and whether the ideas are pursued. They will do so indirectly in their capacity as voters, and—perhaps today more importantly—as lobbyists through campaign groups and social media, acting as countervailing power to the paid members of the lobbying profession. Sending that email message to your elected representative makes a difference. But individuals can influence the extent of inequality in our society directly by their own actions as consumers, as savers, as investors, as workers, or as employers. This is most evident in terms of individual philanthropy, where transfers of resources not only are valuable in themselves but also provide a powerful signal of what we should like to see done by our governments. But, as I have stressed in the case of governments, transfers are only part of the story. Consumers make a difference by buying from suppliers who are paying a living wage, or whose products are fair trade. Individuals, acting on their own or collectively, make a difference by supporting local shops and enterprises. Savers can ask about the salary policy pursued by their shareholder-owned bank; they can transfer their funds to a mutual organisation. As I have stressed in the case of wages, market forces may limit the range of outcomes, but they leave room for other concerns to come into play, such as fairness and a sense of social justice. In our economic lives, as well as in our personal lives, we make many ethical decisions, and—taken together—our decisions can make a contribution to reducing the extent of inequality. I hope that this book has helped readers see how this can come about.

Grounds for Optimism

I have written this book in a positive spirit. I have stressed the importance of looking back in time, but I do not believe that we have returned to a world like that when Queen Victoria was alive. The citizens of OECD countries today enjoy a standard of living that is much higher than that of their great-grandparents. The achievement of a less unequal society in the period of the Second World War and subsequent postwar decades has not been fully overthrown. At a global level, the great divergence between countries associated with the Industrial Revolution is closing. It is true that since 1980 we have seen an "Inequality Turn" and that the twenty-first century brings challenges in terms of the ageing of the population, climate change, and global imbalances. But the solutions to these problems lie in our own hands. If we are willing to use today's greater wealth to address these challenges, and accept that resources should be shared less unequally, there are indeed grounds for optimism.

Glossary

Accrued gains are the increase in the value of an asset that has taken place over a specified period; gains are *realised* only when the asset is sold.

Average tax rate is the proportion of total income that is paid in tax: an average tax rate of 25 per cent means that the person is paying a quarter of his or her income in tax. Contrast this with marginal tax rate (defined below).

Beneficial ownership refers to the ultimate recipient of the income from an asset (and the proceeds from its sale); beneficial ownership is distinct from the legal ownership. For example, a pension fund may legally own shares but the ultimate beneficiaries (beneficial owners) are the pensioners.

Capital income is income generated by the ownership of an asset, and includes interest income, dividends on shares, rent, and capital gains/losses; it may include part of the income accruing to a person who owns a business (self-employment income).

Confidence interval gives the estimated range of values of a quantity that includes, with a given probability (such as 95 per cent), the unknown true value of the quantity in the population.

Correlation is a measure of the association between two variables, such as the earnings of husbands and earnings of wives. The Pearson correlation coefficient is equal to the covariance of the two variables divided by the product of their standard deviations, and lies between −1 (total negative correlation) and +1 (total positive correlation), with 0 indicating no association. The association of two variables can also be measured in terms of the correlation of the ranks.

Decile refers to the value of a variable at each of the nine points that divides the population into tenths when ranked in order. For example, the bottom decile of the income distribution is the income of the person 10 per cent from the bottom; the median is the fifth decile; the top decile is the ninth and is the income of the person 10 per cent from the top.

Difference in differences is a statistical method that seeks to learn about the effect of a policy (or other "treatment") by comparing the *changes* in two groups, one that was affected by the policy and one that was not. In effect it seeks to mimic, using observed data, the approach adopted in controlled experiments.

Discounting refers to the process of valuing income that will be received in the future, allowing for the fact that interest could have been earned if the same amount had been received today; if interest accrues annually at rate r, then the present discounted value of X income received T years in the future is equal to $(1+r)^{-T} X$.

Disposable income refers to income after deducting direct taxes (including social security contributions).

Elasticity measures the proportionate response of an economic quantity to a proportionate change in another variable. For example, the price elasticity of demand shows the change in the quantity demanded in response to a change in the price; an elasticity of 0.5 means that if the price rises by 10 per cent the demand falls by 5 per cent. It is conventional to define the elasticity positively even where, as in this case, the variables move in opposite directions.

Elasticity of substitution of two factors of production (such as labour and capital, or skilled and unskilled workers) refers to the ease of substituting one for the other; if the two factors must be used in fixed proportions, then the elasticity is zero; if they are interchangeable at a fixed ratio, then the elasticity is infinite.

Equivalence scales are used to adjust total household incomes for differences in the needs of the household in terms of size and composition. A simple adjustment is to divide household income by the number of members of the household, giving a per capita figure, but most scales assume that needs rise less than proportionately with the size of the household, as where the scale is taken as the square root of household size. A commonly used scale is the modified OECD scale, which gives 1 for the first adult and 0.5 for additional household members aged 14 or older, plus 0.3 for each child aged under 14.

Europe 2020 is the 10-year growth and jobs strategy for smart, sustainable, and inclusive growth proposed by the European Union in 2010; see http://ec.europa.eu/europe2020/europe-2020-in-a-nutshell/index_en.htm.

Factors of production include capital, land, and labour (where a distinction may be drawn between skilled and unskilled workers).

General equilibrium describes the overall balance of markets in the economy, including markets for factors of production and markets for goods and services. A market is in equilibrium where supply is equal to demand (or supply exceeds demand and the price is zero, as with air).

Gini coefficient is a measure of relative inequality with values lying between 0 (complete equality, everyone gets the same income) and 100 per cent (one person gets all the income); the Gini coefficient may exceed 100 per cent where some people have negative income. The Gini coefficient is defined as half the mean difference divided by the mean; geometrically, it is the area between the Lorenz curve (see below) and the line of equality, divided by the area of the whole triangle.

Gross Domestic Product (GDP) is a measure of national output, usually expressed in annual terms; it can be measured in three different ways: from the total value of production, from total expenditure, and from the total incomes of those engaged in production. It is "Gross" because it is measured before any allowance for the depreciation of capital goods; it is "Domestic" because it refers to the total value of production in a country, rather than Gross National Product (GNP) or Gross National Income (GNI), which refers to goods and services produced by capital and labour belonging to the country.

Gross income of households refers to total income from earnings, capital income, private transfers, and social transfers; it is equal to market income plus social transfers.

Gross National Income (GNI) is a measure of national income and equals Gross Domestic Product minus compensation of employees and property income payable to the rest of the world plus the corresponding items received from the rest of the world.

Hypothecation of a tax refers to the dedication of the revenue collected to a specific expenditure purpose.

Imputed rent refers to the notional income that people get from owning an asset that they use for their own consumption, such as an owner-occupied house.

Inequality Turn is the expression used in this book to describe the change in direction taken by inequality after 1980. Before 1980 inequality in OECD countries had been falling; since then the trend has been reversed and inequality today is higher in many of these countries.

Lorenz curve for a distribution of income is a curve formed by ranking people according to their income, and then plotting their cumulative share of total income as one moves up the distribution. The curve starts at 0 and ends at 100 per cent; if all incomes were identical, the curve would follow the diagonal joining these end points (the line of equality).

Marginal tax rate is the additional tax paid on an additional unit of income: a marginal tax rate of 65 per cent means that, if you earn an additional $1,000, then you pay an extra $650 in tax; it should not be confused with the average tax rate (defined above).

Market income of households refers to total income from earnings, capital income, and private transfers (see Table 1.5).

Material deprivation refers to the lack of particular goods or inability to participate in certain activities; the EU has endorsed indicators of material deprivation.

Median is the "middlemost" value that separates a population into two halves, so that half of the population is below the median and half is above; the median is the fifth decile.

Monopolistic competition denotes the situation where firms have market power but face competition; each firm faces a downward-sloping demand curve for its own product and the location of this curve depends on the decisions of its competitors.

Net worth of a household is the total value at a point in time of its assets minus its liabilities.

Perfect competition describes an economy in which everyone takes market prices as given: that is, they have no power to vary the prices at which they sell or buy.

Poverty trap describes the situation in which a person finds it difficult to rise above the poverty line on account of the deductions from any increase in earnings; an increase in gross earnings leads to only a small increase in net income, because more is paid in income tax/social security contributions and less is received in income-tested transfers.

Primogeniture refers to the practice of wealth, typically landed estates, being left to the eldest child, usually the eldest son.

Production function for an aggregate economy describes the level of output that can be produced with the available factors of production, usually capital and labour, but land and natural resources should also be taken into account when assessing sustainability.

Progressive taxation refers to a tax system in which the amount of tax paid (as a proportion of income) increases with the size of the income, so that, for example, a person on median income pays X per cent in tax and a person above median income pays more than X per cent.

Purchasing Power Parity Standards (PPPS) are rates of currency conversion designed to equate purchasing power in different currencies.

Real rate of interest refers to the rate of interest received after subtracting the rate of inflation (which has reduced the value of an asset denominated in monetary terms).

Reservation wage denotes the minimum wage at which a person will accept a given job; such a wage may form part of a worker's search strategy when seeking employment.

Response rate to a survey refers to the number of people who took part as a proportion of the total number in the original sample drawn.

Salient reduction is defined here in terms of a 3 (or more) percentage point reduction in the Gini coefficient, in the poverty rate, or in top income shares; and of a 5 per cent change in the ratio of the top decile to the median.

Skill-bias in technical progress indicates that one factor of production (skilled workers) is becoming more productive at a faster rate than the other factor (unskilled workers).

Subsidiarity is a principle, originating in Catholic social thought, favouring decentralisation of political action; as applied in European Union law, it requires that the Union should act only if, and insofar as, an action cannot be delivered by member states, operating at the levels of central, regional, or local government.

Tax expenditures are government expenditure programmes that operate through the tax code, allowing exemption against income tax or other taxes for spending on specific items or activities: for example, allowing deduction of private health insurance premiums from taxable income constitutes a form of tax expenditure.

Transfers are payments in cash or provision in kind to provide for particular needs or sets of circumstances; social transfers are those made by governments or official bodies; private transfers are those made by employers or private organisations such as pension funds.

Wage share in national income is the ratio of total compensation (including all employers' costs) to a measure of total national income; the measure of national income may be GDP at market prices or GDP at basic prices (earlier known as factor cost) or may be Net Domestic Product; in some cases, the share of wages includes a proportion of self-employment income.

Welfare state is a general term to describe a set of institutions to ensure health care, education, and social protection for all those who live in a country.

Zero-hours contract is an employment contract that does not guarantee any minimum hours of work; workers may have to be on call to work when needed, but employers do not have to offer them any work or pay them for being on call.

Notes

INTRODUCTION

1 Pew Research Global Attitudes Project, http://www.pewglobal.org/2014/10/16/middle-easterners-see-religious-and-ethnic-hatred-as-top-global-threat/.

2 George Santayana, *The Life of Reason, or, The Phases of Human Progress,* vol. 1: *Introduction and Reason in Common Sense* (New York: Charles Scribner's Sons, 1905).

3 For example, the report of the Friends of Europe makes a powerful case for investment in education and training as part of a broad social investment strategy: *Unequal Europe: Recommendations for a More Caring EU* (Brussels: Friends of Europe, 2015).

4 Stella Gibbons, *Cold Comfort Farm* (London: Allen Lane, 1932), xi. The dust jacket describes this as a "distressingly frivolous story"; the same may perhaps be said of this reference. The endnotes that follow will be limited to providing further explanation, guidance to the sources on which evidence is based, and bibliographic references. It should be noted, however, that "the speech was a lot of *flapdoodle* about the economy" is the example that *Merriam-Webster Dictionary* uses for the word.

CHAPTER 1 SETTING THE SCENE

1 Richard Tawney, *Equality* (London: Allen and Unwin, 1964, first published 1931): 46–47; and John Roemer, *Equality of Opportunity* (Cambridge, MA: Harvard University Press, 1998).

2 Ravi Kanbur and Adam Wagstaff, "How Useful Is Inequality of Opportunity as a Policy Construct?" ECINEQ Working Paper 338 (2014): 1–18, quote p. 5.

3 Joseph E. Stiglitz, *The Price of Inequality* (London: Allen Lane, 2012); and Kate Pickett and Richard Wilkinson, *The Spirit Level,* rev. ed. (London: Penguin, 2010).

4 This phrase is the subtitle of the book by Nolan McCarty, Keith T. Poole, and Howard Rosenthal, *Polarized America: The Dance of Ideology and Unequal Riches* (Cambridge, MA: MIT Press, 2006).

5 Dalton's article (Hugh Dalton, "The Measurement of the Inequality of Incomes," *Economic Journal* 30 [1920]: 348–361) was selected by the Royal Economic Society in its 125th anniversary celebrations as one of the outstanding articles published in the *Economic Journal* in that period. See Anthony B. Atkinson and Andrea Brandolini, "Unveiling the Ethics behind Inequality Measurement: Dalton's Contribution to Economics," *Economic Journal* 125 (forthcoming, 2015).

6 Amartya Sen, *On Economic Inequality* (Oxford: Clarendon Press, 1973), 16.

7 John Rawls, *A Theory of Justice* (Cambridge, MA: Harvard University Press, 1971).

8 Plato, *The Laws* V.744e (New York: Dutton, 1960), quote p. 127. I owe this reference to Ray C. Fair, "The Optimal Distribution of Income," *Quarterly Journal of Economics* 85 (1971): 551–579, quote p. 552.

9 Rawls, *A Theory of Justice*, 92.

10 Amartya Sen, *The Idea of Justice* (London: Allen Lane, 2009), 66.

11 Amartya Sen, *Development as Freedom* (Oxford: Oxford University Press, 1999).

12 See the website of the United Nations Development Programme: http://hdr.undp.org/en/content/human-development-index-hdi.

13 For further references to the capability approach, see the website of the Human Development and Capability Association: https://hd-ca.org/.

14 Anthony B. Atkinson, "Bringing Income Distribution in from the Cold," *Economic Journal* 107 (1997): 297–321.

15 Hugh Dalton, *Some Aspects of the Inequality of Incomes in Modern Communities* (London: Routledge, 1920), quote p. vii.

16 Agnar Sandmo, "The Principal Problem in Political Economy: Income Distribution in the History of Economic Thought," in Anthony B. Atkinson and François Bourguignon, eds., *Handbook of Income Distribution*, vol. 2A (Amsterdam: Elsevier, 2015), 3–65, quotes pp. 22, 60–61. The reference is to Gerard Debreu, *Theory of Value* (New York: John Wiley, 1959).

17 N. Gregory Mankiw, *Principles of Microeconomics*, 7th ed. (New York: Worth, 2007), and *Essentials of Economics*, 7th ed. (New York: Worth, 2014).

18 In contrast, the new teaching materials being produced by the INET CORE project give prominence to economic inequality. Under the question "What economics is about," the second of the four answers is learning "What explains the wealth and poverty of nations and people," http://core-econ.org/about/.

19 Robert E. Lucas, "The Industrial Revolution: Past and Future," *The Region, 2003 Annual Report of the Federal Reserve Bank of Minneapolis*, 5–20, quote p. 20.

20 Robert M. Solow, "Dumb and Dumber in Macroeconomics" (2003), available online at https://wwwo.gsb.columbia.edu/faculty/jstiglitz/festschrift/Papers/Stig-Solow.pdf.

21 It bears his name, but in fact the basic statistic—the mean difference—had already been proposed some thirty years earlier by two German scholars, Carl Christopher von Andrae and Friedrich Robert Helmert, as Gini generously acknowledged: Corrado Gini, *Variabilità e Mutabilità* (Bologna: Paolo Cuppini, 1912), 58n. Those interested in the history of statistics may know that Professor Helmert was also an early discoverer of the chi-squared distribution.

22 The weights are given by 2(1F) where F is the rank of the person in the distribution. See Anthony B. Atkinson and Andrea Brandolini, "On Analysing the
World Distribution of Income," *World Bank Economic Review* 24 (2010): 1–17.

23 For an introduction to measures of economic inequality, see Stephen P. Jenkins and Philippe van Kerm, "The Measurement of Economic Inequality," in
Wiemer Salverda, Brian Nolan, and Timothy M. Smeeding, eds., *The Oxford
Handbook of Economic Inequality* (Oxford: Oxford University Press, 2009):
40–67.

24 Herman P. Miller, *Income Distribution in the United States* (Washington, D.C.:
Bureau of the Census, 1966), quote p. 2. As he shows, the U.S. Census figures
up to the 1960s suggested that the reduction in inequality had come to an end
by 1944.

25 The taxpayers in the top 1 per cent change from year to year. However, downward mobility is limited. Of those in the top 1 per cent aged 35–40 in 1987, 24
per cent were in the top 1 per cent twenty years later, and 70 per cent were in
the top 10 per cent. See Table 1 in Gerald Auten, Geoffrey Gee, and Nicholas
Turner, "Income Inequality, Mobility, and Turnover at the Top in the US, 1987–
2010," *American Economic Review* 103 (2013): 168–172.

26 Robert M. Solow, "Income Inequality since the War," in Ralph E. Freeman, ed.,
Postwar Economic Trends in the United States (New York: Harper and Brothers,
1960), quote p. 135.

27 Suppose that the tax/transfer system can be approximated over most of the income range by a constant tax rate and a uniform benefit for everyone (an assumption that is a reasonable first approximation). A gross income of Y becomes a net income of $(1-t)Y + A$, where t is the tax rate and A is the benefit
paid to everyone (this can be thought of as the value of the personal tax allowance). Since A is the same for all, the Gini for disposable income is $(1-t)$ times
the Gini for market income (Y) divided by the ratio of average disposable income to average market income. Then, if government spending on goods and
services (health, education, defence, etc.) absorbs 20 per cent of tax revenue,
the latter ratio is equal to 80 per cent. Suppose further that the Gini coefficient
of market incomes is 50 per cent. The reduction in the Gini for disposable income from an increase Δt in the tax rate is then 0.5 times Δt divided by 0.8.
Inverting this relationship, it follows that the required increase in the tax rate is
equal to 0.8/0.5 (=1.6) times the desired reduction in the Gini for disposable
income.

28 For reviews of income inequality in OECD countries, see Andrea Brandolini
and Timothy M. Smeeding, "Income Inequality in Richer and OECD Countries," in Salverda, Nolan, and Smeeding, eds., *The Oxford Handbook of Economic Inequality*, 71–100; Salvatore Morelli, Timothy M. Smeeding, and Jeffrey
Thompson, "Post-1970 Trends in Within-Country Inequality and Poverty," in

Atkinson and Bourguignon, eds., *Handbook of Income Distribution,* vol. 2; and OECD, *Divided We Stand: Why Inequality Keeps Rising* (Paris: OECD, 2011).

29 Martin S. Feldstein, "Rethinking Social Insurance," *American Economic Review* 95 (2005): 1–24, quote p. 12.

30 Brian Abel-Smith and Peter Townsend, *The Poor and the Poorest* (London: G. Bell, 1965); and Anthony B. Atkinson, *Poverty in Britain and the Reform of Social Security* (Cambridge: Cambridge University Press, 1969).

31 The Europe 2020 target is described on the European Commission website: http://ec.europa.eu/europe2020/targets/eu-targets/. See also Anthony B. Atkinson and Eric Marlier, "Living Conditions in Europe and the Europe 2020 Agenda," in Anthony B. Atkinson and Eric Marlier, eds., *Income and Living Conditions in Europe* (Luxembourg: Publications Office of the European Union, 2010), 21–35.

32 The EU threshold is set at 60 per cent of the median equivalised household disposable income in the country in question, and therefore rises, or falls, in line with median income.

33 For an analysis of the mid-term situation for the Europe 2020 Strategy, see Hugh Frazer et al., "Putting the Fight against Poverty and Social Exclusion at the Heart of the EU Agenda: A Contribution to the Mid-Term Review of the Europe 2020 Strategy," OSE Paper 15 (2014), Observatoire Social Européen, Brussels.

34 Social Protection Committee, *Social Europe: Many Ways, One Objective* (Luxembourg: Publications Office of the European Union, 2014), quote p. 7.

35 John Donne, *Meditations XVII, Devotions upon Emergent Occasions* (London: Nonesuch Press, 1962), quote p. 538. Richard H. Tawney, "Poverty as an Industrial Problem," in *Memoranda on the Problems of Poverty* (London: William Morris Press, 1913).

36 Adam Smith, *An Inquiry into the Nature and Causes of the Wealth of Nations* (London: Routledge, 1903, first published 1776), quote p. 78. Milton Friedman and Simon Kuznets, *Income from Independent Professional Practice* (New York: National Bureau of Economic Research, 1945), quote p. 84.

37 For more information about equivalence scales, see Anthony B. Atkinson, Bea Cantillon, Eric Marlier, and Brian Nolan, *Social Indicators* (Oxford: Oxford University Press, 2002), 98–101.

38 See Rolf Aaberge, Audun Langørgen, and Petter Lindgren, "The Distributional Impact of Public Services in European Countries," Statistics Norway Research Department Discussion Paper 746 (2013), http://www.ssb.no/en/forskning/discussion-papers/_attachment/123883?_ts=13f50d54ab8.

39 These figures are from the World Top Incomes Database (WTID): http://topincomes.g-mond.parisschoolofeconomics.eu/.

40 George Eliot, *Silas Marner: The Weaver of Raveloe* (Edinburgh: William Black-wood, 1861).

41 Bill Gates, "Why Inequality Matters," review of Piketty, *Capital in the Twenty-First Century* (2014), http://www.gatesnotes.com/Books/Why-Inequality-Matters-Capital-in-21st-Century-Review.

42 Dirk Krueger and Fabrizio Perri, "Does Income Inequality Lead to Consumption Inequality?" *Review of Economic Studies* 73 (2006): 163–193, quote p. 163. Dale Jorgenson, "Did We Lose the War on Poverty?" *Journal of Economic Perspectives* 12 (1998): 79–96, quote p. 79. Bruce D. Meyer and James X. Sullivan, "Winning the War: Poverty from the Great Society to the Great Recession," *Brookings Papers on Economic Activity* (Fall 2012): 163–193, quote p. 163.

43 Orazio Attanasio, Erik Hurst, and Luigi Pistaferri, "The Evolution of Income, Consumption, and Leisure Inequality in the US, 1980–2010," NBER Working Paper No. 17982, April 2012, http://papers.nber.org/tmp/69610-w17982.pdf.

44 Mark A. Aguiar and Mark Bils, "Has Consumption Inequality Mirrored Income Inequality?" NBER Working Paper No. 16807, http://papers.nber.org/tmp/69610-w17982.pdf, quote p. 2.

45 John Sabelhaus et al., "Is the Consumer Expenditure Survey Representative by Income?" Finance and Economics Discussion Series, Divisions of Research & Statistics and Monetary Affairs, Federal Reserve Board, Washington, D.C.

46 Jonathan D. Fisher, David S. Johnson, and Timothy M. Smeeding, "Measuring the Trends in Inequality of Individuals and Families: Income and Consumption," *American Economic Review, Papers and Proceedings* 103 (2013): 184–188, quote p. 187.

47 B. Seebohm Rowntree, *Poverty: A Study of Town Life* (London: Longmans, Green and Co., 1901, new ed. 1922), quote p. 117.

48 Mollie Orshansky, "Counting the Poor: Another Look at the Poverty Profile," *Social Security Bulletin* 28 (1965): 3–29, Table E on p. 28.

49 James Tobin, "On Limiting the Domain of Inequality," *Journal of Law and Economics* 13 (1970): 263–277, quote p. 264. Tobin's essay is well worth reading today. He was a Nobel Prize–winning economist at Yale, who served on President Kennedy's Council of Economic Advisers. When approached about this post, Professor Tobin initially resisted, identifying himself as "an ivory tower economist." "That's all right, professor," Kennedy replied, "I am what you might call an ivory tower president." (Obituary for James Tobin in *Yale Bulletin and Calendar,* vol. 30, no. 22, 15 March 2002).

50 See Alessio Fusco, Anne-Catherine Guio, and Eric Marlier, "Characterising the Income Poor and the Materially Deprived in European Countries," in Atkinson and Marlier, *Income and Living Conditions in Europe,* pp. 133–153.

51 Brian Barry, "Social Exclusion, Social Isolation and the Distribution of In-

come," *CASEpaper* 12, Centre for Analysis of Social Exclusion, London School of Economics, quote p. 8.

52 Barbara Wootton, *The Social Foundations of Wage Policy* (London: Allen and Unwin, 1955).

53 There are interesting websites that allow you to enter your income and then tell you where you are in the income distribution of your country. For a number of countries, there is the website created by GivingWhatYouCan: https://www. givingwhatwecan.org/get-involved/how-rich-am-i. For the US, there is http:// www.whatsmypercent.com/. For the UK, the Institute for Fiscal Studies has created http://www.ifs.org.uk/wheredoyoufitin/.

54 Jan Pen, *Income Distribution* (London: Allen Lane, 1971), quote p. 9.

55 Polly Toynbee and David Walker, *Unjust Rewards* (London: Granta, 2009), quote p. 25.

56 See sources for Figure 1.1.

57 Website of the Institute for Fiscal Studies: see sources for Figure 1.2.

58 Difference by ethnic groups is an important topic that I do not cover here. As far as top incomes are concerned, in the United States in 2013, 5.7 per cent of Non-Hispanic White households had a total money income (before taxes and non-cash benefits) of $200,000 or more a year. The corresponding figures for Black and for Hispanic households were only a third of that rate (1.8 per cent). (For Asian households, in contrast, the proportion was higher at 8.5 per cent.) These figures are from the U.S. Bureau of the Census, *Income, Poverty, and Health Insurance Coverage in the United States: 2013*, Table A-1. In the UK in 2010 to 2013 (3-year average), out of all households 22 per cent had incomes of £52,000 a year or more, a figure that was exceeded by Asian/Asian British, where it was 25 per cent, but for Black/African/Caribbean/Black British households, the figure was 16 per cent and for Bangladeshis it was 11 per cent. The figures are from Department of Work and Pensions, *Family Resources Survey (FRS) United Kingdom, 2012/13* (London: Department of Work and Pensions, 2014), Table 2.6.

59 http://www.infoplease.com/business/economy/cost-living-index-us-cities. html, downloaded 1 January 2015.

60 U.S. Bureau of the Census, *Income, Poverty, and Health Insurance Coverage in the United States: 2013*, Table A-4.

61 Sophie Ponthieux and Dominique Meurs, "Gender Inequality," in Atkinson and Bourguignon, eds., *Handbook of Income Distribution*, vol. 2A, quote p. 1008.

62 The figures for the US college ratios by gender are from Claudia Goldin, Lawrence F. Katz, and Iyana Kuziemko, "The Homecoming of American College Women: The Reversal of the College Gender Gap," *Journal of Economic Perspectives* 20(4): 133–156. The figures for the OECD are from Ponthieux and Meurs, "Gender Inequality."

63 Doris Weichselbaumer and Rudolf Winter-Ebmer, "A Meta-Analysis of the International Gender Wage Gap," *Journal of Economic Surveys* 19: 479–511, quote p. 508.

64 Stephen P. Jenkins, *Changing Fortunes* (Oxford: Oxford University Press, 2011), quote pp. 360 and 361.

65 Peter Gottschalk and Robert Moffitt, "The Rising Instability of U.S. Earnings," *Journal of Economic Perspectives* 23 (2009): 3–24.

66 Wojciech Kopczuk, Emmanuel Saez, and Jae Song, "Earnings Inequality and Mobility in the United States: Evidence from Social Security Data since 1937," *Quarterly Journal of Economics* 125 (2010): 91–128, quote p. 91.

67 Rebecca M. Blank, *Changing Inequality* (Berkeley: University of California Press, 2011), quote p. 93.

68 The mathematical formula is $\delta + \varepsilon g$, where δ is the pure discount rate, ε is the elasticity of the marginal value of consumption, and g is the growth rate of consumption per head.

CHAPTER 2 LEARNING FROM HISTORY

1 Simon Kuznets, "Economic Growth and Income Inequality," *American Economic Review* 44 (1954): 1–28.

2 Arthur Sakamoto, Hyeyoung Woo, Isao Takei, and Yoichi Murase, "Cultural Constraints on Rising Income Inequality: A U.S.–Japan Comparison," *Journal of Economic Inequality* 10 (2012): 565–581; and Dierk Herzer and Sebastian Vollmer, "Inequality and Growth: Evidence from Panel Cointegration," *Journal of Economic Inequality* 10 (2012): 489–503. The first article refers to a variety of sources, but the data are consistent with those from the LIS Key Statistics (see above); the second article uses data from the University of Texas Inequality Project described by James K. Galbraith, "Inequality, Unemployment and Growth: New Measures for Old Controversies," *Journal of Economic Inequality* 7 (2009): 189–206.

3 The adjustment is made on the basis of the official estimate that these changes could account for half of the recorded increase: David H. Weinberg, "A Brief Look at Postwar U.S. Income Inequality," *Current Population Reports, P60-191,* U.S. Census Bureau, Washington, D.C., footnote 3. See also Richard V. Burkhauser et al., "Recent Trends in Top Income Shares in the USA: Reconciling Estimates from March CPS and IRS Tax Return Data," *Review of Economics and Statistics* 94 (2012): 371–388.

4 The same problem arises today if a survey is based on landline telephones. According to the Pew Research Center, "the latest estimates of telephone coverage by the National Center for Health Statistics found that a quarter of U.S. households have only a cell phone and cannot be reached by a landline telephone. Cell-only adults are demographically and politically different from those who

live in landline households; as a result, election polls that rely only on landline samples may be biased." http://www.pewresearch.org/2010/10/13/cell-phones-and-election-polls-an-update/.

5 Jesse Bricker et al., "Changes in U.S. Family Finances from 2010 to 2013: Evidence from the Survey of Consumer Finances," *Federal Reserve Bulletin* 100 (2014): 1–41, quote p. 1.

6 Maria L. Mattonetti, "European Household Income by Groups of Households," *Eurostat Methodologies and Working Papers* (Luxembourg: Publications Office of the European Union, 2013), Table 3. The pattern follows that found in earlier comparisons of survey data and national accounts, such as Anthony B. Atkinson, Lee Rainwater, and Timothy M. Smeeding, *Income Distribution in OECD Countries* (Paris: OECD, 1995), Table 3.7.

7 For fuller discussion of the use of income tax statistics to estimate top income shares, see Anthony B. Atkinson, Thomas Piketty, and Emmanuel Saez, "Top Incomes in the Long Run of History," *Journal of Economic Literature* 49 (2011): 3–71; and Andrew Leigh, "Top Incomes," in Wiemer Salverda, Brian Nolan, and Timothy M. Smeeding, eds., *The Oxford Handbook of Economic Inequality* (Oxford: Oxford University Press, 2009): 150–174.

8 It is not obvious how this affects the comparison. If all units are weighted equally, as in the estimates in Figures 1.1 and 1.2, then the impact of moving from a couple-based to an individual-based system depends on the joint distribution of income. If all rich people have partners with zero income or are unmarried, then the top shares may be raised by the move to an individual basis. A larger total of tax units means that one has to go further down the distribution to find the top X per cent. On the other hand, if the richest tax units are couples who share their incomes equally, then the move may reduce top shares.

9 See the country studies reported in Atkinson and Piketty, *Top Incomes*; and Anthony B. Atkinson and Thomas Piketty, eds., *Top Incomes: A Global Perspective* (Oxford: Oxford University Press, 2010).

10 For a dated but detailed comparison in the UK of the New Earnings Survey (the predecessor of the Annual Survey on Hours and Earnings) and the Family Expenditure Survey (predecessor of the Family Resources Survey), see Anthony B. Atkinson, John Micklewright, and Nicholas H. Stern, "Comparison of the FES and New Earnings Survey 1971–1977," in Anthony B. Atkinson and Holly Sutherland, eds., *Tax-Benefit Models* (London: STICERD, LSE, 1988), 154–222.

11 An impressive study based on the collection of individual data on estates is that by Thomas Piketty, Gilles Postel-Vinay, and Jean-Laurent Rosenthal, "Wealth Concentration in a Developing Economy: Paris and France, 1807–1994," *American Economic Review* 96 (2006): 236–256. They collected informa-

tion on everyone dying in Paris in each of ten selected years between 1807 and 1902.

12 Centraal Bureau voor de Statistiek, *Statistiek der Rijksfinanciën 1936* ('s Graven-hage: Drukkerij Albani, 1936), Table XV.

13 This fruitful line of research was initiated by Thomas Piketty, "Income In-equality in France, 1901–1998," *Journal of Political Economy* 111 (2003): 1004–1042, and *Les hauts revenus en France au XXe siècle* (Paris: Bernard Grasset, 2001).

14 Zvi Griliches, "Economic Data Issues," in Zvi Griliches and Michael D. Intri-ligator, eds., *Handbook of Econometrics* (Amsterdam: Elsevier, 1986), vol. 3, quote p. 1509.

15 Statistics Canada, *Income in Canada 2005*, Catalogue 75-202-XIE (Ottawa: Sta-tistics Canada, 2007), p. 125.

16 Strictly the calculation yields 3 1/8: the change in the Gini coefficient for net income is 5/8 times the change in the marginal tax rate.

17 Thomas Piketty, *Capital in the Twenty-First Century*, trans. Arthur Goldham-mer (Cambridge, MA: Belknap Press of Harvard University Press, 2014), quote p. 275.

18 From the World Top Incomes Database. In the case of the UK, the data relate to the share of the top 0.1 per cent. The comparisons are between 1914 and 1945 except for France (1915), Japan (1947), Sweden (1912), Norway (1913 and 1948), Netherlands (1946), and Denmark (1908).

19 Josiah Stamp, *The Financial Aftermath of War* (London: Ernest Benn, 1932), quote p. 34.

20 Piketty, *Les hauts revenus en France*, quote pp. 272–279.

21 Stephen P. Jenkins, Andrea Brandolini, John Micklewright, and Brian Nolan, eds., *The Great Recession and the Distribution of Household Income* (Oxford: Oxford University Press, 2013), 16–20. See also Anthony B. Atkinson and Sal-vatore Morelli, "Inequality and Banking Crises: A First Look," paper pre-pared for Global Labour Forum 2010, http://www.nuffield.ox.ac.uk/Users/Atkinson/Paper-Inequality%20and%20Banking%20Crises-A%20First%20Look.pdf; and Anthony B. Atkinson and Salvatore Morelli, "Economic Crises and Inequality," Human Development Research Paper 2011/06 (New York: United Nations Development Programme, 2011), http://dl4a.org/uploads/pdf/HDRP_2011_06.pdf.

22 Richard M. Titmuss, *Problems of Social Policy* (London: HMSO and Long-mans, Green and Co., 1950), quote p. 506.

23 Claudia Goldin and Robert Margo, "The Great Compression: The Wage Struc-ture in the United States at Mid-Century," *Quarterly Journal of Economics* 107 (1992): 1–34, quote pp. 23 and 27.

24 Paul Krugman, *The Conscience of a Liberal* (New York: W. W. Norton, 2007), see pp. 47–52.

25 Richard B. Freeman, "The Evolution of the American Labor Market, 1948–80," in Martin Feldstein, ed., *The American Economy in Transition* (Chicago: University of Chicago Press, 1980), quote p. 357 and Figure 5.1.

26 Nan L. Maxwell, "Changing Female Labor Force Participation: Influences on Income Inequality and Distribution," *Social Forces* 68 (1990): 1251–1266, quote p. 1251.

27 Lynn Karoly and Gary Burtless, "Demographic Change, Rising Earnings Inequality, and the Distribution of Personal Well-Being, 1959–1989," *Demography* 32 (1995): 379–405, quote p. 392.

28 Jeff Larrimore, "Accounting for United States Household Income Inequality Trends: The Changing Importance of Household Structure and Male and Female Earnings Inequality," *Review of Income and Wealth* 60 (2014): 683–704.

29 Wojciech Kopczuk and Emmanuel Saez, "Top Wealth Shares in the US, 1916–2000: Evidence from the Estate Tax Returns," *National Tax Journal* 57 (2004): 445–487, longer version in *NBER Working Paper* 10399.

30 George F. Break, "The Role of Government: Taxes, Transfers, and Spending," in Martin Feldstein, ed., *The American Economy in Transition* (Chicago: University of Chicago Press, 1980), Table 9.17. The figures are for percentages of "nonrecession GNP."

31 Karoly and Burtless, "Demographic Change," quote p. 392.

32 Richard Goode, *The Individual Income Tax* (Washington, D.C.: Brookings Institution, 1964), quote p. 283. I owe to this source the quotations from Joseph Schumpeter, *Capitalism, Socialism and Democracy* (New York: Harper and Row, 1962), 3rd ed., quote p. 381; and Irving B. Kravis, *The Structure of Income* (Philadelphia: University of Pennsylvania Press, 1962), quote p. 220.

33 See, for example, Figure 2.1 in Anthony B. Atkinson and Joseph E. Stiglitz, *Lectures on Public Economics* (New York: McGraw-Hill, 1980, reprinted by Princeton University Press, 2015).

34 The proportions in poverty come from Anthony B. Atkinson and Salvatore Morelli, *Chartbook of Economic Inequality*, http://www.chartbookofeconomicinequality.com/.

35 Thomas Piketty, "Income, Wage, and Wealth Inequality in France, 1901–98," in Anthony B. Atkinson and Thomas Piketty, eds., *Top Incomes*, quote p. 50.

36 These figures are from Anthony B. Atkinson, "Increased Income Inequality in OECD Countries and the Redistributive Impact of the Government Budget," in Giovanni A. Cornia, ed., *Inequality, Growth, and Poverty in an Era of Liberalization and Globalization* (Oxford: Oxford University Press, 2004), 221–248. See also Anthony B. Atkinson, "What Is Happening to the Distribution of In-

come in the UK?" *Proceedings of the British Academy* 82 (1992): 317–351; and Anthony B. Atkinson and John Micklewright, "Turning the Screw: Benefits for the Unemployed 1979–88," in Andrew Dilnot and Ian Walker, eds., *The Economics of Social Security* (Oxford: Oxford University Press, 1989), 17–51.

37 Richard Hauser, "Personal Primär- und Sekundärverteilung der Einkommen unter dem Einfluss sich ändernen wirtschaftlicher und sozialpolitisch Rahmenbedingungen," *Allgemeines Statistisches Achiv* 83 (1999): 88–110 (my translation).

38 Hannu Uusitalo, "Changes in Income Distribution During a Deep Recession and After" (Helsinki: National Institute for Health and Welfare, STAKES, 1999).

39 Secretary-General, "Editorial," in OECD, *Divided We Stand* (Paris: OECD, 2011), quote p. 18.

40 Michael F. Förster and István G. Tóth, "Cross-Country Evidence of the Multiple Causes of Inequality Changes in the OECD Area," in Anthony B. Atkinson and François Bourguignon, *Handbook of Income Distribution*, vol. 2B (Amsterdam: Elsevier, 2015), quote p. 1803.

41 OECD, *Divided We Stand*, quote p. 292; the coverage figures are from Figure 7.5. They include a range of unemployment insurance and assistance benefits; for details, see Herwig Immervoll, Pascal Marianna, and Marco Mira D'Ercole, "Benefit Coverage Rates and Household Typologies: Scope and Limitations of Tax-Benefit Indicators," *OECD Social, Employment and Migration Working Paper* 20, OECD, Paris, 2004.

42 Nicholas Kaldor, "Alternative Theories of Distribution," *Review of Economic Studies* 23 (1955–6): 83–100, and "A Model of Economic Growth," *Economic Journal* 67 (1957): 591–624. It should be noted that the constancy of the share of wages does not appear in the "new" Kaldor facts listed by Charles I. Jones and Paul M. Romer, "The New Kaldor Facts: Ideas, Institutions, Population, and Human Capital," *American Economic Journal: Macroeconomics* 2 (2010): 224–245. They refer instead to the constancy of the college-educated / high-school-educated wage premium, which is discussed in the next chapter.

43 Klaus Heidensohn, "Labour's Share in National Income: A Constant?" *Manchester School* 37 (1969): 295–321, quote p. 304. The figures given below are from Table 1.

44 Piketty, *Capital,* quote p. 221.

45 Loukas Karabarbounis and Brent Neiman, "The Global Decline of the Labor Share," *Quarterly Journal of Economics* 129 (2014): 61–103.

46 David Ricardo, Preface to *Principles of Political Economy* (London: Dent, 1911, first published 1817).

47 It is not, however, a movement in one direction. After 1981, with the sale of so-

cial housing, its share fell, and the past two decades have seen, with the rise in buy-to-let, a revival of the share of private landlords, which reached 18 per cent in 2011.

48 The Gini coefficient is then equal to the difference between the share of workers in the total population and their share of total income—see Anthony B. Atkinson and John Micklewright, *Economic Transformation in Eastern Europe and the Distribution of Income* (Cambridge: Cambridge University Press, 1992), Ch. 2.

49 Daniele Checchi and Cecilia Garcia Peñalosa, "Labour Market Institutions and the Personal Distribution of Income in the OECD," *Economica* 77 (2010): 413–450, quote to Table 7. There is a 95 per cent confidence interval for the coefficient extending down to 0.4.

50 Jesper Roine and Daniel Waldenström, "Long Run Trends in the Distribution of Income and Wealth," in Atkinson and Bourguignon, *Handbook of Income Distribution,* vol. 2A, Table 7.A2. The Luxembourg Income Study has been extended to cover wealth in the Luxembourg Wealth Study, but the earliest data relate to 1994.

51 This takes account of the break in the series between 1959 and 1960—see Anthony B. Atkinson, James P. F. Gordon, and Alan Harrison, "Trends in the Shares of Top-Wealth-Holders in Britain, 1923–81," *Oxford Bulletin of Economics and Statistics* 51 (1989): 315–332.

52 In the US, for the period since 1980, the evidence from different sources points in different directions: see Emmanuel Saez and Gabriel Zucman, "Wealth Inequality in the United States since 1913: Evidence from Capitalized Income Tax Data," Working Paper 20625, National Bureau of Economic Research; and Wojciech Kopczuk, "What Do We Know about Evolution of Top Wealth Shares in the United States?" *Journal of Economic Perspectives,* forthcoming.

53 Christopher L. Erickson and Andrea Ichino, "Wage Differentials in Italy: Market Forces, Institutions and Inflation," in Richard B. Freeman and Lawrence F. Katz, eds., *Differences and Changes in Wage Structures* (Chicago: University of Chicago Press, 1995): 265–306, quote p. 265. Andrea Brandolini, "The Distribution of Personal Income in Post-War Italy: Source Description, Data Quality, and the Time Pattern of Income Inequality," *Giornale degli Economisti e Annali di Economia* 58 (1999): 183–239; Ignacio Visco, "The Indexation of Earnings in Italy: Sectoral Analysis and Estimates for 1978–79," *Rivista di Politica Economica* 13 (1979): 151–183; Marco Manacorda, "Can the Scala Mobile Explain the Fall and Rise of Earnings Inequality in Italy? A Semiparametric Analysis, 1977–1993," *Journal of Labor Economics* 22 (2004): 585–613, Magnus Gustavsson, "Trends in the Transitory Variance of Earnings: Evidence from Sweden 1960–1990 and a Comparison with the United States," *Working Paper* 2004:11, Department of Economics, Uppsala Universitet; Tor Eriksson and Markus Jäntti,

"The Distribution of Earnings in Finland 1971–1990," *European Economic Review* 41 (1997): 1736–1779.

54 Checchi and Garcia Peñalosa, "Labour Market Institutions," quote to Table 7, where the figures cited are based on the 95 per cent confidence interval around the estimated coefficient.

55 Piketty, *Les hauts revenus en France*, quote p. 165 (my translation).

56 Joop Hartog and Nick Vriend, "Post-War International Labour Mobility: The Netherlands," in Ian Gordon and Anthony P. Thirlwall, eds., *European Factor Mobility* (London: Macmillan, 1989). On France, see in Piketty, *Les hauts revenus en France*, Ch. 3.

57 "Incomes Policy," Wikipedia, downloaded 5 October 2014.

58 See Jenkins et al., *The Great Recession*, pp. 14–16.

59 International Labour Office, *Year Book of Labour Statistics 1961* (Geneva: International Labour Office, 1961), quote p. 202.

60 OECD, *Historical Statistics* (Paris: OECD, 1997), Table 2.15.

61 See OECD, *Divided We Stand*, Chs. 3 and 4; and Anthony B. Atkinson and Andrea Brandolini, "From Earnings Dispersion to Income Inequality," in Francesco Farina and Ernesto Savaglio, eds., *Inequality and Economic Integration* (London: Routledge, 2006): 35–64.

62 Calculations of the distributions among workers (including part-time and self-employed) and the entire working population are given in Figures 4.1 and 4.6 of OECD, *Divided We Stand*.

63 The study of the impact on inequality of rising unemployment in the Nordic countries in the late 1980s and early 1990s concluded that "a recession sets several complex mechanisms in motion, and a large model with interactions between income components is probably required to understand the evolution of income distribution during rapidly rising unemployment." Rolf Aaberge, Anders Björklund, Markus Jäntti, Peder J. Pedersen, Nina Smith, and Tom Wennemo, "Unemployment Shocks and Income Distribution: How Did the Nordic Countries Fare during Their Crises?" *Scandinavian Journal of Economics* 102 (2000): 77–99.

64 See Anthony B. Atkinson, "Social Exclusion, Poverty and Unemployment," in Anthony B. Atkinson and John Hills, eds., *Exclusion, Employment and Opportunity*, CASEpaper 4 (London: LSE, STICERD, 1998): 1–20.

65 Amartya Sen, "Inequality, Unemployment and Contemporary Europe," *International Labour Review* 136 (1997): 155–171, quote p. 169.

66 Source: *SEDLAC*, CEDLAS (Universidad Nacional de La Plata) and The World Bank, (http://sedlac.econo.unlp.edu.ar/eng/), downloaded 5 October 2014.

67 Facundo Alvaredo and Leonardo Gasparini, "Recent Trends in Inequality and Poverty in Developing Countries," in Atkinson and Bourguignon, *Handbook of Income Distribution*, vol. 2, quote p. 726.

68 Giovanni Andrea Cornia, ed., *Falling Inequality in Latin America* (Oxford: Oxford University Press, 2014), quote p. 7.

69 Nora Lustig, Luis F. Lopez-Calva, and Eduardo Ortiz-Juarez, "Deconstructing the Decline in Inequality in Latin America," in Robert Devlin, Jose Luis Machinea, and Oscar Echeverria, eds., *Latin American Development in an Age of Globalization: Essays in Honor of Enrique V. Iglesias,* 2013.

70 Alvaredo and Gasparini, "Recent Trends," quote p. 732.

71 Armando Barrientos, "On the Distributional Implications of Social Protection Reforms in Latin America," in Cornia, *Falling Inequality,* quote pp. 356 and 358.

72 Source: Atkinson and Morelli, *Chartbook.*

73 OECD, *Divided We Stand,* quote p. 22.

CHAPTER 3 THE ECONOMICS OF INEQUALITY

1 It is also evident that the list could be extended. I do not, for instance, discuss the relation between income inequality and immigration. The economics of immigration is an important topic in itself. It is less clear that it is a major factor causing a rise in overall income inequality. David Card, in his analysis of the issue in the US, concluded that "the presence of immigration can account for a relatively small share (4–6 percent) of the rise in overall wage inequality over the past 25 years." "Immigration and Inequality," *American Economic Review, Papers and Proceedings* 99 (2009): 1–19, quote p. 19.

2 Jan Tinbergen, *Income Distribution: Analysis and Policies* (Amsterdam: North-Holland, 1975).

3 The elasticity of substitution measures the proportionate fall in the demand for one factor (relative to the other) in response to a rise in the relative price. If a 10 per cent rise in the relative wage of skilled workers leads to a 10 per cent fall in the relative demand, then the elasticity is equal to 1. The extension of the concept to more than two factors raises a number of definitional problems—see Charles Blackorby and Robert Russell, "Will the Real Elasticity of Substitution Please Stand Up? (A Comparison of the Allen/Uzawa and Morishima Elasticities)," *American Economic Review* 79 (1989): 882–888.

4 See, for example, Daron Acemoglu and David Autor, "What Does Human Capital Do? A Review of Goldin and Katz's *The Race between Education and Technology*," *Journal of Economic Literature* 50 (2012): 426–463, quoted footnote 10, which gives a clear account of this point.

5 The present value calculation takes account of the fact that income earned in future years is worth less than income earned today. Earnings of £1 today would accumulate to $£e^{rT}$ if saved for T years in an account paying interest at rate r. It is assumed in this calculation that the working life is the same for both skilled and unskilled workers.

6 Adam Bryant, "In Head-Hunting, Big Data May Not Be Such a Big Deal," interview with Laszlo Bock, *New York Times,* June 19, 2013.

7 Sir John Hicks, *The Theory of Wages* (London: Macmillan, 1932), quote p. 124.

8 The long-run steady state is unstable where the elasticity of substitution is greater than 1, and the economy diverges to the point on the innovation possibility frontier where unskilled-labour augmenting technical progress is zero (taken to be the lower limit). See Charles Kennedy, "Induced Bias in Innovation and the Theory of Distribution," *Economic Journal* 74 (1964): 541–547; Paul Samuelson, "A Theory of Induced Innovations along Kennedy-Weisäcker Lines," *Review of Economics and Statistics* 97 (1965): 444–464; and Emmanuel Drandakis and Edmund S. Phelps, "A Model of Induced Invention, Growth and Distribution," *Economic Journal* 75 (1965): 823–840. The induced innovation literature of the 1960s is well summarised by Daron Acemoglu, "Localized and Biased Technologies: Atkinson and Stiglitz's New View, Induced Innovations, and Directed Technological Change," *Economic Journal* 125 (2015), where he discusses the more recent literature on "directed" technological change, to which he has made a major contribution.

9 Anthony B. Atkinson and Joseph E. Stiglitz, "A New View of Technological Change," *Economic Journal* 79 (1969): 573–578.

10 David H. Autor, Frank Levy, and Richard J. Murnane, "The Skill Content of Recent Technological Change: An Empirical Exploration," *Quarterly Journal of Economics* 118 (2003): 1279–1333; David H. Autor, Lawrence F. Katz, and Melissa S. Kearney, "The Polarization of the U.S. Labor Market," *American Economic Review, Papers and Proceedings* 96 (2006): 189–194; and Acemoglu and Autor, "What Does Human Capital Do?"

11 Kenneth Arrow, "The Economic Implications of Learning by Doing," *Review of Economic Studies* 29 (1962): 155–173, quote p. 156.

12 Steven Chu, Romanes lecture, University of Oxford, November 2014.

13 Robert M. Solow, *The Labor Market as a Social Institution* (Oxford: Basil Blackwell, 1990), quote p. 3.

14 Eric Newby, *The Last Grain Race* (London: Secker and Warburg, 1956).

15 Peter Diamond, "Wage Determination and Efficiency in Search Equilibrium," *Review of Economic Studies* 49 (1982): 217–227, quote p. 219.

16 E. Henry Phelps Brown, *The Inequality of Pay* (Oxford: Oxford University Press, 1977).

17 W. Bentley MacLeod and James M. Malcomson, "Motivation and Markets," *American Economic Review* 88 (1998): 388–411, quote p. 400.

18 Truman Bewley, *Why Wages Don't Fall During a Recession* (Cambridge, MA: Harvard University Press, 1999), quote pp. 84–85.

19 This pay norm model is described in Anthony B. Atkinson, *Is Rising Inequality Inevitable? A Critique of the Transatlantic Consensus* (Helsinki: UNU/WIDER, 1999); and Anthony B. Atkinson, *The Changing Distribution of Earnings in OECD Countries* (*The Rodolfo De Benedetti Lecture Series*) (Oxford: Oxford University Press, 2008), Note 2.

20 OECD, *Divided We Stand* (Paris: OECD, 2011), Figure 1.18.

21 Stephen Nickell and Richard Layard, "Labour Market Institutions and Economic Performance," in Orley Ashenfelter and David Card, eds., *Handbook of Labor Economics*, vol. 3.3 (Amsterdam: Elsevier, 1999), 3029–3084, quote p. 3078.

22 Jelle Visser, "Wage Bargaining Institutions—from Crisis to Crisis," *European Economy Economic Papers* 488 (2013), European Commission, Brussels, quote p. 4.

23 David Card, Thomas Lemieux, and W. Craig Riddell, "Unions and Wage Inequality," *Journal of Labor Research* 25 (2004): 519–562, quote p. 555.

24 Trade Union Congress website (http://www.tuc.org.uk), downloaded 24 October 2014.

25 Daron Acemoglu, Philippe Aghion, and Giovanni L. Violante, "Deunionization, Technical Change, and Inequality," *Carnegie-Rochester Conference Series on Public Policy* 55 (2001): 229–264. I owe this reference to Andrea Brandolini, "Political Economy and the Mechanics of Politics," *Politics and Society* 38 (2010): 212–226.

26 Mark Carley, "Trade Union Membership 2003–2008," in *European Industrial Relations Observatory On-Line* (Dublin: European Foundation for the Improvement of Living and Working Conditions, 2009).

27 Michael F. Förster and István György Tóth, "Cross-Country Evidence of the Multiple Causes of Inequality Changes in the OECD Area," in Anthony B. Atkinson and François Bourguignon, eds., *Handbook of Income Distribution*, vol. 2B (Amsterdam: Elsevier, 2015), 1729–1843, quote p. 1775.

28 When I was a student in Cambridge, writing such a production function would have provoked a lively debate. "What is capital?" is a question that I heard frequently asked by Joan Robinson. There are indeed issues that need to be addressed regarding capital aggregates, but for the present purpose the construction serves.

29 There is a borderline case, where the elasticity is equal to 1, and the rate of return falls by the same proportion as the stock of capital rises. This leaves the capital (profits) share unchanged over time. This is the case of the Cobb-Douglas production function, where output Y is given by $aL^{\beta}K^{1-\beta}$, where a and β are constants. The story is that Professor (later Senator) Paul Douglas found the factor shares to be broadly constant and asked his mathematician colleague, Charles Cobb, what function would generate this result. It had earlier been suggested by the celebrated Swedish economist Knut Wicksell.

30 Daron Acemoglu and James Robinson, "The Rise and Fall of General Laws of Capitalism," *Journal of Economic Literature*, forthcoming. The review by Robert S. Chirinko, "σ: The Long and Short of It," *Journal of Macroeconomics* 30 (2008): 671–686, stresses the tension between evidence from short-run data and the long-run parameter in which we are primarily interested. It is also nec-

essary to distinguish gross and net. As has been shown by Matthew Rognlie, "A Note on Piketty and Diminishing Returns to Capital," available at http://www.mit.edu/~mrognlie/piketty_diminishing_returns.pdf, the elasticity defined in terms of the production function and rate of return net of depreciation is less than the gross elasticity defined before depreciation.

31 Alfonso Arpaia, Esther Pérez, and Karl Pichelmann, "Understanding Labour Income Share Dynamics in Europe," *European Economy Economic Papers* 379 (2009), European Commission, Brussels, quote p. 2. They go on to say that "not only has the labour share fallen over the past three decades, but it may decline further in the future as a result of capital accumulation and an increasing share of skilled labour in total employment."

32 Lawrence H. Summers, "Economic Possibilities for Our Children," The 2013 Martin Feldstein Lecture, *NBER Reporter* 4 (2013): 1–6. Denoting the first use of capital by K_1 and the second by K_2, the aggregate production function becomes $F(K_1, AL + BK_2)$, where A and B depend on the level of technology. The task-based approach adopted by Autor, Katz, and Kearney, "The Polarization of the U.S. Labor Market," also treated the case where robots are perfect substitutes for labour (in the performance of routine tasks).

33 If (1/A) workers contribute as much as (1/B) robots, then robots are not employed where the ratio of the wage to the rate of return is less than A/B. Where the ratio of the wage to the rate of return is equal to A/B, then both are employed.

34 Carl Benedikt Frey and Michael Osborne, "The Future of Employment: How Susceptible Are Jobs to Computerisation?" Oxford Martin School Working Paper (2013), http://www.oxfordmartin.ox.ac.uk/downloads/academic/The_Future_of_Employment.pdf.

35 James E. Meade, *Efficiency, Equality and the Ownership of Property* (London: Allen and Unwin, 1964).

36 Paul Samuelson, "Review," *Economic Journal* 75 (1965): 804–806, quote p. 805.

37 Michael Kalecki, "Class Struggle and the Distribution of National Income," *Kyklos* 24 (1971): 1–9, quote p. 3.

38 This analysis combines the wage bargaining model (where unions recognise the effect on employment) with the model of monopolistic competition described by Avinash Dixit and Joseph Stiglitz, "Monopolistic Competition and Optimum Product Diversity," *American Economic Review* 67 (1977): 297–308.

39 John K. Galbraith, *American Capitalism: The Concept of Countervailing Power* (London: Hamish Hamilton, 1952).

40 Office for National Statistics, *Ownership of UK Quoted Shares, 2012* (London: Office for National Statistics, 2013), Table 1.

41 Andrea Brandolini, "Nonlinear Dynamics, Entitlement Rules, and the Cyclical Behaviour of the Personal Income Distribution," Centre for Economic Performance Discussion Paper 84, London School of Economics, July 1992.

42 As in the macro-economic literature on heterogeneous agents, see Vincenzo Quadrini and José-Victor Rios-Rull, "Inequality in Macroeconomics," in Anthony B. Atkinson and François Bourguignon, eds., *Handbook of Income Distribution*, vol. 2B (Amsterdam: Elsevier, 2015), 1229–1302.

43 U.S. Census Bureau, *Educational Attainment in the United States: 2013*, Table 1: "Educational Attainment of the Population 18 Years and Over."

44 World Bank, Data on labour force with tertiary education: http://data.worldbank.org/indicator/SL.TLF.TERT.ZS.

45 These calculations assume that the upper tail of the earnings distribution is Pareto in form. The Pareto distribution was first proposed by Vilfredo Pareto at the end of the nineteenth century, and takes the mathematical form that the proportion of the population with earnings of Y and above is proportional to $Y^{-\alpha}$, where α is known as the Pareto coefficient. It is a property of the Pareto distribution that the mean income above Y is equal to $\alpha/(\alpha-1)$ Y. In the UK, the Pareto coefficient fell from around 4.5 in 1977 to 2.8 in 2003 (source: Anthony B. Atkinson and Sarah Voitchovsky, "The Distribution of Top Earnings in the UK since the Second World War," *Economica* 78 (2011): 440–459), and these values are the basis for the figures given in the text. For example, the value of α = 4.5 yields 4.5/3.5 (= 1.29) times Y. To move from the top decile to the top percentile requires earnings to rise by a factor of $10^{1/\alpha}$.

46 Jacob S. Hacker and Paul Pierson, "Winner-Take-All Politics: Public Policy, Political Organization, and the Precipitous Rise of Top Incomes in the United States," *Politics and Society* 38 (2010): 152–204.

47 See Atkinson, *The Changing Distribution of Earnings in OECD Countries*, Ch. 4.

48 Anthony B. Atkinson, "The Distribution of Top Incomes in the United Kingdom 1908–2000," in A. B. Atkinson and Thomas Piketty, eds., *Top Incomes: A Global Perspective* (Oxford: Oxford University Press, 2010), 82–140, Figure 4.11.

49 Thomas Piketty and Emmanuel Saez, "Income and Wage Inequality in the United States, 1913–2002," in Atkinson and Piketty, *Top Incomes*, quote p. 153.

50 Jon Bakija, Adam Cole, and Bradley T. Heim, "Jobs and Income Growth of Top Earners and the Causes of Changing Income Inequality: Evidence from U.S. Tax Return Data," Williams College Department of Economics Working Paper, 2010–22 (revised 2012).

51 Alfred Marshall, *Principles of Economics*, 8th ed. (London: Macmillan, 1920).

52 Thomas Lemieux, W. Bentley MacLeod, and Daniel Parent, "Performance Pay and Wage Inequality," *Quarterly Journal of Economics* 124 (2009): 1–49.

53 Hacker and Pierson, "Winner-Take-All Politics," p. 203.

54 Hacker and Pierson, "Winner-Take-All Politics," p. 192.

55 Facundo Alvaredo, Anthony B. Atkinson, Thomas Piketty, and Emmanuel Saez, "The Top 1 Per Cent in International and Historical Perspective," *Journal of Economic Perspectives* 27 (2013): 3–20, Table 1. The source of the results for

the US is Christoph Lakner, "Wages, Capital and Top Incomes: The Factor Income Composition of Top Incomes in the USA, 1960–2005," forthcoming. The US results are compared with those for Norway in Rolf Aaberge, Anthony B. Atkinson, Sebastian Königs and Christoph Lakner, "Wages, Capital and Top Incomes," forthcoming. Earned income is defined as wages plus pensions plus two-thirds of business (self-employment) income.

56 John Kay and Mervyn King, *The British Tax System* (Oxford: Oxford University Press, 1980), quote p. 59.

57 This is true for men, but not necessarily for women. If we look at the top 1 per cent in terms of income, we find that women were seriously under-represented. In Canada, for example, in 2010, women accounted for only 21 per cent of those with gross incomes in the top 1 per cent (Statistics Canada, "High-Income Trends among Canadian Taxfilers, 1982 to 2010," release 28 January 2013), and in the United Kingdom in 2011 the corresponding figure was 17 per cent (Anthony B. Atkinson, Alessandra Casarico, and Sarah Voitchovsky, "Top Incomes and the Glass Ceiling," forthcoming). There is a distinct "glass ceiling."

CHAPTER 4 TECHNOLOGICAL CHANGE AND COUNTERVAILING POWER

1 "The Future of Jobs: The Onrushing Wave," Briefing, *Economist,* 18 January 2014.

2 John M. Keynes, "Economic Possibilities for Our Grandchildren," originally pubiished in *The Nation and Athenaeum* (11 and 18 October, 1930), reprinted in *Essays in Persuasion* (London: Macmillan, 1933), part V, ch. 2.

3 McKinsey roundtable discussion, "Automation, Jobs, and the Future of Work," December 2014, edited transcript.

4 Remarks by Hunter Rawlings, quoted in American Academy of Arts and Sciences, *Restoring the Foundation* (Cambridge, MA: American Academy of Arts and Sciences, 2014), quote p. 10.

5 Mariana Mazzucato, *The Entrepreneurial State* (London: Anthem Press, 2014), quote pp. 96 and 101.

6 Mazzucato, *The Entrepreneurial State,* quote p. 193.

7 Steven Johnson, *How We Got to Now* (New York: Riverhead Press, 2014), quote p. x.

8 Office of Science and Technology Policy, *American Competitiveness: Leading the World in Innovation* (Washington, D.C.: Domestic Policy Council, 2006), quote p. 4.

9 William J. Baumol and William G. Bowen, *Performing Arts: The Economic Dilemma* (New York: Twentieth Century Fund, 1966).

10 William J. Baumol, *The Cost Disease: Why Computers Get Cheaper and Health Care Doesn't* (New Haven: Yale University Press, 2012).

11 In this book, I do not discuss at length the need for human capital investment,

as this case has been made extensively, notably with regard to early childhood. See, for example, James J. Heckman, "Going Forward Wisely," Speech to the White House Early Childhood Education Summit, 10 December, 2014, Center for the Economics of Human Development, University of Chicago.

12 *Quaker Faith and Practice: The Book of Christian Discipline of the Yearly Meeting of the Religious Society of Friends* (London: Quaker Books, 1995), quoted paragraph 23.57.

13 Milton Friedman, "The Social Responsibility of Business Is to Increase Its Profits," *New York Times Magazine,* 13 September 1970.

14 Kenneth J. Arrow, "Social Responsibility and Economic Efficiency," *Public Policy* 21 (1973): 303–318, quote pp. 313 and 314.

15 Website of MBA Oath: http://mbaoath.org/.

16 Jonathan B. Baker, "The Case for Anti-Trust Enforcement," *Journal of Economic Perspectives* 17 (2003): 27–50, quote p. 27.

17 Robert Bork, *The Anti-Trust Paradox* (New York: Free Press, 1978), quote p. 66.

18 Senator Sherman, *21 Congressional Record* 2728 (1890). I owe these and other references to Shi-Ling Hsu, "The Rise and Rise of the One Percent: Considering Legal Causes of Inequality" (Florida State University College of Law, Public Law Research Paper 698; FSU College of Law, Law, Business and Economics Paper no. 14–11, 2014).

19 Hsu, "The Rise and Rise of the One Percent," quote p. 24.

20 For an illustrative analysis of the relation between market structure and exclusion from the supply of goods, see Anthony B. Atkinson, "Capabilities, Exclusion, and the Supply of Goods," in Kaushik Basu, Prasanta Pattanaik, and Kotaro Suzumura, eds., *Choice, Welfare and Development* (Oxford: Clarendon Press, 1995): 17–31.

21 For an analysis of the distributional implications of banking provision, see Babak Somekh, "Access to Banking and Income Inequality," in "Income Inequality and Consumer Markets" (D.Phil. thesis, University of Oxford, 2012).

22 The passage from Henry Simons is from Tobin, "On Limiting the Domain of Inequality," *Journal of Law and Economics* 13 (1970): 263–277, quote p. 264.

23 Hsu, "The Rise and Rise of the One Percent," quote p. 4.

24 Joseph Stiglitz, *The Price of Inequality* (London: Allen Lane, 2012), quote p. 64.

25 John T. Addison, Claus Schnabel, and Joachim Wagner, "The (Parlous) State of German Unions," *Politics and Society* 28 (2007): 3–18, figures from p. 8.

26 Ben Roberts, "Trade Union Behavior and Wage Determination in Great Britain," in John T. Dunlop, ed., *The Theory of Wage Determination* (London: Macmillan, 1957), 107–122, quote p. 110.

27 See, for example, Bruno Palier and Kathleen Thelen, "Institutionalising Dualism: Complementarities and Change in France and Germany," *Politics and So-*

ciety 38 (2010): 119–148; and Patrick Emmenegger, "From Drift to Layering: The Politics of Job Security Regulations in Western Europe," *Politics and Society* (2015).

28 Colin Crouch, "The Snakes and Ladders of 21st Century Trade Unionism," *Oxford Review of Economic Policy* 16 (2000): 70–83, quote p. 77.

29 The indexation of benefits and tax thresholds in the face of rising (or falling) prices and real incomes is an important issue not discussed here. Studies in Europe have shown that the rate of indexation may be more consequential for the evolution of poverty than explicit policy reforms: see Alari Paulus, Holly Sutherland, and Iva Tasseva, "Indexation Matters: The Distributional Impact of Fiscal Policy Changes in Cross-National Perspective," University of Essex, December 2014.

CHAPTER 5 EMPLOYMENT AND PAY IN THE FUTURE

1 Jean-Claude Juncker, *A New Start for Europe: My Agenda for Jobs, Growth, Fairness and Democratic Change: Political Guidelines for the Next European Commission* (Brussels: European Commission, 2014).

2 Robert Salais, Nicolas Baverez, and Bénédicte Reynaud, *L'invention du chômage* (Paris: Presses Universitaires de France, 1986). As they note, there is an interesting difference between the French and English words. The French word goes back to an earlier, and different, usage which referred to "taking one's ease in the heat of the day," whereas, according to the *Oxford English Dictionary*, the word "unemployment" came into common use in Britain as recently as 1895.

3 Michael J. Piore, "Historical Perspective and the Interpretation of Unemployment," *Journal of Economic Literature* 25 (1987): 1834–1850, quote p. 1836.

4 Leslie Hannah, *Inventing Retirement* (Cambridge: Cambridge University Press, 1986), quote p. 21.

5 Isaac M. Rubinow, *Social Insurance* (New York: H. Holt, 1913), quote p. 304.

6 Kees Le Blansch et al., "Atypical Work in the EU," *Social Affairs Series*, SOCI 106 EN (2000), Directorate-General for Research, European Parliament L–2929 Luxembourg.

7 Günther Schmid, "Non-Standard Employment in Europe: Its Development and Consequences for the European Employment Strategy," *German Policy Studies* 7 (2001): 171–210, quote p. 171.

8 OECD, *Employment Outlook 2014* (Paris: OECD, 2014), quote p. 144.

9 James Manyika, Susan Lund, Byron Auguste, and Sreenivas Ramaswamy, "Help Wanted: The Future of Work in Advanced Economies," McKinsey Global Institute Discussion Paper, March 2012, quote pp. 3 and 4.

10 Schmid, "Non-Standard Employment," quote p. 175.

11 Günther Schmid, *Full Employment in Europe* (Cheltenham: Edward Elgar, 2008), Table 5.1. Civil servants and soldiers have been included in the category of "standard employment."

12 European Trade Union Institute, *Benchmarking Working Europe 2012* (Brussels: ETUI, 2012), quote p. 31.

13 European Commission, *Employment and Social Developments in Europe 2013* (Luxembourg: Publications Office of the European Union, 2014).

14 Eurostat website, *Employed Persons with a Second Job* (http://epp.eurostat. ec.europa.eu/tgm/table.do?tab=table&init=1&plugin=1&language=en&pco de=tps00074), downloaded 27 October 2014, series tps00074.

15 *The Guardian,* 28 October 2014, G2, quote p. 12.

16 Andrea Brandolini and Eliana Viviano, "Extensive versus Intensive Margin: Changing Perspective on the Employment Rate," paper for Conference on Comparative EU Statistics on Income and Living Conditions (EU-SILC), Austria, Vienna, December 2012.

17 International Labour Organisation, "Part-Time Work: Solution or Trap?" *International Labour Review* 136 (1997): 557–578, quote pp. 562–563.

18 European Commission, *Employment and Social Developments,* quote p. 41, Chart 28.

19 Richard A. Musgrave, *The Theory of Public Finance* (New York: McGraw-Hill, 1959).

20 Joseph A. Kershaw, *Government against Poverty* (Washington, D.C.: Brookings Institution, 1970), quote p. 91.

21 Peter Gottschalk, "The Impact of Changes in Public Employment on Low-Wage Labor Markets," in Richard B. Freeman and Peter Gottschalk, eds., *Generating Jobs: How to Increase Demand for Less-Skilled Workers* (New York: Russell Sage Foundation, 1998), quote p. 83.

22 Robert H. Haveman, "The Dutch Social Employment Program," in John L. Palmer, ed., *Creating Jobs* (Washington, D.C.: Brookings Institution, 1978): 241–270, quote p. 243.

23 Hyman P. Minsky, *Stabilizing an Unstable Economy* (New York: McGraw-Hill, 1986). The estimated cost of the Minsky programme was 0.055 per cent of Gross National Product, covering some 2 million workers. In September 2014, the total number unemployed in the U.S. were 9.3 million (Bureau of Labor Statistics News Release, U.S. Department of Labor, *The Employment Situation—September 2014,* USDL-14-1796).

24 A zero hours contract is one where the employer has discretion to vary the employee's working hours from full-time to zero. There are good reasons for banning such contracts, and in any case their legality in the UK has been questioned: see Ewan McGaughey, "Are Zero Hours Contracts Lawful?" 29 November 2014, http://ssrn.com/abstract=2531913.

25 Kershaw, *Government against Poverty,* quote p. 92.

26 Established in 2014, see http://ec.europa.eu/social/main.jsp?catId=1079.

27 David T. Ellwood and Elisabeth Welty, "Public Service Employment and Mandatory Work: A Policy Whose Time Has Come and Gone and Come Again?" in Rebecca Blank and David Card, eds., *Finding Jobs: Work and Welfare Reform* (New York: Russell Sage Foundation, 2001): 299–372, quote p. 300.

28 Melvin M. Brodsky, "Public-Service Employment Programs in Selected OECD Countries," *Monthly Labor Review* 123 (2000): 31–41, quote p. 34.

29 Lane Kenworthy, *Egalitarian Capitalism* (New York: Russell Sage Foundation, 2004), quote p. 153.

30 European Commission, *Employment and Social Developments,* the heading to Section 5.1 of ch. 2.

31 Ive Marx and Gerlinde Verbist, "The Policy Response: Boosting Employment and Social Investment," in Wiemer Salverda et al., eds., *Changing Inequalities and Societal Impacts in Rich Countries* (Oxford: Oxford University Press, 2014): 265–293, quote p. 271.

32 OECD, *Extending Opportunities: How Active Social Policy Can Benefit Us All* (Paris: OECD, 2005), quote p. 8.

33 Winston Churchill MP, Hansard House of Commons, 24 April 1906 155: col 1888.

34 The adoption of this definition owes much to the research of the Low-Wage Employment Research (LoWER) network. See Claudio Lucifora and Wiemer Salverda, *Policies for Low-Wage Employment and Social Exclusion in Europe* (Milan: Franco/Angeli, 1998); and "Low Pay," in Wiemer Salverda, Brian Nolan, and Timothy Smeeding, eds., *The Oxford Handbook of Economic Inequality* (Oxford: Oxford University Press, 2009), 257–283.

35 Centre for Research in Social Policy, "Uprating the UK Living Wage in 2013," CRSP Working Paper 2013, University of Loughborough.

36 Low Wage Commission, *Work That Pays: The Final Report of the Low Pay Commission* (London: Low Pay Commission, 2014), quote p. 22.

37 Low Pay Commission, *National Minimum Wage Report 2014* (London: HMSO, 2014), quote paragraph 37.

38 Anthony B. Atkinson and Sarah Voitchovsky, "The Distribution of Top Earnings in the UK since the Second World War," *Economica* 78 (2011): 440–459.

39 High Pay Centre, *Reform Agenda: How to Make Top Pay Fairer* (London: High Pay Centre, 2014).

40 *Impact and Performance Report for Traidcraft 2013–14,* quote p. 42.

41 Will Hutton, *Review of Fair Pay in the Public Sector: Final Report* (London: HMSO, 2011), quote p. 3.

42 High Pay Centre, *Reform Agenda,* quote p. 17.

43 Evidence from the Annual Survey of Hours and Earnings, ONS website, Table

1.7a, http://www.ons.gov.uk/ons/rel/ashe/annual-survey-of-hours-and-earnings/index.html.

CHAPTER 6 CAPITAL SHARED

1 J. E. Meade, *Efficiency, Equality, and the Ownership of Property* (London: G. Allen and Unwin, 1964), quote p. 48.

2 Josiah Wedgwood, *The Economics of Inheritance*, new ed. (London: Pelican Books, 1939), 115–116.

3 Geoffrey Brennan, Gordon Menzies, and Michael Munge, "A Brief History of Equality," *Economics Discipline Group Working Paper* 17 (2014), UTS Business School, University of Technology Sydney.

4 Christine Schwartz, "Earnings Inequality and the Changing Association between Spouses' Earnings," *American Journal of Sociology* 115 (2010): 1524–1557, quote p. 1528.

5 John Ermisch, Marco Francesconi, and Thomas Siedler, "Intergenerational Economic Mobility and Assortative Mating," IZA Discussion Papers 1847, Institute for the Study of Labor, Bonn, 2005.

6 Kerwin Kofi Charles, Erik Hurst, and Alexandra Killewald, "Marital Sorting and Parental Wealth," *Demography* 50 (2013): 51–70.

7 Francesca Bastagli and John Hills, "Wealth Accumulation, Ageing, and House Prices," in John Hills et al., eds., *Wealth in the UK* (Oxford: Oxford University Press, 2013): 63–91, quote p. 65.

8 These figures are from Bastagli and Hills, "Wealth Accumulation," Table 4.1.

9 European Central Bank, "The Eurosystem Household Finance and Consumption Survey: Results from the First Wave," *Statistical Paper Series* 2 (2013): quoted Table 1.2.

10 Colin Jones and Alan Murie, *The Right to Buy* (Oxford: Blackwell, 2006), quote pp. 178 and 179.

11 John Hills and Howard Glennerster, "Public Policy, Wealth, and Assets: A Complex and Inconsistent Story," in Hills et al., *Wealth in the UK*, 165–193, quote p. 187.

12 Regeneris Consulting and Oxford Economics, *The Role of Housing in the Economy: A Final Report by Regeneris Consulting and Oxford Economics* (Altrincham: Regeneris Consulting Ltd., 2010), quote pp. 8 and 71.

13 Office of Fair Trading, *Defined Contribution Workplace Pension Market Study* (London: Office of Fair Trading, 2013), OFT1505, quote p. 16 and Figure 6.2. This study found that in 2013 the median charge (by assets) for contract and bundled-trust schemes was 0.71 per cent.

14 As described by the UK Office for National Statistics: Karen Grovell and Daniel Wisniewski, *Changes to the UK National Accounts: Financial Intermediation*

Services Indirectly Measured (London: Office for National Statistics, 2014), quote p. 2.

15 John Kay, *Other People's Money* (New York: Public Affairs, 2015). I am grateful to John Kay for permission to quote from the prepublication version.

16 Jan Pen, *Income Distribution: Facts, Theories, Policies,* trans. Trevor S. Preston (New York: Praeger, 1971), 50. If the distribution is represented in terms of the cumulative shares of total income, then the share of the bottom groups is negative. This means that the curve showing the cumulative share in total income of different proportions of the population—a curve known as the Lorenz curve—lies initially below zero. This is particularly an issue with the measurement of the inequality of wealth, where it leads to higher values for the Gini coefficient. If there are enough people with negative wealth, then the Gini coefficient can theoretically exceed 100 per cent.

17 Edward N. Wolff, "Recent Trends in Household Wealth in the United States: Rising Debt and the Middle-Class Squeeze—an Update to 2007," Levy Economics Institute of Bard College, Working Paper 589 (2010), Tables 1 and 2.

18 Jesse Bricker et al., "Changes in U.S. Family Finances from 2010 to 2013: Evidence from the Survey of Consumer Finances," *Federal Reserve Bulletin* 100 (2014): 1–41, quote p. 3.

19 Bricker at al., quote p. 26.

20 Jean-Claude Juncker, *A New Start for Europe: My Agenda for Jobs, Growth, Fairness and Democratic Change: Political Guidelines for the Next European Commission* (Brussels: European Commission, 2014), quote p. 8.

21 International Monetary Fund (IMF), *World Economic Outlook (WEO) April 2014: Recovery Strengthens, Remains Uneven. World Economic and Financial Surveys,* quote p. 1.

22 Meade, *Efficiency, Equality,* quote p. 44.

23 I owe this to Robert J. Shiller, "The Invention of Inflation-Indexed Bonds in Early America," *NBER Working Paper* 10183, December 2003. As he observes, there may well be earlier precedents.

24 Available from the website of the U.S. Social Security Administration under the heading of "Social Insurance History" (http://www.socialsecurity.gov/history/paine4.html).

25 Peter Lindert and Jeffrey Williamson, "English Workers' Living Standards during the Industrial Revolution: A New Look," *Economic History Review,* sec. ser. 36 (1983): 1–25, quoted Table 2.

26 Bruce Ackerman and Anne Alstott, *The Stake-Holder Society* (New Haven: Yale University Press, 1999).

27 Cedric Sandford, *Economics of Public Finance* (Oxford: Pergamon Press, 1969); and Anthony B. Atkinson, *Unequal Shares* (London: Allen Lane, 1972), ch. 11.

28 Julian Le Grand, "Markets, Welfare and Equality," in Julian Le Grand and Saul Estrin, eds., *Market Socialism* (Oxford: Oxford University Press, 1989); and Julian Le Grand and David Nissan, *A Capital Idea: Start-Up Grants for Young People* (London: Fabian Society, 2000).

29 Eligibility (in 2014) for Child Benefit is limited by requirements that both parent and child satisfy "presence and residence conditions," and that the claimant satisfy the "right to reside test."

30 Julian Le Grand, "A Demogrant," in *Motivation, Agency and Public Policy* (Oxford: Oxford University Press, 2006), 120–136.

31 President Dwight Eisenhower, *State of the Union Message* (January 1960).

32 John Hills, "Counting the Family Silver: The Public Sector's Balance Sheet 1957 to 1987," *Fiscal Studies* 10 (1989): 66–85.

33 See Samuel Wills, Rick van der Ploeg, and Ton van den Bremer, "Norway is right to reassess its sovereign wealth fund" (VoxEU) http://www.voxeu.org/article/norway-right-reassess-its-sovereign-wealth-fund.

34 James Meade, "Full Employment, New Technologies and the Distribution of Income," *Journal of Social Policy* 13 (1984): 129–146, quote p. 145.

CHAPTER 7 PROGRESSIVE TAXATION

1 More precisely, the after-tax share would follow the *average* retention rate.

2 This graph is an updated version of Figure 4 in Facundo Alvaredo, Anthony B. Atkinson, Thomas Piketty, and Emmanuel Saez, "The Top 1 Per Cent in International and Historical Perspective," *Journal of Economic Perspectives* 27 (2013): 3–20.

3 Michael Brewer, Emmanuel Saez, and Andrew Shephard, "Means-Testing and Tax Rates on Earnings," in Stuart Adam et al., *Dimensions of Tax Design: Mirrlees Review,* vol. 1 (Oxford: Oxford University Press, 2010), 90–173.

4 Brewer, Saez, and Shephard, "Means-Testing," quote p. 110. The calculation involves not only the elasticity but also the shape of the income distribution, as described by them. See also Anthony B. Atkinson, *Public Economics in an Age of Austerity* (Abingdon: Routledge, 2014), ch. 2.

5 2012 Budget Speech, *Hansard* 31 March 2012, column 805.

6 Brewer, Saez, and Shephard, "Means-Testing," quote p. 110.

7 James Mirrlees et al., *Tax by Design: Mirrlees Review, The Final Report* (Oxford: Oxford University Press, 2011), quote p. 109.

8 Thomas Piketty, Emmanuel Saez, and Stefanie Stantcheva, "Optimal Taxation of Top Incomes: A Tale of Three Elasticities," *American Economic Journal: Economic Policy* 6 (2014): 230–271.

9 William S. Vickrey, "Measuring Marginal Utility by Reactions to Risk," *Econometrica* 13 (1945): 215–236; and James A. Mirrlees, "An Exploration in the The-

ory of Optimum Income Taxation," *Review of Economic Studies* 38 (1971): 175–208.

10 See, for example, Stanley S. Surrey and Paul R. McDaniel, "The Tax Expenditure Concept and the Budgetary Reform Act of 1974," *Boston College Law Review* 17 (1976): 679–737, reference on p. 693.

11 HM Revenue and Customs, *Estimated Costs of the Principal Tax Expenditure and Structural Reliefs*, Table 1.5, 2013–14 figures.

12 See the Mirrlees Review, *Tax by Design*, p. 335.

13 HM Revenue and Customs, *Estimated Costs* (2013–14 figures), quoted Table 1.5.

14 Mirrlees, *Tax by Design*, quote p. 490. The Review proposes (pp. 338–340) the alternative solution of exempting employee pension contributions from NIC, to put them on the same footing as employer contributions: i.e., an EEE regime. Since the Review accepts that the absence of any T is indefensible, it goes on to propose that that NIC be levied on pensions in payment (at a rate in 2010–11 of 21.1 per cent on pensions up to the upper earnings limit), thus creating an EET regime for both sets of contributions. This proposal has the merit of putting contributions on the same basis, but, as the Review recognises, the tax would be unfair on those who had already paid NIC (in effect they would be in a TET regime). It is therefore suggested that the charge on pensions be phased in. Phasing would, though, worsen a second problem which is that the reform would postpone tax revenue to a substantial extent—at a time when budgetary problems are severe.

15 HMRC tax receipts website, https://www.gov.uk/government/statistics/hmrc-tax-and-nics-receipts-for-the-uk; and *Inland Revenue Statistics* (London: HMSO, 1987), Table 1.1.

16 Thomas Piketty, "On the Long-Run Evolution of Inheritance: France 1820–2050," *Quarterly Journal of Economics* 126 (2011): 1071–1131.

17 Anthony B. Atkinson, "Wealth and Inheritance in Britain from 1896 to the Present," CASEpaper 178 (2013): 1–40, STICERD, London School of Economics.

18 Gerald R. Jantscher, "Death and Gift Taxation in the United States after the Report of the Royal Commission," *National Tax Journal* 22 (1969): 121–138, quote p. 122.

19 Quoted in Robert B. Ekelund and Douglas M. Walker, "J. S. Mill on the Income Tax Exemption and Inheritance Taxes: The Evidence Reconsidered," *History of Political Economy* 28 (1996): 559–581, quote p. 578.

20 HM Revenue and Customs, *Main Tax Expenditures and Structural Reliefs*, Table 1.5, https://www.gov.uk/government/uploads/system/uploads/attachment_data/file/302317/20140109_expenditure_reliefs_v0.4published.pdf.

21 Robin Boadway, Emma Chamberlain, and Carl Emmerson, "Taxation of

Wealth and Wealth Transfers," in Adam et al., *Dimensions of Tax Design*, 737–814, quote p. 798.

22 Edwin Cannan, *The History of Local Rates in England*, 2nd ed. (Westminster: P. S. King, 1927), quote p. 1.

23 This applies to England and Scotland. In Wales, in contrast, a revaluation was carried out in April 2005 (based on April 2003 property values) and a higher ninth band, I, was introduced.

24 Mirrlees, *Tax by Design*, quote p. 383.

25 Average Council Tax bill from Department for Communities and Local Government, "Council Tax Levels Set by Local Authorities in England 2014–15 (revised)," *Local Government Finance Statistical Release*, 23 July 2014. For average house price, see source to Figure 7.4.

26 These figures are from Andy Wightman, "Listen Up, Griff Rhys Jones, the Mansion Tax Is the Soft Option," *The Guardian*, 5 November 2014.

27 John Flemming and Ian Little, *Why We Need a Wealth Tax* (London: Methuen, 1974), quote p. 33.

28 Denis Healey, *The Time of My Life* (London: Penguin Books, 1990), quote p. 404. He went on to say that "I suspect the Conservative Party is even more unhappy that Mrs Thatcher promised to abolish the rates [local taxes] without having the slightest idea what to put in their place." In fact, the answer which she came up was the UK Poll Tax that led to her downfall.

29 Martin Weale, "Commentary," in Adam et al., *Dimensions of Tax Design*, 832–836, quote p. 834.

30 Stuart Berry, Richard Williams, and Matthew Waldron, "Household Saving," *Bank of England Quarterly Bulletin* 49 (2009): 191–201, quote p. 191.

31 Ehsan Khoman and Martin Weale, "The UK Savings Gap," *National Institute Economic Review* 198 (2006): 97–111, quote p. 105.

32 Weale, "Commentary," quote p. 834.

33 Thomas Piketty, *Capital in the Twenty-First Century* (Belknap Press of Harvard University Press, 2014), quote p. 533.

34 Piketty, *Capital*, quote p. 515.

35 Oxfam blog, "Number of Billionaires Doubled since Financial Crisis as Inequality Spirals Out of Control," http://www.oxfam.org.uk/blogs/2014/10/number-of-billionaires-doubled-since-financial-crisis-as-inequality-spirals-out-of-control, 29 October 2014.

36 Piketty, *Capital*, quote p. 515.

37 Groupe de Travail sur les nouvelles contributions financières internationales, *Rapport à Monsieur Jacques Chirac, Président de la République*, Paris, December 2004.pp

38 Piketty, *Capital*, quote p. 525.

39 Richard A. Musgrave and Peggy B. Musgrave, *Public Finance in Theory and Practice*, 5th ed. (New York: McGraw-Hill, 1989), quote p. 373.

40 George F. Break and Joseph A. Pechman, *Federal Tax Reform* (Washington, D.C.: The Brookings Institution, 1975), quote p. 78.

CHAPTER 8 SOCIAL SECURITY FOR ALL

1 Ive Marx, Brian Nolan, and Javier Olivera, "The Welfare State and Anti-Poverty Policy in Rich Countries," in Anthony B. Atkinson and François Bourguignon, *Handbook of Income Distribution*, vol. 2B (Amsterdam: Elsevier, 2015), 2063–2139, quote p. 2081.

2 Anthony B. Atkinson, "What Is Happening to the Distribution of Income in the UK?" *Proceedings of the British Academy* 82 (1993): 317–351.

3 Michael Brewer, Emmanuel Saez, and Andrew Shephard, "Means-Testing and Tax Rates on Earnings," in Stuart Adam et al., *Dimensions of Tax Design: Mirrlees Review*, vol. 1 (Oxford: Oxford University Press, 2010), 90–173, quote p. 143.

4 European Commission, *The Social Situation in the European Union 2008* (Brussels: Directorate-General for Employment, Social Affairs and Equal Opportunities, 2009), quote p. 45.

5 Manos Matsaganis, Alari Paulus, and Holly Sutherland, "The Take-Up of Social Benefits," Research Note, European Observatory on the Social Situation, 2008, quote pp. 3–4.

6 Dean Plueger, "Earned Income Tax Credit Participation Rate for the Tax Year 2005," *IRS Research Bulletin* 500 (2009): 151–195, quote p. 179.

7 Brian Abel-Smith and Peter Townsend, *The Poor and the Poorest: A New Analysis of the Ministry of Labour's Family Expenditure Surveys of 1953–54 and 1960* (London: Bell, 1965).

8 HM Revenue and Customs, *Child Benefit, Child Tax Credit, and Working Tax Credit* (London: HM Revenue and Customs, 2012), quote p. 13.

9 Clair Vickery, "The Time-Poor: A New Look at Poverty," *Journal of Human Resources* 12 (1977): 27–48; and Anthony B. Atkinson, *Poverty in Europe* (Oxford: Blackwell, 1998).

10 Michael E. Rose, *The Relief of Poverty, 1834–1914* (London: Macmillan, 1972), quote pp. 63–64.

11 Lord Beveridge, *Social Insurance and Allied Services* (London: HMSO Cmd 6404, 1942), quote p. 12.

12 James J. Heckman, "Going Forward Wisely," Speech to the White House Early Childhood Education Summit, 10 December, 2014, Center for the Economics of Human Development, University of Chicago.

13 Timothy M. Smeeding and Jane Waldfogel, "Fighting Child Poverty in the United States and United Kingdom: An Update," *Fast Focus* no. 8 (2010): 1–5, quote p. 2.

14 HMRC, *Child Benefit Statistics: Geographical Analysis August 2013*, quote p. 7.

15 James A. Mirrlees, "An Exploration in the Theory of Optimum Income Taxation," *Review of Economic Studies* 38 (1971): 175–208.

16 See Rolf Aaberge, Ugo Colombino, and Steinar Strøm, "Do More Equal Slices Shrink the Cake? An Empirical Investigation of Tax-Transfer Reform Proposals in Italy," *Journal of Population Economics* 17 (2004): 767–785; and, for Norway, Rolf Aaberge and Ugo Colombino, "Using a Microeconometric Model of Household Labour Supply to Design Optimal Income Taxes," *Scandinavian Journal of Economics* 115 (2013): 449–475.

17 Moreover, one has to be careful about using the term "choice"; childlessness may also not be a "choice."

18 Amelia Hill, "Cash-Strapped Parents Choosing to Have Only One Baby, Survey Finds," *The Guardian*, 31 October 2014.

19 For this arithmetic, see Tobin, "On Limiting the Domain of Inequality," *Journal of Law and Economics* 13 (1970): 263–277, quote p. 265.

20 Even if it were feasible, the sensitivities surrounding the criteria for qualifying for citizenship mean that I have considerable doubts about the wisdom of attaching a monetary reward—in the form of the basic income—to the acquisition of citizenship.

21 Jurgen De Wispelaere and Lindsay Stirton, "The Public Administration Case against Participation Income," *Social Service Review* 81 (2007): 523–549, quote p. 540. The next quotation is from page 545. See also by the same authors, "The Many Faces of Universal Basic Income," *Political Quarterly* 75 (2004): 266–274.

22 Philippe Van Parijs, "Why Surfers Should Be Fed: The Liberal Case for an Unconditional Basic Income," *Philosophy and Public Affairs* 20 (1991): 101–131. John Rawls, "The Priority of Right and Ideas of the Good," *Philosophy and Public Affairs* 17 (1988): 251–276, note 7.

23 Horacio Levy, Christine Luetz, and Holly Sutherland, "A Guaranteed Income for Europe's Children?" in Stephen P. Jenkins and John Micklewright, eds., *Inequality and Poverty Re-Examined* (Oxford: Oxford University Press, 2007), quote pp. 209–231. See also Manos Matsaganis et al. "Reforming Family Transfers in Southern Europe: Is There a Role for Universal Child Benefits?" *Social Policy and Society* 5 (2006): 189–197.

24 The idea of such a "pension-tested" increase in the state basic pension was first suggested to me by Tony Lynes, who was the source of much wisdom on social security and who sadly died in 2014. It is described in greater detail in Anthony B. Atkinson, "State Pensions for Today and Tomorrow," in Anthony B. Atkinson, ed., *Incomes and the Welfare State: Essays on Britain and Europe* (Cambridge: Cambridge University Press, 1995), 305–323. (I proposed the approach to the late Donald Dewar, when he was spokesman for the Labour Party in the

mid-1990s, but it was not favoured by the then Shadow Chancellor, Gordon Brown).

25 Peter Kenway, *Should Adult Benefit for Unemployment Now Be Raised?* (York: Joseph Rowntree Foundation, 2009).

26 I am most grateful to Kenway, *Should Adult Benefit,* note 10, for having documented so fully the series that he used. This has allowed me to readily update the values in Figure 8.2.

27 The quotation is from Kenway, *Should Adult Benefit,* quote p. 13; the poverty rate is from Figure 2.

28 Josh Bivens, "Historically Small Share of Jobless People Are Receiving Unemployment Insurance," *Economic Snapshot* (Washington, D.C.: Economic Policy Institute), 25 September 2014.

29 John Hills, *Good Times, Bad Times* (Bristol: Policy Press, 2014), quote p. 261. He cites evidence that "half of those surveyed thought that 40 per cent or more of spending was on the unemployed" (p. 259).

30 Anthony B. Atkinson and John Micklewright, "Turning the Screw: Benefits for the Unemployed 1979–88," in Andrew Dilnot and Ian Walker, eds., *The Economics of Social Security* (Oxford: Oxford University Press, 1989), 17–51.

31 Anthony B. Atkinson, *Public Economics in an Age of Austerity* (Abingdon: Routledge, 2014), ch. 3, sec. 4. The discussion in the Mirrlees Review is in James Mirrlees et al., *Tax by Design: Mirrlees Review, The Final Report* (Oxford: Oxford University Press, 2011), pp. 126–128.

32 Edward J. McCaffery and Joel Slemrod, "Toward an Agenda for Behavioral Public Finance," in Edward J. McCaffery and Joel Slemrod, eds., *Behavioral Public Finance* (New York: Sage, 2006), 3–31, quote pp. 7 and 9.

33 *Public Finance* website, 18 August 2014.

34 Mutual Information System on Social Protection (MISSOC) Database of the European Commission.

35 In addition, with the social insurance approach and with the participation income, the present benefit cap, limiting the total paid to people aged 16 to 64, would be abolished.

36 United Nations, *Millennium Development Goals Report 2014* (New York: United Nations, 2014), quote p. 9.

37 Harry G. Johnson, *Economic Policies towards Less Developed Countries* (London: Allen and Unwin, 1967), quote p. 118. I owe my interest in the subject to the study by Ian Little and Juliet M. Clifford, *International Aid* (London: Allen and Unwin, 1965).

38 Johnson, *Economic Policies,* quote p. 119.

39 Jim Murphy, interviewed by Mary Riddell, "National Interest," *Fabian Review* 126 (Autumn 2014), quote p. 16.

40 For views on the effectiveness of aid in stimulating growth that run counter to this, see Martin Ravallion, "On the Role of Aid in the *Great Escape*," *Review of Income and Wealth* 60 (2014): 967–984; and Channing Arndt, Sam Jones, and Finn Tarp, "What Is the Aggregate Economic Rate of Return to Foreign Aid?" UNU-WIDER Working Paper 2014/089. The latter states on p. 2 that "the large majority of up-to-date empirical studies in the economics literature have found positive impacts."

41 Angus Deaton, *The Great Escape* (Princeton: Princeton University Press, 2013), quote p. 312.

42 According to the *Global Humanitarian Assistance Report 2014* (Bristol: Development Initiatives, 2014), "the international community responded to the dramatic scale of need in 2013 with a record $22 billion in funding. This was a significant increase.... Yet even at these record levels of funding, under two-thirds (65%) of the needs outlined in the UN-coordinated appeals were met in 2013," quote p. 13.

43 Channing Arndt, Sam Jones, and Finn Tarp, "Assessing Foreign Aid's Long-Run Contribution to Growth in Development," *World Development*, forthcoming, quote p. x.

44 David Miller, *National Responsibility and Global Justice* (Oxford: Oxford University Press, 2007), quotes from pp. 266–267.

45 *The Guardian,* 2 December 2014.

46 Amartya Sen, *The Idea of Justice* (Cambridge, MA: Harvard University Press, 2009), quote p. 8.

CHAPTER 9 SHRINKING THE CAKE?

1 See, for example, Anthony B. Atkinson and Joseph E. Stiglitz, *Lectures on Public Economics* (New York: McGraw-Hill, 1980), Fig. 11-5, where the well-being of individuals is represented by their utilities.

2 Jonathan D. Ostry, Andrew Berg, and Charalambos G. Tsangarides, "Redistribution, Inequality, and Growth," IMF Staff Discussion Note SDN/14/02, February 2014, quote p. 4, http://www.imf.org/external/pubs/ft/sdn/2014/sdn1402.pdf.

3 B is excluded because if wages rise (fall) when there is excess demand (supply) for workers, then B is unstable. If there is any slight deviation, then the economy moves off either upwards to A or downwards to C.

4 Harvey Leibenstein, "The Theory of Underemployment in Densely Populated Backward Areas," in *Economic Backwardness and Economic Growth* (New York: John Wiley, 1963), ch. 6.

5 See Carl Shapiro and Joseph E. Stiglitz, "Equilibrium Unemployment as a Worker Discipline Device," *American Economic Review* 74 (1984): 433–444.

6 Martin Feldstein, "Introduction," in Martin Feldstein, ed., *The American Economy in Transition* (Chicago: University of Chicago Press, 1980), quote p. 4.

7 Jose Harris, *Unemployment and Politics* (Oxford: Oxford University Press, 1972), see p. 307.

8 See Anthony B. Atkinson and John Micklewright, "Unemployment Compensation and Labor Market Transitions: A Critical Review," *Journal of Economic Literature* 29 (1991): 1679–1727.

9 David Card, Raj Chetty, and Andrea Weber, "The Spike at Benefit Exhaustion: Leaving the Unemployment System or Starting a New Job," *American Economic Review, Papers and Proceedings* 97 (2007): 113–118, quote p. 113.

10 The argument is developed more formally in Anthony B. Atkinson, *The Economic Consequences of Rolling Back the Welfare State* (Cambridge, MA: MIT Press, 1999), ch. 7.

11 For a review of the literature on inequality and growth, see Sarah Voitchovsky "Inequality and Economic Growth," in Wiemer Salverda, Brian Nolan, and Timothy M. Smeeding, eds., *The Oxford Handbook of Economic Inequality* (Oxford: Oxford University Press, 2009): 549–574.

12 It should be noted that this is not the same as the growth of GDP measured in terms of Purchasing Power Parities (PPP), since the change in the PPP rates, which are essentially a multilateral calculation, do not necessarily correspond to the rates of domestic inflation, which are measured using only national statistics. See Anthony B. Atkinson, Eric Marlier, and Anne-Catherine Guio, "Monitoring the Evolution of Income Poverty and Real Incomes over Time," Second Network for the Analysis of EU-Statistics on Income and Living Conditions (Net-SILC2) Working Paper, 2015.

13 China may have high inequality because it has grown fast.

14 Steven N. Durlauf, "Econometric Analysis and the Study of Economic Growth: A Skeptical Perspective," in Roger Backhouse and Andrea Salanti, eds., *Macroeconomics and the Real World*, vol. 1 (Oxford: Oxford University Press, 2001), 249–262. The reference in the quotation is to Steven N. Durlauf and Danny T. Quah, "The New Empirics of Economic Growth," in John B. Taylor and Michael Woodford, eds., *Handbook of Macroeconomics* (Amsterdam: North Holland, 1999): 235–308.

15 Ostry, Berg, and Tsangarides, "Redistribution."

16 Ostry, Berg, and Tsangarides, "Redistribution," quote p. 17. The final quotation in this paragraph is from page 4.

CHAPTER 10 GLOBALISATION PREVENTS ACTION?

1 "History of Globalization," "Modern Globalization," http://en.wikipedia.org/wiki/History_of_globalization, downloaded 19 January 2015.

2   See also Anthony B. Atkinson, "Globalization and the European Welfare State at the Opening and the Closing of the Twentieth Century," in Henryk Kierz-kowski, ed., *Europe and Globalization* (London: Palgrave Macmillan, 2002): 249–273.

3   Isaac M. Rubinow, *Social Insurance: With Special Reference to American Conditions* (New York: Williams and Norgate, 1913), quote p. 26.

4   Moses Abramovitz, "Welfare Quandaries and Productivity Concerns," *American Economic Review* 71 (1981): 1–17, quote pp. 2–3.

5   James M. Buchanan, "The Fiscal Crises in Welfare Democracies with Some Implications for Public Investment," in Hirofumi Shibata and Toshihiro Ihori, eds., *The Welfare State, Public Investment, and Growth* (Berlin: Springer, 1998), 3–16, quote p. 4.

6   Michel Camdessus, IMF Managing Director, as reported in *The Observer,* 21 September 1997.

7   In 1844 the French economist Jules Dupuit gave a very clear explanation: "if a tax is gradually increased from zero up to a point at which it becomes prohibitive, its yield is at first nil, then increases by small stages until it reaches a maximum, after which it gradually declines until it becomes zero again" (translated in Kenneth J. Arrow and Tibor Scitovsky, eds., *Readings in Welfare Economics* (London: Allen and Unwin, 1969), quote p. 278.

8   Joe Minarik, "Tax Expenditures in OECD Countries," Presentation to Meeting of Senior Budget Officials, 4–5 June 2009, OECD, Paris, http://www.oecd.org/governance/budgeting/42976288.pdf, slide 22.

9   Paul Krugman, "Competitiveness: A Dangerous Obsession," *Foreign Affairs* 74/2 (1994): 28–44, quote p. 44, and "Making Sense of the Competitiveness Debate," *Oxford Review of Economic Policy* 1996 (Autumn): 17–25, quote p. 24.

10   Richard Tawney, *Equality,* 2nd rev. ed. (London: Unwin Books, 1931), quote p. 270.

11   Migration Advisory Committee, *Migrants in Low-Skilled Work: The Growth of EU and Non-EU Labour in Low-Skilled Jobs and Its Impact on the UK: Summary Report* (London: Migration Advisory Committee, 2014). The quotations are from pages 1 and 38.

12   Danny Dorling, "Overseas Property Buyers Are Not the Problem: Landlord Subsidies Are," *The Guardian,* 10 February 2014, http://www.theguardian.com/commentisfree/2014/feb/10/overseas-property-london-landlord-subsidies. See also Danny Dorling, *All That Is Solid* (London: Penguin, 2014).

13   John Hilary, *The Transatlantic Trade and Investment Partnership* (Brussels: Rosa Luxemburg Stiftung, 2014), quote p. 6.

14   I owe this quotation to Leif J. Eliasson, "What Is at Stake in the Transatlantic

Trade and Investment Partnership?" Saar Expert Papers 2/2014, http://jean-monnet-saar.eu/wp-content/uploads/2013/12/10_07_14_TTIP-Eliasson.pdf.

15 Ranjit Lall, "Beyond Institutional Design: Explaining the Performance of International Organizations," ms. in prep.

16 OECD Press Release, 17 September 2014, and oral reply to questions.

17 Pierre Gramegna, Press Conference at Ecofin Council, Brussels, 11 November 2014.

18 Robert Marjolin, chair, "The Marjolin Report," *Report of the Study Group: Economic and Monetary Union 1980* (Brussels: European Commission, EMU–63, 1975), quote p. 34.

19 Donald MacDougall, chair, "The MacDougall Report, vol. 2," *Report of the Study Group on the Role of Public Finance in European Integration* (Brussels: European Commission, 1977), quote p. 16.

20 See Eric Marlier and David Natali, with Rudi Van Dam, eds., *Europe 2020: Towards a More Social EU?* (Brussels: Peter Lang, 2010).

21 For a telling critique of the jobless household component, see Sophie Ponthieux, "Evolution of AROPE over Time: A Focus on (Quasi-) Joblessness," paper presented at the International Conference on Comparative EU Statistics on Income and Living Conditions (Net-SILC2), Lisbon, October 2014.

CHAPTER 11 CAN WE AFFORD IT?

1 England Royal Commission on the Taxation of Profits and Income, *Minutes of Evidence Taken before the Royal Commission on the Taxation of Profits and Income. First [etc.] Day. 21 June 1951, etc.* (London, 1952), Question 444.

2 We were, of course, helped by the fact that the speech was interrupted by Alex Salmond, at the time a young Scottish Nationalist MP, who was then ejected from the House of Commons, which delayed proceedings.

3 I am most grateful to them for making these calculations, while making clear that I alone am responsible for the conclusions. The model is described in Paola De Agostini and Holly Sutherland, *EUROMOD Country Report: UK 2009–2013* (EUROMOD: University of Essex, June 2014).

4 De Agostini and Sutherland, *EUROMOD Country Report*, quote p. 59.

5 For a survey of work in this area, see Michael P. Keane, "Labour Supply and Taxes: A Survey," *Journal of Economic Literature* 49 (2011): 961–1075.

6 Congressional Budget Office website, *Processes,* https://www.cbo.gov/content/processes.

7 The eligibility conditions should be coordinated with those for Child Benefit, so that those not eligible for the participation income are covered by Child Benefit, and to avoid any disincentive to remaining in education where the PI

is higher than the Child Benefit. It may in fact be better to pay Child Benefit to the minimum school-leaving age and PI beyond that age.

8 In the calculation of Child Tax Credit, the gross amount enters; for other income-tested benefits account is taken of the income tax paid on the addition to Child Benefit.

9 De Agostini and Sutherland, *EUROMOD Country Report,* quote p. 72.

THE WAY FORWARD

1 Quoted in Martin S. Feldstein, "On the Theory of Tax Reform," *Journal of Public Economics* (1976): 77–104, quote p. 77.

Contents in Detail

List of Tables and Figures

Figure Sources

FIGURE 1.1: Based on Anthony B. Atkinson and Salvatore Morelli, *Chartbook of Economic Inequality,* http://www.chartbookofeconomicinequality.com/. The underlying sources of the US data are as follows. Overall inequality: "Annual Social and Economic Supplement to the Current Population Survey," from *Income and Poverty in the United States: 2013* (Washington, D.C.: U.S. Bureau of the Census, 2014), http://www.census.gov/content/dam/Census/library/publications/2014/demo/p60-249.pdf, Table A-3, "Selected measures of equivalence-adjusted income dispersion," where it has been assumed that half of the recorded change between 1992 and 1993 was due to the change in methods (1.15 percentage points has been added to the values from 1992 back to 1967). This series is linked backwards at 1967 to the series from 1944 given by E. C. Budd, "Postwar Changes in the Size Distribution of Income in the U.S.," *American Economic Review, Papers and Proceedings* 60 (1970): 247–260. Income share of top 1%: Thomas Piketty and Emmanuel Saez, "Income Inequality in the United States, 1913–1998," *Quarterly Journal of Economics* 118 (2003): 1–39; updated figures from Saez's website, http://eml.berkeley.edu/~saez/. Poverty rate: Before 1959 from Gordon Fisher, "Estimates of the Poverty Population under the Current Official Definition for Years before 1959," mimeograph, Office of the Assistant Secretary for Planning and Evaluation, U.S. Department of Health and Human Services, 1970, Table 6. Since 1959 from the U.S. Bureau of the Census website, Historical Poverty Tables, Table 2; and U.S. Bureau of the Census publications, *Income and Poverty in the United States: 2013,* Table B1. Individual earnings: Based on the Current Population Survey (CPS) from the OECD iLibrary, most recent data available at http://www.oecd-ilibrary.org/employment/data/oecd-employment-and-labour-market-statistics_lfs-data-en. These data are linked at 1973 to the estimates of Lynn A. Karoly, "The Trend in Inequality among Families, Individuals, and Workers in the United States: A Twenty-five Year Perspective," in Sheldon Danziger and Peter Gottschalk, eds., *Uneven Tides* (New York: Russell Sage Foundation, 1994), Table 2B.2; and at 1963 to the estimates in Anthony B. Atkinson, *The Changing Distribution of Earnings in OECD Countries* (Oxford: Oxford University Press, 2008), Table T.10. The last of these sources provides information about the definition of the population covered and the time period, which differ across the sources.

FIGURE 1.2: Based on Anthony B. Atkinson and Salvatore Morelli, *Chartbook of Economic Inequality,* http://www.chartbookofeconomicinequality.com/. The underlying sources of the UK data are as follows. Overall inequality: Gini coefficient of equivalised (modified OECD scale) disposable household income for all persons in the United Kingdom (Great Britain up to 2001/02) are from the website of the Institute for Fiscal Studies: http://www.ifs.org.uk/. The data from 1961 to 1992 (financial year 1993/94) are from the Family Expenditure Survey, and thereafter from the Family Resources Survey. The Gini earlier series ("Blue Book series") values are from Anthony B. Atkinson and John Micklewright, *Economic Transformation in Eastern Europe and the Distribution of Income* (Cambridge: Cambridge University Press, 1992), Table BI1; the figure for 1938 is from the Royal Commission on the Distribution of Income and Wealth, *Report No. 7, Fourth report on the Standing Reference,* Cmnd.7595 (London: HMSO, 1979), p. 23. Income share of top 1%: World Top Incomes Database (WTID), http://topincomes.g-mond.parisschoolofeconomics.eu/. Poverty rate: from the website of the Institute for

Fiscal Studies (before housing costs series), as described above. Individual earnings: Earnings data from Annual Survey of Hours and Earnings, covering all full-time workers on adult rates whose pay for the survey period was not affected by absence, linked backwards to take account of changes in methodology in 2006 and 2004, linked backwards in 2000 to the data from the New Earnings Survey (NES) from Atkinson, *The Changing Distribution of Earnings in OECD Countries*, Table S.8, taking the series back to 1968 (when the NES began), linked backwards to the income tax data (Schedule E earnings) from the same source, Table S.7.

FIGURE 1.3: LIS Key Figures, http://www.lisdatacenter.org/data-access/key-figures/download-key-figures/, downloaded 30 November 2014.

FIGURE 1.4: Poverty rates from LIS Key Figures, http://www.lisdatacenter.org/data-access/key-figures/download-key-figures/, downloaded 30 November 2014. Top income shares from the World Top Incomes Database, http://topincomes.g-mond.parisschoolofeconomics.eu/, downloaded 9 December 2014.

FIGURE 1.6: Data for 2000 and earlier are from website of Angus Maddison, *Historical Statistics of the World Economy*, GDP measured at 1990 PPPs, http://www.ggdc.net/maddison/oriindex.htm. Data for 2020 and later are from the Long-term Baseline Projections from OECD Economic Outlook No. 95, May 2014, Dataset, GDP at 2005 US$ PPPs. The series for the UK and the US have been linked using the Maddison values for 2008 and the OECD values for 2010; the figures for China and India did not appear to need adjustment.

FIGURE 2.1: Top income shares from the World Top Incomes Database, http://topincomes.g-mond.parisschoolofeconomics.eu/, downloaded 27 September 2014. Gini coefficients: see Sources for Figures 1.1 (US) and 1.2 (UK); for Denmark, the coefficients are from Anthony B. Atkinson and Jakob Søgaard, "The Long Run History of Income Inequality in Denmark," *Scandinavian Journal of Economics*, forthcoming, Figure 4.

FIGURE 2.2: Data for Finland, Norway, and Sweden from Anthony B. Atkinson and Salvatore Morelli, *Chartbook of Economic Inequality*, http://www.chartbookofeconomicinequality.com/. Data for top shares for Denmark from the World Top Incomes Database, http://topincomes.g-mond.parisschoolofeconomics.eu/, downloaded 27 September 2014; for the source of data for the Gini coefficient for Denmark, see Figure 2.1 Sources.

FIGURE 2.3: Anthony B. Atkinson and Salvatore Morelli, *Chartbook of Economic Inequality*, http://www.chartbookofeconomicinequality.com/.

FIGURE 2.4: Thomas Piketty and Gabriel Zucman, "Capital Is Back: Wealth-Income Ratios in Rich Countries, 1700–2010," *Quarterly Journal of Economics* 129 (2014): 1255–1310, online appendix table A50, http://gabriel-zucman.eu/capitalisback/. No data are given in the original source for the 1950s for Australia, Canada, Italy, or Japan.

FIGURE 2.5: Anthony B. Atkinson and Salvatore Morelli, *Chartbook of Economic Inequality*, http://www.chartbookofeconomicinequality.com/.

FIGURE 2.6: Socio Economic Database for Latin America and the Caribbean (SEDLAC), (CEDLAS and The World Bank), http://sedlac.econo.unlp.edu.ar/eng/, downloaded 5 October 2014.

FIGURE 2.7: Anthony B. Atkinson and Salvatore Morelli, *Chartbook of Economic Inequality*, http://www.chartbookofeconomicinequality.com/.

FIGURE 3.2: UK Annual Survey of Hours and Earnings (ASHE), and the New Earnings Survey (NES) that preceded ASHE; data for 2006 and after are from the website of the UK Office for National Statistics (ONS); data before 2006 are from Anthony B. Atkinson, *The Changing Distribution of Earnings* (Oxford: Oxford University Press, 2008), Tables S4 and S5. The series are linked forwards in 2000 to join the NES and ASHE data, and in 2004 and 2006 to take account of changes in the methodology.

FIGURE 5.1: I am grateful to David Hendry for supplying this series: David F. Hendry, *Macroeconometrics: An Introduction* (London: Timberlake Consultants, 2015).

FIGURE 5.2: Eurostat, *Labour Market Policy—Expenditure and Participants, Data 2010* (Luxembourg: Publications Office of the European Union, 2012). The UK data are from the 2008 publication because no data were supplied by the UK government for the 2010 report. The expenditure in the UK in 2008 related to the—since abolished—New Deal for 18–24 Voluntary Sector and Environment Task Force options.

FIGURE 5.3: European Commission, *Employment and Social Developments in Europe 2013* (Luxembourg: Publications Office of the European Union, 2014), Chart 34, p. 158.

FIGURE 5.4: International Labour Organization (ILO), *Global Wage Report 2012/13,* Figure 28.

FIGURE 6.1A: The wealth shares are from Anthony B. Atkinson and Salvatore Morelli, *Chartbook of Economic Inequality;* total wealth series is based on Facundo Alvaredo, Anthony B. Atkinson, and Salvatore Morelli, "Top Wealth Shares in the UK: 1895 to 2010." Wealth is adjusted to 2000 prices using the composite consumer price index constructed by the Office for National Statistics: Jim O'Donoghue, Louise Goulding, and Grahame Allen, "Consumer Price Inflation since 1750," *Economic Trends* 604 (March 2004): 38–46, Table 1.

FIGURE 6.1B: See Figure 6.1A Sources. National income figures for 1923, 1937, and 1950 are from Charles H. Feinstein, *Statistical Tables of National Income, Expenditure and Output of the U.K. 1855–1965* (Cambridge: Cambridge University Press, 1976), Table 1, column 13 (net national product). Figures for 1975 are from *United Kingdom National Accounts 1997 (The Blue Book)* (London: HMSO, 1997), Table 1.1. The *Blue Book 1997* provides a figure for 1996, but the change to the European System of Accounts 1995 means that figures for later years are not given on the same basis. The 1996 figure has been updated to 2000 by the increase in gross value added at current basic prices from the *Blue Book 2005,* Table 1.4.

FIGURE 6.2: Money interest rate from Bank of England, Statistical Interactive Database, Interest and exchange rates data, Quoted household interest rates, Deposit rates, Fixed rate bonds, and Time (notice accounts), http://www.bankofengland.co.uk/boeapps/iadb/. Rate of inflation from UK Office for National Statistics (ONS), United Kingdom National Accounts online dataset, Consumer Price Index (all items), variable CDID.

FIGURE 6.3: UK Office for National Statistics (ONS), United Kingdom National Accounts online dataset, variables CGRX for the net worth of general government (since 1987) and YBHA for GDP. Net worth of general government and public corporations before 1987 from UK National Accounts 1990, Table 12.12 (1979 to 1986), UK National Accounts 1987, Tables 11.6–11.8 (1975 to 1978); C. G. E. Bryant, "National and Sector Balance Sheets 1957–1985," *Economic Trends* 403 (May 1987), Table A1 (1966, 1969 and 1972); and Alan R. Roe, *The Financial Interdependence of the Economy 1957–1966* (Cambridge: Chapman and Hall, 1971), Table 34 (1957 to 1963).

FIGURE 6.4: Assets under management from website of Sovereign Wealth Fund Institute, http://www.swfinstitute.org/fund-rankings/, downloaded 15 November 2014. GDP figures from World Bank, World Development Indicators, GDP by country, http://data.worldbank.org/products/wdi. Figures for Alaska and Texas from US Bureau of Economic Analysis, *Quarterly Gross Domestic Product by State, 2005–2013,* news release 20 August 2014, Table 3.

FIGURE 6.5: See sources for Figure 6.3: Total government revenue from UK oil and gas.

production (not including gas levy) from *Statistics of Government Revenues from Oil and Gas*

Production, Table 11.1, adjusted to real values using the UK Office for National Statistics (ONS) long-term indicator of prices of consumer goods and services, CDKO.

FIGURE 7.1: Share of top 0.1% from the World Top Incomes Database, downloaded 15 October 2014. Marginal retention rate calculated as 1 minus the top income tax (and super-tax or surtax) rate, from annual reports of the Inland Revenue/HM Revenue and Customs and HMRC website, https://www.gov.uk/government/publications/rates-and-allowances-income-tax/rates-and-allowances-income-tax.

FIGURE 7.2: Income shares are from the World Top Incomes Database, http://topincomes.g-mond.parisschoolofeconomics.eu/, downloaded 15 October 2014. Top marginal retention rate data are from Alvaredo et al., "The Top 1 Per Cent," Figure 4, with new data added for Denmark supplied by Jakob Søgaard (the Danish tax rate for the earlier period is taken as that for 1967, in view of the major tax reform in 1966). The data start later for Ireland (1975), Italy (1974), Portugal (1976), and Spain (1981). For Switzerland, the data end in 1995. The data have been updated since the publication of Alvaredo et al., but a linear regression in logarithmic form yields a coefficient of 0.45, close to their reported value of 0.47.

FIGURE 7.3: Author's calculations. The property values are related to Council Tax bands in April 1991 using the UK Office for National Statistics (ONS) average house price series, monthly and quarterly tables, Table 12, for England and Wales, all dwellings, http://www.ons.gov.uk/ons/rel/hpi/house-price-index/september-2014/stb-september-2014.html, downloaded 19 December 2014, taking quarter 2 for 1991 and quarter 2 for 2014.

FIGURE 8.1: UK Office for National Statistics (ONS), United Kingdom National Accounts online dataset, http://www.ons.gov.uk/ons/rel/naa1-rd/united-kingdom-national-accounts/the-blue-book—2013-edition/tsd--blue-book-2013.html, using variables ACHH, EKY3, and NZGO. The data in that source for 1999 to 2003 for Child Benefit include tax credits and have been replaced by the data for Child Benefit in Table 5.2.4S of the National Accounts Blue Book for 2006. The data for Child Benefit before 1987 are from the Family Benefits entry in the National Accounts Blue Books for 1987, Table 7.2; 1982, Table 7.2; and 1963–1973, Table 39.

FIGURE 8.2: US data from U.S. Bureau of the Census, *Income, Poverty, and Health Insurance Coverage in the United States: 2013,* Table B-2; UK data from Department for Work and Pensions, *Households Below Average Income 1994/95–2010/11* (London: Department for Work and Pensions, 2012), Table 4.2tr.

FIGURE 8.3: LIS Key Figures, http://www.lisdatacenter.org/data-access/key-figures/download-key-figures/, downloaded 30 November 2014. Figures are for 2010 except Brazil (2011), Japan (2008), Guatemala and South Korea (2006), Hungary and Sweden (2005), Austria, Czech Republic, India, Peru, Switzerland, and Uruguay (2004), China (2002), and Belgium (2000).

FIGURE 8.4: Household consumption expenditure series ABPB and the total population series EBAQ from 1954 from the UK Office for National Statistics (ONS), Blue Book tables online, http://www.ons.gov.uk/ons/rel/naa1-rd/united-kingdom-national-accounts/the-blue-book—2013-edition/tsd--blue-book-2013.html, downloaded 4 November 2014. Population data for 1948 to 1954 are from C. H. Feinstein, *Statistical Tables of National Income, Expenditure and Output of the U.K., 1855–1965* (Cambridge: Cambridge University Press, 1976), Table 55, where the (minor) break in the series in 1950 has been ignored. Unemployment rates are from the Institute for Fiscal Studies website, Unemployment benefit rates, downloaded 4 November 2014. The benefit rate is that ruling on 1 July of each year.

FIGURE 8.5: OECD, *Divided We Stand* (Paris: OECD, 2011), Figure 7.5.

FIGURE 8.6: OECD Compare your country—Official Development Assistance 2013 website, downloaded 2 November 2014. Aid is expressed as a percentage of GNI.

FIGURE 9.3: Gini coefficients from LIS Key Figures, http://www.lisdatacenter.org/data-access/key-figures/download-key-figures/, downloaded 23 November 2014. GDP annual growth rates from World Bank, World Development Indicators, http://databank.worldbank.org/data/views/reports/tableview.aspx#, annual percentage rate of growth of GDP per capita based on constant local currency. These have been cumulated from 1990 (in some cases later years) to 2013 and the average growth calculated.

FIGURE 10.1: OECD Social Expenditure Database (SOCX), Table "From gross public to total net social spending, 2011," http://www.oecd.org/social/expenditure.htm, downloaded 25 November 2014.

FIGURE 11.2: Calculations using the UK module of EUROMOD (see text).

Index

Aaberge, Rolf, 327n63

Aaron, Henry, 17

Abel-Smith, Brian, *The Poor and the Poorest,* 23, 211

Abramovitz, Moses, on social security programs, 265

Acemoglu, Daron: on decline in unionisation, 94; on elasticity of substitution, 96

Ackerman, Bruce: on asset-based egalitarianism, 169, 171; on minimum inheritance, 169, 171

Addison, John T., on German labour unions, 128

Aghion, Philippe, on decline in unionisation, 94

Aguiar, Mark A., on savings rates, 34

Aid. *See* International development aid

Akerlof, George: *Efficiency Wage Models of the Labor Market,* 251; on efficiency wages, 251, 252

Alaska, sovereign wealth fund in, 175

Alstott, Anne: on asset-based egalitarianism, 169, 171; on minimum inheritance, 169, 171

Alvaredo, Facundo: on reduction of inequality in Latin America, 78, 79–80; on minimum wage in Brazil, 79–80

Andrae, Carl Christopher von, 316n21

Antitrust, 126

Apple, 119

Argentina: top income share in, 78; economic inequality in, 78, 79; reduction in economic inequality in, 78, 79; poverty in, 79

Arndt, Channing, on international aid effectiveness, 235, 345n39

Arpaia, Alfonso, on labour income share, 96, 331n31

Arrow, Kenneth: on learning by doing, 88; on ethical codes, 125; on social responsibility, 125

Asset values, 31; accrued vs. realised gains, 32

Assortative mating, 160

Attanasio, Orazio, on consumption inequality, 34

Austen, Jane, *Mansfield Park,* 158

Austerity programmes, 118, 205

Australia: economic inequality in, 22, 23, 26, 55, 56, 81, 259, 260; poverty in, 26; top income share in, 56; share of wages in national income, 69; minimum wage in, 149; sovereign wealth fund in, 175; tax rates for top 1 per cent in, 182; child poverty in, 215; economic growth in, 259, 260; social spending in, 269

Austria: economic inequality in, 22, 259; unemployment benefits in, 67, 255; share of wages in national income, 68; nonstandard employment in, 136, 138; part-time work in, 138; public job creation in, 142; poverty in, 146; housing wealth in, 162; means-tested benefits in, 210, 211; child poverty in, 215; unemployment insurance coverage in, 227, 228, 230; economic growth in, 259; social security in, 266; social spending in, 269

Autor, David, 88

Baker, Jonathan, 126

Bakija, Jon, on US taxpayers in 0.1 per cent, 107

Baltic states: nonstandard employment in, 136; poverty in, 146

Bank of England, 138

Bankruptcy, 103

Banks: as too big to fail, 124; regulation of, 127; fees charged by, 164–165; secrecy of, 276. *See also* Financial-services sector

Barrientos, Armando, 80

Barry, Brian, 37

Bastagli, Francesca, on housing wealth, 161

Baumol, William J.: on productivity, 121; on public services, 121; Baumol effect, 121–122